SOUTH CAROLINA FIRE-EATER

Lawrence M. Keitt
S.C.

South Carolina Fire-Eater

The Life of Laurence Massillon Keitt, 1824–1864

Holt Merchant

The University of South Carolina Press

Published by the University of South Carolina Press
Columbia, South Carolina 29208

www.sc.edu/uscpress

Manufactured in the United States of America

23 22 21 20 19 18 17 16 15 14   10 9 8 7 6 5 4 3 2 1

Library of Congress Cataloging-in-Publication Data

Merchant, Holt.
South Carolina fire-eater : the life of Laurence Massillon Keitt, 1824–1864 / Holt Merchant.
pages cm
Includes bibliographical references and index.
ISBN 978-1-61117-349-9 (hardbound : alk. paper) — ISBN 978-1-61117-350-5 (ebook)
1. Keitt, Laurence M. (Lawrence Massillon), 1824–1864. 2. Legislators—United States—Biography. 3. United States. Congress. House—Biography. 4. United States—Politics and government—1849–1861. 5. Secession—South Carolina. 6. United States—History—Civil War, 1861–1865—Biography. 7. Generals—Confederate States of America—Biography. 8. Orangeburg County (S.C.)—Biography. I. Title.
E415.9.K27M47 2014
328.73'092—dc23
[B]

2013041101

Frontispiece: Laurence M. Keitt, representative from South Carolina.
Courtesy of Library of Congress.

This book was printed on a recycled paper with 30 percent postconsumer waste content.

CONTENTS

ILLUSTRATIONS

ACKNOWLEDGMENTS

A project that consumes forty years from start to finish accumulates a significant number of obligations along the way. I returned to my alma mater in 1970 before I had completed work on my Ph.D. at the University of Virginia. Allen Moger, one of my undergraduate professors, then chairman of the Department of History proposed that I write a biography of Laurence Keitt. He explained that Ollinger Crenshaw, another much-admired professor at Washington and Lee University, had begun work on the project but died before he could get very far into it. I had the good sense not to ask who Keitt was or why I should write about him, adopted his suggestion, and set out in pursuit of a man that consumed much of the next six years—summers at libraries at the University of Virginia, Duke University, the University of North Carolina at Chapel Hill, the University of South Carolina, and the Calhoun County Historical Commission in St. Matthews, South Carolina—including nights and weekends that I could steal from the more pressing business of writing lectures, meeting classes, grading papers, and sitting on committees.

During these six years of struggle, I accumulated debts to a long list of wonderful men and women. Paul Gaston, my mentor at the University of Virginia, kindled my enthusiasm for the history of the South and occasionally even soothed my anger. His careful reading of every version of the manuscript saved me from errors of both fact and interpretation. And Michael Holt read the final version and helped me to understand more fully the heart and mind of a surprisingly complex politician. His knowledge of the years immediately preceding the Civil War prevented me from falling into traps best known to historians of the antebellum South. And a small army of librarians, many of whose names I have over the intervening years forgotten, deserve better from me. I do nevertheless want to single out William Erwin of Duke University and Jeanne Ulmer of the Calhoun County Historical Commission, who helped to make a difficult task easier than I had any right to expect. Finally, I would like to thank Anna Claytor, who typed the final version; my wife, who typed every other version; and the John M. Glenn Fund of Washington and Lee that made three summers away from Lexington less painful than they otherwise would have been.

In 1976 I completed the work and put the manuscript on the shelf, where for thirty years I let it gather dust. But during the summer of 2007, I was sitting on a beach in North Carolina reading the second volume of William W. Freehling's monumental *Road to Disunion* and noticed that Freehling had discussed Keitt's contributions to the sectional crisis, wondered where he had looked for information, turned to his footnotes, and noticed he had referenced my research. My reaction to that discovery scattered a sizable flock of seagulls. Later that year, I came upon the excellent half-chapter on Keitt in Eric H. Walther's *The Fire-Eaters.* Together, the two historians almost had convinced me that Keitt deserved another look. Then, in the spring of 2008, Bill Freehling came to Washington and Lee to preside over a seminar on sectionalism. While he was here, he urged me to revise the manuscript for publication. I took his advice, obtained a sabbatical from the university, devoted my time away from teaching to research and writing, and in nine months converted my earlier efforts into what I hope will be a useful book.

During those nine months, I accumulated still more debts—to Vaughan Stanley, Richard Grefe, and Elizabeth Teaff, librarians at Washington and Lee who greatly eased the task of locating sources and checking facts; to Henry Fulmer and Graham Duncan of the South Caroliniana Library, who aided my search for information about the postwar struggles of Keitt's widow Susanna, a real-life prototype of the fictional Scarlett O'Hara; and to Thomas Litzenburg, a literary craftsman who relentlessly held up the prose of Jane Austen and R. D. James, whose clarity and grace he was convinced every historian should do his best to emulate. Debts are owed also to Jennifer Ashworth, who has typed and advised and retyped; to Washington and Lee, which has provided financial support at crucial moments; and to Alexander Moore, acquisitions editor at the University of South Carolina Press. And most of all, I owe an enormous debt to Becky, to whom I have been married for almost fifty years. She has typed and edited and encouraged, and every bit as important, worked, run our home, and looked after our two sons—children when I began this project but middle-aged now—and protected me from the distractions of the world. She has brought light and joy into my life; I love her more than she can possibly know.

Introduction

In September 1860, the *New York Leader* published a description of Congressman Laurence M. Keitt of South Carolina that would have agitated the enemies and surprised the friends who read it. It was not the physical description of the man that would have attracted their attention. He was, as the anonymous author wrote, tall, "broad shouldered, deep-chested, and powerful." He had dark brown curly hair that was rapidly receding, a full beard, blue-gray eyes, a florid complexion, irregular features, a deep scar on the right side of his forehead, a small mouth, and "a general air which reminds one of King Henry the Eighth." His voice was "clear and ringing," his gestures graceful, his imagination fervid, and his appearance overall commanding.

It was the author's analysis of Keitt's many virtues and few faults that would have angered his enemies and amused his friends. They may have laughed at his satirical version of the American Revolution in which South Carolinians threw tea into Boston harbor and battled redcoats at Lexington and Bunker Hill while terror-stricken New Englanders looked on from a safe distance. They would surely have added to the number of faults the reporter had identified and severely reduced the number of his virtues.

In his private life, the unknown author attested, Keitt was generous to a fault, cordial, hospitable, "full of dash and daring, brave as a lion and prodigal as a lord," and unfailingly loyal to his friends. That last trait had been responsible for involving him in "transgressions of doubtful taste." He had been only a bystander when Preston Brooks caned Charles Sumner and later when Henry Edmundson struck John Hickman with "a slight switch." He was unjustly accused of participating in the encounters, had stood by his friends, and so been reviled for acts he did not commit. If he had done anything else, he would have abandoned his friends and violated the code of honor that shaped his life. Nothing he did was truly open to censure.

In public, the writer continued, Keitt was a "South Carolinian all over." He believed without reservation in the gospel according to John C. Calhoun, "the alpha and omega of his faith," and had no equal in preaching "that disasterous [*sic*] doctrine." In Congress, he quickly established himself as a masterful orator, though a bit too fond of metaphor and paradox. His speeches attacking the Know Nothings and defending the admission of Kansas to the Union won widespread applause, even from men who rejected his arguments. He was a true scholar who lectured learnedly and with great success on ancient civilizations, the superiority of southern culture, the morality of slavery, and the need to annex Cuba.

Before he was elected to Congress in 1854, Keitt had graduated from South Carolina College, studied law in the offices of Henry Bailey and James L. Petigru, and served five terms in the lower house of the South Carolina legislature. There, he had championed the secession of his state from the Union, alone if necessary. When he entered Congress, he continued to advocate that radical policy. Unlike Calhoun, who dedicated the last half of his political career to making the Union safe for slavery and slaveholders, Keitt was certain that slavery could never be secure inside the Union, and converted secession from a weapon into an end in itself. He was willing to work with Democrats when their short-run interests coincided with his own, but never willing to tie himself to the party, even when it was led by men as sympathetic to the South as Franklin Pierce and James Buchanan. He refused to support radical schemes like the reopening of the international slave trade because they threatened to destroy the unity of the lower South.

Near the end of his career in the House of Representatives, after a long and tumultuous courtship, Keitt married "the truly beautiful and accomplished" Suzanne Sparks and exchanged his first love—politics—for his second. Much too soon, his extended honeymoon tour of Europe was interrupted by John Brown's raid on Harpers Ferry, and he returned to Washington to look after the needs of his state and section, dragging along his unhappy bride who had anticipated spending years, not mere weeks, abroad.

Back in South Carolina, Keitt campaigned relentlessly to take his state out of the Union, with the rest of the South if possible, alone if necessary. Abraham Lincoln's election ensured his success. He was a member of the state convention that voted for secession, the delegation that tried to convince Buchanan to evacuate Fort Sumter, and the committee that wrote the rules for the convention that established the Confederacy. He was deeply dissatisfied with the Constitution the convention drafted, but back in Columbia he worked hard to convince the voters to ratify the fundamental law of the new nation. He was a member of the Provisional Congress, but once the initial excitement subsided, he became bored, resigned his seat, went home, raised the Twentieth South Carolina Infantry, and was elected its colonel. For much of the war, his regiment took part in the defense of Charleston harbor. Keitt himself was in command of forces on Sullivan's Island and intermittently of Morris Island, the site of the heroic but doomed assault of the Fifty-fourth Massachusetts Infantry on Battery Wagner. He was in command of the battery when the Confederates finally evacuated the island.

Near the close of his service outside Charleston, Keitt conceded in a letter to his wife that the Confederacy could not win its war for independence. He had done as much as any man in calling down death and destruction on his beloved South. After the war was over, he promised her, he would do everything in his power to rectify the mistakes he had made. The insight came a decade too late. Soon after he finished writing, the Twentieth was ordered north to the Army of Northern Virginia. There Keitt took command of a brigade and, unaware that war in the field was not the romantic adventure he imagined, launched a frontal assault against Federal cavalry defending a crossroads at Cold Harbor. The brigade was routed, and Keitt was mortally wounded. He died the next day.

There was no typical southern fire-eater, though historians have argued that there was. The fire-eater was, according to William L. Barney and others, a young man whose formative years coincided with the escalation of sectional hostility. He had not taken part in the process of nation-building that had united North and South in a common cause. He was far more concerned with the welfare of the South than the nation as a whole. His earliest memories were of nullification and slave revolts and northern threats to the peculiar institution. He had discarded the view common a generation earlier that the Union was a confederation of equal and sovereign states, valuable because of the essential services it provided. For him it was an unequal coalition in which a northern majority dominated and exploited a southern minority.[1]

The man historians have described as a typical fire-eater was a lawyer or a planter or both. If he did not live in South Carolina, he had probably been born there. If he had continued his education after leaving an academy, it was at a school like South Carolina College whose faculty preached the virtues of free trade, decentralized government, and slavery. If he had not inherited wealth, he was engaged in a frantic effort to acquire land and slaves. The 1850s were not a favorable time for young men on the make. The price of everything they needed to establish plantations was soaring, the price of raw cotton had stabilized, and it was becoming increasingly difficult for even talented, hard-driving men to raise themselves into the plantation gentry. If he wanted to buy land in the West, he ran into Free Soil opposition to the spread of slavery into the territories. If he wanted to buy slaves as inexpensively as possible, he ran into abolitionist opposition to reopening the African slave trade.

If the fire-eater belonged to any political party, he was a state-rights Democrat because the party catered to his prejudices and promised to relieve his economic frustrations. It approved expansion into the Caribbean to increase the supply of available land, reopening the slave trade to reduce the cost of labor, and free trade to lessen the cost of doing business with Europe. Ultimately southern demands for economic independence from the North could not be separated from demands for political independence as well.

For many historians the typical fire-eater resembled William L. Barney's portrait of Robert Barnwell Rhett: "a rash and ultra man . . . , frequently bent upon extreme and desperate courses, very excitable and unstable and intolerant and contemptuous of all about him, with neither tact or discretion and without sympathy or popularity with the great mass of men." He was an ideologue, not a politician; he was loyal to principles, not parties. He was "bold, impetuous, uncompromising, greedily ambitious . . . [a] swaggering hothead plotting to break up the Union." His addiction to abstract principle and his aversion to political discipline made him an outsider isolated from the process of decision-making at every level of government. He remained an outsider until the dramatic events of the late 1850s confirmed his dire predictions and allowed him to shape the politics of secession to his own specifications.[2]

Keitt did share traits and experiences that set radicals off from politicians whose views were less extreme and actions less precipitous than their own. Even among those men, he stood out as an elitist, a southern nationalist, a romantic, and a superb speaker. He was fiery, impetuous, frequently violent in defense of his honor and the honor of his state, but he was not an outsider. He owned plantations and slaves, and was not at all worried that he was losing his standing in society. His position among the gentry was entirely secure. He was not isolated from the centers of political power. In Washington, he had little influence on the day-to-day activities of the federal government and in eight years did not draft even a single piece of legislation, but he did play a critical role in the legislative battles of the era. Nor was he worried that the spread of Jacksonian democracy would overwhelm his state's traditional republican government. South Carolina was the least democratic state in the Union and promised to remain so far into the future. Nor did he seem particularly concerned by the economic problems posed by federal tax policy or the declining productivity of his state's plantations, the emigration of its people, or the erosion of its political influence. Finally, he was not moved by bouts of panic or insanity. Even if South Carolina were not too big to be a madhouse, he was in no danger of becoming an inmate. He was instead a champion of slavery and a way of life that was impossible without it. He understood the indispensable role that slavery played in the life of the South, and his decision—and the decision of men like him—to fight to the death to defend it was entirely rational if not defensible by the standards of the nineteenth-century South. It was a decision for which Keitt paid with his life.

ONE

"See that you rear a new Union"

According to stories still repeated in Calhoun County, the first Keitt came to South Carolina from Bermuda shortly before the Revolutionary War. Around 1760, George Kitts settled on Big Bull Swamp just west of Orangeburg, married Dorothy Whetstone, and began to acquire land and slaves. The marriage produced five children, a daughter and four sons. In 1812 three of the sons changed their family name to "Keitt," apparently because they preferred the look and sound of the new spelling.[1]

Around 1819 George Keitt, the youngest of the four brothers, married Mary W. Wannamaker, the daughter of a prominent planter and Methodist minister, Rev. Jacob Wannamaker. About the same time, the bride's father gave the couple a tract of land and a house—"Puritan Hall"—some two miles west of St. Matthews in Orangeburg District. In time, the gift became the nucleus of a sizeable estate; when he died in 1861, George Keitt was the master of approximately twenty-five hundred acres and more than fifty slaves.[2]

Long after the war, Sue Keitt fondly recalled Christmas visits to Puritan Hall, where fires blazed in every room and her father-in-law dispensed food and drink with lavish abandon. Like so many plantation homes in the lower South, it is best described as "frontier Georgian" or perhaps "Georgian primitive." It was a two-story frame building, painted white, with a sharply pitched roof and enormous stone chimneys at each end. In front, a porch ran the length of the lower story, with a much smaller porch set above it. In the rear a T-shaped wing almost as wide as the main house ended in three identical gables. A wide central hall ran from front to rear. Judged by the standards established by tidewater planters, the house was not large. There were six rooms on the main floor, but only two above. Perhaps the usual out-buildings compensated for the small number of bedrooms. Hand-carved mantels, wide-board flooring, and seven acres of flower gardens made up in luxury whatever the house lacked in size. It was there that Laurence Massilon Keitt was born on October 4, 1824.[3]

Keitt received his early education at St. Matthews Academy, where he was "famous for foot races, the gift of gab, and for never wincing when . . . flogged."[4] In 1838 he attended Mt. Zion Academy in Winnsboro, where he spent a year preparing to enter college.[5] When Keitt enrolled at South Carolina College in the fall of 1839, the school was a bastion of conservatism in a conservative state. It was small—during Keitt's four years, it enrolled between 150 and 169 students instructed by six professors—but influential far out of proportion to its size. Founded early in the nineteenth century, primarily to prepare young men to exercise political power in ways that would benefit their state, the college quickly became a breeding ground for sectional-minded lawyers and politicians. During the fifteen-year presidency of Thomas Cooper, it graduated students well drilled in the virtues of state rights, slavery, and free trade. After Cooper's retirement in 1834, professors like James H. Thornwell, Maximilian LaBorde, and Robert Henry continued to defend the South's conservative social and political institutions. From these men students learned that they must accept the world as they found it. They must not attempt to alter the state of society but acknowledge and defend it against the attacks of its enemies.[6]

Cooper and his successors were astoundingly successful at passing along their conservative ideals. Students left their classrooms to become "attorneys for a cause," not "liberals, equalitarian Democrats or zealous reformers eager to dissect South Carolina's institutions." Of course, not every graduate of the college emerged a champion of strict construction and a foe of the federal government. But for every Unionist like William Aiken, the college produced at least two dozen secessionists like James H. Hammond, Louis Wigfall, and Leonidas W. Spratt.[7]

At South Carolina College, Keitt absorbed "a smattering of Greek and Latin, was introduced to metaphysics and logic, [and] learned something about chemistry." He was most strongly attracted to the study of history and political economy, and to Francis Lieber, the arch-dissenter who had begun his long and uncomfortable association with the college five years before. Lieber was a prolific writer and an effective teacher who introduced modern methods into his classroom, alternated lectures and recitations, and used maps, globes, and other aids to hold the attention of his students. He refused to discuss his more controversial opinions in public, but his ideas inevitably antagonized the community in which he lived. He was a skeptic among evangelical Christians, a gradual emancipationist among slaveholders, and a Unionist among disciples of John C. Calhoun. Lieber did not succeed in indoctrinating Keitt with his liberal ideals. However great Lieber's influence may have been when he was a student, it had entirely dissipated by the time Keitt entered public life. In 1848, when Keitt was elected to the lower house of the South Carolina legislature for the first time, he was totally committed to the sectionalist views of his Orangeburg constituents. But Lieber did inspire in him a respect for scholarship and a love of the history of his state that produced practical results during his years in the legislature.[8]

Throughout his four years at the college, Keitt was a member of the Euphradian Society, one of two organizations—the other was the Clariosophic Society—founded in 1806 to transform students into polished orators. At a school whose graduates commonly pursued careers that demanded skill in public speaking, the societies occupied positions of real importance. During his senior year, Keitt was one of the Euphradian Society's four presidents.

When the college was in session, the Euphradians met every Saturday. A typical program included two speeches and three debates, with two members speaking on each side. Politics was by far the most frequent subject for debate, but almost without exception, Keitt's topics were historical or literary. Would Socrates have been justified in leaving prison when solicited by Crito? Was Aaron Burr treated justly by the government of the United States? In a state of single blessedness, does a male or a female possess more advantages? Was Coriolanus justified in fighting against his country? In the margin of his minute-book, the Euphradians' secretary noted that the last topic had "elicited much debate and also a most eloquent and able speech from L. Keitt."[9]

It appears that the Euphradians failed repeatedly to conduct their meetings in an orderly manner. The constitution of the society forbade a long list of improprieties and prescribed fines to be levied against members who committed them. Miscreants paid as little as twelve cents for spitting on the carpet, carving on the furniture, falling asleep, or laughing out loud, and as much as five dollars for attending a meeting while intoxicated. "Non-performance in debate" cost offenders fifty cents. Compared to his colleagues, Keitt was not a conspicuous scoff-law, but he did pay more than two dozen fines—most of them for committing minor offenses—during the years he was an active member of the society.[10]

Keitt graduated from South Carolina College in 1843 with a "reputation for talents which would have given him a higher mark on the college roles but for general and desultory reading, which always weigh heavily with professors and tutors."[11] Soon afterward, he went to Charleston to read law in the offices of James L. Petigru and Henry Bailey. Formerly state attorney general and a member of the lower house of the legislature, Petigru in 1843 was the acknowledged leader of the South Carolina Bar. During the 1830s he had been an outspoken opponent of nullification, and he continued to defend the Union until his death in 1863. Bailey was the state attorney general in 1843. Keitt was admitted to the South Carolina Bar in 1844 and opened a law office in Orangeburg soon after.[12]

No doubt the practice of law consumed most of Keitt's time from 1844 until his election to the U.S. House of Representatives in the spring of 1853. Unfortunately, the details of his career are beyond recovery. During its march northward from Savannah early in 1865, Sherman's army destroyed every courthouse in its path. The fifty-mile swath it cut included Orangeburg and every town in which Keitt is likely to have practiced.[13] None of Keitt's letters from the period have survived, so it is impossible to prove from documentary evidence that he ever tried a case. Still, it is reasonable to assume that his practice flourished, if only because his neighbors would not have elected an unsuccessful attorney to public office and kept him there for fourteen years.

In the fall of 1848, the voters of Orangeburg District elected Keitt to the lower house of the South Carolina legislature for the first time. David F. Jamison had occupied the seat for six years but retired after the 1847 session, and Keitt defeated two other candidates, Lewis E. Conner and Paul S. Felder, by wide margins. He held the seat continuously until his election to Congress in 1853.[14]

In Columbia, Keitt quickly discovered that much of his time would be consumed in satisfying the demands of his constituents. He presented a petition from "sundry citizens" asking the state to construct a new road; he submitted a report from a grand jury describing the condition of the Orangeburg courthouse and recommending that it be enlarged; he introduced a petition from the elders of Four Hole Baptist Church asking for incorporation, one from a constituent demanding additional compensation for a slave the state had executed, and one from "sundry citizens" requesting permission to form a militia company. And he tried repeatedly to have the name of Saxe-Gotha District changed to "Lexington."[15]

Not all of Keitt's activities in the legislature were so prosaic. Early in his public career he became entangled in the controversy surrounding the Bank of the State of South Carolina. Throughout the nineteenth century, the bank had provided an adequate supply of credit to meet the needs of the state's planters and businessmen. South Carolina did not participate in the rapid economic expansion of the 1820s and early 1830s; the officers of the bank had conducted its affairs in a conservative manner, and both the state and its bank escaped the panics of 1837 and 1839 largely unscathed. Business failures were rare, and the bank suspended specie payments for only a short period in 1837.[16]

In spite of the success of the state-owned bank, it came under attack by some of the state's most prominent politicians, among them James H. Hammond, Whitemarsh Seabrook, and Christopher G. Memminger. Governor Seabrook denounced the bank as a "dangerous institution, anti-republican in its character and tendency." It was ridiculous, he insisted, for a state committed to the independent treasury to violate so conspicuously the principle that demanded the separation of bank and state. The longer the state extended the rights and privileges of the "moneyed corporation," the greater would be its evils.[17]

During Keitt's first campaign for the legislature in 1848, "Many Citizens" demanded to know if he would vote for a resolution requiring the bank to publish a list of legislators who owed it money. In his reply Keitt argued that publication would serve no purpose except to gratify idle curiosity. The resolution implied that the bank had bribed members of the legislature to secure favorable treatment. Passage would produce distrust of the legislators and reflect unfavorably on the honor of the state. If such a bill reached the floor of the House, he would vote against it.[18]

Keitt moved quickly to the heart of the controversy. He was not an advocate of the bank, the candidate told his constituents, and he wished the state were rid of it. But its destruction would curtail private and public credit, bankrupt individuals, and impose a heavy burden on the state. The bank posed complex problems that could be solved only by "wise statesmanship," not by the "head over heel remedies of political quackery." He would not participate in a "wild and hasty scheme" to destroy it, but he would support any measure to separate the bank and the state that would not administer too great a shock to the state's economy. Years later, Keitt recalled that his letter had attracted so much criticism that no politician in St. Matthews Parish had dared to support him. But his gamble had been successful; the voters had elected him to the legislature by a wide margin.[19]

Keitt's response to "many citizens" could have reflected his belief that legislators had no obligation to support measures they opposed, however popular they might be with their constituents. Or it could even have revealed his contempt for voters who were not part of the planter elite. But much more likely is that what it revealed was his fear that the battle over the bank would distract the voters from the only battle that truly concerned him—the state's battle with the federal government.

Keitt was never seriously interested in the fiscal measures debated by the legislature. It is doubtful that he knew very much about the operations of the Bank of South Carolina or understood its importance to the state's business community. But in 1849, when opponents of the bank introduced legislation that would prevent it from discounting the notes of other banks and the legislature launched into a heated debate, he recognized the gravity of the situation. They must unite and settle the question once and for all, he told the members of the House. They must not allow the bank to distract their attention from more important problems. "Domestic agitation" would only paralyze the state during the confrontation with the federal government that was inexorably approaching. The state must be prepared to defend its interest in the territories against the demands of the Free Soilers. Keitt and other enemies of "domestic agitation" easily warded off criticism of the bank, and after the 1849 session, federal relations all but monopolized the attention of the legislature.[20]

Of all his activities in the legislature, Keitt was proudest of his successful campaign to protect the state's archives. He had been interested in history even before his studies with Francis Lieber at South Carolina College. For some years he had dabbled in the pre-Columbian history of the United States, and he was collecting material for an "ante-colonial" history of the state which he hoped to write when political tensions had somewhat relaxed.

In 1849 Keitt suggested that the legislature send an agent to Europe to collect "historical memorials." He was certain that archives in Copenhagen contained evidence that white men had reached South Carolina in the tenth century. Unfortunately, the legislators were caught up in the "political chaos" of the period, and his proposal encountered "general indifference."[21]

Keitt's suggestion that the legislature construct a fireproof building to house the archives met with more success. In 1850 he was appointed to a committee to consider the proposal. The committee recommended that the state begin construction of the building at once and transfer the archives as soon as the first floor was ready to house them. When additional funds were available, it could complete the building. The legislature agreed, and work on the building began in 1851.[22]

On December 15, Keitt delivered the principal address at the laying of the cornerstone. He told a large crowd that it was the duty of South Carolina to "impress itself on the mind of the world" and warned that it could succeed only if it gathered up and preserved the records of its noble past. In 1788 fire had swept through the State House and destroyed a portion of the archives, but in the records that escaped the flames, the story of the glorious past lived on. The records recounted the story of the brave sons of South Carolina: Marion and Sumter and Moultrie, who had fought to free the land from English tyranny; Rutledge and Pinckney and Gadsden, who raised up a mighty nation out of "weltering chaos"; Calhoun and Lowndes and Cheves, who defended the state from the assaults of the foes of slavery and state rights. "As you are rearing a new hall here," Keitt admonished his audience, "see that you rear a new union, to save and defend you. Act so that whatever else may perish, Carolina may live."[23] Keitt's conclusion, "interrupted by warm expressions of approbation," clearly revealed that, however much history interested him, politics interested him considerably more.[24]

Keitt's career in the South Carolina legislature coincided almost exactly with the state's struggle to protect its interests in the territories acquired during the Mexican War. The Wilmot Proviso, introduced into Congress for the first time in the summer of 1846, barred slavery from any lands Mexico might cede to the

United States at the end of the war. The proviso passed the House, failed repeatedly in the Senate, and raised issues that refused to go away. By 1848 the efforts of Free Soilers to prevent the spread of slavery into the West had provoked southern congressmen to strike back. Robert Barnwell Rhett, who represented South Carolina's Seventh District in the House of Representatives, exactly reflected the beliefs of his constituents when he argued that neither the Congress nor a territorial legislature had the power to exclude slavery from any part of the land ceded by Mexico.[25]

In Orangeburg District slaves outnumbered white people by almost two to one, and people who thought about such things were acutely aware of the need for plantation agriculture to expand into the West, if not for themselves, then for their sons and daughters. In the district emotions ran high. Early in November, a mass meeting at the courthouse in Orangeburg approved resolutions that Keitt introduced into the legislature a month later. The meeting unanimously resolved that the "continued agitation of the slavery question" by the northern people, their legislatures, and their representatives in Congress exhibited "a want of national courtesy." The meeting endorsed the Missouri Compromise but insisted that South Carolinians would not submit to additional restrictions on their right to carry slaves into any territory acquired by their blood and treasure. If the Congress tried to apply the Wilmot Proviso to any territory south of the 36° 30' line or to carry out any similar action, the state's representatives must withdraw from Congress and the legislature must adopt measures to deal with the emergency.[26] Meetings throughout the state approved similar resolutions. The legislature was not ready for the state to act alone and resolved only that South Carolina was prepared to cooperate with the rest of the South to resist federal tyranny.[27]

By the fall of 1849, prominent South Carolina politicians were convinced that the legislature should call a convention of the slaveholding states to confront the problem posed by the Wilmot Proviso, but they were acutely aware of their state's radical reputation and hesitated to act for fear that they would alienate the rest of the South. At this critical juncture, a convention in Mississippi proposed that representatives from the southern states meet in Nashville the following June.[28]

At a legislative caucus called to consider the Mississippi proposals, Keitt spoke "strongly and eloquently" in favor of sending delegates to the convention. The federal government, he said, "driven on by the lust of power, and the fell spirit of fanaticism," was determined to close the West to slavery. South Carolina must act at once. It must co-operate with the rest of the South to "avert the common calamities impending over us." The legislators agreed, and on December 9, voted to participate in the convention, appointed four delegates-at-large, and recommended that each congressional district appoint two more.[29]

During the same session, Keitt introduced resolutions condemning the personal liberty laws enacted by the legislatures of four northern states. In a "speech of considerable ability," he quoted the provisions of the U.S. Constitution that required states to deliver up fugitive slaves to their owners, argued that the laws passed by the four states violated the Constitution, and asked the Committee on Federal Relations to consider legislation to protect the state's slaveowners. Two years before, he had told John C. Calhoun he would introduce a bill to prohibit the state from collecting debts owed to any citizen of a state that refused to enforce the law. In another series of resolutions, Keitt commended the South Carolina congressmen who had refused to vote for any candidate for Speaker of the House of Representatives who was "in the slightest degree tainted with unsoundness on the slavery question," and endorsed the argument of one congressman that the adoption of the Wilmot Proviso or the abolition of slavery in the District of Columbia would automatically dissolve the Union.[30]

Late in March 1850, Keitt presided over a public meeting at Orangeburg Court House to nominate delegates to the convention in Nashville. In a "succinct and summary manner," Keitt explained the causes of the hostility between North and South. The South, he insisted, must share equally in the common property of the Union. It must not hesitate to defend its right to carry slaves into the West. It must act promptly; timidity and irresolution would be disastrous. When he had finished speaking, the meeting agreed to send representatives to Walterboro where the Seventh Congressional District would select its delegates to the convention. Keitt declined a nomination to attend; the convention, he argued, must be composed of men widely known and respected for their wisdom and experience. At Walterboro, representatives from every parish in the district elected David F. Jamison and Robert Barnwell Rhett to represent them in Nashville.[31]

In Washington, Congress struggled to solve the problems posed by the Mexican cession. In January, Senator Henry Clay of Kentucky introduced a series of bills designed to silence southern threats of disunion and satisfy moderates of both North and South.[32] His proposals satisfied neither side; first John C. Calhoun and then William H. Seward insisted that compromise was impossible. The South, said Calhoun, would concede nothing whatever. If the North wanted to save the Union, it must acknowledge the right of the slaveholding states to take slaves into the territories, enforce the fugitive slave provisions of the Constitution, and stop all agitation against slavery. Finally, it must ratify a constitutional amendment to restore the balance of power between the sections. If it refused, it must accept the destruction of the Union. Speaking for the Free Soil North, Seward appealed to a "higher law" that transcended the Constitution and predicted that the progress of civilization would soon extinguish the peculiar institution wherever it existed. Daniel Webster warned the South that peaceful secession was impossible and begged the two sections to compromise their differences. Lewis Cass and Stephen A. Douglas spoke in the same vein, but without success.[33]

Early in June, with the Congress hopelessly deadlocked, the long-awaited convention of southern states assembled in Nashville. Fire-eaters like Keitt who expected the delegates to dissolve the Union were painfully disappointed. Only nine states had sent delegations, and only two—from South Carolina and Mississippi—enjoyed much support at home. After nine days of debate, the convention condemned the compromise measures under consideration in Washington, approved the extension of the Missouri Compromise line to the Pacific Ocean as the fairest way to divide the new territory between the two sections, and refused to discuss means of defending southern interests in the territories until the Congress had acted. In Orangeburg, Keitt concluded that the southern ultimatum was really a surrender.[34]

In South Carolina the radicals refused to acquiesce in the actions of either the southern convention or the Congress when in September it enacted piecemeal the compromise measures it had earlier rejected in a single bill.[35] All over the state, newly organized southern rights associations appealed to the people to resist the most recent federal aggression. During a meeting at Orangeburg Court House, Keitt traced the history of the wrongs the North had perpetrated against the South and insisted that it was time for the cotton states to dissolve the Union and form a new confederacy. If the rest of the southern states refused to cooperate, South Carolina must act alone. The *Charleston Mercury* reported that the speech "riveted the attention and kindled the feelings of his audience into burning indignation against [their] oppressors." Following the speech, the meeting adopted a constitution for the Orangeburg Southern Rights Association and appointed committees of correspondence and public safety.[36]

The 1850 session of the legislature devoted itself almost exclusively to the state's rapidly deteriorating relations with the federal government. At first it appeared that the fire-eaters were in complete control, but on November 28, Keitt introduced the resolutions he had sponsored at Orangeburg the previous month. The rhetoric was radical, but the recommendations were unexpectedly moderate, evidence that he doubted the secessionists could convince the legislature to approve genuinely radical measures. The government of the United States, he told the legislators, was a confederacy of sovereign states that could exercise only powers delegated to it by the states. Each state had the right to decide when the government had violated the Constitution and to determine the most effective mode of redress. Each state had the right to secede from the confederacy at any time without opposition or explanation. The people of the North had organized societies to despoil them of their property, instigated insurrections of their slaves, and prevented federal officers from returning fugitives to their rightful owners. They had monopolized the territory taken from Mexico; they had abolished the slave trade in the District of Columbia; they had debased the people of the South in the eyes of the world. The proper remedy for the aggression of the northern states, he asserted, was secession. Rather than submit to the tyranny of the federal government, South Carolina must secede, alone if necessary.[37]

At this point, the thrust of Keitt's remarks suddenly changed. He could have demanded that the state answer the northern challenge by withdrawing from the Union. Instead he urged a more moderate course; he advised legislators to call for a southern congress to meet in Montgomery in April 1851, with power "to carry out every act of sovereignty," and for a state convention to meet in July to ratify the actions of the congress. After almost three weeks of maneuvering, the legislature approved the resolutions but called for the southern congress to meet in January 1852 and refused to set a date for the state convention. The decision to delay any action for more than a year was a major victory for moderates who strongly opposed independent action by the state.[38]

All over the South, the movement to answer the Compromise of 1850 with force began to break down. Sectional bitterness ebbed rapidly, and no state responded to the legislature's call for a southern congress. At this juncture, the South Carolina radicals could have acknowledged the failure of the secession movement and waited for a more auspicious occasion. Instead, they agreed to make the October 1851 elections for delegates to the southern congress a test of strength and launched a frenzied campaign to win support for their candidates.[39]

Unionists made up only a tiny minority of the state's electorate, and the campaign quickly became a contest between radicals who favored immediate secession and moderates who favored secession but only with the cooperation of at least one other southern state. Keitt, entirely recovered from his flirtation with moderation, stumped the Seventh Congressional District from end to end and occasionally crossed into neighboring districts. Beginning in the spring, he repeatedly addressed meetings convened by local southern rights associations. South Carolina, Keitt told his audiences, had already taken a stand against the compromise measures adopted by the Congress in 1850. It was desirable for the state to act in concert with the rest of the South, but at present, cooperation was impossible. South Carolina could not wait any longer without calling down dishonor on itself or endangering its rights and liberties. It must act independently and at once.[40]

On election day, Keitt saw his work go for nothing. In the Seventh District the two secessionist candidates—Robert Barnwell Rhett and G. W. Duncan—polled almost 65 percent of the vote, but in every other district, cooperationists won impressive victories. Statewide, they attracted seventy-five hundred more votes than the radicals.[41]

In spite of the lopsided vote, the meaning of the election was unclear because a sizeable minority of the radicals, Keitt among them, refused to admit defeat. In a series of resolutions he introduced into the legislature early in December, Keitt argued that rejection of immediate secession did not mean the voters opposed all forms of resistance. Many of the cooperationist candidates had declared that the state must not submit to the wrongs inflicted by the federal government and had suggested means of resistance short of secession. The legislature must set a date for the state convention it had authorized during its previous session so that the people could adopt the most expeditious means of defending themselves against federal aggression.[42]

Keitt's resolutions set off a brief debate easily won by the radical majority. With help from a handful of cooperationists, the radicals scheduled the convention for the fourth Monday in April, 1852.[43] It was a pathetic gesture; even its supporters admitted that the meeting would do little more than reinforce the state's reputation for radicalism. In the end the politicians met in Columbia, debated half-heartedly for five days, resolved that South Carolina would remain in the Union solely for reasons of expediency, and adjourned. Keitt was not there to share in the embarrassment.[44]

By mid-summer 1852, the bitterness created by the secession movement had begun to wane. In February of the following year, Keitt compared politics in low-country South Carolina to "a pool with not even the wing of a devil to trouble its waters." Carefully avoiding political controversy—"he's a fool who rakes up the mud of a pond when he means to drink its waters"—he turned his attention to other matters. In October, he addressed a joint session of the Calliopean and Polytechnic Societies of the Citadel Academy, arguing that education provided the strongest defense of conservative belief and action. And a month later he tried unsuccessfully to prevent a duel between his brother, Dr. William J. Keitt, and one of his closest colleagues, Olin M. Dantzler. Apparently Dantzler had questioned Dr. Keitt's courage. The doctor demanded that Dantzler retract his remarks, and when he refused, challenged him. In an exchange of fire, Dr. Keitt was hit but not seriously wounded. Keitt himself was never reluctant to resort to violence to settle his own quarrels, and on the surface his effort to resolve his brother's dispute with Dantzler seemed out of character. Perhaps he was afraid one or both men would be seriously hurt or even killed. More likely he believed attacks on abolitionists like Charles Sumner and Galusha Grow were justified but confrontations between southern patriots were not.[45]

During the 1852 session of the legislature, Keitt spoke at length only once, to defend South Carolina's peculiar method of choosing presidential electors.

The appointment of electors by the legislature, he argued, upheld the republican spirit of the U.S. Constitution. It faithfully reflected the popular will, and was at once the simplest and least expensive mode of selection. To put the selection into the hands of the people would threaten the state's sovereignty, transfer the loyalty of the people to the federal government, and lead from change to change until the entire Constitution was overthrown. It would consolidate both the state and central governments, and create a democracy of mere numbers; it would destroy genius and morality, statesmanship and freedom. Keitt carefully skirted the most important argument in favor of retaining the present system. Like Calhoun, he believed the legislature must not provoke discussion of any issue that might divide the white population of the state. If the legislature put the choice of electors into the hands of the people, political factions would spring up, political unity would vanish, and the state's ability to resist the incursions of the federal government would be seriously compromised.

A reporter for the *Charleston Mercury* called the speech "able and eloquent." The young legislator had spoken with less than his usual ardor but with "greater strength" than ever before. In every respect he had lived up to his exalted reputation. The reporter obviously approved of Keitt's efforts to fend off the Jacksonian political democracy that had swept over the rest of the nation. Keitt must have known that the efforts of conservative leaders to win popular support for nullification during the 1820s had spun out of control and very nearly cost the landed gentry its monopoly of political power in South Carolina. He was determined to avoid a second experiment in democratic politics.[46]

Late in 1852, Keitt suddenly discovered that the political waters were not as calm as he had supposed. Hearing that William F. Colcock would not run for reelection to the House of Representatives from the Third District, Keitt announced his candidacy and began canvassing for votes. In February 1853 he learned that the reports of Colcock's retirement had not been accurate. In a letter to the *Charleston Mercury*, W. F. Hutson—a member of the legislature from Colleton District and a close friend of the incumbent—announced that Colcock would run for reelection and suggested that Keitt withdraw from the race. Keitt was genuinely embarrassed. He was perfectly aware that in most congressional elections in South Carolina, the leading politicians in a district got together, agreed on a candidate, and the man they selected ran unopposed. He had unwittingly violated the rules of the game, scarcely a month after his well-publicized defense of government by the elite. He replied to Hutson's letter in the same issue of the *Mercury*. He would not be a candidate for Congress in opposition to Colcock. When it was reported that the congressman would not stand for reelection, a few of Keitt's friends had suggested that he run for the vacancy. His candidacy was predicated on Colcock's retirement.[47]

In March, Colcock was elected without opposition to his second term in the House, but almost immediately after the election, President Franklin Pierce appointed him collector of the Port of Charleston, and he resigned his seat. In the scramble that followed, Keitt was the front-runner from the start. Four other Third District politicians—George P. Elliott, Isidore Lartigue, J. A. Strobhart, and William A. Owens—announced their candidacies. By early April only Owens, a lawyer from Barnwell District, was still in the race. Keitt reflected the political views of the district more accurately than Owens, who favored secession only in cooperation with the rest of the lower South. He apparently did not campaign on the issues, but he must have realized that his support for state rights and his opposition to tariffs and internal improvements were widely known and would win the votes of a majority of the electorate. A month later, the *Charleston Mercury* reported that he had won majorities in three of four districts—Owens carried only Barnwell—and was elected by "a large majority." In fact, he carried the district by only 200 out of 3,400 votes cast. In July, he resigned his seat in the legislature and began preparations to leave for Washington when Congress convened in the fall.[48]

Six years in the legislature had given Keitt a superb political education. He had sharpened his legislative skills, improved his oratorical prowess, expanded his grasp of the issues, and demonstrated the popularity of his radical opinions. Most important, he had confirmed his suspicion of the Federal government and his determination never to compromise the interests of his state and section. He was, in short, well prepared to take his place among the fire-eaters in the lower house of the Congress.

TWO

"Trample upon your hosannas to the Union"

Keitt's career in the House of Representatives coincided almost exactly with the struggle between North and South for control of Kansas. He arrived in Washington late in 1853, in time to throw himself into the fight over the organization of the territory. Seven years later, when he resigned his seat and led South Carolina out of the Union, the English Compromise was only eighteen months old.[1] During the years when the outcome was in doubt, he played a conspicuous and frequently destructive role in the struggle, consciously sacrificing the nation's peace and prosperity to a vain attempt to safeguard what he believed were the vital interests of his state and section. His inflammatory rhetoric, enormously effective on the floor of the House or on the stump, contributed immeasurably to the growth of sectional hostilities.[2]

Keitt went off to Washington determined to speak his mind regardless of whom he might offend and to avoid tying himself to any party or platform. At the start of the session, most Democrats supported Linn Boyd of Kentucky for Speaker of the House. All but one of the delegates from South Carolina supported James L. Orr, a conditional Unionist from Anderson District in the mountainous northwest corner of the state. Orr had led the opposition to secession in 1852, and Keitt refused to vote for him and instead supported John S. Millson of Virginia.[3]

In January 1854, before he was comfortably settled in his rooms at Flint's Hotel—on E Street, just off Pennsylvania Avenue—or in his seat at the rear of the House,[4] Stephen A. Douglas introduced into the Senate a bill to organize the Nebraska Territory. Douglas, the junior senator from Illinois and a leading candidate for president, was an outspoken advocate of westward expansion and popular sovereignty. Organization of the territory would clear the way for construction of an intercontinental railroad west from Chicago, encourage settlement, and ensure his future prosperity. For a territorial bill to pass the Congress, it had to attract the support of the South, and to do that, it had somehow to surmount the barrier to the expansion of slavery erected by the Missouri Compromise.

Douglas first tried to solve the problem by pushing it aside and pretending it did not exist. In its original form, his bill provided that the territory would enter the Union with or without slavery as its constitution prescribed. Southern congressmen realized that the proposal would exclude slaves until the territory applied for statehood and, led by Senator David Atchison of Missouri and the F Street Mess, forced Douglas to amend the bill, first by granting the people of the territory the right to decide the question, and then by declaring the compromise "inoperative and void" and opening the area north of 36° 30' to settlement by slaveholders. Finally, Douglas divided the territory in two, implying that one would be settled by Free Soilers and the other by slaves and slave owners.[5]

Administration support and a large, well-disciplined Democratic majority made it virtually certain that, even in the face of a ferocious assault by "Independent Democrats," the measure would sooner or later pass the Senate. Early in March, it did. In the House, however, victory was far from assured. Northern Free Soilers, convinced that the "Slave Power" was conspiring to extend its boundaries simultaneously southward into the Caribbean and westward into the plains, reacted in fear and anger. The product of an outburst of moral indignation reinforced by political and economic self-interest and encouraged by editors and clergymen as well as politicians, opposition to the bill rapidly gained momentum. Public opinion had no real influence in the Senate, where northern Democrats remained loyal to their party, but in the House it threatened to destroy the Democratic majority and block organization of the territories.[6]

The frenzied northern reaction contrasted initially with southern indifference. In the South radicals had long regarded the Missouri Compromise as a studied insult. Most of them feared that Missouri, surrounded on three sides by Free Soil, would in time be lost to slavery. Loss of the state would contract the boundaries of the South, reduce its influence in Congress, and divert trade that now flowed south toward New Orleans eastward into Chicago. They believed Douglas's bill did not do enough to protect slavery in the territories, and assumed that slave owners would not carry their human property into the West when they could employ it more lucratively in the Deep South. They accepted the bill as simple justice to the South and quietly supported it. Not until abolitionists condemned the measure as "a gross violation of a sacred pledge, a criminal betrayal of precious rights, part and parcel of an atrocious plot" did the South rally behind the measure. Not until the North assaulted its honor and its common sense did the South demand that the Congress approve the bill.[7]

In the House, debate on the bill began in mid-March when it reached the Committee of the Whole. With a vocal segment of the North in revolt, with the South seemingly indifferent to its fate, with northern elections half a year away, Keitt concluded that the bill could not pass.[8] On March 30, he seized the opportunity to address the Congress, not so much to defend the bill but to demand justice for the South. Ignoring the effects of the pneumonia that had confined him to his rooms for some weeks, he spoke for an hour to justify the repeal of the Missouri Compromise and defend the peculiar interests of his state and section.[9]

Keitt based his assault on the Missouri Compromise on two documents: the treaty by which the United States had acquired Louisiana and the U.S. Constitution. In the treaty with France, the federal government had guaranteed that the territory would be incorporated into the Union and the new states admitted as equals of the old. The Missouri Compromise violated that agreement by imposing requirements on the new states not imposed on the old. The government had guaranteed that the inhabitants of the territory would enjoy all the rights of American citizens, but by prohibiting slavery, the compromise deprived them of the right to determine the shape of their domestic institutions.

When the Missouri Compromise closed the Northwest to slavery, Keitt insisted, it violated the Constitution. The federal government was the creation of sovereign and equal states; it could act only as the agent of the states and exercise only powers delegated to it by the states. Under the Constitution, the states had retained the right to determine what was property and had delegated to the federal government only the responsibility to protect that property whatever it might be and wherever it might go. The southern states had decided that slaves were lawful property, and the federal government had no choice but to admit them to the territory and protect them as long as they remained there.[10]

Henry Clay and Daniel Webster had expected the Missouri Compromise to unite the nation after months of debate, but they were wrong. It had produced "unnumbered woes," encouraged the stronger section to trample on the rights of the weaker, and made resistance a law of self-preservation. Near the end of his life, John C. Calhoun had acquiesced in the extension of the compromise line to the Pacific Ocean, but Keitt would not. "Squatter sovereignty"[11] was not an acceptable solution to the problems facing the country. The doctrine, he insisted, threatened to subvert the Constitution and destroy the rights of the South. A territorial legislature had no more power than the Congress to forbid southerners to settle there with their slaves. A territory acquired sovereignty only when it entered the Union. After that it could determine the shape of its domestic institutions. Until that time it could not close its borders to slavery.

Long before he reached the end of his text, Keitt abandoned his constitutional defense of southern rights in favor of threats and denunciations. Northern fanatics, he believed, were determined to imprison slavery where it already existed and then wipe it out of existence. They too had owned slaves, but when they were no longer profitable, sold them, condemned their owners as pirates, induced them to murder their masters, lured them into the North, and left them "to wander, to starve, . . . and to die." The Congress must put an end to the attacks on the rights of the South. And if it refused, the South must confront the foe "with helmet on and visor down and lance couched," conscious of its right and strong in the justice of its cause, confident that the god of battles would give it the victory.[12]

In South Carolina the reaction to Keitt's speech was favorable but restrained. Both the *Charleston Courier* and the *Charleston Mercury* published extended summaries of his remarks, and both congratulated him for his "forceful and eloquent" defense of slavery and the South. The editor of the *Southern Quarterly Review* agreed. The speech was the product of superior industry and intellect, he wrote, and should be conclusive for "every just and appreciative mind."[13]

Almost three weeks later, in a reply to a letter from Olin M. Dantzler, Keitt discussed his opinions in greater detail. Dantzler, a boyhood friend and a prominent politician in Orangeburg District, had congratulated him on the success of his speech and expressed doubts about the Kansas bill. Keitt agreed; as an attempt to settle the slavery question, the bill was the "merest delusion." It did not confront the issue squarely, instead "shuffling and dodging" in an effort to satisfy all shades of political opinion. Popular sovereignty was a snare the South must avoid at all costs. In practice, it would give territorial legislatures authority to act on all domestic questions, including slavery, as long as they did not violate the Constitution. If a legislature enacted a law to prohibit slavery, that law would clearly violate the Constitution, but it was highly unlikely that the Supreme Court would strike it down. The judiciary, he insisted, was always the weakest, most timid branch of any government. If a territorial legislature enacted a law to establish slavery, the Congress would almost certainly refuse to allow it.

The bill, Keitt admitted, did hold out to the South one important benefit; it repealed the Missouri Compromise. Repeal would open Kansas to slavery and prevent Missouri from becoming Free Soil. It would pass the Congress if its friends could stop its enemies from striking out the Clayton amendment or specifically recognizing squatter sovereignty.[14] In spite of its inducements, Keitt was reluctant to support the bill. Southern congressmen who defended it were making a serious error. They were paying too high a price for repeal of the compromise, and in time they would realize it. In the end they would turn against the bill, and with the help of northern representatives who opposed the repeal, they would defeat it. Meanwhile, they should stand back and let the Yankees fight among themselves. He had proposed that no southerner speak on the subject, but several insisted, and he had joined them. He had not really talked about the bill; he had delivered an ultimatum to the North, demanding that it respect the rights of the South in the territories. As for the bill, he had not yet decided how he would vote.[15]

The debate raged on for more than a month after Keitt spoke on March 30. Early in May, as the struggle to force the bill through the House was nearing a climax, the South Carolina fire-eater plunged into a raucous exchange with half a dozen Free Soilers, emerging badly battered but unwilling to concede that he had lost the fight.

On May 3, Keitt objected to a proposal by Israel Washburn of Maine that the federal government grant land in the territories to free blacks. Black people could go to Kansas as property, he insisted, but not as property owners. Washburn interrupted, demanding to know where black people would go if they could not settle in the West. Keitt pounced on the question: abolitionists lured slaves away from their rightful owners, he charged, and then demanded that the federal government give them land to settle. Why did not the abolitionists provide homes for their stolen goods in the North?

Washburn interrupted again. Why, he demanded, could black people not settle in the territories as citizens? Keitt's reply anticipated the ruling of the U.S. Supreme Court in *Scott v. Sandford*: because, he said, theirs was a government of white men. He did not object if Maine chose to make citizens of black men, but the federal government could recognize only white men. The territories were the common property of all the states, and any attempt to admit free black people was an attack on southern institutions and a violation of the Constitution. Turning to Congressman Edward Wade, he asked if black people in Ohio voted or intermarried with white people. Wade replied, "It is just as they please about that." Keitt lashed back at him: "The white man who marries a black woman must be so degraded that even such a connection will elevate him."

The Speaker tried to put a stop to the raucous exchange, but Joshua Giddings of Ohio sarcastically moved to open the territories to persons "more than half white." His intention, he said, was to benefit the descendants of Thomas Jefferson and Martha Washington who otherwise would be barred from settling there. "The gentleman across the way" had said that theirs was a government of white men, but Keitt himself was two-thirds black, if the color of the people of his district were an accurate indication of his complexion. The minority side of the House roared its appreciation.

Next it was the turn of Giddings's colleague, Lewis Campbell. The white race in Ohio, he assured the House, would not be improved by intermarriage with black people, and the citizens of Ohio were not in the habit of marrying them. But, he asked Keitt, if white people did not marry black people in his district, how could he explain the large number of mulattoes who lived there? Raising his voice to make himself heard above the explosion of laughter, the Speaker ruled the question out of order. Keitt was equal to the challenge. Ignoring the Speaker's repeated attempts to silence him, the fire-eater spat out his reply to Campbell: If there were mulattoes in South Carolina, it was because itinerant Yankee schoolmasters and nutmeg venders had spawned them there.[16]

Sooner or later, congressmen converted even discussions of seemingly unrelated matters into debates on slavery and the territories. On May 4, the House was considering ways of stamping out polygamy in Utah. Keitt conceded that the practice was disgusting but questioned the right of the federal government to interfere in the domestic relations of the territory. The government's right to acquire land implied the right to govern it subject to limits imposed by the Constitution. But if the Congress could prohibit polygamy in the territory, it could also prohibit marriage there. Keitt's implication was unmistakable: if Congress could prohibit polygamy, it could also prohibit slavery.

To destroy polygamy, Keitt warned the congressmen, they must increase the powers of the federal government, burst the bands of the Confederacy, and weld the fragments into a consolidated despotism. Polygamy was a "burning shame" to any community, and he would vote to abolish it as quickly as any man, if only Congress had the right. Even if the Congress did prohibit polygamy, no jury in Utah would enforce the law. The government could root out the evil only by imposing a military tyranny over the people of the territory. Before they acted, he advised his colleagues, they should look to the practical difficulties that confronted them, and not to the moral and social enormities alone. Again, his implication was clear: the Congress must not try to stamp out slavery in the territories where it did not have the ability to do the job.[17]

Time after time, debate between the two nearly equal sides threatened to descend into violence. On April 13, Keitt prevented Henry Edmundson of Virginia from assaulting Lewis Campbell of Ohio, a leader of the northern coalition that was trying to defeat the Douglas bill by talking it to death. Enraged by Campbell's attacks on the South and slavery, Edmundson tried to club the man with the butt of his pistol. With help from his friend William Aiken of South Carolina, Keitt pulled Edmundson away from his quarry and prevented a crowd of irate southerners from rushing into the fray. His behavior must have amazed men who knew him well. In the future Keitt would provoke far more confrontations than he prevented.[18] He was rarely willing to overlook an insult to himself or his state, intentional or not, and frequently lashed out at his attackers with fists or cane. During the time he was a member of the House his refusal to govern his notoriously explosive temper repeatedly led him into trouble. His constituents overwhelmingly approved his impetuous behavior, bombastic oratory, and outspoken defense of southern interests, and in his 1854 campaign for reelection he ran unopposed.

In May, Democratic leaders in the House decided to shut off debate and force a vote on the Kansas bill. Alexander H. Stephens took charge of administration forces, maneuvered the bill through a maze of parliamentary pitfalls, and won final approval by a narrow margin, 113 to 100. Unwilling to oppose the repeal of the Missouri Compromise and unable to overcome his hatred for squatter sovereignty, Keitt refused to vote. He was joined by John McQueen of Bennettsville, who represented South Carolina's First District. Only two southern Democrats, John S. Millson of Virginia and Thomas Hart Benton of Missouri, voted against the bill.[19]

Early in the spring of 1854, the struggle for Kansas that had begun in Washington shifted to the territory. Thousands of men, most of them farmers or lawyers or speculators out to make their fortunes, flooded into the area. Some, however, were fire-eaters—planters, politicians, "border ruffians"—determined to protect slavery in Missouri and add another state to the slave block in Congress. For their purposes Kansas was attracting too many settlers from the North, most of them from the Ohio Valley, and too few from the South. It quickly became obvious that, in a confrontation with the Free Soilers, the champions of slavery would come out second best, and they sent their friends in the South desperate appeals for help. For the most part, Kansas was no more violent than any other territory during the early stages of development. But many of the southern settlers were determined to hold onto the territory, even if it meant intimidating voters and stuffing ballot boxes, shooting rival politicians, and burning down rival settlements.[20]

At the start, South Carolinians were largely indifferent to the furor over Kansas, but early in 1856, with the territory already in flames, the fight to make the West safe for slavery finally attracted their attention. South Carolina editors urged each of the state's six congressional districts to raise and equip volunteers to settle the territory. In Keitt's Third District, leaders formed Kansas associations, pledged to migrate to the territory, and canvassed for men and money. Prominent politicians wrote letters to newspapers and addressed mass meetings, calling on their constituents to contribute their money and their sons to the campaign.[21]

In Keitt's district, the initial response was encouraging. At a meeting in Orangeburg, organizers collected more than twelve hundred dollars and turned the money over to an expedition about to leave for the territory. At Whippy Swamp Cross Roads, Gillisonville, and Bell's Cross Roads—and, no doubt, at other villages overlooked by the correspondents of Charleston newspapers—speakers harangued and audiences pledged their support. Fifteen volunteers left the district for Kansas in the spring of 1855, followed a year later by twenty more led by

Keitt's political rival Lewis M. Ayer.[22] The Orangeburg *Southron* published letters from Kansas, one reporting that a thousand South Carolinians were in the territory—almost certainly an exaggeration—and another predicting the imminent outbreak of civil war. By the time the letter appeared in print, prediction had become reality. A third letter reported the sack of Lawrence, boasted that a company of South Carolinians had participated, and begged for more support from home. "Send on men and means," it urged. The abolitionists were too cowardly to fight back; if the South would only do its duty, it would make Kansas a slave state and increase the influence of the slave block in Congress.[23]

Keitt plunged joyfully into the campaign, speaking and writing whenever his congressional duties would permit. Early in 1856, he replied publicly to a constituent who had written about his plans to settle in Kansas. In his letter, published first in the Orangeburg *Southron* and copied widely throughout the state, Keitt stressed the need for slave owners to populate the territory. The climate of Kansas was perfectly suited to growing corn, wheat, and hemp. Men who cultivated the crops with slave labor would expand plantation agriculture into the West, benefit the South, and earn fabulous profits for themselves.

Even more important than the climate of the territory was its location. If Kansas became Free Soil, Keitt warned, it would become a nursery for abolitionists and a haven for fugitive slaves. A free Kansas would slowly but surely destroy slavery in Missouri. State after state would become victims of abolitionist fanatics; state after state would be lost to slavery. The South must wage the battle now, outside its own borders, on the plains of Kansas. For thirty years the South had been preparing for battle; now, at the hour of reckoning, it must not allow Missouri to face the abolitionist hoards alone. The Third District contained more slaves than any other; it had more to lose politically and economically if the North excluded them from the territory; its people must play a prominent part in the struggle. As for himself, said Keitt, he would support any plan they might adopt to seize Kansas for the South.[24]

Early in May, with the campaign apparently successful in South Carolina, Keitt traveled south from Washington to Petersburg, Virginia, to stir up enthusiasm there. Later, he reported that he had spoken to a crowd so large that it had jammed a large hall to capacity. The evening had been a great success; forty-seven men had volunteered to go to Kansas, and the wealthy men of the city had poured out their money for the cause.[25]

Keitt could not have known it at the time, but the southern campaign to send settlers to Kansas would be a miserable failure. Like Keitt, its leaders were skilled at haranguing crowds but inept at organizing projects and seeing them through to successful conclusions. The campaign was badly organized; its leaders recognized the need to coordinate the efforts of the independent Kansas associations that sprang up after 1854 but did little to bring order out of chaos. In the Third Congressional District as in all the others, interest quickly flagged. Men pledged contributions and never paid them; other men volunteered to fight and never left home. In Kansas, expectations of creating a new slave state faded rapidly, wiped out by an influx of northern settlers the South could not match. Too few slaveholders had any real interest in migrating to Kansas or any real desire to go there. Why would a man take slaves into an area in which so many settlers were hostile to the peculiar institution when fertile land, favorable climate, supportive government, and welcoming neighbors beckoned in the Southwest? Why go to Kansas when Texas was clamoring for settlers?[26]

When the first session of the Thirty-fourth Congress convened in December 1855, Keitt and his Democratic colleagues confronted two new parties and another new crisis. A legislature sitting at Shawnee Mission, Kansas, elected by fraud and dominated by slave owners, had expelled the Free Soil delegates and enacted a draconian legal code designed to safeguard slavery in the territory. Its most egregious provisions barred opponents of slavery from holding public office and sitting on juries, disfranchised critics of the Fugitive Slave Act, and made aiding a fugitive a capital offense.

At Topeka, a Free Soil convention had created a rival government, adopted a constitution, and applied for admission to the Union as a free state. Bushwhackings and claim jumpings threatened to plunge the two camps into civil war. President Franklin Pierce and the governors he appointed one after another failed miserably to restore order in the territory.[27]

Before the House could deal with the crisis in the territory, it had to organize, a process that was seriously complicated by the disintegration of the Whig Party and the emergence of the Republicans. The unexpected appearance of the Know Nothings added to the confusion and all but guaranteed that any attempt to elect a Speaker would degenerate into political chaos.

The Native American or Know Nothing Party had appeared in South Carolina for the first time in the autumn of 1854. Under the leadership of John Cunningham, the editor of the *Charleston Evening News*, it grew slowly but steadily, especially in the cities and large towns of the state. On the surface, Know Nothings in South Carolina appeared to share the concerns of nativists in the North. During the two decades that preceded the secession crisis, approximately forty thousand immigrants had taken up residence in the state. By the mid-1850s, some 15 percent of the total population and 30 percent of the white population was foreign born. In 1854 the *Evening News* began to publish editorials denouncing foreigners and Roman Catholics and demanding that the legislature take steps to make the state safe for native Protestants. By strengthening the naturalization and election laws, it could check the growth of the Catholic Church and ensure that America was ruled by "Americans."[28]

In South Carolina fears of foreigners and Roman Catholics had to take a back seat to fears unfamiliar to Know Nothings farther north. To Cunningham and the men around him, the growing strength of the national Democratic Party in South Carolina posed a far greater threat to the political welfare of the state than a handful of alien Papists ever could. Afraid that the efforts of Benjamin F. Perry and James L. Orr to lure the state back into the party would succeed and convinced that the old formulas for warding off Unionists and abolitionists would not, Cunningham was willing to do anything—even to join the Know Nothings—to defend the interests of the state.[29]

From the start it was obvious that Know Nothings in South Carolina would not cooperate with the northern wing of the party. A majority of them objected to planks in the party's platform that pledged to limit the extension of both slavery and the consumption of alcohol and rejected outright its attack on the rights of aliens and naturalized Americans. Cunningham and his followers were not particularly interested in curbing the flow of foreigners and Catholics into the state. The Whig Party in the state had never been strong, and now it was falling apart. The Know Nothing Party provided a convenient screen behind which they could create a southern rights party strong enough to prevent South Carolina Unionists from coaxing the state back into the Democratic Party.[30]

Whatever the reason, South Carolina Know Nothings won a number of victories in local elections soon after the formation of the party. In the fall of 1854, Charleston elected a Know Nothing to the state senate, and the following spring three cities—Charleston, Columbia, and Greenville—elected Know Nothing mayors.[31] The early success of the party alarmed radicals like Keitt who believed it posed a greater threat than the Republicans. If it could gain a foothold in South Carolina, it could split the radical camp and divide the state between two parties, a situation South Carolina politicians had worked hard to avoid. Keitt also feared, probably without cause, that the party could undermine his hold on the Third District and deprive him of his seat in the House at the next election.[32]

The movement to snuff out the Know Nothing menace in South Carolina brought together politicians who had little in common beyond hostility to the new party. Keitt found himself allied uneasily with national Democrats like Orr and Perry, men whose company he usually found uncongenial.[33] At first many of Keitt's new colleagues held back, understandably reluctant to attack a political phenomenon whose popularity seemed to be growing rapidly all along the east coast. Keitt's congressional district was overwhelmingly rural and agricultural; the only ethnic voters were largely German Protestants, and he no saw reason to hesitate. On January 3, soon after the Congress returned from its Christmas recess, he launched an all-out attack on the Know Nothings.[34]

In Europe, Keitt told the Congress, "the heavings of the social strata . . . , the rupture and chaos of industrial relations, and the armed collisions of Governments" had reduced working men to poverty and swollen the flood of immigrants into the United States. From the first the northern states had welcomed the immigrants, exploited their labor, and achieved "miracles of enterprise," throwing bridges across the mountains and building roads over the clouds, but they had also reduced the wages of American labor to the merest pittance. They were too pious to make slaves of black men, but they had trampled down free white men, men of their own race, and made slaves of them instead. "Black slaves you will not have," he sneered, but "white slaves you would make." Now the men they had exploited were fighting back.[35]

The grievances of American workingmen were real, Keitt continued, and they were being exploited by devious politicians, camp followers who hovered around the battlefield to plunder the dead and rifle the baggage. They were like the Jews who followed Jesus, not because he healed the sick and gave sight to the blind, but because he multiplied the loaves and fishes. They had founded a new party, the Know Nothings, and made it "a sanctuary for malcontents and a hospital for changlings."[36]

This new political order, Keitt told the Congress, demanded the extension of the naturalization laws, the exclusion of foreigners from positions of trust and honor, and the proscription of the Roman Catholic Church, but it did not demand an end to immigration, the only way it could rescue American labor from poverty and degradation. It demanded only that the Congress deny the suffrage to any person born in a foreign country, a measure that would not resolve the problems of American labor but would violate the constitutional right of the states to regulate the franchise.[37]

Keitt next quoted Congressman Nathaniel Banks of Massachusetts, who had accused northern capitalists of pushing two-thirds of the people of his state into the gutter and forcing them "to flit along subterranean paths, and conspire in secret against their own Government." The Know Nothing Party was conceived in secrecy; it hid from the light of day; it conspired at midnight and struck down its victims in the dark. Suffrage was the lifeblood of the republic. For the body politic to remain healthy, its citizens must exercise the suffrage freely, intelligently, and with discrimination. When men planned measures in secret and hid them from view, that was impossible. The laws enacted by the government affected the interests of every man, and every man must be free to examine those measures for himself and vote as he saw fit. The way to protect the rights of labor was to abolish immigration, not disfranchise immigrants.[38]

The South, Keitt concluded, must not encourage the growth of the Know Nothings within its borders, or create class distinctions within its white population. In the South labor was not threatened by grinding poverty. Capital and labor were united by bonds of mutual obligation. The franchise was limited to a portion of the community, but no part of that community starved. In the North the franchise was unqualified, but capital and labor recognized no mutual obligation, and a tenth of the laboring population died every year from the lack of food and shelter. The North was free to choose any social system it wanted, but the southern system was superior, and the North would do well to copy it.[39]

Amelia Murray, a British noblewoman with "literary tastes" and a member of Queen Victoria's household, listened to Keitt's speech from the visitors' gallery of the House. It was, she wrote later, "fervid, energetic, argumentative and eloquent." She had heard all of the great orators in Parliament during the past twenty years, but none of them could rival Keitt for eloquence. She had expected to "find a sad lack of talent and political honesty" in the United States, but she had been surprised by the rhetoric and appearance of the congressmen she encountered. That night at Willard's Hotel, she had met Keitt, who had pointed out a number of Know Nothings. One could easily recognize them, he told her, by their "crude, unintelligent style of conversation."[40]

The following day, January 4, Augustus Sollers of Maryland tried to answer Keitt's attack on his party. The Know Nothings, he insisted, wanted only to save the nation from destruction, whether by European paupers or northern abolitionists or southern nullifiers.[41] Sollers's remark associating abolitionists and secessionists and condemning both of them equally was more than Keitt could swallow in silence. He had been a member of the secessionist party in 1850, Keitt told the congressman. He had demanded that South Carolina interpose its sovereignty as a shield between its citizens and the outrages of the central government. He had opposed federal aggression; he had advised the state to abandon the federal compact and if necessary decide the question on the field of battle. But he had acted openly, in the "light of the sun," not like a hired assassin who struck at midnight and the next day "professed to know nothing" about the deed. He owed his allegiance to South Carolina, Keitt continued, and through his state to the federal government. Whenever his state called him home, he would "scorn your clamors, and trample upon your hosannas to the Union."[42]

Observers agreed that Keitt's speech and his reply to Sollers were truly eloquent. A correspondent of the *Charleston Mercury* reported that the speech had "induced deep reflection" in southern congressmen who had committed themselves to the new party. An anonymous letter published in the Boston *American Celt* commended Keitt's "ability, modesty and good sense," and pointed to the importance of Irish votes to the continued success of the South and the Democratic Party.[43]

Devastating as Keitt's assaults on the Know Nothings surely were, they paled in comparison to the abuse southern editors routinely heaped on the party. Its supporters were "murderers, thieves, thugs, orphan killers, brass knucklers, . . . assassins, . . . widow makers, rowdies, bullies, plug-uglies, drunkards, house burners . . . and rioters."[44] Even Keitt would have been impressed by such vivid use of language.

Keitt was sure none of his speeches had won as much popular acclaim as this one attacking the Know Nothings. Sue Sparks, the woman he would marry in 1859, warned that it might turn public opinion against him, but he refused to listen to her. He had not stopped to worry that his speech was indiscreet. The party was "dangerous and demoralizing"; he had struck it, and he would strike it again when he had the opportunity. He knew demagogues could make capital out of the speech, but when a vital principle was at stake, he would never stop to wonder if the multitude thought as he did. He would never "stoop to a namby-pamby dalliance . . . a melodramatic flirtation with public opinion." In the end, Keitt assured her, his constituents would approve his stand and crush the Know Nothings under their heels.[45]

Early in February, Keitt wrote to James Chesnut, a wealthy planter from Camden and a member of the state senate, to justify his attack on the Know Nothings. He would have written sooner, he explained, if he had not gone hunting, stood in a marsh for four or five hours, and caught pneumonia. In South Carolina, Keitt explained, he had largely ignored the new party; in Washington he realized it posed a serious threat to the welfare of the South. It was a coalition of protectionists and Free Soilers. It could never raise the wages of American working men by ending the flow of immigrants into the country; it could do that only be reducing the flow of foreign goods, and to do that it would have to increase the tariff. It had elected Free Soilers to the Congress: Seward, Harlan, Trumbull, and Wilson to the Senate and men of similar ilk to the House. True southerners must do everything in their power, Keitt warned, to ensure that the party did not survive.[46]

After Congress adjourned early in March, Keitt returned to South Carolina to alert his constituents to the menace of the new party. He spoke repeatedly at public dinners and mass meetings, warning that the Know Nothings were really Free Soilers and protectionists in a new guise. Even after Virginia Democrats led by Henry Wise won a series of spectacular victories in the spring of 1855—convincing evidence that the Know Nothings would not take root in the South—he refused to break off the attack.[47] "It requires . . . no great prescience to read the future," he told Sue Sparks late in May. "The Know Nothings are going fast to the wall and out of their debris an insignificant party only can be raised, and that [only] for the time being. Those who thought I had dashed my head against the wall in leading off against them, will see the future disclosed."[48]

Perhaps Keitt was concerned about the approaching elections for the South Carolina legislature. Perhaps he had discovered that Know Nothings made excellent whipping boys, or perhaps he was unwilling to believe the party was really dead. Whatever the reason, the young congressman refused to call a halt to his campaign and spent much of the summer storming through his district, haranguing any crowd that would listen to him. At Whippy Swamp, he called the Know Nothings a "bastard coalition," a corrupt union of northern Democrats and Whigs, abolitionists, and office seekers. At Orangeburg and again at Chick Springs, he warned that the party threatened the vital interests of the South. At a time when southerners should be arming themselves for one great battle in defense of conservatism and state rights, it threatened to distract them with its proscriptions and its bigotry. It promised to preserve American markets for American laboring men but refused to cut off the influx of immigrants. Why? Because the immigrants increased northern representation in Congress and tightened the hold of the Free Soilers over the federal government.[49]

Events in the fall of 1855 finally convinced Keitt that the Know Nothings no longer posed a threat to him or his state. When a group of his constituents invited him to attend a public meeting at Barnwell Court House, he agreed to speak, but not about the Know Nothings. That party, Keitt insisted, "only required a burial service."[50]

Nevertheless, Keitt did take one last swipe at the rapidly dying party. In February 1856, Franklin Pierce asked him to address a campaign rally in Georgetown, a short distance from the capital. The Democrats were facing a critical election, and the president wanted to do everything possible to guarantee a victory over the Know Nothings. Keitt reluctantly agreed to speak. The night of the meeting was cold and windy, the hall was large and crowded, and Keitt had to shout to make himself heard. Afterward, he had to walk a quarter of a mile to a dinner in his honor. Before he arrived, he told Sue, "an ice bolt smote to my very heart." For a time he had feared pneumonia might carry him off, but by the end of the month, he was out of danger, "only weak and petulant." At least the speech had been a success; the Democrats had won the election by three hundred votes. After his appearance in Georgetown, late in 1855, Keitt paid little attention to his old enemies. In 1856 he had new ones to contend with.[51]

When the Thirty-fourth Congress assembled in December 1855, it was badly split among anti-Nebraska Democrats, administration Democrats, southern

Democrats, Republicans, and Know Nothings. The Republican Party was emerging, the Know Nothings were falling apart, a handful of die-hard Whigs were refusing to concede their party was already dead, and no faction could elect a Speaker on its own. The result was a protracted contest at a time when the Congress desperately needed to deal with the crises confronting the nation.[52]

Keitt saved his most revealing comments for his letters to Sue. The old parties, he told her, "already effete," were disbanding and dying out. He could see no real difference between the Know Nothings and the national Democrats. Their proposals for ending the sectional conflict were "quackery." Whatever the future held, he was determined to keep his district conservative or die in the attempt.[53]

During a speech at Barnwell Court House in October, Keitt repeated his assertion that the old parties were dying, victims of their flirtations with the Free Soil doctrines that dominated the North. As to what the state should do, he insisted that it do everything possible to defend its independence and its honor: refuse to send delegates to the Democratic convention in Cincinnati, support the party when it was true and oppose it when false, reject all compromise, refuse to sacrifice duty and honor for place and power.[54]

Keitt and the rest of the South Carolina delegation refused to participate in the Democratic caucus, fearing they might unintentionally commit themselves to vote for a Speaker hostile to the interests of the state. They did support Samuel A. Richardson, a "fat, jovial, tobacco chewing" Douglas Democrat from Illinois, as long as he remained the party's candidate,[55] but neither Richardson nor his Republican rivals—first Lewis Campbell of Ohio and later Nathaniel P. Banks of Massachusetts—could win without the support of the Know Nothings who held the balance of power. They refused to throw their votes to either side, and for weeks ballot followed ballot, caucus followed caucus, and speech followed speech without breaking the deadlock. Keitt's support for Richardson was erratic, more because he was bored than because he was dissatisfied with the Democratic candidate. He voted consistently for Richardson during the early ballots and irregularly as long as he retained the support of the party. On the fifty-fifth ballot, Richardson voted for Keitt.[56]

On December 22, Keitt moved that the balloting be suspended until January 3 so congressmen could spend the Christmas holidays with their families. The House voted down his resolution, but Keitt left Washington anyway.[57] When he returned early in the New Year, the voting was still in progress. In mid-January, the Democratic caucus shifted its support temporarily from Richardson to James L. Orr, the moderate who represented South Carolina's Fifth District, but Keitt refused to go along, voting instead for retired filibusterer John A. Quitman of Mississippi.[58]

Congressmen of both parties consumed hundreds of hours propounding questions to the candidates, trying to force them to discuss the issues and antagonize the Know Nothings whose votes would ultimately determine the election. On January 9, a violent debate disrupted the ninety-second ballot. Replying to repeated accusations that the Know Nothings were to blame for the failure of the House to elect a Speaker, Percy Walker of Alabama insisted that the Democrats were equally at fault. Trying to demonstrate that the Democrats were as badly divided as the Americans, he quoted at length a speech Keitt had delivered at Barnwell Court House during the summer. Keitt had charged that the Democratic Party in the North was uncompromisingly hostile to the extension of slavery into the territories. By quoting "one of their best, their ablest, and most reliable members," Walker was certain he had proved that the Democrats were caught up in a family quarrel even more divisive than the Know Nothings.[59]

The debate was meaningless, wasting time, stirring up personal antagonisms, and accomplishing nothing. All the same, Keitt demanded the right to reply. He was not, he insisted, a member of the Democratic Party. He wore no party collar and would never wear one. He would support any just measure, regardless of the party that endorsed it. He expressed his own opinions, and no man could quote him to prove that the Democratic Party lacked unity.[60]

Keitt indulged in a brief tirade against the Know Nothings and then, prodded by his friend Preston Brooks, admitted that he approved the platform endorsed by the Democratic caucus. The party, he said, in an obvious reference to the Democrats' support for the Kansas-Nebraska bill and the defections it had provoked, was purer then than it had been for many years. It had passed through fire and water, and its impurities had burned away. As long as it remained true to the Constitution and the South, he would support it. He did not want his state to send delegates to the Democratic Convention in Cincinnati, but if the party nominated Franklin Pierce for a second term, he would gladly support its candidate. A correspondent of the *Charleston Mercury* called Keitt's declaration of independence from party shackles the most eloquent speech he had ever made. When he finished, his friends had flocked around his seat to congratulate him. Grasping his hand, William Aiken had exclaimed: "Ah, Keitt, if your lady love had been in the gallery, your victory would have been complete."[61]

By mid-January, the long struggle over the speakership had begun to take its toll. Keitt told Sue Sparks he was "almost broken down." It was less the physical effort than the "unbroken intellectual solicitude" during the endless sessions that exhausted him. The Congress was playing for high stakes; the vote was so close that his might decide the result, but "this keeping the loins of the mind girded up" was rapidly wearing him down.[62]

Keitt's exchange with Russell Sage of New York reflected the growing tension. During a long and tedious cross-examination of the candidates, Sage demanded to know how Richardson would select the members of the committees on naturalization and territories. Keitt interrupted; if the gentleman from Illinois would promise to put Sage on the committees, would the gentleman from New York vote for him? Obviously angered, Sage replied, "Does the gentleman suppose that I can be bought . . . ? A different standard of morality must prevail in South Carolina." Keitt refused to back down: "Well, when that gentleman *dares* to intimate anything of that kind in reference to my State, I will answer him in a specific way. . . . Let him have the courage to do it openly." The exchange ended amid roars of laughter and demands for order. The flare-up passed quickly, and the next day, January 12, both Keitt and Sage apologized for their parts in the disruption.[63]

On the first day of February, the Democrats conceded that neither Richardson nor Orr could win, and transferred their support to Aiken.[64] Keitt worked hard for his colleague, helping to persuade seven southern Know Nothings to switch their votes to the Democratic candidate.[65] It was not enough; on February 2, the House agreed to choose the speaker by plurality vote, and on the 133rd ballot elected Banks over Aiken, 103–100. Banks had been a Democrat and then a Know Nothing. In 1856 he was a Republican, prompting Keitt to label his election a victory for the abolitionists. Keitt had played only a minor part in the squabble. It had ended badly for the Democrats, but now at least the Congress was free to turn its attention to the problems that plagued the nation.[66]

Of all the dilemmas that faced the federal government, the confrontation of North and South in Kansas was by far the most explosive. Faced by the threat of civil war in the territory, an able and courageous president would have acted vigorously to restore order to the territory. Unfortunately, Franklin Pierce was neither able nor courageous. He could have used the army to put an end to the violence; two or three squadrons of cavalry would have been enough to do the job. He could have appointed an impartial commission to investigate the situation; he could have ordered new elections for a territorial government that accurately reflected the will of a majority of the legitimate settlers, but he did none of these things.

Pierce avoided confronting the crisis in the territories as long as he could, and on January 24, when he could delay no longer, sent a special message to Congress describing the violence in Kansas and defending his half-hearted efforts to deal with it. He blamed the collapse of law and order on territorial governors Andrew Reeder, Wilson Shannon, and John Geary, and the northern emigrant aid societies; he defended the actions of the Shawnee Mission Legislature, and he threatened to suppress the free-state movement if it resisted the legitimate government of the territory.[67]

The president's message touched off a long and largely fruitless debate in both houses of Congress that consumed the better part of the next four months. In mid-March, the Lower House created a committee to investigate the charges of fraud and violence each side had hurled at the other. Beyond that one constructive act, it accomplished nothing. Instead, Democrats and Republicans endlessly traded verbal brickbats. Emotions rapidly reached the breaking point; in Congress and in the country at large, talk of secession and war became increasingly common.[68]

Keitt, of course, flung himself joyously into the struggle. On April 7, during a debate already marred by bitter quarreling, he delivered a violent denunciation of what he called the "Nebraska Vendetta." He may have believed it would be his last speech in the House before he resigned his seat to accept a diplomatic post in Italy, and was determined to make it impossible for his enemies to forget him.[69]

Keitt spoke for almost an hour, wandering over a bewildering variety of topics—abolitionist fanaticism, Yankee hypocrisy, Know Nothings and Black Republicans, the superior intelligence and virtue of the South, the one-term principle, the coming presidential election, and the slave trade. He sneered at the abolitionists, "their blood warmed into insolence, the trumpet of philanthropy in their glozing mouths, . . . singing psalms through their noses, [moving] down upon the South like an army with banners; they come to set their venom to do its work, and seal her overthrow with havoc and conflagration. Between the South and such men there must be war." Unwilling to end his assault, he returned to the subject midway through the speech: "Born amid jeers, contempt and scorn, nursed in the haunts of obscurity and fattened upon the offals of the shambles, and the garbage of the gutter, [abolition] has waxed corpulent and audacious. Under the plea of justice, it commits a fraud; and under the pretense of humanity it libels truth."

Keitt treated the Know Nothings no better, calling their platform "a mess of verbiage, insipidities, crudities, flatulent professions and impalpable abstractions." He condemned the free society of the North, plagued by crime and poverty, disease and misfortune. It had produced an army of starving workers, an array of crowded jails, fetid hospitals, and breadless tables. The Good Samaritans of the North could find enough social outcasts on their own doorsteps to occupy their time and charity, if only they would look for them and leave the South to solve its own problems. The North could keep its society if that was what it wanted; the South preferred its own and would defend it to the death.

Yankees were hypocrites hiding behind their pleas for racial justice: "Grinning malignantly from behind the mask of religion," they had committed a monstrous crime against the South. History would convict the North of the sin of enslaving Africans and transporting them to the South, and credit the South for introducing them to civilization and Christianity. It would convict the North of pocketing the profits from their sale, and then marching "through blood and massacre, over burning homes and butchered families" to set them free.[70]

After an hour Keitt finally reached the real subject of his harangue. Public opinion could grapple with only one subject at a time, he told the House; in 1856, that subject was the government of the territories. The South demanded that Congress choose between abolitionist demands and constitutional obligations. The South would not acquiesce any longer in pettifogging subterfuges and slippery evasions, or accept any more pliant leaders and elastic platforms. If the Congress made the wrong choice, if it refused to admit Kansas to the Union because its constitution sanctioned slavery, Keitt warned, the history of the Union would come to a close: "We have reared this Government through toil and travail, through blood and sacrifice; we have invested it with authority, have enriched it with treasuries, and fleets, and armies, and have endowed it with Senates, and courts, and judges; but if it becomes, in our very midst, a foreign government, the South will tear it down from turret to foundation stone. Abolish the inter-state slave trade, and we will trample your usurpation under foot. Repeal the fugitive slave law, and the South will meet you with gauntlets on."[71]

Keitt was enormously pleased by the reception his speech received. It was "even more successful than I even had hoped it would be, " he told his fiancée a week later. He was having it printed and "scattered . . . all over the country."[72] Without exception, southern editors agreed with the congressman's favorable assessment. Too much had already been said about the slavery question, the *Washington Union* told its readers; only a speaker "of no ordinary reputation . . . and abilities" could attract a large audience to a discussion of such a hackneyed subject. For more than an hour, Keitt had held the attention of a packed House, the lobbies, and the ladies' galleries. A number of senators, among them James M. Mason, Andrew Pickens Butler, John Slidell, and David Yulee, had come to the Lower House to hear the speech, and congratulated him warmly at its close.

In a letter to the *Baltimore Republican,* "J.C.M." described the speech as "beyond all odds the best of the session." Keitt's assault on the "vile hypocrisy" of the North had brought two abolitionist congressmen to their feet in a rage, but he had treated them with contempt and chased them "writhing and wriggling back to their seats like whipped curs." He had awed the Black Republicans, and they had quailed before him. The friends of the Union were fortunate to have in Congress so able and earnest a champion. Keitt was, the editor of the *Mobile Daily Register* flatly asserted, "the finest orator in the House, . . . a man of very superior attainments" who had a bright future ahead of him.[73]

Ten days later, in a reply to innocuous remarks by Benjamin Stanton of Ohio, Keitt returned to the subject of Kansas and slavery. Stanton had announced that he would use the approaching presidential campaign to condemn the Pierce administration for its bungling in the territories. The Kansas-Nebraska Act, Keitt admitted, had loosed a whirlwind in the North, and the Republican Party had ridden it into office. By promising to restore the Missouri Compromise, repeal the Fugitive Slave Law, prevent the admission of new slave states, and abolish the domestic slave trade, it had won a plurality in the House of Representatives. It had elected a Speaker and seized control of the legislative machinery. But, he sneered, with the appurtenances of power in its hands, what had the party done to carry out its threats against the South? It was afraid to act boldly and go to the voters for approval; it ignored its manifestoes, swallowed its threats, and masked its principles. It shrank from the issues and "cringing, crawl[ed] to its objectives."[74]

No doubt Keitt enjoyed the laughter his last sally inspired on the Democratic side of the House. For Yankee-baiting invective, even in an age when the boundaries of political decorum were vaguely defined at best, he had few equals and no superiors. His back-to-back assaults preceded Charles Sumner's "Crime Against Kansas" by more than six weeks and may well have helped to provoke it. Certainly they poisoned the atmosphere to the extent that an outbreak of violence was all but unavoidable. Sumner's description of Andrew Pickens Butler was despicable, but no more so than Keitt's all-out assault on the Republicans.

THREE

"He who dallies is a dastard"

At least as early as the fall of 1855, South Carolina politicians began to look ahead to the presidential elections of the following year. Speaking for the state's moderate minority, James L. Orr proposed that it take the novel step of sending delegates to the Democratic nominating convention. During the nullification controversy more than twenty years earlier, South Carolina had cut its ties to both national parties and had never reestablished them. Twice it had intentionally thrown away its electoral votes by casting them for men who had no chance of winning the presidency, John Floyd of Virginia in 1832 and Willie P. Mangum of North Carolina in 1836. Not since the Jacksonians had held the first nominating convention in 1832 had it sent an official delegation to a convention held by any party.[1]

Orr's arguments in favor of rejoining the national Democrats should have been persuasive. The state should support northern friends of the South; it should work to unify the South inside the party; it should press the party to adopt policies that would benefit the South. The proposal gained support, particularly in the up country, and by early spring, led by moderates like Orr and Benjamin F. Perry of Greenville, twenty-three of the state's twenty-nine districts had organized public meetings and elected delegates to a state Democratic convention scheduled for May 5 in Columbia.[2]

South Carolina radicals failed to agree on how best to react. In Fairfield District politicians tried to organize a new party to nominate a southern man with southern principles to run for the presidency. The idea quickly died. Like many of his radical friends—William W. Boyce, John McQueen, Robert Barnwell Rhett—Keitt was sympathetic, but like his friends, he was deeply suspicious of all political parties; they knew that southerners were as likely as anybody else to abandon principles for patronage. As a result, the movement to form a new southern rights party died before it was fairly launched.[3]

The radicals had more success attacking the convention movement head-on. Speaking at Barnwell Court House on October 15, Keitt defended the political course the state had pursued for almost a quarter-century and insisted it was the best possible course for the future. What, Keitt asked, could South Carolina gain by attending the Democratic convention or participating in national politics? The state generally acted with the Democrats, but it must remain free to support the party when it was right and oppose it when it was wrong. The state might acquiesce in compromise measures like the 1852 platform that defended squatter sovereignty, but it must never endorse them. If the state participated in selecting Democratic candidates or writing Democratic platforms, it would be morally obliged to support and defend them, even if they compromised southern interests. The northern wing of the party was uncompromisingly hostile to the extension of slavery into the territories. The president was true to the Constitution and the South, but the party could not be trusted to withstand the onslaught of abolitionism or the lure of patronage. The state must not gamble with its future by tying itself to the Democratic Party; it must remain loyal to the legacy of John C. Calhoun.

Since the birth of the republic, Keitt said, South Carolina had jealously guarded its independence from national politics. As a result, it had exercised far greater influence than its wealth and population could justify. From the beginning its leaders had resisted the temptations of power and patronage held out by the national parties and had loyally served the interests of the South. But no leader could successfully defend his moral purity if the state insisted on tying him to the Democratic Party's northern rabble or dragging him into the cesspool of party politics. The state must stand fast in its ancient faith; it must not sacrifice its principles to win a place in the councils of the Democrats.[4]

The editor of the Orangeburg *Southron* congratulated Keitt for handling an important subject with great ability. It was gratifying, he wrote, to find its young representative rising above the temptations held out by national politics and exhibiting a conservatism worthy of imitation by his older colleagues. The *Charleston Mercury* also praised the speech, calling it "condensed, clear, and comprehensive," and set off a brief but noisy debate with two up-country journals—the Abbeville *Independent Press* and the Edgefield *Advertiser*—that supported the convention movement. The exchange attracted attention only because the Abbeville editor quoted Keitt to defend the Democratic Party.[5]

Keitt was largely successful in his efforts to persuade his constituents to maintain a safe distance between themselves and the national party. At the state Democratic convention in Columbia, his district was not represented. Of the four towns that made up his congressional district—Beaufort, Barnwell, Colleton, and Orangeburg—only Barnwell sent delegates. By boycotting the meeting, however, the radicals allowed moderates to elect representatives to the national convention and to endorse Franklin Pierce for a second term.[6]

Already southern politicians were making clear the price the Democratic Party would have to pay for southern votes. On April 7, pausing partway through his address on "The Politics of the Country," Keitt told the Congress that simple justice entitled the South to name the Democratic candidate for president. R. M. T. Hunter of Virginia or Thomas J. Rusk of Texas would be acceptable to his constituents. The South was willing to waive its claim to the nomination, but in return, the party must allow the South to write the platform. It must acknowledge that the right of a southern man to own a slave was equal to the right of a northern man to own a horse. If the party would write a platform acceptable to the South, the South would accept the nomination of Franklin Pierce or Stephen Douglas. The storm of fanaticism was howling around them, but the South would not abandon men who had been tried and found faithful, but only as long as they did not abandon the South to win election.[7]

A few days later, Keitt again made it clear to House Democrats that southern support for their candidate would not come cheaply. During the coming campaign, he warned, constitutional rectitude would confront abolitionist fanaticism. If the party tried to compromise its principles, if it tried to fight the next election for "the profits of place or the plumage of authority," the South would abandon it to its just desserts. If it tried to avoid the issues or nominate a candidate because he was "available," the South had no interest in its success. It must place its standard in the hands of a man who bore "the scars of conflict, and has the smoke of battle around him"; if not, the South would stand idly by and watch it go down to ignominious defeat.[8]

During a lull in the political warfare, Keitt described the national political situation for Sue Sparks at home in Marlborough District. Everybody in Washington was anxiously awaiting the Democratic National Convention in Cincinnati in early June: "Debates in the House, intrigues in secret and social manipulations"—all were carried out with the nomination in mind. It was still too early to predict who the party's candidate would be. Most insiders thought James Buchanan had the best chance, but Keitt was doubtful. Pierce's hopes for a second nomination were probably dead; southern support guaranteed that the North would oppose him. The Kansas bill had destroyed Douglas. Hunter or Rusk, he thought, was most likely to succeed because so little had been said of them.[9]

In Cincinnati the South Carolina delegation cast its first fourteen ballots for Pierce and its next two for Douglas. After the sixteenth it switched its support to Buchanan, helping to make the old man the unanimous choice of the party. Keitt was not particularly disappointed. He would have preferred Douglas, he told his fiancée, because the senator supported the acquisition of Cuba, but Buchanan would do. He had reluctantly agreed to speak in favor of the ticket.[10]

Keitt's letter to an Orangeburg militia company reflected the sort of half-hearted support he gave the nominee. First, he emphasized his objections to national nominating conventions, "disguised oligarchies, . . . more likely to seduce, betray, or defeat the public will than fairly represent it." Next, he pointed out the two courses open to the South. It could throw away its votes, or it could cast them for one of the existing parties. Of course he would not recommend voting for the Republicans or the Know Nothings, nor would he advocate voting for a man who had no chance to win. He did not agree with Buchanan's views on slavery and the tariff, but he was the only candidate acceptable to the South. If he did not win, the South would have no choice but to secede from the Union.[11]

Not long after Keitt's assault on all things Republican, a brawl in the dining room of Willard's Hotel temporarily diverted his attention from national politics. On May 8, a young congressman from California, Philemon T. Herbert, saved himself from being mauled by half a dozen Irish waiters by fatally shooting one of them. Herbert was Keitt's close friend and political ally, and William W. Boyce, who represented South Carolina's Sixth Congressional District, was his cousin.

Testimony at the coroner's inquest was contradictory. Apparently Herbert had been enraged by a waiter who refused to serve him breakfast—it was almost noon—cursed the man and then struck him, either with a napkin or his fist. The waiter hit Herbert over the head with a tray, the congressman defended himself with a chair, and the brawl was on. Sympathetic bystanders, among them the ambassadors from Austria and the Netherlands and several members of Congress, testified that at least three waiters held Herbert while another battered him with a chair. In real danger of being beaten to death, Herbert drew his pistol and fired a ball through the heart of one of his assailants. At this point, two onlookers charged into the melee, canes swinging, and pulled Herbert away from the furious waiters. Herbert immediately gave himself up to the police, was taken to jail, treated for his injuries, and released on a writ of habeas corpus.[12]

Two days after the shooting, Keitt told Sue it had been a "lamentable affair." A man whose control over his own temper was always insecure, Keitt knew that Herbert could have avoided the fight. He knew too that it would reinforce the abolitionists' image of the southern politician, always ready to bully his inferiors and to resort to force when he did not get his way. Keitt predicted that the Washington grand jury would ignore the shooting and reinforce the abolitionists' belief that southern justice favored the wealthy and powerful over the poor.

Such mindless violence could do only harm to the southern cause.[13] Herbert was tried twice. The first jury deliberated for five days and failed to reach a verdict; the second deliberated for forty-five minutes, found the defendant not guilty of first-degree murder, and released him. The House tabled a resolution to investigate the shooting, and Herbert resumed his seat.[14]

The capital city had not seen the last of the violence. On May 19 and 20, before news of the sack of Lawrence had reached Washington, Charles Sumner delivered a long, meticulously prepared speech he called "The Crime Against Kansas." The speaker's reputation, the events of the past months, and the increasing alienation of North and South ensured that his remarks would be closely followed by friends and enemies alike.

To his friends in New England, Sumner represented everything that was best in the character and intellect of the section. He was exceptionally well educated, highly articulate, idealistic, and incorruptible. Unfortunately, he was also egotistical, humorless, arrogant, self-righteous, and totally intolerant of the opinions of men who saw the world differently from the way he did. Worst of all in the opinion of his southern opponents, he considered himself an unerring judge of moral law and insisted on deciding every political issue according to its precepts. His bitter attacks on slavery, southern politicians, and the South itself had made him, at the time he rose to speak, the most controversial man in the Senate.[15]

Sumner began by attacking the administration's support of the proslavery legislature of the territory, blaming it for all of the violence that had engulfed the area.[16] If he had confined himself to that one topic, he would have emerged unscathed. Instead, he launched a vicious personal assault on three of the administration's staunchest defenders. He singled out James M. Mason, Stephen A. Douglas, and Andrew Pickens Butler and blamed them for the tragic events of the past two years. He compared Butler and Douglas to Don Quixote and Sancho Panza, sallying forth to do battle for slavery and the South. His references to sexual irregularities became increasingly blatant. Butler, he said, had read too many romantic novels, and now thought himself a chivalric knight. He had "chosen a mistress to whom he had made his vows, and who, though ugly to others, is always lovely to him; though polluted in the sight of the world, is chaste in his sight—I mean the harlot slavery. For her, his tongue is always profuse in words. . . . The frenzy of Don Quixote, in behalf of his wench, Dulcinea Del Toboso, is all surpassed."[17]

During a recent speech on Kansas, Sumner charged, Butler had overflowed with rage and "with incoherent phrases, discharged the loose expectoration of his speech" on the people of the territory. He touched nothing he did not disfigure; there was no extravagance, no error he did not repeat. He was incapable of telling the truth; "he cannot open his mouth but out there flies a blunder." Butler was

"Arguments of the Chivalry." Courtesy of Library of Congress, Washington, D.C.

a fit representative of a state whose "shameful imbecility" was created by slavery and revealed throughout its history: "Were the whole history of South Carolina blotted out of existence, from its very beginning down to the day of the last election of the Senator to his present seat on this floor," civilization would lose less than it had already gained by the valiant struggle of Free Soil Kansas against oppression.[18]

Butler was an unlikely target for Sumner's invective. He was a southern gentleman of the old school, a political moderate, a man of unfailing courtesy and charm. The speech on the Kansas issue which Sumner described so offensively had been a restrained statement of the southern position, presented in dignified language, without any direct reference to the abolitionist Senator. Butler had been active in public life since 1818, first as a lawyer, then as a legislator, judge, and U.S. senator. In 1856 he was an old man, widely respected by his colleagues and rapidly approaching the end of his career. He had recently suffered a stroke that impaired his ability to speak and led to his death in 1857.[19]

If Butler was an inappropriate object for Sumner's invective, Preston Brooks was an even less likely instrument of southern vengeance. A hero of the Mexican War, an officer of the Palmetto Regiment that fought its way from Vera Cruz to Chapultepec, Brooks was now a second-term congressman, a man of only modest ability who had won many friends but few distinctions in the House. He was best known for his half-humorous suggestion that congressmen check their sidearms before coming onto the floor. He was not a hothead like Keitt. His conduct during the debates over Kansas had been so moderate that it became a political liability in the western piedmont district he represented. South Carolina politicians were already battling over the right to run for his seat in the November elections.[20]

Knowing almost instinctively that he had to defend his cousin and satisfy the demands of the southern code of honor, Brooks resolved to punish Sumner. On May 21, the day following the speech, he told at least three of his closest friends in the Congress—Henry A. Edmundson of Virginia, James L. Orr of South Carolina, and Keitt—of his intention. All three offered their support, and Keitt demanded without success to be allowed to administer the beating. On the morning of May 21, Brooks and Edmundson waited for several hours on the Capitol grounds, but their quarry did not appear. That evening the two men, this time accompanied by Keitt, went to Gautier's, a restaurant where Sumner frequently dined, but again failed to encounter the senator. Later that night, Keitt left Brooks at his lodgings, too angry even to sleep.[21]

Charles Sumner. Courtesy of Library of Congress

The next day, May 22, Keitt spent the morning in the lobby of the Senate, waiting. At noon, a few minutes before Brooks finally caught up with Sumner, Keitt refused to return to the House with Edmundson. "No," he said, "I can't leave until Brooks does." With that, he turned away from his friend, disappeared behind the screen that stood behind the president's chair, and became involved in a conversation with a constituent, an unwelcome intruder on the scene about to play itself out. The constituent, probably J. G. Mittag, had been watching Sumner, and had just remarked that he would do well to discharge his choler with a dose of mercury, when the sound of a cane breaking over Sumner's head interrupted their conversation. The assault lasted no more than a minute, but the noise attracted the attention of every man in the chamber. Keitt, apparently surprised that Brooks had begun without him, emerged from behind the screen in time to see Sumner break loose from his desk and stagger into the aisle. Three bystanders—Congressmen Edwin B. Morgan and Ambrose S. Murray of New York and Senator John J. Crittenden of Kentucky—went to his rescue. Keitt was amazed that anyone would try to stop the caning Sumner so richly deserved and charged toward the struggling men, brandishing his walking stick and shouting, "Let them alone, God damn you." Afraid that the Carolinian was angry enough to attack the elderly Crittenden, Senator Robert Toombs of Georgia stepped between the two men. Toombs later said he approved the beating and wanted only to ensure that Keitt would not assault a fellow southerner.

By this time, Sumner was lying on the floor, bleeding profusely from wounds on his head and scalp. Brooks, satisfied that he had done his duty, allowed Keitt to take him into a side room and wash a small cut above one eye made by the recoil of his cane. Minutes later, witnesses saw the two men walking together down Pennsylvania Avenue.[22] The public reaction to the bloody encounter was predictable. Brooks, an obscure congressman whose constituents had considered him "a little too national," suddenly found himself transformed into a southern hero. Fire-eaters armed themselves and blustered loudly about imitating him. More than one observer expected the city to rise up and slice the abolitionists' throats. Enemies of slavery made Sumner a martyr for freedom and justice.[23]

Washington was wild with excitement, Keitt told his fiancée a few days later. Brooks had flogged Sumner "well and soundly"; he had combined "in happy proportion freedom of speech and freedom of the cudgel. . . . if the northern men had stood up, the city would now float with blood." Washington was sitting atop a volcano that was about to explode, and he was glad of it. He was tired of stagnation; he would remain in the city until the fires burned themselves out.[24]

In the Senate, James Wilson of Massachusetts and William H. Seward of New York demanded an investigation. Seemingly reluctant to take any action at all, the Upper House elected a committee composed entirely of Democrats. The members deliberated briefly and concluded that the Senate could not punish members of the other house who violated its rules.[25] In the Lower House, Lewis Campbell of Ohio set off a long and quarrelsome debate when he denounced Brooks and Keitt for assaulting Sumner and demanded a committee to investigate the attack and recommend measures to "vindicate the character" of the House. During a seemingly interminable wrangle marked more by parliamentary maneuver than rational discussion, both Keitt and Brooks insisted that they had not plotted the assault in advance. Keitt—no doubt twisting the facts in hope of avoiding the consequence of his rash act—told the House that he had not known the time or the place the assault would take place and had not been present when it began. "I had not the slightest concert with my colleague," he insisted, "nor did I know when or where it would occur." The majority accepted Keitt's dubious protestations, deleted his name from the resolution, and authorized an investigation. The Speaker immediately appointed a committee, a majority of whose members were Republicans. The following day, May 24, it began to take testimony from the first of twenty-seven witnesses—Sumner himself.[26]

All across the country, editors and politicians rushed to take sides. A few northern conservatives blamed Sumner for provoking the caning, and a few southerners criticized Brooks for attacking a man who could not defend himself, but opinions divided largely along sectional lines. Almost every southern newspaper loudly approved the assault, and almost every northern paper condemned it.

The most hysterical response came from the *Boston Atlas.* The editor called Brooks the "Bludgeoner-in-Chief of South Carolina" and insisted the attack was an attempt to silence a man who had exposed southern iniquities in Kansas. Southern slave owners wielding "bowie-knives, bludgeons, and revolvers" had transferred the "reign of terror" from the territory to the nation's capital.[27] The *New York Tribune* condemned both Brooks and Keitt. Keitt, Horace Greeley told his readers, had been Brooks's "fender-off." He had never witnessed a "meaner exhibition of southern cowardice—generally miscalled southern chivalry"; Keitt's conduct proved that democracy was "a delusion and a lie." The *New York Herald* printed an interview with a Doctor Bunting, apparently a Canadian physician. Bunting had witnessed the caning from the visitors' gallery and charged that Keitt had brandished a cane in one hand and in the other concealed a pistol beneath the flaps of his coat. Editor James Gordon Bennett ridiculed both Sumner, the "nigger worshiper" who had presented the Senate with a "stale and loathsome rehash of niggers and niggerism," and the "nigger drivers" who had introduced mob law into the Upper House and made a martyr of a notorious liar. The *New York Times* reported it had learned from a reliable source that Keitt habitually beat his washerwoman. At a protest meeting in Boston, one of many held throughout the North, abolitionist Theodore Parker told the audience that

Keitt had threatened to flog Henry Wilson if he met him in the street. Wilson had defiantly stalked back and forth in front of Keitt's boarding house while the "coward" stood in the doorway too terrified to accept the challenge. Both Keitt and Wilson denied Parker's story.[28]

The reaction of southern editors was every bit as emotional. The *Richmond Whig* rejoiced that Brooks had given "the notorious and foul-mouthed abolitionist . . . an elegant and effectual caning." It regretted only that he had not used "a horsewhip or a cowhide upon his slanderous back. . . . Seward and others should catch it next."[29] The *Richmond Enquirer* suggested that Sumner "ought to have nine-and-thirty early every morning. He is a great strapping fellow, and could stand the cowhide beautifully."[30]

With few exceptions, South Carolina newspapers applauded the assault. The Orangeburg *Southron* expressed its disappointment that Brooks had not used a cowhide, applauded Keitt for seeing the licks well laid on, and regretted he had not had an opportunity to do the same to Henry Wilson. In Washington, "Faineant" told the editor the attack had driven the abolitionists "stark mad." They had turned "the whole kennel of fanatical hounds" against Brooks, and their barking was still ringing through the city, but it would not prevent a true southerner from whipping a Yankee when he deserved it. The Columbia *South Carolinian* thought Sumner had "not gotten a lick more than he deserved," and the *Sumter Watchman* concluded that the beating was the "legitimate dessert of the uncalled for outrage."[31]

Editors in Charleston did not join the chorus of approval. Robert Barnwell Rhett Jr., the radical editor of the *Charleston Mercury*, first condemned the deed as a "plain violation of the right of speech guaranteed by the Constitution," but later reversed himself. Sumner, "the high priest of this lawlessness," had placed himself above the Constitution and forced Brooks to deal with him outside the law. The *Charleston News* declared that Brooks had been "wrong in chastising Sumner, wrong in method and wrong in place." The state had gained nothing from his act.[32]

Editorial criticism did not prevent radicals from organizing mass meetings in cities as large as Columbia and villages as small as Hamburg and Bishopville, voting their approval and ordering "suitable testimonials" sent to Brooks and Keitt. Keitt told Sue that gold-headed canes and invitations to address public dinners and mass meetings were "coming in thick." The editor of the *Carolina Times* invited his readers to visit the newspaper's office where a great quantity of silver plate presented to Brooks was on display. In Orangeburg, a mob burned Sumner in effigy.[33]

Rhett, never one of Keitt's admirers, decided it was time to call a halt to the general rejoicing when he learned that slaves in Columbia had taken up a collection and presented Brooks with still another cane. The editor was clearly amazed; when slaves could take part in the political activities of white men, they presented "a spectacle as disgusting as it is novel." If some slaves could praise white politicians, others could condemn them. If one group could applaud Brooks, another could sympathize with Sumner.[34]

In the Senate, Wilson denounced the "brutal, murderous and cowardly assault." Brooks challenged him, but Wilson refused to fight. Dueling was a crime, he said, "the lingering relic of a barbarous civilization." Keitt had the last word: "The very mention of cold lead," he sneered, had given the "swaggering cobbler" a deathly chill.[35]

On June 2, the investigating committee appointed by the Speaker of the House presented two reports. The report drafted by the Republican majority concluded that Brooks was guilty of assaulting Sumner and recommended that the House expel him. It also concluded that Keitt and Edmundson had known the assault was coming but had done nothing to prevent it, and recommended that the House censure both of them.[36] The minority report compiled by two southern Democrats, Howell Cobb of Georgia and Alfred B. Greenwood of Arkansas, argued that the House lacked authority to try or punish any of its members for participating in the assault and could take no action against them.[37]

The reports set off a protracted debate that involved every member of the South Carolina delegation, and at least twice threatened to erupt into violence. During an exchange between James L. Orr and John Hickman of Pennsylvania, Keitt accused Hickman of voting to print the committee report so that the Republicans could use it as a campaign document. Hickman tried to ignore the interruption, and Keitt bolted from his seat, apparently intending to attack the Pennsylvanian. Sampson W. Harris of Alabama grabbed Keitt's coattail as he went by, held on, and Keitt returned to his seat. Observers were amazed. One speculated that Keitt expected Hickman "to give him the lie" and decided to retaliate in advance.[38]

The debate reached an angry climax on June 21 when Anson W. Burlingame, a Know Nothing from Massachusetts, chose the occasion to rescue his declining political fortunes and to defend his state against the attacks of the Democrats.[39] In the course of his remarks, Burlingame tried to rebut charges Keitt had made more than two months before. Keitt had described the sad plight of New England factory hands, and Burlingame reminded his listeners that Speaker Nathaniel P. Banks had once been an "operative." How sad it was that Banks had not been born a slave in South Carolina where he could have spent his days singing and dancing and basking in the sun. The sarcasm produced a burst of laughter from the Republican side of the House and encouraged Burlingame to invite Keitt to visit Massachusetts, where he could persuade workingmen they were indeed starving. He could see for himself that Massachusetts was the most productive, most prosperous state in the Union.[40]

Burlingame next heaped praise on Sumner and his condemnation of southern outrages in Kansas. The senator, he said, had spoken with severity, but only because he hated tyranny and injustice. He had been provoked, but he had not violated the dictates of decorum. He had been peacefully carrying out the duties of his office when a member of the House "stole into the Senate . . . and smote him as Cain smote his brother." Keitt, whose control over his temper was never very secure, could restrain himself no longer. Without rising from his seat, he exclaimed, "That is false!" Burlingame refused to be interrupted. Declining to "bandy epithets" and assuring Keitt that he was responsible for his language, the congressman continued his description of the assault: "One blow was enough; but it did not satiate the wrath of the spirit which had pursued him through two days. Again and again, quicker and faster fell the leaden blows, until he was torn away from his victim, when the senator from Massachusetts fell into the arms of his friends, and his blood ran down on the Senate floor."[41] If a member of the Senate could be called to account by "some gallant nephew" whenever he was offended, the very existence of the nation was threatened. As for himself, he would say whatever and whenever and wherever he chose, whatever the consequences.[42]

Keitt tried to challenge the sarcastic congressman to a duel, but Brooks challenged him first. Burlingame agreed to a meeting, but for the site designated the Canadian side of Niagara Falls. Brooks knew he would have to face howling mobs on his way north, refused, and Burlingame had the last laugh.[43]

On July 6, accompanied by Keitt, Butler, and a number of others, Brooks appeared in the Criminal Court of the District of Columbia to answer charges that he had assaulted Sumner. After two days of testimony, the presiding judge fined Brooks three hundred dollars, the penalty for half-killing a senator according to the editor of the *Boston Atlas*. A murder would cost six hundred dollars, he calculated, approximately the price of a hundred gutta percha canes.[44]

With the criminal proceedings disposed of, the House was free to act on the recommendations of its committee. On July 14, the resolution to expel Brooks passed, 121–95, well short of the required two-thirds vote, but the South Carolinian immediately resigned his seat. The following day, the House exonerated Edmundson but approved the resolution censuring Keitt by a vote of 106–96. On the sixteenth, the South Carolina fire-eater delivered a "Farewell Address," resigned his seat, and stalked out of the chamber.[45]

Keitt had been waiting impatiently for an opportunity to reply to the Republican attacks against himself and his state, and now the time had finally arrived. Burlingame had accused him of "contankerosity" and compared his rhetoric to "St. Vitus's dance." Worse, he had belittled the history of South

Carolina during the Revolutionary War, and Keitt was determined to set the record straight. Massachusetts claimed sole credit for starting and winning the war, but it was wrong. In Boston patriots had disguised themselves as Indians and waited for darkness before throwing the tea into the harbor; in Charleston they had thrown tea into the harbor in broad daylight. The Mecklenburg Declaration of Independence had preceded the Declaration signed in Philadelphia by more than a year. Carolinians had won the first battle of the war at Moore's Creek Bridge. George Washington had complained bitterly about the "dearth of public spirit, . . . want of virtue, . . . stock jabbing and fertility in all of the low arts" of the New England troops who served under him. During the War of 1812, Boston had grown fat smuggling tea, selling slaves, and lending money to the British. South Carolina would never stoop so low.[46]

His foray into American history completed at last, Keitt turned to the principal subject of his speech. The House had passed a resolution of censure against him, Keitt insisted, only because he had refused to become an informer against his friend or defend a man who had slandered his state and one of its most distinguished sons. He admitted he knew Brooks intended to cane Sumner but insisted he did not know when or where he would administer the punishment. If he had anticipated that his colleague would take his revenge in the Senate chamber, he would have been at the scene when he began the beating.

Realizing that a majority of his audience did not approve of Brooks's conduct or his own, Keitt tried to explain the southern gentleman's way of dealing with insults to himself and his family. There were wrongs, he told the House, that a gentleman could not correct by appealing to a court of law. A gentleman could never restore his honor by consulting an attorney or having his actions weighed in scales held by a judge and jury. His colleague had redressed an insult to his family and his state "in a fair and manly way." He had done neither more nor less than the code demanded.

As for himself, said Keitt, an informer was more despicable than a slanderer, and he would never inform against his friends. As for the opinion of the men who had approved his censure—Black Republicans and abolitionists—he cared nothing. He was ready to appeal their decision to his constituents. The issue would be "sanctity of character on one side, and impunity to slander on the other," and he had no doubt of the result. After an hour he announced his resignation and stalked out of the chamber, followed by the applause of the packed galleries and the hearty congratulations of his friends.[47] Editors throughout the state praised his remarks but seemed disappointed by their essential moderation.[48]

The campaign to fill the seats Keitt and Brooks had vacated began even before the two men announced their resignations. Governor James H. Adams scheduled special elections for July 28, ensuring that there could be no effective opposition.

Brooks was so certain his constituents would return him to the House that he did not even return to South Carolina. Keitt was no less confident; he spent the week before the election touring the Virginia springs.[49]

In a letter published in the *Charleston Mercury,* Keitt defended his decision to resign his seat. Quoting extensively from his farewell speech in the House, he argued that honor and duty forced him to appeal to his constituents to overturn the decision of the Black Republicans. As individuals, their opinions meant nothing to him; as members of the Congress, their censure was an insult to himself and his state that he could not allow to stand.[50]

The editor of the *Mercury* agreed. Men might question the propriety of the actions of their congressman and deplore the tumult he had provoked, but they could not deny that Keitt's only crime had been to defend his state against insults to its honor and patriotism. The North had rallied around Sumner and "silenced his cowardly bleatings in shrieks of freedom and cries of martyrdom." His fanaticism had fanned the fires of abolitionism into fury, and now the voters of South Carolina must sustain the man who had become the special object of Yankee wrath. With libels on the history of their state ringing in their ears, with threats of extermination borne south on every gale, they must defy their enemies and return their representative to Congress.[51]

Similar appeals appeared in newspapers throughout the state. Politicians wrote public letters and organized mass meetings in an attempt to transform the election into a demonstration of southern solidarity. They aroused public opinion to such a peak that a Baptist preacher in Barnwell District who criticized Keitt's part in the caning had to resign his pastorate and flee the state.[52] So certain was the outcome that Governor Adams sent Keitt's certificate of election to Washington before the balloting even began.[53] Running unopposed, he polled all 3,723 votes cast in a district with approximately 4,000 qualified voters. Brooks ran almost as well. Tradition has it that the only vote against him was cast by a distant relative of Charles Sumner.[54] The Orangeburg *Southron* noted that the short campaign and the lack of opposition had no impact on the size of the vote. Uncontested elections were usually dull affairs, but the turnout for this one had been large and enthusiastic, and an expression of unqualified approval of Keitt's conduct.[55]

On August 6, James L. Orr called to the attention of the House that Keitt was present and asked the Speaker to administer the oath of office to his colleague and mess-mate. Duly sworn, the fire-eater resumed his seat in time to plunge headfirst into the never-ending debate on the civil war in Kansas.[56]

Brooks did not have long to enjoy his notoriety. Barely six months after he had caned Sumner, he developed a cold, chills, and a sore throat. In the early evening of January 27, he was in his rooms in Brown's Hotel talking with Keitt and Orr when he suddenly began choking. In no more than thirty minutes, his throat closed and he suffocated. Doctors diagnosed the cause as "violent croup," a nineteenth-century term for diphtheria. An anonymous correspondent of the *Charleston Courier* wrote of Keitt: "his kindred spirit . . . ran to and fro, temporarily crazed at the shock, and rocked as on billows of grief." Keitt informed the House of Brooks's death on January 29, and funeral services were conducted there the following day.[57]

In the interval between his encounter with Sumner and his censure by the House, Keitt accepted an invitation to address the literary societies of the Virginia Military Institute, one of many such invitations inspired by his newly enhanced notoriety. It would be a "great occasion," the *New York Tribune* predicted. Governor Henry A. Wise had agreed to speak at the dedication of a bronze statue of George Washington and to award diplomas to the graduating cadets. Keitt, the editor maliciously suggested, would deliver "an elaborate disquisition of the art of skulking and surprise." His speech would be a warning to his audience never to attack an enemy who was not outnumbered at least three to one and a hymn in praise of men who "fend off" while others make the assault.[58]

In Lexington, Keitt attended the dedication of Washington's statue and spoke briefly at a dinner to honor returning alumni. A participant recalled two years later that his remarks were intensely hostile to the Union.[59] The next day, July 4, he delivered a formal address to an "immense throng" which packed the Presbyterian Church "almost to suffocation." Cadets filled the pews; townspeople who could not find seats in the gallery spilled over into aisles and doorways. Men standing on window ledges blocked out the light and left the church in near darkness.[60]

Keitt was determined that his address would be more scholarly than political and devoted the first half to a comparison of ancient and modern civilizations. Every enduring civilization, he asserted, had to rest on three foundations—the material, the intellectual, and the moral. Ancient Greece had rested on only the first two and had passed away at its zenith; ancient Israel was based on only the third, and it too had perished. The South had inherited the best of both and created a society that was unique and uniquely stable.[61]

Repeating an argument that had long been part of the southern defense of slavery, Keitt asserted that the South's greatest strength lay in its social system. Every society, he continued, had to include a class of ignorant, unskilled people to perform the drudgery that educated, intelligent men avoided as distasteful or degrading. They were, in a phrase later made famous by his friend James H. Hammond, the "mudsill" of society. Where these men and women were content to remain in their assigned sphere and did not engage in "aimless struggles at impracticable advancement," society was harmonious and secure. In the South, society was based on race, and Negro slaves willingly performed menial but necessary tasks, leaving their masters free to devote their lives to higher pursuits. In the North, where society was based on class, every man mistakenly believed he was just as good as every other man, resented the society that exploited him, and governments had to put down endless revolts by embittered laborers.

Life, Keitt warned the cadets, was constant warfare. The school which provided its graduates effective weapons to fight society's battles accomplished its true purpose. The military academy succeeded because it blended reason with faith and freedom with discipline. It prepared men to "embellish civil life, to grapple with the rigors of the wilderness, and on the battlefield to chain victory to their standard." Life would test them severely. The captains of fanaticism were summoning their legions to wreak havoc across the land. A century ago, Virginia had sent her young men out to found a new nation. Now, it was preparing them to "raise up a wall of fire around her handiwork." Now, they must join that "noble band of saints, martyrs, and confessors." With the cheers of his audience threatening to drown out his closing sentences, Keitt implored the graduates to preserve the Old Dominion "unshorn of her political splendor, undimmed in her moral beauty, untarnished in the blazonry of her world-wide fame."[62]

Both Keitt's defense of slavery and his warning that the institution was in real danger were by this time well-worn facets of fire-eating rhetoric, but the cadets reacted as though they were hearing it all for the first time, repeatedly interrupting his remarks with prolonged applause. The reaction of the editors of the two local newspapers reflected the political division of Lexington and the Shenandoah Valley. The *Valley Star,* a Democratic paper closely allied with Keitt's friend and colleague John Letcher, reported that no speaker had ever received a warmer reception. Spectators had repeatedly interrupted his "lofty and impassioned declamation" with "spontaneous and thundering applause." The *Gazette,* a Whiggish paper in a Whiggish town, conceded that Keitt knew a great deal about classical society, but called his analysis hasty and ignored his appeal to southern nationalism. Two years later, the editor wondered if the speech had been part of a conspiracy to poison the minds of innocent young men against the Union.[63]

Keitt spent the time between the adjournment of Congress in August and the opening of the new session in December touring the Virginia springs, mending political fences, and paying political debts. He also found himself drawn into the campaign to elect James Buchanan to the presidency, not so much because he believed Buchanan would be a friend to the South but because he was certain Republican John C. Frémont and Know Nothing Millard Fillmore would not.[64]

Early in September, Keitt interrupted his vacation at White Sulphur Springs to deliver a major address in Lynchburg, Virginia. Speaking to an audience that included two former governors of the commonwealth and an array of local dignitaries, the congressman poured out a torrent of emotional rhetoric and transformed a Democratic campaign rally into a secessionist camp meeting.[65]

Keitt warned his audience that the coming election would determine the fate of the Union. Twenty years ago, abolitionist fanatics had declared war against the South, and for twenty years had pursued their prey with an insatiable vengeance. Every southern concession had encouraged new aggressions; every southern surrender had provoked fresh attacks. Now the South could retreat no further; now the South must stand and fight.

He was as much a lover of the Constitution as any man, Keitt told his audience. But when men asked him to love a Union in which his constituents were not the equals of the rabble who caught codfish and sold wooden nutmegs, when they asked him to love a Union in which the gallant sons of Virginia were not the equals of the poor, crazy constituents of Charles Sumner and Joshua Giddings, then "God help me—I am against the Union! I love the Union to a reasonable extent—I trust none of you love it any more—but when I am asked to put my constituents under the foul domination of such a set of black serpents as Greeley, Sumner, Seward, Wilson, Chase and Giddings, . . . I should rather my State should be a grave yard of martyred patriots than the slave of northern abolitionists."[66] Interrupted again and again by "enthusiastic cheers," Keitt insisted that the South must not remain in the Union "stigmatized, dishonored, reviled, plundered, degraded" by the Republican North. If Frémont were elected, adherence to the Union would be treason to liberty; the southern man who would submit was a traitor and a coward. The North must elect Buchanan to the presidency; the North must recognize southern claims to the territory won by southern blood and treasure in the war against Mexico; the North must concede the right of the South to carry slaves into Kansas. If not, the South must assert its rights or perish in the attempt. "God grant," he concluded, "that [Virginia] may be true . . . in the coming fight."[67]

In South Carolina, newspapers took little notice of the event. The editor of the *Yorkville Enquirer* praised Keitt's "bursts of eloquence which could be no more recorded than the lightning's flash could be daguerreotyped." Papers that ordinarily reported his speeches in detail published only the most spectacular of his remarks, and even those without comment. Outside of the state, reactions varied from the criticism of the *Lynchburg Virginian* to the scorn of the *New York Herald.*

A correspondent told the *New York Times* that Keitt belonged to the "skyrocket class" of orators who dealt in "epithets and bombast" and made up for a decided lack of sense with "swelling periods and portentous threats." The *New York Herald* quoted Gov. John B. Floyd's praise for the speech—"sterling, eloquent, . . . powerful"—and sarcastically agreed. It was a perfect reflection of South Carolina, wrote editor James Gordon Bennett, flashing secession and disunion like lightning from a thundercloud, but his words were only bosh. He had heard, Bennett concluded, that Keitt was planning to stump Pennsylvania for Buchanan. That should cost the Democrats at least thirty thousand votes. Perhaps Frémont would reward him with a seat in his cabinet.[68]

The reaction of the *Lynchburg Virginian* was one of shocked disapproval. Its editor, a Whig turned Know Nothing, acknowledged that Keitt's oratory had been "above average," filled with "gunpowder rhapsodies and volcano metaphors," flashing swords, sounding bugles, and streaming banners, but as a party speech, it had been singularly ineffective. Keitt had not once mentioned Buchanan or proposed a single reason for believing he should govern the nation during the next four years. The speech had not suited the temper of the town. The public mind was already sufficiently inflamed; the South Carolinian need not doubt that Virginia would do its duty when the time for action finally arrived.

In the following issue, the editor of the *Virginian* reported that Keitt's "harangue" had produced in Lynchburg "a general and earnest disapprobation." Almost without exception, the citizens of the town dreaded the evils that would inevitably follow the dissolution of the Union. Secession would do nothing to protect slavery, but it would reduce a great nation to a mess of "miserable, contemptible, squabbling" fragments.[69]

Undeterred by his reception in western Virginia, Keitt appeared at a Democratic campaign rally in Petersburg on September 16 and then returned to South Carolina for a round of stump speeches that consumed the months of October and November. The Petersburg *Southside Democrat* applauded his performance, apparently a near duplicate of his Lynchburg address, citing his "happy hits, withering satire, and frequent bursts of the loftiest eloquence." Keitt had attacked the South's unaccountable apathy in the face of impending danger and appealed for southern unity. He had demolished Frémont and Fillmore and left his audience no alternative but to vote for Buchanan.[70]

Returning to his congressional district for the first time since his censure, Keitt spoke in Orangeburg to a crowd so large that it filled the courthouse and spilled out onto the lawn in front of the building. Newspaper accounts of the speech ignored his assault on Frémont and Fillmore, perhaps because they had become all too predictable, and focused instead on his plea for the legislature to preserve the history of the state. He had turned to a subject that had fascinated him since his student days at South Carolina College, proposing that the state underwrite a study and commission his friend William Gilmore Simms to carry it out. The legislature must not wait, Keitt insisted, until old men died, records moldered into dust, and the deeds of patriotic ancestors were lost forever. At home, her history would inspire patriotism and unity; abroad, it would protect the reputation of the state and, when the time came, justify its secession from the Union. No people that ignored its history long remained great. South Carolina must not betray its heroic past; it must protect "the honor of her dead and the sanctity of her battles."[71]

An anonymous correspondent of the *New York Times* was far more interested in Keitt the fire-eater than Keitt the historian. He had breathed fire from start to finish, the writer insisted, condemned the aggressions of abolitionists, cursed southern Know Nothings as traitors, and half-heartedly defended the Democrats. Buchanan was not the best man for the presidency, Keitt had warned, but he was the best man in the field. Submit to the election of Frémont, and the South was doomed. Submit and she would see "her fields laid waste, her houses in flames, her proud cities sinking down into pestilent marshes." And why should she not form an independent confederacy? Did she lack numbers? Did she lack money and resources? Did she not have ample cause to secede? Faced by a choice between submission and secession, her decision was obvious. Using a phrase he would repeat over and over during the campaign, Keitt drove his point home: "He who dallies is a dastard, and he who doubts is doomed."[72]

Stumping his congressional district from end to end, Keitt addressed large crowds at Barnwell Court House on October 20 and Gillisonville on November 11. Speaking to audiences provided by Judge John B. O'Neall, who twice adjourned sessions of his court so that the congressman could address his constituents, Keitt repeated his well-worn warnings that the South was in danger. At Barnwell, Col. W. A. Owens, perhaps Keitt's most powerful political rival in the Third District and an opponent of separate secession in 1851, argued that South Carolina should leave the Union only if the rest of the southern states agreed to follow her lead. At the end, the meeting ignored Owens's advice and unanimously resolved that the election of Frémont would be grounds for secession, whatever the consequences might be.[73]

After attending innumerable testimonial dinners, delivering innumerable stump speeches—most of them, no doubt, overlooked by the press—and seeing to his reelection to Congress, Keitt found time to prepare an article for *DeBow's Review* that appeared in November 1856. In it he repeated with only minor changes the defense of South Carolina he had delivered in the House of Representatives in July. After so strenuous an autumn, Keitt must have been happy to return to Washington and the new Congress.[74]

In the South, in spite of the note of moral indignation injected into the campaign by radical Republicans, in spite of the threats of secession issued almost hourly by radical Democrats, the presidential election had gone off quietly. Keitt knew long before November that the Know Nothings would not cut into the

Democratic vote in South Carolina, but he must have been shocked by the narrowness of the Democratic victory in the nation at large. Buchanan won slightly more than 1.8 million votes, compared to Frémont's 1.3 million and Fillmore's 875,000. Only the support of old-line Whigs saved him from defeat. The size of the Republican vote forced moderate Carolinians like Perry and Orr to re-examine their assumption that the South could continue to dominate the Democratic Party and through it the federal government. Equally important, it confirmed the most extreme of the radical prophecies. For Keitt and men like him, the election was proof that the South could save itself only by leaving the Union.[75]

FOUR

"Shake the Federal temple from turret to foundation stone"

When the members of the Thirty-fourth Congress returned to Washington late in 1856, few observers could have disagreed with Keitt's assessment that the political climate was "gloomy and ominous." The Democratic victory had changed nothing. At the far end of Pennsylvania Avenue, Franklin Pierce still occupied the White House. The last of his annual messages, an embittered attack on the Republican Party, did little more than give the assembled congressmen more to fight about while they waited for the new administration to take office. In his message, Pierce blamed Free Soilers for all of the violence in Kansas and accused them of attempting to "erect a revolutionary government" in the territory. He insisted that slaveowners had a right to carry their property into all of the territories and charged that the Republicans were working to abolish slavery not only in the territories, but in the entire South. They were preparing the country for war by appealing "to passion and sectional prejudice, by indoctrinating its people with reciprocal hatred, and by educating them to stand face-to-face as enemies rather than shoulder-to-shoulder as friends." The result would be "burning cities, and ravaged fields, and slaughtered populations."[1]

For most of the session, members took turns attacking and defending the president's assertions. Keitt played a minor but acrimonious role in the debate. On December 8, he tried to obtain the floor, the speaker ignored him, and according to a report in the *New York Times,* he "evinced his displeasure by a series of cavortings . . . better suited to a circus clown, convulsing form and features in a mock display of heroics. . . . after the House adjourned, he stationed himself at one of the doors, cane in hand, vowing his purpose to use it upon the speaker on his exit from the hall." Fortunately, Banks left by a different door.[2]

Two days later, during his reply to an attack on Pierce by his old antagonist Israel Washburn, Keitt again insisted that the right of a southern man to own slaves differed in no way from his right to own any other kind of property. Republicans denounced slavery as a moral, social, and political evil and opposed its extension into the territories. But if it were evil, why did they not destroy it in the states? Washburn replied: because under the Constitution they lacked the power to do what they wanted to do. And what, Keitt asked, would the Republicans do next? They would admit free states to the Union one after another until they acquired the power they needed. Then they would alter the Constitution and destroy slavery. Washburn conceded that he would not object if the Constitution were amended to allow Congress to abolish slavery in the states, but he thought it would not be wise to exercise the power at that time. Keitt pressed his opponent harder; did he think it would be wise to abolish slavery at a later time? Washburn tried to evade the question, and Keitt pounced; it was, he insisted, the "evitable tendency" of the Republican Party to make war on slavery wherever it had the power.[3]

Trying to clinch his argument, Keitt charged that the Republicans were revolutionaries. Southern men claimed the right to go into the territories with their slaves as property, and the federal government was obliged to protect that right. Northerners denied their rights, and southerners offered to take the question to the Supreme Court. The Republican Party refused, claiming that it was the right of the majority to determine at the ballot box what was property and what was not. "You substituted the ballot box for the Supreme Court," Keitt insisted, "and sought to supersede the Constitution by an elective despotism." The president was right, Keitt told Washburn; he was plotting a revolution.[4]

The Republicans scored heavily when they pointed out that the northern and southern wings of the Democratic Party could not agree on the meaning of popular sovereignty. On December 11, Humphrey Marshall of Kentucky chided the Democrats for their inconsistency. Marshall, a Whig turned Know Nothing, ridiculed the national Democrats by comparing Keitt's interpretation of popular sovereignty with that of Lewis Cass, the senator from Michigan. Keitt denied that he was a member of the party. The Constitution was a treaty among sovereign states; the United States could not be a nation, and he could not be a national Democrat. Marshall asked Keitt if he were a "sectional Democrat." No, Keitt replied, he was a "Constitutional Democrat." If that were true, Marshall concluded triumphantly, Senator Cass must be an "Unconstitutional Democrat."[5]

Keitt held his usually volatile temper under tight control. One part of the Democratic Party defended the doctrine of "squatter sovereignty," he explained patiently, and the other did not. One part understood that neither the Congress nor a territorial legislature could prohibit slavery in a territory; the other mistakenly believed that either of them could do so. He acknowledged that the powers of a territorial legislature under the Kansas-Nebraska Act depended entirely on judicial construction and predicted that the Supreme Court's decision in the Dred Scott case would sustain the southern version of popular sovereignty. When it did, the northern wing of the Democratic party would accept the ruling in good faith.[6]

It is impossible to know if Keitt's prediction was the product of inside information or simple common sense. Any observer who was aware of the composition of the court could have anticipated the thrust, though perhaps not the breadth, of the verdict. In *Scott v. Sandford,* Chief Justice Roger B. Taney ruled that no African American, slave or free, could be a citizen and so had no right to sue in federal court, that the Congress had no right to prohibit slavery in a territory, and that the Missouri Compromise—repealed by the Kansas-Nebraska Act and perhaps by the Compromise of 1850—was unconstitutional. It was one of the most controversial rulings in all of American history, delighting southern champions of slavery, disgusting their Free Soil opponents, and carrying the nation one more step closer to war.[7]

Washington was every bit as "gloomy and ominous" as Keitt believed, but the situation in Kansas was far worse. Fighting had virtually ended, but the threat of renewed violence remained. In December, when the Thirty-fourth Congress convened for its third and final session, the leaders of the pro-slavery forces were plotting to cement their control over the territory. John W. Geary, the third in a seemingly endless succession of governors, had brought law and order to the territory, but was no match for the Lecompton legislature. It blocked his efforts to reform the legal code, rigged the election of delegates to the constitutional convention, and in March 1857 drove him out of the territory in fear for his life.[8]

Robert J. Walker, a planter and politician from Mississippi but a migrant from Pennsylvania, suited the southerners in Kansas no better than his predecessors. In his inaugural address, late in May 1857, the new governor argued that Kansas lay outside the natural limits of slavery and demanded that the members of the upcoming constitutional convention submit their handiwork to the voters for their approval. If they refused, he warned, the Congress would surely reject it. Convinced that Kansas would be Free Soil and determined that it would be Democratic, he went to work to satisfy as many settlers as possible and to create a party of the center that would exclude only extremists in both camps.[9]

Walker failed completely. The Free Soilers refused to trust him, refused to participate in the election of delegates to the constitutional convention, and forfeited control of the territorial government to men determined to make Kansas a slave state. He fared no better with the pro-slavery faction that assailed him savagely for intervening in the affairs of the legislature. He believed that climate permanently barred slavery from the territory, championed genuine popular sovereignty, and warned that the Congress would not accept a constitution not approved by a popular referendum. By early summer, he was under fire by politicians and editors throughout the South who recognized the threat posed by a genuine referendum, the territory slipping inexorably out of their grasp, and the balance of power in the Congress turning permanently against them. It was a prospect they were determined to resist at almost any cost.[10]

Keitt joined the assault against Walker even before the governor delivered his inaugural address and continued to denounce him until August 1858, when the voters of the territory rejected the English Compromise and laid the statehood issue to rest. At first he limited his attacks to Walker alone, bitterly assailing his attempts to bring Kansas into the Union as a free state. Later, at the very time that the president was withdrawing administration support from the embattled governor, he expanded his attacks to include Buchanan, accusing him of defending a man hostile to the southern cause. Not until early 1858, when Buchanan gave his approval to the work of the Lecompton convention, did Keitt break off his attacks.

On May 22, the fiery congressman used a complimentary dinner given him by the citizens of Cheraw—a hamlet in Marlborough District not far from the plantation owned by his prospective father-in-law—to discuss the political problems facing the South. Responding to a highly flattering toast, he talked for an hour and a half, warning the guests that northern fanaticism aided by southern apathy threatened to blot out the rights of the South in the territories.[11]

Keitt told his audience that he had some confidence in Buchanan's honesty and integrity but doubted his ability to defeat the forces of fanaticism arrayed against him; he had no confidence in the men the president had appointed to office in Kansas, and no confidence in the Democratic Party. Walker was a Pennsylvania bankrupt, and Frederick Stanton, the secretary of the territory, was an unprincipled political gambler. Like the men who had fallen from high estate and paraded the streets of Washington, filled the lobbies of the Congress, thronged the executive departments with their prices "placarded in figures on their foreheads," they were ready to do the will of the highest bidder.[12]

Keitt denounced Walker's decision to submit the Lecompton constitution to the people for ratification before he presented it to the Congress. It was an unprecedented maneuver intended only to hand the state to the Black Republicans. He warned that the South must not look to the Democratic Party for salvation. Every day its northern wing grew more willing to betray the South to secure the spoils of victory for itself. Already it had agreed to levy a protective tariff, admitted California to the Union, and robbed Texas to create Free Soil New Mexico. Now it threatened to drive slaveholders out of Kansas. He had no confidence the party would defend the Constitution and the Union. The country was hopelessly divided. One section was battling for equality and independence, the other for domination. The issue would be decided at the next election.[13]

All over South Carolina, newspapers lavished praise on the speech. The editor of the *Cheraw Gazette* called it "one of the most powerful political speeches it had ever been our good fortune to listen to," and the editor of the *Cheraw Herald* emphatically agreed. If every man south of the Potomac River would endorse Keitt's opinions as heartily as he did, a southern confederacy would soon spring up to right the wrongs the section had endured so patiently for so long.[14]

A month later, Keitt was still blaming Buchanan for "treachery" in Kansas. Writing to Congressman W. Porcher Miles of Charleston, he speculated that "Buchanan [had] a finger in the pie" in Kansas. The president was "a political Mephistopholes [*sic*], . . . a worse rascal [than Walker], an ignorant knave." If he tried to bring Kansas into the Union as a slave state, the northern Democratic Party would desert the administration. To save himself, Buchanan was working to make the territory a free state. But, Keitt predicted accurately enough, his "deuced cunning" would bring him down.[15]

A few days after he wrote to Miles, Keitt delivered a stump speech and found himself at the center of a newspaper war. At Laurenville he described to a large crowd his embarrassment at the course of national politics. He did not want to judge the Buchanan administration unfairly, he said, but he had no confidence that it would deal justly with the South. First, the president had appointed Walker governor of Kansas Territory; then Walker had insisted that the constitution framed by the Lecompton convention be submitted to the people for their approval, knowing that immigrants from the North and apathy in the South would produce a majority against the pro-slavery constitution. It was all part of a conspiracy, Keitt concluded, to drive slaves out of Kansas, make Kansas a free state, and elect a Black Republican to the presidency in 1860.[16]

Late in June the editor of the *Richmond Examiner* discovered an account of the speech in the *Laurensville Herald,* wrote an emotional reply—"The Mask Thrown Off"—and precipitated a bitter debate. The editor praised Keitt for his frankness but denounced his hostility to the president and the Democratic Party. Keitt had attacked Walker and conceded Kansas to the Free Soilers; he had attacked Buchanan and conceded the White House to the Black Republicans in 1860. Henceforth, the editor concluded, Keitt was his enemy.[17]

Keitt jumped at the opportunity to continue his assault on Walker. In a letter to the *Examiner,* he flatly denied both of its charges. He had supported the president in the last election, he pointed out, and he was not hostile to him or his administration. He had denounced the governor, and would continue to denounce him because he had violated the law of the territory and the spirit of the president's inaugural address. Walker had "courted the caresses of the profligate free state rabble" and dictated to the legislature. The Free Soilers had declined to go to the polls and vote for delegates to the constitutional convention in Lecompton, and the governor had no power to interfere with their decision. What right did he have, Keitt demanded, "to coax, wheedle, or drag [them] to the registry office or the polls?" The governor had demanded that the convention submit the finished constitution to the people for their approval, a demand that violated both theory and practice. Fully one-half of the states had not referred their constitutions to the people, and that did not detract one iota from their legitimacy. It was the duty of the governor to carry out the law. If the Free Soilers refused to obey it, the proper remedy was the bayonet. Walker had done everything in his power to bar slavery from the territory. Buchanan must prove he was not in league with the governor by removing him from office without delay.[18]

Dozens of newspapers reprinted Keitt's letter, most of them without comment. Only James Gordon Bennett of the *New York Herald* added fuel to the fire. He compared the South Carolina fire-eater to Lyman Trumbull, the Republican senator from Illinois, and concluded that one radical was as obnoxious as another. Keitt he derided as a "Simon pure secessionist" and "a southern nigger driver." Both men were ready to break up the Union to serve their own selfish purposes.[19]

Keitt did not try to refute the *Examiner*'s accusation that he was hostile to the Democratic Party. He had never surrendered his independence to the party, he insisted, and he never would. He supported the party when it was right and opposed it when it was wrong. He had some confidence in its leaders, but he doubted they had the will to adhere to the Constitution or the strength to defend it against the Republican onslaught. They had repeatedly betrayed the South, sacrificing its interests to buy victories in the North. He denied that he had conceded control of the government to the Black Republicans but warned that they would almost certainly seize it in 1860. Then, the safety of the South would lie only in itself.[20]

On August 3, Keitt wrote a second public letter, this one to state-rights Democrats in Marion District who had invited him to attend a dinner in his honor. Unwilling to interrupt his vacation at White Sulphur Springs, Keitt expressed regret that he could not attend and then reviewed at considerable length the struggle for Kansas. For the first time, he openly admitted that the South could not carry slavery into the territory and laid the blame squarely on Buchanan and his administration. The rival forms of society were about to face each other in battle, Keitt told his audience. "Neither shivering cabinets" nor "convulsive administrations" nor "dying parties" could prevent the conflict nor cushion its shock. In the end, either "northern license or southern law" must triumph.

Three years before, Congress had passed the Kansas-Nebraska Act. Under its provisions, each section pledged to strive honorably to plant its institutions in the new territories. The federal government agreed to remain neutral, encouraging legitimate development and preventing violent confrontations. The Pierce administration had fulfilled its pledge, first censuring and then removing from office the territorial governors who basely betrayed its trust. Unfortunately, the present administration had not followed the lead of its predecessor.[21]

As his first act, Buchanan had appointed Robert Walker governor of Kansas, "a man of broken fortune and sullied reputation, a needy adventurer" who won the confidence of the South and then betrayed it. Together, they tore Kansas from its allegiance to the South and delivered the territory into the hands of Free Soil fanatics. They made Kansas a battleground, "year after year shaken by revolt, stained with blood, wrapped with flames." The South had won every battle, but Buchanan and Walker had stolen the fruits of its victory. Buchanan robbed the South of its triumph, Keitt insisted, and Walker had delivered Kansas into the hand of the Free Soilers. The loss of the territory was a serious defeat, doubly painful because it was lost through the base betrayal of a man appointed by a Democratic president and trusted by the people of the South. The Democratic Party owed its ascendancy to the South. The South had raised Buchanan to the presidency, and the South could pull him down again. No leader was ever safe from the vengeance of an outraged people; no leader ever rose so high that the people could not lay him low. South Carolina must not hesitate to defend the rights of the South against the aggressions of the federal government. When the time for battle finally arrived, "loyalty to party" would be "treason to the South."[22]

In South Carolina, only the *Sumter Watchman* took any notice of Keitt's letter. Perhaps the state's editors had become numb to his denunciations of Buchanan, Walker, and the Democrats. In New York, reactions ranged from sarcastic to perceptive. The editor of the *New York Times* announced that a group of impassioned admirers had invited Keitt to dinner, and with singular modesty had refrained from revealing the bill of fare. He assumed they would serve up southern fire in all of its forms, and hoped they would avoid the cannibalism of another group that had invited a senator to "a barbeque composed of two thousand ladies and gentlemen." However tempted by the promise of southern fire and northern blood, Keitt had declined the invitation. Turning to Keitt's letter, the editor wondered why the congressman persisted in advising his constituents to "bite off their noses and kick their neighbors down the stairs." Keitt's fulminations made him believe the most effective remedy for his afflictions was medical rather than military. At the *New York Herald,* Bennett concluded that the letter was a declaration of war against Buchanan and the northern Democrats. Keitt did not want Kansas admitted to the Union as a slave state. He knew that was impossible. What he did want was the utter destruction of the Buchanan administration, the reconstruction of political parties along sectional lines, and the creation of a southern confederacy. His letter foreshadowed what might be expected from the secessionists in the next session of Congress.[23]

To a strong executive, events in Kansas would have posed grave but not insoluble problems; to one as weak as Buchanan, they presented a dilemma that had no solution. On the one hand, the president recognized his obligation to support Governor Walker in his dealings with the pro-slavery legislature of the territory and to submit the Lecompton constitution to a genuine popular referendum. On the other, he was acutely sensitive to the demands of southern leaders whose support was critical to the success of his administration and genuinely believed that the federal government should protect the South from its enemies. Even more important, he wanted desperately to leave office with the Union intact. For a time Buchanan stood firm, repeatedly assuring Walker that the administration would stand or fall in his defense. But gradually, under unrelenting pressure from events in Kansas and southern politicians who alternately denounced him as a turncoat and played on his fear of secession, his resolve began to crumble. By late autumn, Buchanan had concluded that Walker had to go.[24]

The situation in Kansas was enormously complicated. In June voters had elected delegates to a convention in Lecompton that would draft a constitution for the state. Free staters had known the election was rigged and refused to vote. The result was a convention dominated by men determined to make Kansas a slave state. The convention met from September to November and produced a document that was for the most part unremarkable because it relied heavily on the constitutions of states already in the Union. In two areas, however, it departed sharply from precedent. It included clauses that prohibited the legislature from emancipating slaves already in Kansas unless the owners consented and the state compensated them for their losses and required the legislature to enforce the Fugitive Slave Act. It also required governors to have been citizens for twenty years and prohibited amendment of the constitution for seven years. Its most controversial provision allowed voters to approve the constitution with slavery or the constitution without slavery, but not to reject the constitution as a whole. The provision was an obvious swindle. Even if the voters approved the constitution without slavery, the two hundred slaves already in Kansas would remain in bondage. The property rights of the owners would remain undisturbed.[25]

In October, while the convention was still in session, Kansas held an election for members of the territorial legislature. This time, men who wanted to make Kansas a free state did participate and easily elected a Republican delegate to Congress, but massive fraud produced a territorial legislature dominated by pro-slavery Democrats. Walker threw out enough of the most questionable ballots to hand over the legislature to the Free Soilers. In December, in a referendum boycotted by Free Soilers who knew it too was rigged, voters overwhelmingly approved the Lecompton constitution with slavery. And in January, in still another referendum called by the legislature, free-state voters rejected the constitution by an even greater margin.[26]

This was the situation that confronted Buchanan when Congress returned to Washington early in December 1856. On December 7, the House elected its Speaker, James L. Orr of South Carolina, an up-country moderate in a state dominated by low-country radicals.[27] The next day, it heard Buchanan's fourth annual message, a truly perverse document that defended the Lecompton constitution, urged voters to participate in the referendum later that month, and predicted that admission of Kansas to the Union would put an end to the crisis. He tried to explain away his betrayal of Walker and popular sovereignty by insisting that, when he promised voters an opportunity to accept or reject the constitution, he had meant only the clauses dealing with slavery. The Kansas-Nebraska Act required only that the people have the right to determine their own domestic institutions, not the right to approve the entire constitution. The referendum would give voters the opportunity to settle the slavery question once and for all. On February 2, Buchanan sent the Lecompton constitution to Congress, and with it a last impassioned defense of his actions and a demand that it approve the constitution and admit Kansas to the Union without delay.[28]

Keitt had returned to Washington prepared to wage all-out war on the administration and its Kansas policy, and the president's change of heart must have come as a genuine surprise. Buchanan's defense of the Lecompton constitution and his repudiation of Governor Walker radically altered political alignments in the House and forced Keitt to reconsider his intentions. Confused, convinced that the South could not open Kansas to slavery but unwilling to give up without a fight, he took no part in the savage debate that followed. He did move closer to the administration, slowly repairing his relationship with the president he had spent the summer denouncing as a traitor, and by early February 1858 he was ready to return to the fray.

In November 1857, when the South Carolina legislature had elected James H. Hammond to the Senate to fill the seat left vacant by the death of Andrew Pickens Butler, Keitt had warmly congratulated his old friend on his victory and warned him that he would see "strange moves on the political chess board" when he arrived in Washington. The situation was dangerously unsettled; the administration's hostility toward Walker was increasing rapidly, and nobody knew what the results might be. Buchanan's stand on Kansas would do, but his reasoning was unfortunate. Stephen Douglas, Keitt's choice for president in 1856, had "gone off from us," but he would soon return to the Democratic fold. Congress

James Henry Hammond. Courtesy of South Caroliniana Library, University of South Carolina.

would approve the Lecompton constitution "after a terrible fight," he predicted, but he could not see what the South would gain from it.[29]

Buchanan was determined to ram the constitution through the Congress in as short a time as possible, whatever the cost. In the Senate, dominated by a coalition of southerners and "dough faces," the outcome was virtually certain. Douglas led a determined but clearly hopeless fight to defeat the bill. The Senate debated six weeks—among the speeches was Hammond's "Cotton Is King" oration—but altered few opinions; the administration swung its patronage club with effect and forced reluctant Democrats into line. On March 23, the Lecompton constitution passed the upper house by a comfortable majority.[30]

It was obvious from the start that the decisive struggle would occur in the House of Representatives. There the margin of victory would be extremely narrow, and there was concentrated all of the bitterness generated by four years of almost constant warfare. When the president's message arrived on February 2, the enemies of the administration referred it to a select committee with power to investigate every facet of the constitution-making process in Kansas. Speaker

Orr appointed Anti-Lecompton Democrat Thomas L. Harris of Illinois as chairman but packed the committee with men who wanted to admit Kansas as a slave state. The committee did its part by endorsing the constitution.[31]

For three days the two sides battled without reaching a decision. Then, late in the afternoon of February 5, opposition leaders discovered an unexpected advantage. Dinner parties had depleted the administration's forces. Alexander H. Stephens stalled desperately, demanding roll call after roll call and dispatching messengers to pry friendly congressmen away from fashionable dining rooms all over Washington.[32]

The struggle went on for hour after hour, taking an increasingly heavy toll on the men involved, culminating just before 2:00 A.M. in a "grand row." Galusha Grow of Pennsylvania, the Republican floor leader, had crossed the aisle to confer with anti-Lecompton Democrats. John A. Quitman of Mississippi offered another in the long series of motions designed to consume as much time as possible and prevent a vote until reinforcements arrived. To this tactic, Grow objected "with considerable tartness in his tone of voice, and in a manner that was . . . very offensive." Nearby, Keitt—one of the Democrats called away from dinner to defend the administration, tired, at least a bit intoxicated—lay across two desks, one shoe off and half asleep. Grow's objection came as an unwelcome intrusion. Rousing himself slightly, he growled, "If you are going to object, go back to your own side of the House." Grow, bigger than Keitt and almost as belligerent, refused to be intimidated. "This is a free hall," he replied, "and I have the right to object from any part of it when I choose." Now Keitt was wide-awake and furious: "Wait until I put my shoe on, you Black Republican puppy, and we will see about that." Grow waited: "I shall occupy such place in this hall as I please, and no nigger driver is going to come up from his plantation and crack his whip about my ears."

Keitt hurled himself at Grow, grabbed his throat—or his cravat or the lapels of his coat, depending on the witness—and held on. For a few seconds, Reuben Davis of Mississippi managed to separate the two men, but Keitt broke away and rushed at Grow a second time. From this point accounts of the melee diverge even more dramatically. Grow swung, either missing Keitt completely or knocking him flat on his back and launching a back-alley brawl in front of the Speaker's desk. Dozens of congressmen rushed in, some intent on joining the fray, others on breaking it up.[33] For at least five minutes, they flailed away at each other, ignoring the attempts of the Speaker to call them to order but doing little damage to their opponents. Only John Covode, a Republican from Pennsylvania, thought to bring along a weapon; fortunately, every blow of his stoneware spittoon fell wide of the mark. Sheer exhaustion would eventually have forced the combatants to stop fighting had not the absurdity of what they were doing finally dawned on them first. Cadwallader Washburn of Wisconsin grabbed William Barksdale of Mississippi by the hair, but the hair came off in his hand. Barksdale was embarrassed because few congressmen knew he wore a wig and angry because the rioters were trampling on it. He managed to retrieve the wig but crammed it back on his head wrong-side-out, convulsing the brawlers and ending the riot.[34]

At the next meeting of the House, Keitt expressed "profound regret" that he had disrupted the order and dignity of its proceedings. "I was the aggressor," he admitted, "and whatever responsibility attaches to the act properly belongs to me alone." He insisted that he had emerged from the melee untouched: "If any blow was directed at me I am not conscious of it. I am at least utterly unconscious of receiving any."[35] Keitt hoped the remark would satisfy the requirements of the southern code of honor. Any insult left unanswered would have threatened both his political fortunes and his self-esteem. He could not challenge Grow, who was not a "gentleman," nor could he risk a repetition of the Sumner affair, which had occurred less than a year before. It is possible, of course, that Keitt believed that Grow had not hit him. In a letter to his brother two weeks later, he insisted that

Galusha A. Grow. Courtesy of Library of Congress, Washington, D.C.

the widely circulated story that Grow had struck him was "a foul lie."[36] One of his friends told a *New York Times* correspondent that Keitt had fallen when Davis pulled him away from Grow.[37] Accurate or not, Keitt's assertion allowed him to escape from a difficult situation without serious damage to his reputation.

Most published reactions to the brawl were severely critical. An editorial in the *New York Times* condemned it as "a crying offense against the whole land, and a just reproach to the nation." Any member who provoked a fight should be expelled, but Keitt was an important ally of the administration and a "trusty friend . . . of Lecompton law and Atchison order" and would go unpunished. If the "southern chevaliers" could not behave themselves properly, the sooner they left the Union the better it would be for the peace and safety of all concerned. At least the bully who for years had believed that a man who did not own slaves could be "trodden upon with impunity" had been "elaborately, scientifically, and thoroughly" beaten.[38]

An editor in Ithaca, New York, blamed the fight on Buchanan's "fool-hardy determination" to force the Lecompton constitution through Congress, and one in Charles Town, Virginia, blamed the "vulgar mode of legislation" carried over from the age of Andrew Jackson. A third editor held the Speaker responsible for failing to enforce the rules of the House. Only Horace Greeley refused to treat the incident seriously. The editor of the *New York Tribune* described "some fifty middle-aged and elderly gentlemen pitching into each other like so many Tipperary savages." Most of them, he wrote, owing to their lack of wind and muscle, were incapable of doing each other any real damage.[39]

Most southern papers published reports of the melee without editorial comment. Only one, the *Sumter Watchman,* approved of Keitt's conduct. The editor called it "impulsive and precipitate," but insisted that every blow struck in Congress by a southerner was a blow for the southern cause. Two papers commended Keitt for his "frank-hearted, . . . manly, and generous" apology, and one warned that the southern cause was too important to be risked in the pursuit of personal revenge.[40]

Many of the friends who commented on Keitt's behavior expressed approval, at least in public, but some revealed their embarrassment and concern in conversations they assumed would remain private. In a letter to Hammond, David F. Jamison of Orangeburg District told the senator he was sorry his neighbor "had got into a row with that creature," not because Keitt had kicked the man, but because he had put himself in the wrong by his bullying and bravado.[41] One constituent wrote to Congressman Porcher Miles, "You know that I don't admire brawls, but I never think of the way Kitt [*sic*] used that fellow from Pennsylvania without wishing that the time had come for us to *shoot* instead of *choaking* [*sic*] the negro stealing rascals." Another, a railroad executive from Charleston, wanted to know what ammunition Keitt had used to cause such a furious explosion.[42] William Henry Trescot, the scholarly South Carolina planter then assistant secretary of state, was more measured. "In common with most of the gentlemen whom I meet," Trescot told Miles, "I have a nervous apprehension of some new mortification whenever I hear that a South Carolinian has been distinguishing himself." Referring sarcastically to Keitt's "heroic achievement," Trescott roundly condemned his behavior: "I have heard his conduct very generally discussed and I have heard the expression of but one feeling—that of contemptuous disgust. I am sorry for it. With all his faults and in spite even of [his] crazy rhetoric . . . I like Keitt for many things. He is frank in his nature, honest in his politics and I believe true to his work, but he has sadly depreciated the old Carolina standard and I see no hope of improvement."[43]

In time Keitt's notoriety spread through much of the English-speaking world. In March, *Punch* published a long poem, "The Fight over the Body of Keitt." Beginning "Sing, O goddess, the wrath, the untamable dander of Keitt," it described with tongue in cheek the Lecompton debate and the brawl it provoked. The poem was unsigned, but widely attributed to Oliver Wendell Holmes, who was in London at the time. It appeared in journals all over the North, adding greatly to the unfortunate reputation of its subject.[44]

Aware that every vote for the constitution was critical, the administration worked desperately to force dissident Democrats back into line, wielding the patronage power with brutal efficiency. All over the North, anti-Lecomptonites found themselves pushed away from the public trough. Buchanan Democrats traded jobs, contracts, army commissions, money, even feminine companionship for much-needed votes. In February, Hammond told William Gilmore Simms that "Old Buck" would "buy up enough votes to carry Lecompton high and dry on the finality." He was wrong; in spite of the enormous pressure exerted against them, most foes of the constitution stood firm.[45]

Meanwhile, the debate in the House went on and on. On March 9, Keitt interrupted a discussion of an appropriations bill to return to what was by then a very stale subject. He began by arguing that, under the Constitution, the powers of the Congress in the territories were strictly limited. The Congress had to require a territory to establish a republican form of government and eventually admit it to the Union, but when it had carried out those two functions, it had exhausted its powers. In Kansas the Lecompton convention had satisfied the constitutional requirement by creating three branches of government and dividing the powers of the state among them. Congress could not "look into the minor details of the constitution, or the character of the constituency"; it could not concern itself with the rights of individuals, only the rights of organized societies. It could only admit Kansas to the Union.[46]

Keitt pushed stubbornly on: Congress could not require the Lecompton convention to submit the constitution to a popular referendum. The idea that a convention had to refer its work to the people was a "mischievous doctrine" that reversed the progress of human history and blotted out the experience of the age. Conventions judiciously weighed the interests of every element of society; popular elections elevated passion and self-interest over selfless deliberation. Conventions, he concluded, not popular elections, best expressed the true interest of the community.

Next Keitt turned to the expediency of admitting Kansas to the Union. The South, he told the House, was willing to admit two more free states, Minnesota and Oregon, but the North had sworn to admit no more slave states. If it rejected Kansas because its constitution recognized slavery, he warned, it would "shake this Federal temple from turret to foundation stone." No federal tax gatherer, even if he were backed by all the legions of the North, would ever again tread southern soil. The Republican Party might take possession of the government, but it would clutch only a phantom.

The Lecompton constitution, Keitt assured northern Democrats, was an accurate reflection of the popular will in Kansas. They must not quail before the torrent of fanaticism surging at their backs; they must defy the mob and vote to admit Kansas to the Union. The nation was rapidly drifting toward dissolution. The Democratic Party, its ranks thinned by desertion and broken by assault, had so far prevented its destruction. The party must unite behind the Lecompton constitution, he warned, or the bonds of the Union would surely burst.[47]

In South Carolina, editorial comments on Keitt's speech were uniformly favorable, accurately reflecting the state's determination that Kansas would enter the Union a slave state or not enter at all. In an article widely reprinted in the state's rural papers, the *Charleston Mercury* called the speech "closely reasoned, clear, and logical." It placed the South clearly in the right and strengthened the hearts and hands of its sons to continue the contest. It was an effective vindication of its actions, whatever the consequences. The editor praised the state's congressmen for opposing every effort to amend the bill, and urged them to stand boldly on principle and throw responsibility for the defeat of the constitution on the timid men who were ready to make useless concessions to the fanatics of the free states. The *Abbeville Banner* warned that before the South allowed itself to be "chained to the chariot wheels of the North," it would "shake every pillar in the Federal edifice."[48]

At the end of March, administration leaders tried without success to devise a compromise acceptable to every faction of the party. William Montgomery, an anti-Lecompton Democrat from Pennsylvania, proposed an amendment similar to one the Senate had already rejected. The legislature would submit the entire constitution to a genuine popular referendum. If the voters rejected the constitution, the legislature would call another convention. The administration forces voted down the proposal. Next, the House Democratic caucus appointed a conference committee, ten members from each faction, to work out a solution to the stalemate. The anti-Lecomptonites on the committee pledged to vote for the constitution if its supporters would agree that the voters could amend it at any time. Keitt insisted the constitution could not be amended until 1864; the southerners rejected the offer, and the committee adjourned without accomplishing anything. Keitt realized that Kansas might remain a slave state for only a short time and refused to compromise his beliefs to achieve temporary success.[49]

On April 1, the time allotted to the debate finally expired. Keitt, who had no doubt that the House would reject the constitution, "hitched, and fidgeted, and twisted" in his seat. His colleagues were equally uncomfortable. William Boyce "sat listlessly, his arms drooping on his desk"; Alexander Stephens seemed lost in thought; George Houston of Alabama assumed "the moveless melancholy of an antique statue." Shortly after noon, the House rejected an amendment that would have granted Kansas the right to alter its constitution at once. Then, by a margin of 120 to 112, it approved the Crittenden proposal submitting the constitution to the voters of the state. Cheering broke out in the visitors' galleries, and Keitt, trembling with rage, jumped to his feet to demand they be cleared. Speaker Orr reminded the spectators they were not in a theater, and the noise subsided. Moments later, the House passed the amended bill by an identical vote and sent it on to the Senate. The Upper House rejected the substitute, and the deadlock continued.[50]

To escape the impasse, Stephens invented a bizarre compromise and persuaded William H. English to introduce it to a conference committee of both houses. The authors of the Lecompton constitution had asked the federal government to grant Kansas an enormous amount of public land—23.5 million acres—at the time of its admission to the Union. English, a friend of Buchanan and an anti-Lecompton Democrat from Indiana, reduced the grant to approximately 4.0 million acres, the same amount Congress had given other recently admitted states. He proposed that the Congress couple the land grant with statehood and submit both to a popular referendum. If the voters rejected the reduced grant, they would reject statehood as well and Kansas would remain a territory for at least two more years. To acquire the land, they would have to approve the Lecompton constitution. Its southern supporters vehemently denied that the compromise submitted the constitution to a popular vote, but that in fact is what it did do.[51]

With the aid of administration money and patronage, Stephens and his colleagues won the committee's approval of the scheme and introduced it into both houses late in April. Like the majority of the South Carolina delegation, Keitt opposed the compromise. On April 28, he told the House that it was obnoxious to him, but under the circumstances, it would be well to approve it. The next day, he urged the members not to delay the vote any longer. It was time to get on with the business of running the country.[52]

On the last day of April, both houses passed the English amendment by comfortable margins. Of the South Carolinians, only Milledge Bonham voted against it. Miles undoubtedly expressed the opinion of the others when he wrote Hammond, "We were sick and tired of the whole matter, and felt instinctively that we ought not to vote with Seward, Hale, Wilson, Giddings."[53] Early in August, voters rejected the constitution and the land grant by an overwhelming margin, leaving Kansas a territory until 1861 and disposing of an issue that had plagued national politics for half a decade.[54]

The nation would not escape so easily from the long struggle. The battle for Kansas had destroyed the Whig Party, divided the Democrats along sectional lines, and called the Republicans into being. It had convinced many southerners that their most vital interests could never again be secure inside the Union and carried the South a long way toward secession and civil war.

FIVE

"Like mildew and blast, like pestilence and famine"

Even before the Thirty-fifth Congress adjourned in June 1858, Keitt realized that his actions during the session had displeased constituents at one end of South Carolina's narrow political spectrum—conservatives like William Henry Trescott, who criticized his readiness to indulge in exaggerated rhetoric and even to provoke riots on the floor of the House. He knew, however, that his defiance of the Yankees had won him far more votes than it lost and was confident he could treat attacks from that quarter as politically insignificant, as indeed they were.

Keitt feared that attacks from the other end of the political spectrum posed a genuine threat to his popularity. From the start he had built his career on appeals to southern nationalism. A master of the baroque oratory so admired by antebellum audiences, he had established a seemingly unassailable position by telling his constituents what they wanted to hear in a way they wanted to hear it. His speeches in the House and on the stump reflected the hopes and fears of his low-country constituents. The most vital interests of the South, he warned them repeatedly, could never be entirely safe within the Union. They must not believe that the Democratic Party would protect their interests; when the time came, they must be ready to defend themselves against their enemies' assaults on their peculiar institution.

Keitt was widely known for his emotional explosions, but he was capable of acting coolly, even calculatingly, when circumstances demanded it. His vote in favor of the English Compromise—cast because, he insisted, opposition would have made him the ally of the hated Republicans—was the latest example of his willingness to discard ideological consistency when it seemed reasonable to do so. He must have been surprised when he found himself under attack by low-country radicals who accused him of selling his soul to the national Democratic Party. Every member of the South Carolina delegation had supported Buchanan's fruitless attempt to force Kansas into the Union as a slave state. With the exception of Milledge Bonham, every member had reluctantly voted in favor of the English Compromise. He must have been especially amazed when he discovered that a small but tightly organized clique was prepared to make this suddenly controversial vote the basis of a campaign to unseat him in the fall elections.

As early as May 1858, William A. Owens of Barnwell Court House had told Hammond he was thinking of running for Congress. Four years before, he said, Keitt had promised to retire after two terms and endorse Owens to succeed him. But the previous spring, explaining that his expectations had not really worked out, he had reneged on his promise. Now, Owens told the senator, he would make the race.[1]

Later the same month, John E. Tobin, a lawyer and member of the legislature from Blackville in Barnwell District, wrote Hammond somewhat disingenuously that he too was thinking of running against Keitt. Tobin was in fact already campaigning for the seat, supported by low-country radicals angered by Keitt's apparent embrace of political moderation. The clique, led by Bonham, Charleston banker Benjamin Mordecai, and a number of others, had already selected Tobin to run against Keitt and Gen. James Gadsden to oppose Porcher Miles in the Second District. In the following months, the clique pushed its campaign to unseat the two men, publishing letters in the radical press and stumping crossroads stores and courthouses throughout tidewater South Carolina.[2]

Before Keitt could deal more directly with the challenge to his congressional seat, he had to fulfill a pressing obligation in Charleston. Some time before, he had agreed to deliver the principal oration at the dedication of a statue of John C. Calhoun to be erected on the parade ground of the Citadel Academy. Soon after Congress adjourned in mid-June, he took the train to Charleston, stayed with William Gilmore Simms, and worked at polishing his speech. A few days before the dedication, Simms wrote Hammond that Keitt had read him the speech. It was, he thought, "flowery and flimsy, but portions of it would probably tell upon a popular audience." Keitt was a good fellow who meant no harm, but his vanity and lack of purpose would sooner or later "founder his bateau," even in smooth waters. He was beyond saving, Simms concluded, too stubborn to improve himself or to "pass a single inch higher in political or social stature."[3]

Flimsy or not, Keitt's oration was the high point of a spectacular day-long celebration. At mid-afternoon on June 28, a procession of dignitaries—the governor, the mayor, veterans of the Mexican War, the Ladies' Monument Association—marched from South Bay up Meeting Street to Citadel Square. Keitt

"Birds-Eye View of Charleston, South Carolina, and Its Environs." From *Harper's Weekly,* August 15, 1863, 516–17. Courtesy of Thomas Cooper Library, Rare Books and Special Collections, University of South Carolina.

rode in a "large and magnificent Phaeton, drawn by four splendidly caparisoned grays" and escorted by a guard of honor. All along the route, spectators jammed windows, doors, and even rooftops. At the square, bells tolled, and cannons boomed, clergymen prayed, and choirs sang appropriate airs. Keitt spoke for more than an hour to an enormous crowd that repeatedly applauded his tribute to the great South Carolinian.[4]

Keitt congratulated the ladies of Charleston who had done so much to preserve the memory of their state's greatest statesman and praised Calhoun for the power of his intellect, the force of his eloquence, the purity of his character, and most of all, his sacrifice of his political career to defend the interests of the South.

Before Calhoun, Keitt told his audience, no political philosopher had subjected the division of power between the states and the federal government to rigorous analysis. Calhoun had recognized that the federal government had acquired vastly more power during the War of 1812 and the danger that power posed to the states. He had foreseen all of the evils that plagued the American political system and threatened the peace of the country. He had predicted that sooner or later the federal government would degenerate into an irresponsible democracy; the North would break down the guarantees of the Constitution, ignore the rights of the minority section, and declare unremitting warfare against its domestic institutions.

In his prophecy, Keitt insisted, Calhoun had been entirely correct. More important, Calhoun had devised weapons with which the South might roll back the encroachments of the North. Now, the South must act on the advice of its greatest statesman and unite to defend its safety and its honor. It was confronting the very dangers Calhoun had seen approaching. For a generation fanatics had violated the Constitution and perverted the Union. The South must not allow either to endure if, instead of a protection, they became a fortress from which its political rights were assailed and its domestic institutions overthrown.[5]

Two weeks later, Simms described for Hammond the humiliating conclusion of the day's events. "That good, foolish fellow Keitt," he told his friend, "got drunk after or during his oration, and was with difficulty carried from the stand and into the Citadel." Keitt usually had no difficulty holding his liquor, but a mixture of beverages and long hours in the sun had done him in. Say nothing of it, Simms cautioned Hammond; if the story got out, it would compromise the congressman in the eyes of his constituents. Two or three were eager to take his seat in the House, and would use the story to discredit him.[6]

If Keitt had consumed more whiskey than he could handle, he had escaped its effects three days later when he described the day's events to his friend Porcher Miles. "The 28th went off beautifully," he told the congressman, who was in New York tending to business. "About 30,000 people" had come out to hear him speak. All in all, the oration had been a conspicuous success.[7]

The editor of the Charleston *Mercury* agreed wholeheartedly with Keitt's assessment. He praised the speech for its "glowing description, keen discrimination, and . . . original thought." At times it was impassioned, but on the whole it had been quieter and simpler than his typical production. A letter to the *Sumter Watchman* commended Keitt's "fervid imagination, his enthusiastic ardor and patriotism, his eminent literary achievements, and his devotion to the memory of Calhoun." However the day may have ended, Keitt was obviously pleased with his speech and the reaction of the radical press. He understood, as his opponents did not, that the invitation to speak had been a splendid opportunity to reemphasize his devotion to his state and section. He had seized the opportunity and made the most of it.[8]

With the dedication of the Calhoun monument safely behind him, Keitt was free to turn his attention to mending political fences. The letters he wrote to Hammond during this time—no doubt he was corresponding with other political allies, but only the Hammond letters have survived—provide a brief account of his preparations for the coming election. More important, they reveal his reluctance to undertake an active campaign, his momentary doubt that he could retain his seat in the House, and finally his confidence that he would win an overwhelming victory.

Keitt's almost instinctive aversion to canvassing against Tobin or Owens or both was a product of his republican ideology. He was a masterful politician, equally at ease dining in Charleston's aristocratic townhouses and eating barbecue at Round O or Whippy Swamp, as adept at bargaining in smoke-filled rooms as at rough-and-tumble stump speaking. But he had grown up in a political culture that discouraged overt competition. Established politicians typically sat in the House or Senate for a few years and then returned to private life. Outsiders rarely challenged incumbents, instead waiting for deaths or retirements before offering themselves as candidates for public office. In 1853 Keitt had abruptly abandoned his campaign for a seat in the House of Representatives when he learned that incumbent William F. Colcock had decided to run for reelection. It had been an intensely embarrassing experience; still, he had abided by the rules of the political game, and he expected his rivals to do the same.

Keitt's displeasure was also a product of his determination that South Carolina should be ready to defend its institutions against the incursions of the federal government. The state could mount an effective defense only if it first achieved political consensus, only if its leaders first agreed among themselves about the goals the state should pursue and the means it should employ to achieve them. Overt political competition could do nothing to unify public opinion, nothing to prepare the people to face the dangers that lay ahead. At best, it would momentarily divert attention from issues of genuine significance; at worst, it would publicize disagreements over policies or personalities and weaken the state's ability to resist the assaults of its enemies. Finally, Keitt knew that South Carolina had resisted the surge of Jacksonian democracy more successfully than any other state. He believed that men like himself, because they were better educated and more disinterested, were uniquely qualified to govern. If members of the elite competed among themselves for office, they would turn over to ordinary voters the power to determine the men who would hold office and the measures they would pursue. It was a prospect that made him shudder. For Keitt, in short, political competition was an unmitigated evil, but it was an evil that in 1858 he could not avoid.[9]

Late in June, less than a week before his speech in Charleston, Keitt told Hammond he had heard rumors that Tobin planned to attack his vote in favor of the English Compromise. He was confident that he could win reelection by "an overwhelming majority," Keitt told the senator, and without any real difficulty, but he was afraid the campaign might create "agitation," both inside the state and abroad. Keitt reminded Hammond that he too had supported the English bill and asked him to express his opinion publicly. If he would take "decided ground," he would settle public opinion once and for all.[10]

Following an accidental meeting with Tobin on his way home from Charleston, Keitt again asked Hammond for help. Tobin had told Keitt he had not yet decided whether he would run. Keitt, apparently trying to gain a psychological advantage over his opponents, assured Tobin that he was ready to defend his record and accept the judgment of the voters. After their conversation, Keitt told his old friend, he had concluded that Tobin would not run. But if he were forced to canvas, he would "take it right bravely, make the fur fly," win by as large a majority as possible, and "silence the clamor" of his radical critics. However confident he may have been, he ended his letter by begging the senator to take a stand on the English Compromise: "You have the state; for God's sake, keep it, or we'll go to pieces."[11]

Hammond, reluctant to alienate either political faction but unwilling to disappoint his friend, spoke out and quickly found himself assailed by angry radicals. During informal remarks to dinner guests at his plantation near Beech Island in July and in a prepared address at Barnwell Court House in October, he defended the South Carolina congressmen who had voted for the English bill and argued that, in its relations with the federal government, the state should adopt a policy of watchful waiting. Only a "substantial issue," Hammond insisted, should cause the state to leave the Union.[12]

Keitt was not at Beech Island to hear Hammond's controversial remarks. He did not attend the gathering, he explained to Hammond, because he had heard that Milledge Bonham would be there. Bonham was the only member of the South Carolina congressional delegation who had voted against the English Compromise, and Keitt was afraid their meeting would lead to violence. He did not object to Hammond's conciliatory remarks but, he insisted, the election of a Black Republican president would be the event that broke up the Union.[13]

Aware that he could not rely on Hammond, Keitt spent much of the summer stumping his district for votes. At an Independence Day celebration in Orangeburg, he tried once again to justify his vote for the English Compromise. The bill, he explained, did not submit the Lecompton constitution to popular approval; it submitted only an ordinance that granted a generous tract of land to Kansas when the territory became a state. Congress had done the same for every other state admitted to the Union in the nineteenth century.[14]

In August, Keitt interrupted a vacation at Glenn Springs to attend a political rally at nearby Williamston in the northwest corner of the state. He was aware that the crowd of fifteen hundred shared the conditional unionism of Fifth District Congressman James L. Orr and was careful to emphasize the more moderate facets of his own opinions. He told his audience that he had gone to Washington determined to fight Buchanan's Kansas policy, but when he reached the city, he discovered that the president had somehow been converted to southern principles. On the Kansas question, the administration had fought for the true interests of the South. The English bill had established the right of a slave state to enter the Union. Buchanan had worked for ratification of the Lecompton constitution and had not conceded the right of the people to vote on the completed constitution.

The administration deserved the confidence of the South, Keitt told the crowd, and he had supported it ungrudgingly. The president was sound, and the Democratic Party was purer than it had been in years, now that the majority had driven away its "tainted, timid, and feeble members" from the North. Under an administration like Buchanan's, the South could remain in the Union. But, he warned, the Black Republicans were going to win the presidency in 1860, and then the South would have to secede. The South, Keitt repeated, must unite to defend its cherished rights and institutions. Referring obliquely to the controversy created by his vote for the English bill, he insisted that no "practical issue" any longer confronted the state. Its leaders must not invent specious arguments that divided the people and diverted their attention from the genuine problems that threatened the state. They must cultivate harmony and prepare the people to strike for the common good when the "practical issue" appeared.[15]

Keitt's speech stirred up a hornet's nest in tidewater South Carolina, where his unaccustomed moderation met far less approval than in the mountainous Fifth District. The Orangeburg *Southron* concluded that newspaper accounts of the rally could not be correct. Reports that Keitt took "national ground almost as strong as Col. Orr" were "utterly at variance with his avowed political principles" and did him a grave injustice. The Columbia *South Carolinian* defended its version of the speech, insisting that it was consistent with Keitt's activities during the last session of Congress.[16]

In the midst of the furor, Benjamin F. Perry, the unionist editor of the Greenville *Southern Patriot,* noted with approval the unexpected moderation of his state's preeminent fire-eater: "Senator Hammond has given the death blow to disunion and revolution. Orr and Keitt go with him—they are as conservative now as I am."[17] The reaction of the state's radicals was less retrained. Concluding that Keitt had sold out to the national democracy, men like James H. Adams and Maxcy Gregg roundly denounced their former ally. In his *Appeal to the State Rights Party of South Carolina,* James D. Tradewell of Columbia assailed Keitt for speaking at a meeting organized by national Democrats and his praise of Orr and Buchanan for being "unnecessarily strong": "The recent lion of the Third Congressional District, a while since the vehement denouncer of the National Democracy, who refused to go into its caucus at Washington to vote for the nomination of its sweaty leader in South Carolina for Speaker, under alternate lashing and petting, has tamed down into its disgusting apologist, declaring that of its fidelity, he should entertain no doubt in advance."[18]

The key to success for the South Carolina radicals in their campaign to unseat Keitt and Miles was the support of the *Charleston Mercury,* the most influential of the state's secessionist newspapers. At first the Rhetts cooperated, publishing letters like the one written by "York," who bitterly assailed "the vaultings and summersets" of the state's two congressmen. Keitt had been the staunchest defender of state rights, or so it seemed. But now the fire-eater had become a "pap eater," ready to hoodwink the people and join the scramble for loot at the coming Democratic convention in Charleston. The people, he predicted, would make him pay at the polls for his betrayal.[19]

However much the Rhetts disapproved of Keitt's apparent conversion to political moderation, however many angry editorials they published, they could not flatly endorse the radical campaign to snatch away his seat in the House. During the spring, a group led by Hammond, Miles, and Keitt had saved the *Mercury* by secretly investing at least $20,000 in the financially troubled paper. Moreover, Keitt and Miles were the channel through which federal patronage flowed to the *Mercury.* If the Rhetts completely alienated the "moderates," they would cut their own throats. Being sensible men, they refused to wield the knife and worked instead to lure Keitt and his friends back into the radical fold.[20]

By early autumn, the radical "cabal" was close to collapse. Without the endorsement of the *Mercury,* Tobin and Gadsden could not win, but Keitt did not know it. In October he warned Miles that Benjamin Mordecai and his friends were well organized and promised his full support in his campaign against James Gadsden. If Miles were "pressed," he wrote, he could lend him some border votes from the Colleton district. In the end, Miles did not need assistance from anybody; Gadsden withdrew from the race only days after Keitt had made his dubious offer.[21]

If Keitt had in fact drifted into the "national current" as James Tradewell alleged, evidence of his apostasy was exceedingly hard to find in the fall of 1858. At Whippy Swamp, where he delivered his final speech before the votes were cast, Keitt was once again the fire-eating radical. Wary of repeating the mistakes of the past months, he abandoned the moderate tone of his Williamston address and flailed away at "abolitionist fanatics" and "Black Republican puppies." He devoted perhaps two-thirds of his speech to a defense of his vote in favor of the English Compromise, arguing in much the same terms he had employed before: the bill submitted the Kansas land ordinance but not the Lecompton constitution to popular approval; it sacrificed no southern principle and conceded no southern advantage.

After talking for almost an hour, Keitt turned to "subjects of practical and pressing significance." When he first entered the Congress, he told the crowd, there was an insignificant number of abolitionists in the House and only two in the Senate, but their numbers had swelled, and now they dominated the House and threatened to control the Senate:

> Like mildew and blast—like pestilence and famine—abolitionism has swept through the free states, and girdled them round with a belt of deadly influences. If there be any power to stay the ravages of this deadly sirocco, it has not been exerted. . . . I have seen the Whig Party die; its legions dissolve, its glories melt away; and its proud banner . . . folded over the grave of its great leader; and the Black Republican Party, an amalgam of isms, a base conglomerate of opposing elements tied together by fanaticism, step into the field, instigated by hatred of the South, and greed of sectional power. . . . It has formally announced its intention to abolitionize every department of the government, and use them to the overthrow of slavery.[22]

What means, Keitt asked, should the state adopt to ward off the approaching catastrophe? After such a tirade, his answer was surprisingly restrained. It must cooperate with the Buchanan administration and the Democratic Party until they betrayed its principles or threatened its safety. The president had done all he could to defend the rights of the South. Even if the party wavered, he would stand firm. Agitation had driven the timid and wavering out of the party; it had weakened the party in the North and strengthened it in the South, and the whole structure had fallen into southern hands. The party was purer now than it had been for many years. The friends of southern rights were acting with it, and the state could do no less. But, Keitt concluded, if the party betrayed the state, if Congress admitted Kansas to the Union before its population reached 93,000, if the Black Republicans elected the president in 1860, South Carolina would not shrink from its last and fiercest battle. It would take its revenge, and the Union would fall in ruins.[23]

During the week before the election, Tobin withdrew from the race, and Keitt was reelected without opposition. Miles was only slightly less fortunate; General Gadsden reversed his decision to drop out of the contest and lost by a substantial margin.[24] Not even his uncontested victory freed Keitt from the unpleasant task of defending his recent conduct. In November, more than two weeks after the election, the editor of the *Sumter Watchman* demanded to know why he had consorted with national Democrats at Williamston. In his reply, Keitt turned to a new and more persuasive justification and finally laid the affair to rest. He had attended the meeting as the guest of James L. Orr who was retiring from Congress. The occasion demanded that he avoid controversial subjects and speak only in generalities. He had not modified his views or said anything inconsistent with his principles. This last explanation was effective; editors who had been pursuing the subject relentlessly since late summer turned to more pressing problems—among them the election of a senator.[25]

At the same time that Keitt's enemies were trying to take away his seat in the House, his friends were trying to elect him to the Senate. In 1857 a number of editors had proposed that the legislature appoint him to the Upper House to fill the vacancy created by the death of Andrew Pickens Butler.[26] Keitt's role in the election was unclear, even at the time. At least one politician, John Cunningham of Charleston, was sure Keitt would not be a candidate, but others were equally certain he would. Some thought he favored James H. Hammond for the office, but M. C. M. Hammond thought Keitt was supporting Gov. John L. Manning. In the end, the legislature elected Hammond to fill the vacancy.[27]

In May 1858 the death of Josiah Evans created a second vacancy in the upper house. This time, Keitt was a serious candidate to fill the empty seat. In a letter to his brother, Hammond described a visit from the young congressman. Keitt had tried to count votes in the legislature and in the process scribbled all over a letter Hammond had written but not mailed. Keitt had genius, he told his brother, and would make a better senator than many of the men generally mentioned for the office.[28]

Keitt could do little more than correspond with influential politicians and inspire friendly editorials, but his campaign nevertheless took a toll on his usually buoyant demeanor. Keitt himself recognized the change. In August he told Hammond, "I am so grave and long-visaged you'd think I was a preacher." His concern was well justified; with at least half a dozen acknowledged candidates for the office, he knew "the public mind" and his hope for election were both "utterly unsettled."[29]

Keitt received relatively little public support from the state's radical newspapers and politicians. The *Mercury* endorsed Robert Barnwell Rhett, and the others divided their support, the majority going to First District Congressman John McQueen. An editorial that appeared first in the Richmond *South* commended Keitt's "commanding abilities and fascinating deportment." His accomplishments equaled those of any man his age in any country in the world. South Carolina must place him in the Senate, the writer insisted, where he could best employ his talents to advance the interests of the state. The South must send the most talented and courageous of its sons to Washington to stop Seward and his friends from fulfilling their threat to "rule us out of political existence." A number of South Carolina newspapers copied the editorial, but otherwise Keitt's candidacy received little public support.[30]

Almost from the start, it was obvious that the election would strain the political unity Keitt prized so highly. In December the legislature split four ways, dividing among nationalists, moderates, and two factions of radicals. The national Democrats, the weakest of the factions, supported Christopher Memminger and John L. Manning, but without much hope of electing either man. The most extreme of the radicals who favored reopening the international slave trade and opposed any cooperation with the Buchanan administration or the Democratic Party supported Gov. James H. Adams. More pragmatic radicals could not agree on a single candidate and split their votes among Rhett, McQueen, and Keitt. James Chesnut, the candidate of moderates, was the principal beneficiary of the radicals' inability to agree on a candidate.[31]

Until the fourth ballot, Keitt attracted no votes at all. On the fifth, he picked up most of Rhett's votes and a handful of McQueen's and held them through the eighth ballot. At his peak, he had only 30 of the approximately 80 votes he needed for election. In the end, the most radical state in the Union elected its second moderate senator. On the ninth ballot, aware that Keitt could not win and determined that Adams would not, the more pragmatic of the radicals switched their support to Chesnut. The nationalists followed, giving Chesnut the victory over Adams, 92 to 54.[32]

Immediately after his defeat, Keitt announced that he would retire from public life when his current term in the House expired. The unexpected announcement—almost certainly the result of Sue Sparks's demands that Keitt marry her and take her to live in Europe—caused a flurry of campaign activity in the Third District. The next election was almost two years away, but half a dozen politicians hurriedly announced their availability. None of them could know that, when Keitt finally vacated his seat in the House in December 1860, it would remain empty for almost eight years.[33]

SIX

"Lance couched, helmet on, and visor down"

Long before Keitt took his seat in the House of Representatives for the first time, southerners had drawn the outlines of the pro-slavery argument and filled in most of the details. Reacting in part to internal pressures, in part to the first feeble attacks of the abolitionists, they had discarded the defense employed by the founding fathers who admitted that the institution was a blot on southern society but insisted it could not be safely expunged. The founding fathers, they concluded, had been badly mistaken. Slavery was not "a necessary evil"; it was a "positive good."[1]

Keitt arrived in Washington just as the defense of slavery was taking a new and far more militant turn. No longer satisfied simply to parry abolitionist thrusts, men like George Fitzhugh and William J. Grayson were transforming the southern defense of slavery into an all-out assault on northern society. To this ideological transformation, Keitt contributed nothing at all. But from his seat in the House, he dinned into the ears of a captive audience—congressmen, newspaper reporters, spectators—the ideas of Grayson and Fitzhugh as well as those of more traditional apologists like Thomas R. Dew, William Gilmore Simms, William Harper, Thornton Stringfellow, James H. Thornwell, and many others. Without Keitt and fire-eaters like him, their ideas could not have circulated as widely either inside or outside the South. With his assistance, they achieved widespread notoriety.[2]

Keitt's efforts to justify the peculiar institution frequently inspired visitors to the House to record their impressions of his fiery rhetoric and exaggerated behavior. One of the most colorful accounts is a description of a speech entitled "Southern Resources" that he delivered on January 15, 1857:

> Col. K. appears quite young, not more, we should think, than thirty, and has a strikingly bouyant [*sic*], frank, and independent expression. His fiery and impetuous temperament is evident in his whole deportment, and even in the aspect of his desk, which generally presents a wilderness of papers, envelopes, pamphlets, etc. dispersed in all directions like people in a panic.
>
> Col. K. commenced his speech in a low and rather indistinct tone, and it was not till he had spoken for several minutes that his powerful voice began to expand. . . . But when he came to allude to the constant agitation of the slavery question in which the Republican Party indulged, all the bitterness of his nature poured forth. With a remorseless hand, he stripped off the disguises of that party, and treated them as executioners might treat culprits bound to the wheel. . . . One moment he dived, with an actual bodily diving, down into the abyss of his subject, to fish up an argument, then nailed the argument with such reprehensive thumps upon the innocent mahogany before him, until the articles upon it had a really tremendous motion. The loose papers seemed to have the palsy; the ink kept up a chilly chattering in its stand; one paper (the Mercury) incessantly nodded; another (the Courier) as if in contradiction, incessantly shook its head; dear old John Adam's [*sic*] extracts shuddered under the blows as if they were hurt; a little box of Paris pens danced like volatile Frenchmen. Only the slender sticks of English sealing wax stood firm. . . .
>
> [Keitt's] rapid and fervent manner had a riveting interest. His appearance of feeling too, was irresistible. In a knowledge of whatever subject he undertakes, and a facility of developing it in imposing language, this gentleman need not shrink from a comparison with a single contemporary rival in the House.[3]

Keitt rarely wasted an opportunity to warn an audience against the menace of abolition. Twenty years ago, it had been only a tiny cloud on the horizon no bigger than a man's hand; now it darkened the entire sky. Twenty years ago, it had been born "amid jeers, contempt and scorn," but "nursed in the haunts of obscurity . . . fattened upon the offals of the shambles, and the garbage of the gutter," it had waxed "corpulent and audacious." Twenty years ago, men had broken up its meetings, dishonored its leaders, and trampled its petitions under foot, but it refused to die. It subverted churches and schools, tore down old political parties, and raised up out of their ruins a new party "atrocious in its purpose, furious in its energy and unsparing in its vengeance." Now it controlled the governments of ten states, occupied every avenue to the public mind, made lecture hall and press and pulpit pay tribute to its malignancy. Into its heart was burned the pronouncement of its "fiendlike leader," John Quincy Adams: emancipation must come, even if it costs the lives of half a million southern men.[4]

Recent events, Keitt warned, had given Adams's threat an "appalling significance." The whirlwind of fanaticism had swept over the North; abolitionism had stalked into the Congress with the tread of a conqueror. It stood in an unbroken column, defiled the Constitution, and decreed the utter destruction of the South. Unchecked, it would repeal the Fugitive Slave Law, restore the Missouri restriction, and suppress the coastal slave trade. Unopposed, it would exclude new slave states from the Union and abolish slavery in the District of Columbia. But that, Keitt repeatedly declared, the South would never allow. It would meet the foe with "lance couched, helmet on, and visor down"; it would call on the god of battles, secure in the knowledge that he would grant it the victory.[5]

Keitt based much of his defense of slavery on his study of history—"the earliest traditions of races, the written records of societies, and the comparative legislations of antiquity." He was convinced, Keitt told the Congress in January 1857, that slavery was a "primordial fact, rooted in the origin of things." The existence of slavery in all times and in all countries was unmistakable in every book and poem and code of law to which modern man had access. Its origin was so ancient that no man could find its fountainhead; its origins were lost in the mists of the past. In the days of Abraham when the only law was the covenant between God and man, the Hebrews owned slaves. In the days of Homer, centuries before the dawn of recorded history, the bards sang of slavery. From the days of Aristotle, pagan philosophy viewed slavery as an integral part of society. From the days of Romulus, pagan law recognized slavery as a legitimate institution. The oldest law-givers regulated slavery, but they did not create it; when they framed the earliest human constitutions, it had the hoar of ages upon its face. It was an "aboriginal thing." However much they might regret it, abolitionists could not deny that in all times and all places, slavery had been an established fact of human existence. Moreover, he predicted, it always would be.[6]

On other occasions, Keitt turned to American history for material to rebut the abolitionist argument. Speaking to the House in January 1860, he readily acknowledged that the framers of the Constitution had been opposed to slavery. But, he insisted, when the leaders of the Republican Party appealed to the sentiments of the fathers of the republic and ignored their deeds, they committed a fraud. Unfettered by political precedent, imbued with the teachings of the French Encyclopedists, these opponents of slavery wrote a Constitution that recognized the institution. Now the Republican Party, its hands tied by law and precedent, was struggling desperately to do what the founding fathers had refused to do—transform the Constitution into an abolitionist tract. That the South would never allow.[7]

Thomas Jefferson had bought Louisiana from France, Keitt continued, and created an empire for slavery. If he had truly condemned the institution as the Republicans insisted, why did he allow the South to carry slaves into the new territory? James Monroe and James Madison had denounced the Missouri Compromise as a violation of the Constitution. If they had truly opposed the extension of slavery into the West as the Republicans insisted, why did they not praise it instead?[8]

Earlier, Keitt had cited the history of New England to support his argument. Had the North, he asked, always been so "ambitious of negro equality?" Had it always been so "clamorously philanthropical?" Again, the answer was obvious. In 1643, he reminded his audience, the New England colonies had formed a confederation and enacted a law that required members to render up runaway servants on the testimony of a single witness. But now, he sneered, the great-grandsons of those colonists demanded writs and jury trials to protect the rights of runaway slaves.[9]

The saintly hypocrites of the North, so eager to extend the blessings of equality to the black population of the South, were strangely reluctant to concede the same rights and privileges to black people living within their own borders. Ohio restricted the franchise to white people. Indiana prohibited black people from testifying in court except against other black people. New Hampshire and Vermont required every able-bodied white man to bear arms in defense of the state but denied the privilege to Black people. Massachusetts prohibited the marriage of blacks and whites. But men from those states denounced the South because its governments were unrepublican.[10]

Angered by northern charges that slavery was a sin and all slave owners sinners, Keitt repeatedly asserted that the institution was "founded upon an inextinguishable law of God." On at least three occasions he returned to the argument, attempting to prove that slavery was indeed sanctioned by divine law. In May 1858, Keitt told the Congress that he grounded his defense of slavery on "the muniments which the hand of the Almighty has reared." When God revealed his law to the Hebrews, speaking to Moses in the crash of thunder and the flash of lightning, he sanctioned slavery and regulated its character. That law remained unchanged until God revealed his will to his people a second time and sent his son to be a witness of the new covenant. Christ came to fulfill the law, not to destroy it; slavery existed throughout the civilized world, but he did not condemn it. From the summit of the mount, he dispensed the law, but he did not decree an end to it. He preached to the multitudes, but he did not denounce it. He told his disciples that he came to set son against father and mother against daughter, but not that he came to set slave against master. He told them he came to bring not peace but the sword, but never did he tell the slave to turn that sword against his master.[11]

Christ sent his apostles out to preach the Gospel to all the nations of the earth. Of all the men who went out to teach the gentiles, Paul was the most zealous. In his letter to the Ephesians, he wrote: "Servants, . . . be obedient to them that are your masters, according to the flesh, with fear and trembling, in singleness of heart, *as unto Christ*; not with eye-service, as men-pleasers, but as the servants of Christ, doing the will of God." If there were no other foundation than this for the rights of the slaveholder, it alone would be sufficient to protect him against the assaults of fanatics and hypocrites.[12]

Paul transmitted the law of God to his successors and they to their successors in an unbroken line "down the steep of ages" to the present day. But now men sought to substitute a sickly philanthropy for the precepts of the creator. They repudiated the Mosaic law, repudiated the teachings of the savior, repudiated the instructions of the apostles until, in one crowning act of impiety, they repudiated the word of God and declared slavery a crime against God and man.[13]

Who, Keitt demanded, were the true "perpetrators of sin?" Who were the true "workers of iniquity?" Was it the people of the South who looked to God's law to guide their institutions, who abided by God's teachings? Or was it the people of the North who from the moment they emancipated their slaves and abandoned the slave trade discovered that slavery was an abomination? Did they truly believe they were the special agents of God? Could they who lived so long with slavery in their midst, who went to the dark places of the earth to make slaves of helpless Africans, by quoting scripture perverted by fanaticism and fouled by hypocrisy compel the people of the South to believe that slavery was a crime?[14]

In his defense of slavery, Keitt relied most heavily on historical and religious arguments, but in fending off abolitionist assaults, he occasionally took advantage of southern social theories as well. Every society, Keitt told the Congress, must rest on a substratum, its laboring classes. Where that substratum was content, society was stable and prosperous, but where it was restless, society was shaken by riot, anarchy, and despotism. In the South, society was never disfigured by convulsions and violence as it was in the North. Southern society embodied aristocracy without exclusiveness and democracy without licentiousness. It was stable because it was founded on genuine distinctions of race, and not on artificial discriminations of class.[15]

The African was destined to occupy the lowest reaches of society; he was fit only for slavery. In every society, there was an infinite variety of jobs to be done. The ruder and coarser tasks were necessary and honorable, but required little more than brute strength to carry them out. Tasks that contributed to the advancement of civilization required men of intelligence and education. Every society recognized its privileged orders, by custom if not by law. In the North, society admitted some men to office and excluded others, distributed wealth and honors to some men and not to others. In the South, slaves performed the ruder functions of society and left their masters free to engage in the affairs of state. Differences of race and color strengthened the distinction between menial and intellectual labor. The wide divisions between slave and master prevented the growth of envy and hatred, and the character of the slave exempted him from the struggle to attain a higher niche in society.[16]

Northern men insisted that slavery degraded the white man as well as the black, and that between master and slave there could be only undying hatred. In truth the relationship was one of kindness and consideration on the one hand and respect and obedience on the other. When, Keitt asked, had southern slaves died of cold or hunger? When had they been cast out to die of starvation and pestilence and old age? Only the factory operatives of the North suffered such a fate. When had southern slaves turned against their masters, wielding fire and sword in an orgy of destruction? Only the operatives of the North created such convulsions.[17]

In every nation save one, the laboring class had risen in rebellion against the government. Only in the South did it accept its condition without resorting to violence and bloodshed. In the South, slavery benefited the white man because it enabled him to perform the more intellectual duties of society, and the black man because it gave him the support, the guidance, and the protection he could not live without. It benefited both races because it saved society from the convulsions that plagued the rest of the civilized world.[18]

Northern men boasted loud and long about their superior intelligence and virtue, Keitt complained, but their boasting was a sham and a delusion. They pointed to their splendid civilization: its arts, its commerce, its cities, its monuments. But they did not boast about its crime and poverty and disease. They concealed its hoards of starving operatives, its crowded jails and fetid hospitals. Over them, they threw a mantle, not of charity but of oblivion. If they preferred their society, Keitt told the northern congressmen, they were free to keep it. If they were truly Good Samaritans, they could find sufficient victims along their own waysides to occupy their time and charity to the fullest. The South neither asked nor needed their vagabond philanthropy. It spewed out no sore-encrusted beggars, no canting clergymen, no pickpockets and swindlers. The North might hold tight to its society if that was what it wanted; the South preferred its own and meant to keep it.[19]

Nowhere in his defense of slavery did Keitt invoke the pseudo-scientific arguments introduced during the 1850s by Josiah Nott, John H. Van Evrie, and Samuel Cartwright. No doubt, his ties to the Methodist church—however nominal they may have been—and his heavy reliance on the religious justification for slavery prevented him from exploiting their new discoveries. He could not base his defense of slavery on a literal interpretation of the Bible and then reject the biblical account of creation. Forced to choose between separate creations of unequal races and the single creation described in Genesis, he opted for the latter.[20]

The economic argument could have been a powerful weapon in his defense of slavery, but Keitt rarely used it either. He was fond of quoting statistics to prove that the South had the resources to establish and maintain an independent confederacy. He frequently boasted that the South's twelve million people, almost one million square miles of territory, and more than $175 million in agricultural produce annually were critical to the economic health of the nation. He believed beyond any doubt that the destruction of slavery would cripple the economy of the nation and the western world. He warned Congress that emancipation would topple King Cotton from his throne and reduce the most powerful governments on earth to heaps of rubble. Without the agricultural produce of the South, "the civilized world would avert her face, the advance of nations would be arrested and every throne in Europe would be reduced to dust and ashes."[21] This, perhaps, was the strongest justification of all, but Keitt rarely invoked the economic prosperity of the South and the nation to buttress his defense of slavery. Perhaps he believed his argument was strong enough as it was.

Keitt defended slavery and the South in terms familiar to every southern radical of the 1850s. His arguments differed in no important way from those habitually employed by dozens of apologists for the peculiar institution. But in one way he differed significantly from his radical colleagues. He was occasionally willing to cooperate with southerners in Congress whose moderation he condemned. He worked with Alexander Stephens and others who believed the annexation of Cuba would solidify the position of the South in the Union. He opposed Stephens's efforts to keep the South in the Union, and he understood that support for annexation could antagonize his radical allies and jeopardize the unity he himself believed was essential to the welfare of the section. He was convinced nevertheless that annexation would strengthen the South politically and economically, and in time convince his radical friends that he was correct. For the same reasons, he was willing to work with the moderates to defeat the radicals' efforts to revive the international slave trade.[22]

From the beginning of his political career, Keitt argued that the South could best defend slavery by extending its borders southward into the Caribbean. He arrived in Washington in time to take part in the angry debate over the Pierce administration's awkward attempts to annex Cuba, interrupting his maiden speech in the House of Representatives on the constitutionality of tonnage duties to warn that the United States would soon have to intervene in Cuba. For the next half-dozen years, he repeatedly insisted that the federal government must take whatever action was necessary to acquire the island. Few of his speeches on any subject ended before he had repeated the demand.[23]

In October 1854—more than two weeks before American ministers meeting in Ostend drafted their notorious manifesto[24]—Keitt addressed a meeting of his constituents at Barnwell Court House. Cuba, he warned, posed a "question of great delicacy and vital interest." The South could not allow the island to become "a tropical den of free negroes" or fall into the hands of a European power. Spain was too weak to hold it much longer, and when it fell from her lifeless fingers, it would inevitably fall to the United States. There were three ways the nation might acquire Cuba. He did not care whether it was by conquest or purchase or annexation, if only because all three would face obstacles. If the South tried to take the island by force, Spain would free the slaves; if by purchase, the North would impose the Wilmot Proviso; if by annexation, Cuba must first establish its independence. Keitt did not care which means it used; he cared only that "the South must, should, and would have Cuba—and have it slaveholding."[25]

Sue Sparks, the young woman Keitt married in 1859, feared that Cuba was political dynamite and begged him to say nothing that might jeopardize his career. Keitt's reply combined youthful bravado with a sure knowledge of his constituents. A man was timid indeed, he told her, who in a great cause cowered from "political crucifixion." He would speak about Cuba at the first opportunity: "I am for Cuba—and leave the consequences. . . . I am willing to risk the future." Three months later, he told her he expected to overwhelm the opponents of expansion in South Carolina. His proposal would "rattle the bones in the charnel house of this state."[26]

For a time it seemed that Sue was right. In January 1855, William W. Boyce attracted considerable support from southern congressmen when he warned the administration not to annex Cuba in the face of Spanish objections. Boyce, who represented South Carolina's Sixth District, argued that the United States already had enough land to satisfy all its needs; later, after Cuba had won its independence, the nation could extend its borders into the Caribbean. When the fruit was ripe, it would drop into American hands, but the administration should do nothing to encourage it to fall.[27]

In a letter to James Chesnut, Keitt admitted that Boyce's speech had been "a very fine effort," but totally rejected his friend's conclusions: "Cuba we must and will have, and that speedily too. . . . I regard the acquisition [of the island] as certain as a law of nature." Every Democrat in the South was in favor of annexation, and the party would make it a major issue in the next presidential election.[28]

Keitt was wrong when he predicted that the South would unite behind the administration's attempt to acquire Cuba. Even in the lower South, expansion into Latin America did not win universal approval. In South Carolina, Keitt's friend Hammond led the fight against the acquisition of additional territory in the tropics, and his views won considerable support among the state's radicals. Robert Barnwell Rhett, W. W. Boyce, William Gilmore Simms, James Gadsden, I. W. Hayne, and others echoed his objections. In the South Carolina congressional delegation, only Keitt actively supported the administration's Cuba policy; the other members were either indifferent or openly hostile.[29]

By the mid-1850s, most South Carolina radicals had concluded that the administration's aggressive foreign policy threatened to divert attention from more vital southern interests. Like Keitt, they believed that slavery could never be entirely safe as long as the South remained in the Union; unlike Keitt, they believed that the annexation of territory in the tropics was a sop the administration held out to the South to block movement toward secession. Opponents raised additional objections. Some feared that annexation would drain slaves out of the upper South and transform the area into Free Soil; some doubted that the country could easily absorb the "island's mongrel populations"; and some feared competition from Cuban cotton, sugar, and tobacco. Finally, some believed that the South already had enough undeveloped land to last for generations to come.[30]

Toward the end of the decade, Keitt's support for Caribbean imperialism forced him into an awkward alliance with southern moderates like Alexander Stephens, who saw the expansion of slavery into the tropics as the best way to protect southern rights without resorting to secession. Only by absorbing Cuba, Stephens argued, could the South maintain a viable political position within the Union. Keitt rejected the argument but persisted in supporting the administration's ill-fated campaign to drive the nation's borders southward into the Caribbean. If the South remained in the Union, new territories would lead in time to new slave states and additional representatives in Congress. If the South seceded, they would be part of a larger, more powerful, more prosperous confederacy.[31]

In the spring of 1855, Keitt addressed a large crowd gathered at Orangeburg Court House. Months after Pierce had abandoned the attempt to acquire Cuba and win the gratitude of the South, he demanded that the administration seize the island, whatever the cost. Cuba, Keitt told his audience, only sixty miles off the coast of Florida, commanded the entrance to the Gulf of Mexico, the only effective outlet for the commerce of the great Southwest. In the hands of Great

Britain or some other maritime power, it could blockade the Mississippi River and put an end to the prosperity of the American West; in the possession of the United States, it would contribute immeasurably to the prosperity and security of the nation.[32]

The government Spain imposed on the Cuban people was so tyrannical, Keitt argued, that the threat of rebellion was never entirely missing from the island. By itself, the cruelty of the Spanish government did not justify American intervention, but in time it would force the Cuban people to revolt, and successful revolution would throw the island into the hands of its former slaves. "Seething and fermenting with a needy and licentious negro mob," protected by English imperialism and northern fanaticism, Cuba would pose an immediate threat to the domestic tranquility of the South. Every nation had a right to see to its own safety; a successful slave revolt would amply justify American annexation of the island, even in the face of Spanish resistance.[33]

For more than thirty years, every administration had pledged that it would use force to oppose any attempt to seize the island, whether by ambitious Europeans or rebellious black people. But now, with British warships patrolling American waters and searching American vessels, with revolts erupting all across the island and threatening to submerge its people in a sea of blood, Franklin Pierce did nothing. His administration stood "driveling out passion and writhing in gymnastic contortions" while Cuba was "barbarized by emancipation" and "desolated by negro turbulence." The administration would not act; if the South wanted Cuba, it would have to act alone.

Shifting his ground, Keitt began to describe an idea he had presented to the House of Representatives four years earlier, a new twist to an old argument and a new approach to a familiar goal. The Constitution, he argued, had created a league of sovereign states, but the federal government had overrun its boundaries and taken for itself the powers of an oriental despotism. It had taxed the South and subsidized the North; it had impoverished one section and enriched the other. To save itself, Keitt continued, the South must restructure the federal government by adjusting the political relationship between the states and the central government, reserving for each state complete control over its domestic institutions and leaving the Confederacy only the power to conduct war and foreign relations. With such a government, the South would be safe from the "pharisaical inter-meddling and barbarous philanthropy" of the North. The North was pillaging the resources of the South; under a confederation, each section would develop its own energies and foster its own interests.

How was the South to construct such a government? "Southern patriots," Keitt told his audience, must assist the victims of Spanish tyranny to throw off colonial rule and establish an independent government in Cuba. They must add

Cuba to the Union, but only after the North had agreed to reorganize the federal government according to southern demands and made it a government of strictly limited powers. Northern fanatics would rage against their demands, but northern bankers and businessmen would sacrifice their abolitionist allies to win a share of Cuban wealth. If they refused, the South must dissolve the Union and keep Cuba for itself.[34]

In South Carolina, reaction to Keitt's speech was largely favorable. The *Charleston Mercury* called it "a very vigorous and striking effort," but ten days later published an anonymous attack on his extraordinary proposal. "Brutus" insisted that reforming the federal government was impossible, as was acquiring Cuba until the South was out of the Union. Keitt should stop wasting his breath arguing for unattainable goals and get on with the job of establishing a southern confederacy. When that was done, Cuba would fall naturally into its waiting arms.[35]

A few weeks later, Keitt received a surprisingly cordial letter from Assistant Secretary of State A. Dudley Mann. Mann told Keitt that his speech was "decidedly the ablest document that has been prepared on the subject," and urged him to circulate it as widely as possible. Keitt, he predicted, was at the start of a long and brilliant career in national politics. The young congressman was amazed; he thought he had lashed out at the administration and was fortunate to escape unscathed. "I struck them almost with ungloved hand," he told Sue Sparks, "but they do not strike back."[36] In fact Keitt had been far less critical of the administration than he supposed. His speech had been a defense of a key administration policy, and he should not have been surprised when Mann thanked him for his efforts. In the end, they came to nothing; even before Keitt delivered his speech at Orangeburg, hostile reaction in both Europe and the United States had forced the administration to abandon its attempt to acquire Cuba and put an end to American filibustering in the Caribbean.[37]

After his failure in 1855, Pierce made no further attempt to acquire Cuba from Spain, either by purchase or conquest, but his successor failed to learn from his unhappy experience. Late in December 1857, James Buchanan initiated secret negotiations with Spain to purchase the colony. Success, he hoped, would distract attention from the Democrats' domestic failures, placate the South, and reunite the party. In his second annual message to the Congress, in December 1858, he called Cuba "a constant source of injury and annoyance" to the American people. Spanish officials had "insulted our national flag and inflicted injuries on . . . our citizens." The United States had repeatedly attempted to acquire the island "by honorable means," but Spain refused to sell. Cuba was too important to leave in foreign hands. The government must take whatever steps were necessary to obtain it.[38] Early the next year, administration leaders introduced into the Congress a bill appropriating the $30 million that Buchanan needed to bribe

Spanish officials reluctant to part with the island. The request set off a raucous debate, and before it was over, few Republicans had missed the opportunity to condemn the administration's efforts to extend the borders of the Slave Power and few southerners the opportunity to defend them.[39]

Keitt entered the debate on January 19, 1859, after it was well under way, hoping to influence congressional opinion without expending much time and effort preparing an original speech. He resurrected his Orangeburg speech, and with very few changes delivered it in the House. To support his argument, he cited the same authorities and even the same statistics, now some four years out of date. For thirty years, Keitt reminded the House, every administration had promised the American people the United States would acquire Cuba when the situation was right. Now that time had finally arrived. It would confront serious obstacles, he conceded, but no nation ever attained any great object without risk or sacrifice. The island was so critical to the economic prosperity and military security of the United States, and its government so tyrannical, that the administration must adopt whatever means were necessary to take control of it.[40]

At this point, David Ritchie of Pennsylvania interrupted. Did Keitt believe the United States could seize any country whose government he did not approve? Keitt fired back: "Have we not causes of war with Spain sufficient to justify us in the judgment of history? Have not our rights been invaded, our honor touched, and our flag insulted, while all redress had been denied? . . . And if, for these indignities and wrongs, we submitted our disputes with Spain to the arbitrament of the sword, and tore Cuba from her grasp, what nation could rebuke us?" The only honorable recourse was war.[41]

Keitt was unaccountably pleased with his speech and wasted no time getting it into print. Robert Barnwell Rhett, the editor of the *Charleston Mercury,* was more realistic. He agreed that Cuba would contribute to the economic prosperity and military security of the nation. More important, it would strengthen slavery in the South, but the hope of creating new slave states there was pernicious and "utterly delusive." The speech did nothing to change the votes of congressmen hostile to annexation. Both houses refused to appropriate the $30 million the administration wanted to persuade Spanish officials to sell the island, who in any event would have rejected the bribe and refused to sell.[42] And so the South's quixotic attempt to extend its boundaries into the tropics came to an end.

Keitt's support for the Latin American version of manifest destiny—in fact, his scheme to seize Cuba and turn it over to the United States in exchange for significant revisions in the U.S. Constitution—helps to explain his sympathy for filibusterers like John A. Quitman and William Walker and his attempts to convince the federal government to support their schemes. He was acquainted with Quitman and approved his ill-fated attempt to take Cuba. The similarity of their plans to annex the island suggests that the two men were collaborators, at least to the extent of sharing ideas. In the end, Quitman's plans collapsed. In spite of its interest in acquiring Cuba, the Pierce administration announced it would prosecute violations of the neutrality laws. Quitman could still recruit troops, but he could not raise enough money to support an expedition. The efforts of his friends to persuade Congress to repeal the neutrality laws came to nothing, and military preparations in Cuba reduced the prospect for success even further. In April 1855, Quitman abandoned his mad scheme, ran successfully for a seat in the House of Representatives, and became Keitt's staunch friend and political ally.[43]

Keitt also championed the schemes of William Walker, the "gray-eyed man of destiny." In 1855 Walker and a band of filibusterers intervened in a civil war in Nicaragua; Walker put himself at the head of the government, accumulated enemies rapidly, and in mid-1857 an uprising forced him to flee the country.

Walker was determined to return, and late in 1857, aided by prominent southerners who approved his plans to reestablish slavery in Nicaragua and annex the country to the United States, he launched a new expedition to the Caribbean. This time, his stay in Nicaragua was even shorter. U.S. Navy Commodore Hiram Paulding blocked his ascent up the San Juan River, forced him to surrender, and sent him back to the United States to stand trial for violating American neutrality laws.[44]

Walker's arrest set off a political explosion in the South. Four state legislatures approved resolutions praising the filibusterer and denouncing Paulding. Editors and politicians assailed Buchanan for defending Paulding and refusing to compensate Walker. On January 6, Keitt joined Quitman and Sen. Robert Toombs of Georgia in Petersburg, Virginia, where they roundly criticized Walker's arrest before a crowd that packed the largest hall in the city.[45]

The protest soon moved to Washington. Replying to its request for information, Buchanan told the Senate that, by seizing Walker on Nicaraguan soil, Paulding had "committed a grave error," but an error mitigated in part by the officer's conviction that he was acting in the best interest of his country. Nicaragua could not complain that Paulding had violated its territorial rights because his action had in fact saved that country from a "dreaded invasion." He had released Walker, Buchanan told the senators, but he would continue to enforce the neutrality laws. It was the duty of the United States to protect its weaker neighbors from marauders sailing from American ports. The president's remarks—and his annual message in which he asked Congress to strengthen the neutrality laws—set off a debate in both houses that lasted throughout January 1858, revealed the depth of southern support for Walker, and increased the hostility between the northern and southern wings of the Democratic Party.[46]

Early in January, Keitt leaped joyfully into the fray. In a short but pointed speech, he criticized Buchanan's request for a stronger neutrality law. The president already had authority to employ the army and navy to prevent filibustering expeditions from sailing from American ports, and now he had asked for additional authority to hunt down American citizens on the high seas and arrest them on foreign soil. The neutrality laws limited the jurisdiction of American courts to offenses committed no more than three miles from shore, but the president wanted power to punish offenses committed beyond that limit. Buchanan wanted to enforce the law by exercising the powers of a despot.

Next, Keitt attacked the administration's handling of the Walker affair. One naval officer, Commander Frederick Chatard, had allowed the expedition to disembark in Nicaragua because he lacked the authority to prevent it and was called home in disgrace. A second officer—Commodore Paulding—had sent men ashore, arrested Walker and his men, and was treated as if he were a hero. Keitt insisted the administration would not knowingly defend an officer who had broken the law, and was at a loss to explain its conduct toward Paulding.[47]

Keitt's remarks won the approval of both the *Charleston Mercury* and the *Charleston Courier,* and may explain why he continued to take part in a debate that his colleagues ignored.[48] He made no more formal speeches, but he repeatedly harassed Paulding's apologists. On one occasion, John Haskin of New York told the House it should vote Paulding a medal for his services. He himself was not "tinctured with any sickly sentimentality" toward filibustering expeditions, Haskin explained. He favored "national filibustering" but opposed private ventures because they hampered the administration's efforts to acquire territory in Latin America. Keitt interrupted; did Haskin think nations could steal from their neighbors but individuals could not? The New York Democrat extricated himself neatly from the trap. Walker, he said, had tried to commit petty larceny and failed; northern Democrats wanted the nation to commit grand larceny and do it successfully.[49]

Keitt entered the debate for the last time January 14 when he recommended that the House refer the neutrality laws to a special committee for study and revision. The debate had demonstrated that the laws were vague and misleading. Legal experts could not agree on the meaning of the laws nor the extent to which they granted the president power to use the navy to prevent expeditions from fitting out in the United States. Penalties for violating the laws were severe, and there should be no misunderstanding about their application. The nation must discharge its international obligations, but not at the cost of violating the rights of its own citizens. The Congress must not allow the president to extend his authority by interpreting international law to suit himself.[50]

In the end, the House Judiciary Committee refused to act on Keitt's proposal. In January 1859 the full House soundly defeated a resolution censuring Commodore Paulding and narrowly approved a substitute praising his actions. When Keitt asked the House to repeal the law that prohibited citizens from taking part in foreign wars, it refused. His resolution received strong support in the lower South, weaker support in the upper South, and none at all in South Carolina. Keitt's closest friends were convinced he was wasting his time pursuing unattainable goals. Walker fared even worse. In 1860 during his fourth filibustering trip to Latin America, he was arrested by a British naval officer and executed by a Honduran firing squad.[51]

In 1853, responding to much the same pressures that provoked Keitt to throw himself into the campaign to acquire a southern empire in the Caribbean, Leonidas W. Spratt demanded that Congress reopen the international slave trade. Almost alone, the editor of the *Charleston Standard* set out to force southerners to confront the dilemmas inherent in a slaveholding society.[52]

Spratt argued that importing slaves would increase the population of the South, increase southern representation in Congress, and make it possible for the section to defend its vital interests inside the Union. A fresh infusion of Africans could halt the erosion of slavery in the upper South and allow the expansion of plantation agriculture into the territories. It could reduce the price of slaves, increase the profits of established planters, and make it easier for ambitious farmers to become owners. By holding out the prospect of higher profits and greater social mobility, it could defuse the class antagonisms that threatened to disrupt sectional unity. Finally, it could stop the immigration of white laborers from Europe so feared by the Know Nothings.[53]

Spratt's demands attracted limited but highly vocal support, particularly in the cotton states of the lower South. In South Carolina, only Robert Barnwell Rhett from among the state's most prominent leaders publicly endorsed the proposal, but he did have the support of a number of less influential men: Edward Bryan, Maxcy Gregg, Milledge Bonham, William H. Trescot, James H. Hammond's brother M. C. M. Hammond, and two of Keitt's rivals from the Third Congressional District, George P. Elliott and Olin M. Dantzler.[54] Keitt himself stayed clear of the battle until November 1856 when, in his annual message to the legislature, Governor James H. Adams called for reviving the international traffic in slaves. It was, he asserted, the only possible way to restore the economic prosperity and political equality of the state, and to bestow the benefits of Christianity and civilization on benighted Africans.[55]

Keitt rarely passed up an opportunity to praise his state's institutions—political, social and economic—but rarely spoke in public about its problems.

He knew that South Carolinians, black and white alike, were fleeing the state by the thousands, bound mostly for the new lands opening up in the Southwest. He knew that migration was costing the state talent, capital, and political influence. In his lifetime, the state's representation in Congress had fallen from nine to six, and if it had remained in the Union after 1860, it would have fallen to four. Perhaps Keitt was encouraged that migration was spreading radical ideas into the Southwest; perhaps he believed that rapid increases in the price of cotton and slaves made the loss of population less threatening; or perhaps he did not understand the true significance of the problem.[56]

Keitt had little sympathy for the men agitating to reopen the slave trade, whatever their reasons. He had devoted his public career to defending the peculiar institution; he was acutely sensitive to northern attacks on the trade, and he could not ignore the threat they posed to slavery itself. If the slave trade were piracy, Adams had told the legislature, the slave must be plunder and slavery must be wrong. If it were wrong to buy and sell black people, it must also be wrong to own them. If it were wrong to buy slaves in Africa, it must also be wrong to buy them in South Carolina. Faced by this intellectual dilemma, Keitt decided that to defend slavery, he had to defend the international slave trade.

Unlike many of his radical colleagues—Rhett, Spratt, Gregg, and the rest—Keitt refused to demand that Congress repeal the statutes outlawing the trade, not on ideological grounds but on purely practical grounds, not because the trade was wrong but because it was inexpedient. Like congressmen Porcher Miles and William Boyce, he had given up all hope of protecting the interests of his state as long as it remained in the Union. Beginning in 1848, when he first entered the legislature, he had repeatedly argued that secession was the only effective solution for the problems facing South Carolina. He believed the time when the majority of southerners would accept his solution was rapidly approaching, and he was determined not to alienate the moderates among them by championing a controversial cause. He understood that the addition of large numbers of Africans would reduce the value of slaves, reduce the wealth of the men who owned them, and hurt the very men he represented in Congress. He also understood that it would hurt border-state owners whose sale of slaves to the lower South was the source of much of their income. He feared it would impoverish white laborers, inundate the South with untamed savages, and increase the threat of slave revolts. Finally, he knew it would outrage the humanitarian sympathies of the civilized world. His state and section had to be ready to secede when the time came, and to be ready they had to be united. Even its advocates admitted that agitation to reopen the slave trade would never persuade the Congress to amend the law, but it could destroy southern unity and delay the movement toward southern independence.[57]

Adams's proposal attracted hostile criticism from all parts of the South and set off a short but fierce debate in Congress. In the House, Emerson Etheridge of Tennessee introduced a resolution that condemned the proposition as "shocking to the moral sentiment of the enlightened portion of mankind." Any action by the Congress to legalize the "horrid and inhuman traffic" would earn "the reproach and execration of all civilized and Christian people."[58]

Like Keitt, southerners who objected to both the slave trade and to the Tennessee Whig's emotional denunciation of it found themselves in an uncomfortable position. One after another, they explained to the House that they opposed reviving the trade but would not vote for the Etheridge resolution because of its implied criticism of slavery itself. When that failed, Keitt resorted to parliamentary maneuvers to prevent the House from acting on the resolution. In the end, it passed by a wide margin.[59]

Hoping to mollify radical southerners, James L. Orr introduced a second resolution: to repeal the laws prohibiting the African slave trade would be "inexpedient, unwise, and contrary to the settled policy of the United States." The resolution seemed to reflect Keitt's position on the issue, but his vote was one of only eight cast against it. He did not try to explain his opposition, but it seems probable that he voted with the minority because the resolution skirted the real reason he objected to reopening the trade, not because it was "contrary to the settled policy of the United States" but because it threatened to undermine southern unity and block the campaign for southern independence.[60]

In spite of the reluctance of many southern leaders to discuss the subject, the movement to revive the slave trade refused to go away. In the summer of 1858, an American naval vessel brought the slave ship *Echo* into Charleston harbor. When the Navy had seized the vessel off the coast of Cuba, one-third of its cargo of 450 black people was dead or dying. Federal authorities arranged to send the surviving Africans to Monrovia as wards of the American Colonization Society and charged the captain and crew of the slaver with piracy. In the South, public opinion condemned enforcement of the law, and the press roundly criticized the grand jury that indicted Captain Edward Townsend and his crew. In U.S. Circuit Court, Justice James M. Wayne of Georgia and Judge A. G. Magrath of South Carolina made it impossible for the government to prove its case, and even though the men were obviously guilty, the jury found in favor of the two defendants.[61]

Three months later, the *Wanderer,* a slave ship built in New York and owned by Charles A. L. Lamar of Georgia, landed 300 black people—half of its original cargo—near Brunswick, Georgia. Evidence of the event surfaced late in 1858, shortly after the slave traders had held an auction and delivered the Africans to their new owners. Federal marshals seized the ship, but a grand jury refused to return an indictment, and Judge Magrath refused to permit the government to move the case from Charleston to Savannah. When the *Wanderer* was sold at auction, bidders were suspiciously scarce, and the owner regained his ship for a fraction of its real value. At this point, northerners logically concluded that southern judges and juries had conspired to nullify the laws prohibiting the trade.[62]

Early in 1859 the revival of the slave trade and the failure of the federal government to put an end to it forced the Congress to confront the disagreeable subject. During a debate over an appropriations bill, Keitt objected to a grant of thirty thousand dollars to the American Colonization Society to support the black people rescued from the *Echo.* James Dowdell of Alabama complained that the federal government was behaving like a missionary society, and J. L. M. Curry of Alabama charged that it was spending money to educate ignorant savages. Keitt, supported by Porcher Miles and Milledge Bonham, protested that the grant was illegal as well as misguided. A law enacted in 1819, he told the Congress, empowered the president to return slaves imported illegally into the United States, but it did not give him the authority to support them in Liberia. The president had no authority to "convert the Government into a huge grocery" and dole out provisions to liberated Africans. Instead of teaching the black people that they must work in order to eat, it would prepare them for a life of indolence, vice, and crime. If the government were truly interested in their welfare, it would leave them in the South, where kindhearted masters would teach them to lead productive lives.[63]

Keitt also objected because the appropriation would support the American Colonization Society, an organization that had become "a rickety stipendiary of the government." It had "sprung up in the night," a product of "the hot and sickly vapors of a morbid sentimentality." It was supported only by old maids and hypocritical politicians, and was rapidly approaching its well-deserved demise. He would not vote to allow the government to prostitute itself for the benefit of misguided northern philanthropy.[64]

Keitt flatly denied that he wanted to revive the African slave trade. The Congress would approve the trade when it became an economic necessity, he predicted, but for the moment, agitation could serve no practical purpose. Only stand aside, he advised, and let the problem find its own solution. In the interval, he said, "I would sweep from the statute-book every interference with slavery; I would repeal the law declaring the slave trade piracy; I would withdraw our slave squadron from the coast of Africa; and I would leave slavery unintervened against, wherever the power of the country stretches. The power of the free States keeps the Government from intervening in our favor. I would disarm it from intervening against us."[65]

Keitt was willing to attack the laws that prohibited the African slave trade but not to demand their repeal. His refusal to cooperate with radicals working to reopen the trade forced him to cooperate with men like Perry and Orr, men regarded as fire-eaters outside the South but moderates inside South Carolina. The situation was not all that unusual; he had worked with Unionists like Alexander Stephens in the effort to annex Cuba. This political flexibility, this willingness to cooperate with men whose political ideas he rejected was an unexpected characteristic in a man widely known as an uncompromising radical. Only his dedication to secession and his readiness to do whatever was necessary to achieve it explain his seeming moderation in pursuit of an unmistakably radical goal.

SEVEN

"*Take the fetters from your heart*"

When Congressman Keitt arrived in Washington for the first time late in 1853, he found himself in a city with a distinctly southern flavor. Life there was slow paced, provincial, often lacking in creature comforts. The weather was frequently foul: hot and humid in summer, the season when the fortunate few fled to the mountains, and cold and wet in winter. Many of the public buildings were still unfinished, and many of the streets were still unpaved. Defenses against disease and crime and fire were mostly inadequate. But the city was rapidly changing. Handsome brick and stone buildings with gas lights and hot and cold running water were going up. The Library of Congress had opened; the Washington Monument was slowly rising; work on an aqueduct to bring water from the Great Falls of the Potomac was underway; architects were designing the dome of the Capitol. Still, the city remained "a shambling, dilapidated, ill-planned town." The creek residents ironically called the Tiber was an open sewer, and the bridges over the Potomac threatened to collapse into the river.[1]

Only the wealthiest and most prominent of the nation's lawmakers brought their families to Washington. A very few rented or purchased homes in the city, and others installed their wives in hotels for the winter, but most left their families at home, lived in boarding houses scattered around Capitol Hill, and ate in "messes" segregated according to politics and geography. In 1853 the largest of the hotels, the National, was threatening to succumb to years of abuse and neglect, but its cuisine, superior only by Washington standards, helped its patrons overlook its shabby interior. A complete renovation in 1855 did not save it the following year from an outbreak of dysentery virulent enough to cause prolonged illness and even death. Among the victims were James Buchanan, who eventually recovered, and Keitt's friend John Quitman, who did not. Brown's Hotel catered almost exclusively to southerners; James L. Orr dined there with J. L. M. Curry and Clement C. Clay of Alabama, and L. Q. C. Lamar of Mississippi. Years later, Clay's wife recalled that Yankee congressmen feared even to enter the lobby, so hostile was the atmosphere. Willard's was the third of the capital's most prominent hotels. Keitt found lodgings at Flint's Hotel on E Street just off Pennsylvania Avenue.[2]

The White House, normally a center of social activity for official Washington, was quiet in 1853. Franklin Pierce and his wife were in mourning for their only son, killed in a railroad accident shortly before the president took office. Their dinners and receptions were somber affairs. Pierce had no talent for small talk; his wife was frequently sick or depressed; his menus were uninspired, and his wine flowed sparingly. Among the Cabinet officers, only Secretary of the Treasury James Guthrie entertained with enthusiasm.[3]

During the four years that the dour New Englander presided uncomfortably over the government, southern hostesses dominated Washington society. Keitt's friend Mrs. William Aiken vied with Mrs. Robert Toombs and Mrs. Howell Cobb to provide the city's most elaborate hospitality. To their balls and dinners came the elite of the capital: congressmen, diplomats, scholars, military officers. There, they dined at tables laden with linen and crystal and silver, and bounteously supplied with food and drink. There, they gossiped and flirted and danced until the early hours of the morning.[4]

Into this new life, Keitt fit quickly and easily. A newspaper report of his first speech to the House of Representatives, a defense of tonnage duties, informed its readers that the young congressman was "prodigiously popular" with the reigning belles of the city. Whenever he was not attending to his legislative duties, he was attending to the ladies, "dancing, conversing, and acquitting himself to the honor of his native state." "Happy fellow!" another editor wrote enviously; "No wonder he speaks with such effect."[5]

A letter Keitt wrote to his sister soon after he arrived in Washington reflected the excitement of his first forays into society. The city was crowded, he told her, unusually crowded for so early in the season. Pretty girls were everywhere. He was particularly taken by a Miss Badger, "a decidedly pretty and intellectual girl," the daughter of a senator from North Carolina. He did not particularly like her father's "federal notions" but supposed he could convert her to more acceptable opinions. No matter; a number of married ladies had offered to chaperon him during the winter and promised their sisters and cousins would keep him company. He had asked some younger wives to give him a second chance, and one married to an elderly senator seemed ready to agree! Keitt's sister had just returned from the Christmas dances in Columbia, and he wanted to know who

Suzanne Mandeville Sparks Keitt. Courtesy of the South Caroliniana Library, University of South Carolina.

had been there. Had the girls missed him? Had she promised any of them his hand? Was it worth his while to keep the engagement? Clearly Keitt was not about to succumb to the weight of his new duties in the House.[6]

Keitt had known of Susanna Sparks for years but did not meet her for the first time until the summer of 1854. Her father, Samuel Sparks, was a prominent planter from Marlborough District; in 1850 he was the master of "Mandeville," a plantation of some twenty-five hundred acres worked by 151 slaves. Her mother was the former Ann Harry.[7]

Keitt must have discovered soon after they began exchanging letters that Miss Sparks conformed imperfectly if at all to the vision of feminine perfection usually conjured up by antebellum southerners. She was, to be sure, an unusually attractive young woman. She obviously overwhelmed a gentleman who met her for the first time in the winter of 1854. Miss Sparks, he wrote, was "a lady of magnificent form. . . . a modest display of jewels finely adorn her fair brow and lovely arms, a sweet glow mantles upon her cheek, and a bewildering beauty flashes from her eye, and encircles her dream-like form." She was, he concluded, "the acknowledged beauty of the Pee Dee country."[8] She dazzled even Benjamin F. Perry, the crusty editor of the Greenville *Southern Patriot,* who called her "the beauteous belle of the great Pee Dee." Perry's compliments so turned her head that Keitt objected twice in little more than a week. First he asked if she had "waved the necromancy wand over Perry," who was "gazetting all your ball movements," and a few days later complained that the editor's obvious admiration was making her vain and conceited.[9]

Keitt soon learned that Sue's intelligence easily matched her beauty. In his earliest letters, the young congressman wrote mostly of the social life of the capital city: a grand ball at Willard's Hotel, a dinner with Jefferson Davis, a masquerade at the home of Senator William Gwin of California—he had gone dressed as Charles XII of Sweden.[10] But he discovered soon enough that her real interests lay elsewhere, and he began to write about more serious matters: political maneuvering on the floor of the House, the pre-colonial history of South Carolina, the latest novels of his friend William Gilmore Simms. Soon he was asking for her opinion of his speeches and pouring out his ideas on politics and philosophy. Frequently his letters seemed more like political treatises than the professions of love he meant them to be.

In a letter he wrote in January 1855, Keitt tried to relieve Sue's fear that his recent attack on the Know Nothings was indiscreet. He had not stopped to wonder, he told her, if there was much discretion in what he was doing. When a vital principle was at stake, he did not care whether "the multitude" thought as he did. His position required him to teach as well as be taught. He did not care if he made enemies. They could be useful; just knowing they were ready to pounce on his mistakes kept his nerves braced and his mind clear and strong. He might wear down under the strain, but at least he would not rust out through indolence.

Seven years earlier, Keitt recalled, during his first canvass for a seat in the legislature, his defense of the Bank of South Carolina excited so much animosity that not one politician in his parish dared to support him. But his audacity had won the respect of the voters, and they had elected him to four consecutive terms before sending him on to Congress. From that experience he had learned he must never "stoop to a . . . melodramatic flirtation with public opinion." He would make up his mind on an issue and stick to it, whatever the consequences.[11]

Apparently "Miss Sue" was not convinced because a month later Keitt returned to the subject. She had called his audacity "calculated," and he tried to answer the charge. She had asked if he would "espouse a cause" that would jeopardize his career, and he had insisted that, if there were no necessity to express an unpopular opinion, he would not do it. It was the duty of every man in public life to acquire as much influence as he could, not for selfish reasons but to serve the common good. He would not needlessly sacrifice his influence or seek a Quixotic fight, but he would do whatever duty required. He had never shrunk from controversy, and he never would. Office was pleasant and power was tempting, but he would never stoop to "ignoble trickery" to win an office or to retain one. The man who "cowered in a great cause from fear of political crucifixion" was timid indeed, and the one who "courted the pain and thorns of the cross" was a fool.[12]

In June, Keitt was still expressing contempt for democratic politics and demagogic politicians. "I would not have that popularity which flows from supple hypocrisy," he insisted,

> or seeks the trappings and geegaws of office only to be the wonderment of fools and gaping children. . . . Such popularity makes a man not powerful, but a mere office occupant. Such popularity makes a man's intellect a mere bauble loaned, at intervals, to popular caprice, or a juggler's ball for knaves to conjure and trick with. . . .
>
> Power with me must be won by superiority, at least by haughty self-independence and assertion, and not by dexterous trimming and whinning [*sic*] submission. It must be the power of leading, not following. I'd rather write my own political epitaph than hold that power which is held by him who whiffles, whines, and crouches homage. I'll be submissive to one purer than myself, never to an equal, must less an inferior.[13]

In July, Keitt began to think about devoting a part of the summer to concentrated study to prepare himself for his career in national politics. He would soon be thirty-one, he told Sue. He had a most promising future and might fairly aspire to any office. So far, he had found it easy to deal with the measures that came before the Congress and to match wits with his colleagues, but that was not enough. The public men of the nation were weak and fell far short of his standards of scholarship, learning, and cultivation. He was determined to outdo all of them.

In Washington, Keitt continued, men had flattered him by declaring that he had "established a new style of elocution—imaginative, declamatory, and yet somewhat logical." Now he must work to deserve their praise. He would give up the "languid indolence, the heartless frivolities, and worthless dalliances" of the watering places; he would take his books into the mountains "away from the haunts of men" and prepare himself for future greatness. South Carolina was "small in number and resources," but "around its head is the aureole of undying fame. Small as it is, it is classic ground." Its sons had won undying glory, and he must make himself worthy of that great legacy. He might be able to do the state no lasting service, but at least he would try.[14]

By mid-July, Keitt's sense of duty had overcome his indolence. He had rented rooms ten miles from Greenville, he told Sue, and for six weeks would "ignore politics and study the past."[15] On July 29, he reported he had been "on my little mountain, eleven hundred feet above Greenville," for two weeks, and planned to stay there for ten more days; by then, he would have read every book he had brought with him. Already he had "explored the vast, entangled, and intricate system of metaphysics." During his studies at South Carolina College, "its subtle distinctions, its nice refinements, its scholastic formulas" had fascinated him. Now, he had given the subject his time and energies and had fathomed its very depths. It had taught him to "look inwardly with a steady gaze, to pick out, examine, and then replace the springs of thought and the eyes of the mind."[16]

Obviously pleased with his achievement, Keitt rambled artlessly on. There was, he said, "a rapture in intellectual strife." The republic of letters had no patronage to bestow, no offices to distribute, but the scholar who winnowed out a truth or established a principle or discovered a law of nature won more than a "blazing garter or a flaunting ribbon"; he achieved immortality.[17] On August 12, Keitt left his mountaintop for a few days at Glenn's Springs. There he visited an aunt, met fifty or sixty people, attended two balls, and returned home, ready to resume his political duties.[18]

Occasionally Keitt wrote to Sue about the practical side of his life in politics, describing stump speeches, analyzing critical issues, rehearsing arguments, predicting the future of the South and the nation. About a speech in Charleston he wrote, "politicians must keep themselves before the people. Even the gods of old sometimes showed themselves and paid tribute to the principle of humanity." And about a speech he was writing for Barnwell Court House, he told her, "It will be Ishmaelitish; I mean to strike upon the right hand and upon the left. . . . I'll keep my own district conservative, or I'll perish in the struggle."[19]

Early in January 1855, Keitt told Sue that the Congress was debating a Pacific Railroad bill. It was "a grand idea," he thought, because it would make it possible to reach the East by traveling west. But construction was impracticable because the tracks would have to traverse fifteen hundred miles of wilderness and cross deserts the army of Xerxes could not have penetrated. In May 1856, he told her about the murder of an Irish waiter in Willard's Hotel, shot to death by a young congressman from California. A few weeks later, he described Brooks's assault on Sumner and the "wild excitement" it had produced. Throughout the year, he filled his letters with politics, describing intrigues in the Congress and speculating about the identity of the man the Democrats would run for president. By the summer of 1856, Sue could have been one of the best informed women—on politics, at least—in all of South Carolina.[20]

In the summer of 1854, when Keitt first met "the beauteous Miss Sparks," neither he nor she suspected that romance might develop out of their chance encounter. Keitt admitted later that he was only looking for "a listener," and Sue was still recovering from an earlier relationship gone wrong. She had been engaged to Henry Harrington, the son of a wealthy and socially prominent South Carolina planter. Harrington had suddenly and without explanation married another girl, leaving Sue psychologically devastated, unable to keep from doubting herself and the people closest to her, unable to throw off her emotional depression. At first she refused to believe that Keitt's attentions were serious. She thought his flattery was insincere and his attempts at gallantry pompous and absurd. Equally troublesome for Keitt, a year at Barhamville Academy near Columbia had awakened Sue's interest in music and painting, and she was determined to go to Europe for further study. Marriage, she thought, especially to an ambitious politician, would shatter that dream beyond repair.[21]

Keitt persevered. In letters filled with love and understanding, he begged Sue to forget her doubts and fears. "Why, in the name of God," he asked, did she "allow your old habits to re-settle upon your . . . spirit?" Friends had betrayed her, stabbed her through her affections, and she had cultivated indifference to mask her feelings, but a woman capable of anguish was also capable of love. She had to throw off her "dreamy dalliance," her "worship of broken dreams," and take a new hold on life. Society had a claim upon her that she could not deny.[22]

In March of 1855, during a visit to the Sparks plantation, Keitt proposed. Sue may have accepted his offer and then had second thoughts. She refused to believe he was sincere and forced the young congressman to insist repeatedly that his love for her was real. "I cannot imagine what you think me to be," he told her angrily. He despised "sentiment whipped into froth" as much as she did. He had promised her he would not trifle with her affections, and as God was his judge, he had not. His world was not a dancing school; his life did not begin at ten at night and end at four in the morning. He was not one of her fashionable things of buckram. In the "artifices of life," he would "counterfeit" because that was expected; in affairs of the heart, he would never toy with her affections.[23]

"I have thought, I have thought again. Again I have thought over my offer," Keitt wrote in the spring of 1855, and "I still adhere to it." The previous winter, he had hesitated to reveal his love for her. He had wanted to see if her image would fade when he returned to Washington. He had wanted to test his love by the most terrible of all trials—the praises of powerful men and the flatteries of beautiful women. Men had proposed brilliant matches for him, and he had rejected all of them. They had cast no shadow over the image of her he carried in his heart. Men had offered him high positions, and he valued them only because in her sight, he must not seem utterly insignificant.[24]

He knew full well his position in Washington, Keitt told her. There was nothing in it to cheapen his self-esteem. He had scanned his future, and there was nothing in it "troublously dark"; if there were, he would not offer to share it with her. He asked her frankly to give him an answer to his proposal; if she agreed to marry him, she would make him the happiest man on earth: if she did not, he would "take up my cross and press steadily on."[25]

In May, Sue succumbed to Keitt's persistent courtship and again agreed to marry him, but she exacted a terrible price. She demanded that he give up politics and take her to Europe. If he asked, she told him, Franklin Pierce would give him an Italian consulate for a few years. When they returned home, he must retire from politics and become a gentleman planter. Keitt hesitated and then agreed: "I once thought nothing on earth could tempt me from the path of political ambition," but for her, he would give it up forever. For her, he would make any sacrifice. He would carry her away as soon as she was ready to go, plant her in any soil and clime she chose, keep her there as long as she desired.[26]

The couple exchanged daguerreotypes, Sue dressed in a riding habit, Keitt posing stiffly, his hand resting on top of a marble column. Keitt was overjoyed: "I keep your likeness by me as a chastening and holy token," he told her, "as a covenant that makes me a far better man. . . . I almost fear it is only the gorgeous vision of my excited fancy." Sue was critical of his portrait, and he tried to explain the discomfort she saw in it. He had tried to have his portrait made in a "tribunitive attitude," but could not hold his hand still and had to steady it on a pedestal. If his face were cold or imperious, it had caught neither affliction from her. Experience more than nature had made him appear severe. "Rough passages and fiery experiences" had given him a texture usually bestowed by age alone. Five years earlier she might have trifled with him and produced no lasting result; now the furrows she plowed into his soul were impossible to erase.[27]

But still Sue hesitated, forcing Keitt to beg her to make up her mind. "I do not think it is in your heart to torture me cruelly and needlessly," he wrote early in the fall. She must tell him what she meant to do. If she meant for them to be strangers, she must tell him frankly and he would abandon all his hopes. If she meant to be his wife, she had only to tell him so; the uncertainty was preying on his mind; only she could relieve his distress.[28]

However hard he tried, Keitt could not persuade his fiancée to commit herself once and for all to marry him. "Dismiss the wrecks of your dreams," he told her; they were "miasmic vapors" that "minister to a sensibility that is already rubbed raw." The world had filled her with distrust and doubt, but she must cast off its binding spell. Late in the fall, he had still not succeeded in winning her confidence. "I beg of you one favor," he wrote in November. "Do not any more cavil at and disparage yourself." When he offered her his hand and heart, he offered them to her as she was, and she had accepted them as she was. She would not be half so precious to him if she were different. She must not belittle herself, Keitt begged; she must not deface the image of her he carried in his heart.[29]

During Christmas festivities at "Mandeville," Sue promised Keitt she would marry him late in January, and the congressman returned to Washington elated that she would soon be his wife. Shortly after he reached the capital, however, she abruptly put an end to his euphoria. Responding to still another of her cheerless letters, he begged his fiancée to dismiss her doubts. "Take the fetters from your heart," he urged; "Curb not too harshly your womanly impulses." If she would only give herself to him, he would devote his life to removing the "weeds and tares" from her soul.[30]

It could not have surprised Keitt when, late in January, Sue postponed their wedding until the following winter. Her excuse must have satisfied him; in spite of the turmoil she was creating in his life, his letters contained only love and understanding. He tried repeatedly, almost desperately to reassure her: she had made a better man of him; she had given his life new meaning; she was too good for him, but he was struggling to make himself worthy of her love. He made a hurried trip to "Mandeville," failed to change her mind, and reluctantly altered his plans for the coming year.[31] Sue might not have loved him as much as he loved her, or she might have been reluctant to give up the life of a much-sought-after belle, or to leave her family and friends. Keitt might have agreed to the postponement because he was madly in love with her, or because he was reluctant to give up his seat in the Congress when the fight for Kansas was reaching a climax and every vote could be decisive.[32]

Governor James H. Adams agreed to stifle Keitt's "inchoate act of resignation" from the Congress, but Franklin Pierce was less cooperative. The president had promised to appoint him to an Italian consulate, but he was unwilling to keep the post vacant for almost a year. He was confident that he could find a post equal to it or better when Keitt was ready to occupy it. In another month, Keitt had completed his arrangements to leave the House once the battle over Kansas had ended. He would make one last speech for the administration, he explained, and in return, Pierce would give him the consulate he so much wanted. He would resign his seat in the Congress, and the following winter he would carry his bride off to Europe. He would restore her soul.[33]

Keitt should have realized that Sue had once again decided not to marry him. The clues were obvious enough. Early in the spring, she stopped answering his letters; he complained, and she wrote more often. He reported that his defense of the administration's Kansas policy had been even more successful than he had hoped; now Pierce was obliged to give him a post in Italy. He described the activities of Washington's social elite. The fight over the speakership had delayed the start of the season, and Lent had cut it short before it was properly launched,[34] but now the city's hostesses were determined to make up for lost time. The Aiken ball had been a "magnificent affair;" gossips had it that Adelle Cutts—soon to be the second Mrs. Stephen A. Douglas—was engaged to four men at once; all the girls were wearing white dresses with black flounces. However fascinating Keitt's letters may have been, Sue showed little interest.[35]

The evidence continued to pile up. Keitt's friend William Gilmore Simms visited Society Hill; Sue avoided him, Simms was offended, and Keitt tried to make excuses for her. She was "a spoiled and beautiful belle," he told the author, and he should have searched her out. Keitt's sister asked if Sue had unpleasantly broken off their engagement. At a wedding party attended by both women, Sue had refused to speak to her.[36]

In July, in the midst of the controversy stirred up by Brooks's assault on Sumner, Keitt learned the truth. A letter from Sue was waiting for him when he returned from Lexington, where he had addressed the literary societies of the Virginia Military Institute. She accused him of trifling with her affections; he wrote one reply, thought better of it and wrote another, longer and more passionate than the first. Ten times he had offered to release her from her promise to marry him, Keitt reminded the unhappy girl. Even after he had rearranged his life to suit her, he had offered to release her. The last time, he had sworn he would not offer again, and still she had refused. He might be a reckless man; he feared he was, but he would never stain his soul by lying. He would never release her from her promise to marry him, he raged, but then regained control of his emotions, and in the second version of the letter released her "promptly and fully" from her promise. But, he concluded, "we can never meet again, and, if we should, it must be as strangers."[37]

One close observer of the capital's social scene pronounced it "minutely monotonous." At every reception and every party, the same band played the same music, the food was prepared by the same chef, the guests were the same, the gowns were the same. Keitt did not care. He threw himself into the social whirl, attended a seemingly endless round of balls and dinners and receptions, escorted the city's most eligible belles. Milledge Bonham laughed, "We must limit Keitt as to the Belles. He will interfere too much with the other single men of the mess." Keitt gave a supper for the president's cabinet at which he shocked the city's gourmets by serving chops and oysters with an "irreproachable sherry." One guest suggested sarcastically that a "grapphic dilineation [*sic*] of the feast should be preserved . . . for the benefit and encouragement of future statesmen."[38]

The following year, Keitt was the frequent companion of Harriet Lane, who was serving as mistress of the White House for her bachelor uncle James

Buchanan. She was almost thirty years old, had blonde hair, deep violet eyes, and regular features. Washington gossips were almost invariably kind, complimenting her quiet courtesy, her dignity, and her excellent taste. Virginia Clay, the wife of Senator Clement C. Clay of Alabama, remarked that she had Keitt "at her feet."[39]

For a time Keitt competed for Miss Lane's affections with Congressman Thomas Clingman of North Carolina and the British ambassador, Lord Lyons. Then suddenly, in September 1858, he made a "flying visit" to "Mandeville" where he and Sue reconciled their differences and she again agreed to marry him. On May 18, 1859, the much-delayed wedding finally took place at her home. Immediately after a ceremony conducted by Rev. D. X. Lafar, the couple left for New York, and on the twenty-sixth, sailed for Europe on the steamship *Persia.*[40]

Evidence of the Keitts' activities on the continent is sparse; a couple of letters from Keitt to political colleagues and a handful from Sue to her family are all that remain from what must have been a voluminous correspondence. In mid-August, Keitt interrupted their tour of the German spas long enough to write to James H. Hammond and Olin M. Dantzler. Since June, he reported, he and Sue had seen much of Europe—England, France, Belgium, Holland, Prussia, and a number of the German duchies—and had been both "pleased and disappointed." London was a noble old city, but Paris was garish, all gilt and tinsel and pasteboard. Its mad excitement seemed to intoxicate most Americans, but he had grown tired of it in less than a month. Of all the countries they had visited, he liked Holland best. It was a "splendid spot," its cities teeming with industry, its crops tilled by the most enterprising farmers he had ever encountered. Belgium was a "fine and fertile province" whose people he was at a loss to explain. The Belgians were a branch of the Franks and had Celtic blood running in their veins, but they were "heavy, ponderous, even sluggish" people. Perhaps centuries of tyrannical government and oceans of strong beer had destroyed their character. In Antwerp he had seen some excellent paintings by Reubens and Van Dyke.[41]

The watering places in Germany—Johannesberg, Rudesheim, Hochheim—Keitt thought both charming and efficacious. If a man stayed at Schwallbach long enough, he could grow a new liver. The cathedral at Cologne was "a great old monument," and the city itself with its tolling bells, brightly lighted houses, and barges gliding phantom-like down the river fascinated him. The beauties of the Rhine existed mostly in legend and story; the grapes that grew on the banks of the river were worth far more than the ruined castles and picturesque villages. The wine was inexpensive; vintages that sold for twenty dollars at home brought only eight in Europe, and he could not understand why some enterprising American had not struck up a trade. German innkeepers were swindlers, and

German cooks were barbarians. "You may take for granted," Keitt told Hammond, "that if a German dish is not sour, it is greasy, and if not greasy, then it is sour."[42]

Keitt the politician was fascinated by the failures of European governments and Keitt the slave owner by the living conditions of the European poor. The instability of the French government he blamed on the character of the French people—"antic," skeptical, a strange mixture of "sleep and sensation." The "seditious element" in Paris was enormous; no French government could last very long unless it rested on the bayonet. In Prussia, what struck Keitt first was "the clang of muskets and the clink of spurs." Hatred of the French was widespread; soldiers were everywhere; the slightest incident, he thought, would touch off another war.[43]

All over Europe, Keitt reported, the peasants were "wretchedly poor." They worked long hours, lived on potatoes and rye bread, and if they ate meat once a month, considered themselves fortunate. Government was corrupt, taxes oppressive, and military service compulsory. Europe was "a bad place for a poor man," he concluded; compared to German peasants, slaves in South Carolina lived like princes. In a week, he and Sue would leave Cologne for a tour through Switzerland and Italy. He expected to return home in November in time for the opening of Congress.[44]

Sue's letters were full of delighted chatter: she had had her picture made sitting on a donkey; the American ambassador to France had just died; she was going to Lauterbach with a lady from Philadelphia; she had entertained friends from home, among them Thomas Clingman, James Y. Mason, and Edwin DeLeon; Paris was "gay and beautiful." She expected to spend the winter in Paris and to travel in Egypt and Palestine the following spring. Keitt wanted to return to Washington before Congress convened, but she thought he should stay in Europe. If he stayed out of the country, he could avoid the "little disputes" that were making politics so complicated, go home in time for the next election, and stand for the Senate.[45]

In October events in the United States destroyed Sue's plans to remain in Europe indefinitely. Late in the month, news of John Brown's raid on Harpers Ferry reached Keitt in Paris, along with urgent pleas from his colleagues to return home. Keitt was unable to resist. Faced with the unexpected collapse of her plans, Sue was heartbroken. For years she wrote from Paris, she had clung to dreams of travel and study in foreign lands. She had crossed two thousand miles of ocean to see all of Europe, and now she had to settle for "a little flying tour among the flat-headed Dutch and disgusting Swiss." She was within a week of visiting Egypt, two weeks of Palestine, and two or three days away from Spain and Rome, and now she would never get to see any of them. She had not learned a word of French. Palm trees and nutmegs, Italy and Wales and Scotland, all would be sacrificed to politics, and "How I hate the word." Keitt offered to leave her with an American couple they had met in Paris, but Sue refused. Bitterly disappointed, she returned with her husband to the United States. They arrived in Orangeburg on November 8, in good health and with time to attend a round of parties before Congress convened early in December.[46]

EIGHT

"Style, beauty, and high training"

The Keitts arrived in Washington on December 3, two days before Congress was scheduled to convene, and took up temporary lodgings at Brown's Hotel. In a letter to her mother, Sue described the trip north from "Mandeville" and at the same time revealed the fears of a young bride facing life in an unfamiliar city. The weather during the trip was "oppressively hot," she complained; the dust from the locomotive was annoying, and in North Carolina the scenery was "dull in the extreme." Worst of all, the boat ride up the Potomac was rough, and she had suffered from sea sickness. "I had the blues dreadfully coming on," Sue admitted. "I *did* want to stay at home this winter, for I don't like Washington, and . . . I want to rest and ride and fatten up, and . . . keep you and Father company for a little while.[1]

The Thirty-sixth Congress convened at a singularly inauspicious time. On December 5, John Brown had been dead less than seventy-two hours, executed for his bungled attempt to provoke a slave revolt at Harpers Ferry. The tolling of bells and firing of minute guns that marked his death in the North convinced most southerners that the Yankees would gladly see them murdered in their beds. Inspired by a mixture of fear and anger, mobs unleashed a reign of terror, tarring and feathering, flogging and riding on rails anyone who seemed even slightly tainted with abolitionism. At mass meetings, otherwise rational men voted to boycott northern goods, burn northern books and journals, banish northern professors and clergymen. Politicians conferred and denounced and threatened, half of them afraid that the long-awaited dissolution of the Union was at hand and half afraid it was not.[2]

The House plunged at once into a prolonged, emotional battle to elect a Speaker. Unlike in the Senate where the Democrats enjoyed a comfortable majority, in the House the two parties were almost even divided. The Republicans nominated John Sherman of Ohio and the Democrats Thomas Bocock of Virginia, but neither party could elect its candidate without coming to terms with the remnant of Whigs and Know Nothings that held the balance of power.[3]

On the first day, J. B. Clark of Missouri introduced a resolution condemning Hinton Rowan Helper's *Impending Crisis of the South* and declaring that "no member . . . who has indorsed [*sic*] and recommended it . . . is fit to be Speaker of the House."[4] It was a clever strategy; Helper had tried to convince non-slaveholding southerners that the peculiar institution undermined their prosperity and must be eliminated, by violence if necessary. Sherman was one of eighty-six Republicans who had signed a letter soliciting funds to reprint the book as a campaign document. Southern congressmen objected loudly, and Sherman denied that he had even read the tract, but the damage was done. No southerner of any party would vote for a man who advised poor white people to revolt against slavery; without the votes of border-state Whigs and Know Nothings, Sherman could not win.[5]

Keitt was certain that the Republicans who endorsed the book had been familiar with its contents. In 1858, he told the House, a Republican senator—William H. Seward of New York—had proclaimed an "irrepressible conflict" between North and South. He had sowed the seeds of destruction, and now the nation was reaping the fruit. Nine months ago, Republicans had endorsed Helper's book, scattered it across the length and breadth of the country, and provoked a bloody attack against the South. Now they asked the South to believe that only at that moment had they discovered that its doctrines were infamous and its effect outrageous. "Gentlemen," Keitt lectured his opponents, "that will not do. The South here asks nothing but its rights. As one of its representatives, I would have no more; but as God is my judge, . . . I would shatter this Republic from turret to foundation stone before I would take one tittle less."[6]

From the start administration Democrats resolved to go to any lengths to prevent the Republican plurality from organizing the House. Aware that victory in the battle to elect a Speaker would allow Republicans to dominate the standing committees and investigate persistent rumors of corruption in the executive branch, they brought business in the House to a standstill. Their interminable speeches and dilatory motions confused their opponents and provided time for negotiations with the border-state Know Nothings whose votes would eventually determine the winner.[7]

On December 22, during the interval between the eighteenth and nineteenth ballots, Keitt took the floor to urge Democrats and Know Nothings to unite and elect a Speaker. At a time when southern property, southern rights, the very existence of the southern people were at stake, they must put aside all petty dissensions and join together to defend the integrity of the Constitution. The blood spilled at Harpers Ferry by one section waging war on the other was not yet dry. There was an indissoluble connection between the principles of the Republican Party and the assault launched by madmen against the state of Virginia. Republicans claimed they could not have foreseen the consequences of their acts, but how could they proclaim war to the knife against the institutions of the South and not expect deluded fanatics to enlist in the fight?[8]

It was the duty of all Democrats and Know Nothings, Keitt insisted, to unite with the South in a common war against the Republican Party. There was no unconquerable antagonism between their two parties. Let the Know Nothings select a candidate from the ranks of the Democrats or the Democrats a candidate from the ranks of the Know Nothings. If they would unite behind a single candidate, they could easily elect him.[9] It was good advice, "Leo" told the *Charleston Courier*, but it fell on deaf ears. Know Nothings, northern Democrats, and southern Democrats all rejected the arrangement.[10]

As days and then weeks passed without a conclusion to the struggle, the mood of the House became increasingly ugly. Congressmen went to the floor, armed with knives and pistols, and abandoned rational debate in favor angry harangues. In the gallery, spectators punctuated the most vicious thrusts with applause, hisses, and raucous laughter.[11] The Democrats seemed willing to destroy the Congress rather than let it fall into the hands of the Republicans. From Columbia, Gov. William H. Gist offered to send ten thousand armed men if the state's congressmen decided to resist Sherman's election with force. He preferred a peaceful solution, Gist told Porcher Miles, but he would wade in blood rather than submit to a Republican victory: "If you . . . decide to make the issue of force in Washington, write or telegraph me, and I will have a regiment in or near Washington in the shortest possible time."[12]

On December 16, George N. Sanders, an agent for the Navy Department in New York City and a notoriously corrupt political operator, assured Miles and Keitt that the confusion in Congress was creating a conservative reaction in the North. If they could sustain the excitement, they would frighten the Yankees into surrendering. "Don't organize," he wired the Carolinians; "earnest revolution going on all over the North. Adjourn Congress until after holidays and all come here." Sanders had been trying since 1851 to maneuver Stephen A. Douglas into the White House. To win support for the "Little Giant," he had promised the Democratic vice-presidential nomination to both William Lowndes Yancey of Alabama and Francis W. Pickens of South Carolina, and offered Porcher Miles $1.5 million and the speakership of the House for their support. Hurry here with

Keitt, he told Miles in an intentionally cryptic letter, and help me complete my negotiations. "I'll return with you in one week and elect you Speaker sure."[13]

Nothing came of Sanders's bizarre proposal. Keitt tried twice to convince the House to adjourn for Christmas, but the members refused. Miles and Keitt did not go to New York, much to Sue's displeasure, and Miles was not elected Speaker. Evidence of how Sanders expected to fulfill his extravagant promises, or even that he did intend to fulfill them, is entirely missing.[14]

Meanwhile, Sue Keitt was finding her new life anything but agreeable. "I detest Washington," she wrote her sister-in-law soon after her arrival in the capital. "I never fancied politics and the talk of politicians, and here I have *nothing* else. I am tired out of old John Brown, Black Republicans, and the fussing and quarreling for the Speaker." A great many ladies had called, but they insisted on discussing the same topics. She had not visited the Congress or the White House; she heard quite enough of politics at home.[15]

Accustomed to the constant bustle of a large plantation and not yet caught up in the life of the city, Sue complained frequently of boredom and loneliness. At the end of her first week in Washington, she wrote unhappily to her brother-in-law, William J. Keitt. Her husband had gone off again to "that national *bauble* [*sic*], the House," leaving her to find her own entertainment. She had no news of things in Washington, Sue told Keitt; she had seen nobody that day, and "fear of a stray bullet in the head" had kept her from going to the House. In spite of her protests, political matters were already finding their way into her letters. The Democrats thought they had intimidated the Black Republicans, she reported. If they could withdraw Thomas Bocock and bring forward some man who could satisfy all of the factions, they could elect a Democratic Speaker. But, she wondered, would the South unite behind him?[16]

Sue Keitt's slowly emerging fascination with politics mingled incongruously with her realization that the game her husband was determined to play out to its conclusion could end in tragedy. Writing late in December, she revealed her anxiety and her husband's increasing desperation. "O Alex," she told her brother,

> We are having frightful times here. War at any moment, and no knowing who may fall. Mr. Pryor, Clingman, and Mann[17] have just left the parlor, saying that all hope for a Democratic speaker is gone, and the Southerners are resolved a Black Republican shall not take the chair. They are armed and determined to fight to the knife there on the floor of Congress, and either take possession of the Capital or fall. . . . Mr. Keitt has gone with them off to a caucus at Mr. Pryor's. What they will determine on I don't know. I begged Mr. Mann to go with them to try and quiet them. . . .

> You can't imagine the state of feeling here. Bowie knives and revolvers are the companions of every Southern member. These are fearful times, and gloom and the most fearful suspense and expectation prevail over the city. Heaven help us all.[18]

Unwilling to wait for the House to organize, President Buchanan inaugurated the new social season and provided Sue with an antidote for her boredom. Late in December, the Keitts suddenly found themselves caught up in an almost continuous round of levees, dinners, and balls. At first, longing for the simple pleasures of life on the plantation, Sue was reluctant to become involved. "Mr. Mann says the President is anxious to see me," she reported to her family at "Mandeville," "but I have no fancy for the story-telling old man." But Keitt wanted her to go, and Buchanan had particularly requested to meet her, so she would have to visit the White House, if only to pay her respects to Harriet Lane.[19]

Despite her good intentions and the demands of Victorian etiquette, as Christmas approached, Sue had still not paid her first call on the president. On December 22, she told her mother that Buchanan had again asked to see her. Senator John Slidell had told him she was "one of the handsomest women that had been to Washington"; after that, she had to go. At the White House, she met Harriet Lane, whom she pronounced "fine looking and very agreeable" but decidedly "not handsome." She was fascinated by the old president who made himself as charming as he was able and pressed her to come back often. "He has one of the most quizzical faces I ever saw," she reported, "head and mouth twisted to one side, and then the erratic performance of that *famous eye*!"[20]

As the days passed and the House failed to organize, Sue realized she might not be able to spend Christmas in New York as she had planned. They had not yet elected a Speaker, Sue told her mother, and she was quite provoked by it. Her new friend George Sanders had invited them to spend the holidays in the city, and the Democratic Party had subscribed five thousand dollars to hold a ball in her honor. Keitt had tried twice to persuade the House to recess until after New Year's Day, but both times he had failed.[21]

Much to her displeasure, Sue had to spend the Christmas season in Washington. It was, she complained to her mother, "very dull." On Christmas Day, Keitt went off to dine with Miles and the rest of the South Carolina delegation, leaving his young bride to amuse herself as best she could. When her husband did not reappear until two A.M., she was furious. Keitt saved himself from a tongue-lashing by describing at great length the last conversation of the evening. Too tipsy to be discreet, Senator Hammond had admitted to Keitt that his own wife had no style.[22] But Keitt's wife, he told his friend, had "style, beauty, and high training," and he must make something of himself to be worthy of her. After that, Sue laughingly asked her mother, how could she be angry with him any longer?[23]

The events of the next few weeks wiped out Sue's disappointment. The Keitts moved into new rooms at the Lafayette House on F Street and gave a dinner for a dozen southern senators and congressmen. Sue was the guest of honor at a dinner given by the Russian ambassador, the Count de Stoeckl, another given by the president's cabinet, and a ball thrown by the German minister, the Baron von Gerolt. Somehow, she found time to dine at the White House and visit the Congress for the first time.[24]

On the day after Christmas, Sue told her mother, she had visited the House. The experience had clearly unnerved her. Was this disorderly mob really the Congress of the United States, she wondered, "the assembled wisdom of the nation, the legislature of a mighty people?" Could "wise resolves, noble enterprises and great statesmanship" really come from lawmakers such as these? From the quiet of her sitting room Sue described the turmoil she had witnessed on the floor of the House: "Some [congressmen] were reading papers—some smoking—others in noisy groups talking, and others again in the partial oblivion of drunken sleep, heads reclining and feet elevated upon the benches—pages running hither and thither, supplying the wants of those inclined to discuss the merits of the Christmas luxuries, eggnog and apples—Three or four speakers on one side throwing impertinent sarcasms at bloody slaveholders—as many fire eaters on the other side endeavoring to out do each other in defiant threats at the same—the importunate raps of the Speaker's mallet, and the vain cries of Order, Order."[25]

Sue found the dinner given her by the president in January and the reception that followed far more enjoyable. There she met the elite of official Washington society: Madame Bodisco, the American wife of a former Russian minister, a handsome woman despite her enormous bulk, who wore a court dress rumored to have cost fifty thousand dollars; Lord Lyons, the middle-aged British ambassador who was courting Harriet Lane and pretending he was not; Mrs. John J. Crittenden, the wife of the senator from Kentucky, a sixty-year-old belle who wore sky-blue silk dresses with lace flounces, short sleeves and low necklines, and pink roses in her curls, as though she were still young; John McQueen, the congressman from Marlborough District, who was so stout that he reminded Sue of the rabbits inflated by cruel boys until their skins split open. McQueen's wife could not get along with anybody in Washington, and so he left her at home. Vice-President John C. Breckinridge, a charming gentleman from Kentucky, had promised Keitt an important post in the next administration.[26]

Sue "has had a beautiful success," Keitt bragged to her family. The president had "taken a chivalric devotion to her" and persisted in telling everybody that she was "the most cultivated and fascinating woman he has ever met in Washington." Keitt was obviously enjoying her triumph, basking in the reflected glory of the reigning belle of the season.[27]

But for Sue the excitement generated by the endless round of receptions and dinners and balls soon paled, and she began to long for her family and friends in South Carolina. "I am heartily tired of this Washington life," she told her father. Dinner parties and balls crowded one after the other, and receptions almost every day. The women did nothing but visit and talked of nothing but politics. They called once, and if she did not immediately return their visits, they were offended. It took all her time just to return the calls and all her money to hire carriages, and all for people who cared nothing for her and for whom she cared even less. The city was filled to overflowing with "rowdy Congressmen, importunate office seekers, fast young ladies, and insipid dancing young men," decidedly not the sort of people she wanted to know. Thank God Lent would soon put an end to the mad scramble.[28]

When Washington became almost suffocating, Sue turned to a handful of close friends for comfort. She was particularly fond of the Hammonds and their daughter Kate. As long as the Keitts remained in Washington, Mrs. Hammond treated Sue as a daughter. The senator became her beau and excited the jealousy of his younger and less fortunate colleagues.[29]

The Washington social whirl took a toll on the time and energy of the congressmen involved but could not completely divert the attention of the members from the business at hand. After Christmas, Keitt and his Democratic colleagues returned to the task of finding a candidate for the speakership acceptable to administration Democrats, anti-Lecompton Democrats, Whigs, and Know Nothings alike. In the end, it was a feat they could not accomplish.

Early in January, Keitt was still trying to put together a winning coalition. The Know Nothings, he insisted, could nominate a Democrat for the speakership, and the Democrats would unite behind him, or the Democrats could nominate a Know Nothing, and their combined votes would elect him. Democrats who voted for a "Native American"—a Know Nothing—did not endorse Know Nothing principles, but any congressman who voted for John Sherman became a Republican by that act alone. Republican hostility to slavery forced every other party to join forces against them. Any Democrat who voted for a Know Nothing for Speaker did no more than express his opposition to the Republicans, but any congressman who voted for a Republican endorsed the fanatical attitude of that party toward slavery and would have to accept responsibility for his dastardly act. He would not vote for a Democrat or a Know Nothing who attracted Republican votes, Keitt announced; he would not allow the Republicans to determine the Speaker.[30]

The Know Nothings stubbornly refused to come to terms, and Keitt became increasingly discouraged about the prospects for a Democratic victory. "Things [are] as gloomy here as ever," he wrote his old friend O. M. Dantzler. The southern Know Nothings had picked a fight with the Democrats and were trying to make a deal with the Republicans. The government was drifting into chaos: "I wish to God it were wrecked already."[31]

On January 25, Keitt tried one more time to persuade the House that a Republican victory in the battle for the speakership would lead inevitably to the dissolution of the Union. The party's principles were a declaration of war against the South. The party condemned the Fugitive Slave Law, endorsed the Wilmot Proviso, demanded the restoration of the Missouri Compromise line, refused to admit new slave states to the Union or allow slavery to expand into the tropics. The ascendancy of the party would destroy the character of the government by converting a confederacy of sovereign states into a despotism of mere numbers. It would inaugurate a struggle more terrible than war, pestilence, and famine because it would be a war of civilizations embittered by all the horrors of internecine strife.[32]

And why, Keitt asked, did the Republican Party do all these things? Because, it said, slavery is immoral and unjust. But slavery is in fact the cornerstone of the South and the world. Without the produce of the South, all progress would come to an end: "The civilized world [would] avert her face, . . . and every throne in Europe [would] be reduced to dust and ashes." But the South stood on "right, truth, and justice. . . . She has no more compromises to make. She ought never to have made the first one." If she were pressed any farther, she would "burst the bonds which unite her with her faithless confederates, pull down the Federal temple . . . and go forth to meet the future, leaning on the arm of the Almighty. . . . She will fulfill her destiny."

The South had made a history and a civilization, and had matchless resources, a splendid domain, and a gallant people to defend them. Why then, Keitt asked, did she hesitate to proclaim her independence? Because she lay under the spell of past glories and current hopes that the North would ensure her safety within the Union. But day by day that spell was dissipating, and when her last hope was gone, his state would act, alone if necessary. The federal government would not dare to attack a state that seceded from the Union. The entire South would rush to her defense, and the republic would perish in blood and fire.[33]

Newspapers throughout South Carolina published the text of the speech, most of them without comment. The *Charleston Courier* did note that its "terrible denunciation of impending disruption" had badly scared the more timid observers in the galleries. Keitt revised the speech, had it published as a pamphlet, and scattered it throughout the state.[34]

Late in January, it appeared for a few minutes that the administration forces had won the speakership after all. On the thirty-ninth ballot, a coalition of Buchanan Democrats, anti-Lecompton Democrats, and Know Nothings combined to give Know Nothing William N. H. Smith of North Carolina a majority of the votes cast. Before the clerk could announce the result, a handful of Douglas men withdrew their support and deselected him. Keitt was furious. They had taught him a lesson he would never forget, Keitt raged at the four men who had switched their votes. They had taught him never to attach any importance to anything they said, but to recognize them by the flag that waved over them—the pirate flag of the Black Republicans.[35]

Three days later, on January 30, the Republicans finally put together a winning coalition. John Sherman withdrew, clearing the way for William Pennington of New Jersey, a candidate acceptable to northerners of all three parties. Pennington was a longtime Whig whose political affiliation was now conveniently obscure. The Democrats countered by switching from Smith to John A. McClernand, an anti-Lecomptonite from Illinois. To this point, Keitt had voted for every candidate the Democratic caucus nominated, but he refused to support a man he believed was a Republican in disguise. On the forty-fourth and final ballot, all but one of the South Carolina delegation—J. D. Ashmore—threw their votes to certain losers. Pennington attracted the support of a handful of old Whigs, won the speakership by a single vote, and the battle finally came to an end.[36]

Realizing that the House had finally elected a Speaker, Keitt browbeat the clerk who had been ineptly presiding since early December and took the floor. When he withdrew from the race, Sherman had consoled himself by insisting that the battle had demoralized the Democratic Party, but it was the Republicans, Keitt insisted, who should be demoralized. For eight weeks they had failed to elect their candidate to the speakership. They had accepted a compromise candidate, an old-line Whig who had defended the Fugitive Slave Law and agreed that the government should protect slavery wherever it was economically profitable. They had deselected Smith by pledging to pack the Ways and Means Committee with old Whigs and to enact a protective tariff on iron and coal. Honest men would not "traffick" in votes, and the Republicans had tried in vain to conceal what they had done. It was not the Democrats who were demoralized, Keitt told the House; it was the Republicans.[37] Sue Keitt emphasized the positive aspect of the Democratic failure; after all, she told Carrie Sparks, they had defeated Sherman.[38]

Late in February the routine of congressional debates and White House receptions was suddenly cut short for Keitt by the news that his brother, Dr. William J. Keitt, had been murdered by slaves on his plantation outside Palatka, Florida.[39] Keitt immediately left for St. Matthews to console his father, who was recovering from a long illness. There, he learned that the slaves had attacked his brother when he was sick in bed and cut his throat from ear to ear. Neighbors had dragged one of the murderers out of jail and lynched him. An article in the Ocala *Home Companion* reported that the slave confessed his guilt, refused to implicate his accomplices, showed no remorse, and watched the preparations for his execution with "stolid indifference." The same men hanged another slave the following day and sold at least three more out of the state.[40]

In her diary, Mary Chesnut recorded a more complex version of Keitt's death:

> Dr. Keitt was one of the kindest of men and masters. But he was passionate and impulsive, not warranted to act reasonably if he was too much excited about anything. He had some chronic ailment—was always ill. A friend said: Keitt, yours is a strange case. I begin to think these villainous negroes are trying to poison you. . . .
>
> As soon as his friend left, a negro woman brought him a cup of tea. In stirring it, a white powder became evident, settled at the bottom of the cup. In a moment he believed what his friend had suspected.
>
> He dashed the tea in her face.
>
> "You ungrateful beast, I believe you are trying to poison me."
>
> Next morning he was found with his throat cut from ear to ear.[41]

Obituaries praised Dr. Keitt as an outstanding member of his community. He had graduated from the Medical College of South Carolina in Charleston, practiced for a time in St. Matthews, and served in the state legislature. In 1853 he had purchased a plantation near Ocala, Florida; it was there that he was murdered. Keitt took some consolation from the belief that the murderers were not house servants. All of them were field hands, and one had not been raised on his father's plantation; his brother had only recently bought him from Virginia. That news sent the editor of the *Sumter Watchman* into a rage. The laws of Maryland and Virginia allowed owners of "murderers, incendiaries [and] thieves" to sell them south when they should be executed on the spot.[42]

The effect on Keitt of his brother's death is difficult to assess. The identity of the killers could have reinforced the belief held by many slave-owners, a belief Keitt clearly shared, that slavery was a "positive good" for slaves and masters alike. In return for labor, obedience, and respect, slaves received food, clothing, shelter, medical care, and protection. Owners wanted to believe that slaves understood and appreciated the benefits they derived from this system of mutual duties and obligations. More than that, they wanted to believe that the slaves closest to them, their domestic servants, were loyal to them and even loved them. The shock they experienced when those slaves violated their expectations could be overwhelming. The relief that Keitt felt when he learned that his brother's killers were not men and women who had prepared his meals, cleaned his house, laid out his clothes, or saddled his horse was palpable.

The murder of his brother, along with the rumors of slave unrest and abolitionist activity that were becoming increasingly common, confirmed Keitt's determination that the South must maintain absolute control over its domestic institutions. The report that his brother's plantation had been "marked down on John Brown's bloody map with a red cross," evidence that the abolitionist had selected him for destruction, confirmed his belief once and for all that the South must go to any lengths to protect itself from outside interference. During much of 1858, his speeches and letters had been marked by moderation—at least by what passed for moderation in South Carolina. But the campaign that culminated in his reelection to the House of Representatives late that year convinced him that his constituents were committed to a radical resolution to the sectional crisis and that he could campaign for separate secession without jeopardizing his political career. After his brother's murder, he embraced a radicalism so intense, so frenzied, that it sometimes seemed to pass beyond the bounds of reason—not literally beyond the bounds of reason, of course. Keitt knew that the prosperity, the stability, the very existence of the South depended on slavery. He was convinced that the institution was right and just, and he was determined to do whatever was necessary to protect and preserve it. If that meant "rending the Union from turret to foundation stone," so be it. The murder alone does not explain the change in Keitt's behavior; his fear of enemies whose power seemed to be increasing by the day easily accounted for that. But his emotional reaction to the death of his brother surely did contribute to the radicalism of his words and actions.

His brother's murder was not the only violent episode in which Keitt was involved. In mid-February, Congressman Henry Edmondson of Virginia accosted John Hickman of Pennsylvania outside the House of Representatives and called him a slanderer and a coward. Witnesses could not agree about what happened next. Edmondson either slapped Hickman or hit him over the head with a cane or knocked off his hat or knocked him down. Keitt grabbed Edmondson and ordered Hickman, "Pick up your hat and go away; [I] can't hold this man all day!" Hickman did as he was told, and once again Keitt stopped a fight rather than starting one. Two months later, he acted as a second for Roger Pryor when he challenged John F. Potter of Wisconsin to a duel. Potter chose Bowie knives, and Pryor refused to fight.[43]

While Keitt was in St. Matthews consoling his father, Sue wrote to George N. Sanders and A. D. Banks, the two men who were managing Stephen Douglas's campaign for the presidency. Three months earlier, she had openly expressed her hatred of politics and her longing to return to Europe. Now she argued that her husband was the only logical running mate for Douglas in his bid for the presidency in 1860.[44]

Douglas, Sue reminded the two men, could win the office only if he could attract the undivided support of southern Democrats. His "recent defection" during the battle for Kansas had made him "suspicious and unreliable" to most southerners, and he could regain their support only by arranging for a southern "ultra" to run with him. He could not go to the Senate for a running mate, she argued, because no prominent southerner would give up his seat in the Upper House for less than first place on the ticket; he could only go to the Lower House for a suitable candidate. He had to select a man whose views were known, whose talent was recognized, and whose courage was unmistakable. "Who stands out, *head and shoulders* above the throng," she asked? Who satisfied all the requirements? Who could guarantee success for Douglas? To her, the answer was obvious.

Sanders had suggested that James H. Hammond would be the best choice for vice-president, but Sue insisted that the party could not make a worse choice. Hammond was "a man whose appetite is the thing of the greatest moment, whose splendid intellect is the slave of a damaged liver and a morbid spleen! . . . a man effete, blazed, rusted out!" Hammond was afraid that Douglas would involve the country in an unnecessary war, but she and Keitt believed that a foreign war would be the best way to "relieve internal brawls, quell home conflicts, smooth away sectional jealousies, [and] save the Republic." She was interested in Keitt; Sanders and Banks were interested in Douglas; their interests might well serve them both.

"You called me ambitious the other day," Sue reminded Banks, and he had been right. But she was "not ambitious of wearing a smaller hoop than Mrs. Thompson, a bigger bonnet than Mrs. Davis, talk more than Mrs. Clay, or have brighter diamonds than Mrs. Guinn [*sic*]."[45] She had set her sights on nobler goals than those; she was "ambitious to win the power of high authority, wear the dignities of high station, and blazon a page of History." Perhaps he would think her ambition mad, Sue told Banks, and perhaps it was, but even the presidency would not satisfy her. The president exercised only a cramped authority for four years; he had only a negative power, no greater than "a woman's in love affairs . . . the *Veto*." As for what would satisfy her soaring ambition, she did not say. Perhaps she hoped that Keitt might one day take his place in history as the founder of a great nation.

Keitt was going to resign his seat in the House, Sue told Banks. The two of them were going to travel in Europe, study, and prepare themselves so that they would be ready to "grasp the skirts of Happy Chance" when opportunity presented itself. As for the immediate future, she had many influential friends who would be attending the Democratic convention in Charleston. If Douglas made Keitt a truly generous offer, she could persuade them to vote for him.[46]

To advance her plans for winning Keitt the nomination, Sue wrote to her father asking for his help. "Times are quiet here except for President making," she told him. She favored Douglas because "Southern men can rule him and get what they want—and then he is in favor of Cuba and all those other Southern enterprises." The Douglas men were very active, and some of the most influential wanted to run Keitt for vice-president. Could he take a few trusted friends to the state convention in Columbia and see that delegates friendly to her husband went to the national convention in Charleston?

Sue was looking well beyond the vice-presidency. With Douglas in the White House, she explained, effective opposition to the annexation of Cuba would vanish. The South would "get new territory, enlarge herself, and spread her institutions, and cut loose from the North." Who, she asked, would be a more logical choice to be the president of the new confederacy than the vice-president of the old one?[47]

Sue's letters revealed an astonishing personal transformation. Three months earlier, she had wanted only to escape from Washington and its political turmoil. Now she was scheming to make Keitt the president of a republic that did not yet exist. Three months before, she had been pathetically grateful to the Hammonds for sheltering her from the buffetings of the city. Now she was slandering the senator to assist her husband's political advancement. Now she was boldly acknowledging an ambition so overweening that it might well have embarrassed Aaron Burr or James Wilkinson.

Sue's letters also revealed a woman well versed in political skullduggery. She believed only "available" candidates, men not closely associated with the political controversies of the time, could be elected to national office. She was planning for Keitt to resign from the Congress in an attempt to make him less controversial and more available. Like William H. Seward, she believed a foreign war would distract attention from domestic disputes and prevent a premature dissolution of the Union. And she believed that, in spite of his past heresies, Douglas's sympathy for imperialistic ventures into the Caribbean made it safe for a southern politician to support his campaign for the presidency. How much Sue's letters reflected her own opinions and how much those of her husband is impossible to know. Keitt's attempts in 1860 to get South Carolina newspapers to publish Douglas's speeches suggest that he had a hand in her maneuvers, but by waiting until Keitt was away from Washington to write to Banks and Sanders, Sue suggested even more strongly that she was acting alone.

In the end, nothing came of the scheme. The debacle perpetrated by the Democrats at their convention in Charleston destroyed even the slight possibility that Sue's dreams might become reality. For the nation the destruction of the Democratic Party made the election of Abraham Lincoln and the secession of the lower South all but inevitable. For the Keitts it made cooperation with the Douglas Democrats impossible, and dissolved their dreams of political glory inside the Union. It did not, however, put an end to their dreams of founding a new nation.

NINE

"Fidelity to the Union is treason to the South"

With the struggle for the speakership finally over, congressmen turned their attention to long-neglected business, none of it immediately related to slavery or secession. The Congress enacted a homestead bill, and Buchanan vetoed it. The House approved a slight upward revision of the tariff, but the Senate killed it. Neither house could agree on a route for a railroad to the Pacific coast.[1] Keitt showed some interest in the tariff—he condemned the bill as unjust and unnecessary—but none at all in the other issues. In the course of the session, he defended the members' franking privilege, arranged for the dedication of Clark Mills's statue of George Washington, attacked a bill liberalizing divorce in the District of Columbia, and defended the administration of the federal armories against Republican charges of incompetence and corruption.[2] He delivered his only extended speech during a debate on Utah territory, conceding that polygamy was a "high moral offense" but insisting that Congress did not have the power to declare it a crime in Utah or any other territory. It could not condemn the morals and manners or shape the social institutions of any community. And if it tried, it did not have the ability to enforce its edicts. Keitt's real concern was, of course, the growing power of the federal government and the threat it posed to the interests of his state and section. He could hardly concede to the government the power to stamp out polygamy in a territory and then deny it the power to abolish slavery in a state. If the government recognized the legitimacy of polygamy in Utah, however unpopular the practice might be in the rest of the country, it could hardly deny the legitimacy of slavery in the South.[3]

Like everyone else in Washington, Keitt had his attention riveted on Charleston. There, for nine days in April, the Democratic Party struggled to nominate a president and draft a platform for the coming election. For Keitt hundreds of miles away and powerless to affect the result, it was an enormously frustrating

"The Seceding South Carolina Delegation."
From the cover of *Harper's Weekly*, December 22, 1860.
Courtesy of Thomas Cooper Library, Rare Books and Special Collections.

time. Only once did he have any influence on the course of events. On April 26, when the delegates from South Carolina realized that the convention would not endorse a territorial slave code, they asked the state's congressmen for advice.[4] In a flurry of telegrams, Keitt and his colleagues urged the delegates to bolt the convention. Four days later, the South Carolinians joined the delegations from the other cotton states when they stalked out of the hall.[5] It is impossible to know how many of the bolters anticipated the consequences of their actions. Perhaps most of them believed that, by putting pressure on free-state delegates, by turning one more time to the tactic that had worked repeatedly in the past, they could force the party to endorse a territorial slave code or nominate a man more sympathetic to their interests than Douglas. Surely none of them imagined that they were bringing about the very catastrophe that some of them were trying to avoid—not only secession and war, but death, destruction, defeat, and the end of the peculiar institution.[6]

There was no presidential campaign in South Carolina. John C. Breckinridge, nominated in Baltimore by the southerners and "doughfaces" who bolted the Democratic convention a second time, ran unopposed. Few politicians conceded him even a slight chance to win the election or even to create a deadlock in the Electoral College and throw the decision to the House of Representatives. For Keitt and the radicals, that was unimportant. For them his candidacy was valuable because it promised to unite the South, make a Republican victory all but certain, and force even conservative southerners to think seriously about dissolving the old Union and creating a new one.[7]

Even before the disruption of the party at Charleston, radicals in Congress had assumed that defeat was inevitable and begun working to guarantee that, when it came, the South would be united in support of secession. In her memoirs, Mrs. Roger A. Pryor, the wife of a fire-eating congressman from Virginia, described the meetings in the library of her home in Washington. There assembled R. M. T. Hunter and Muscoe Garnett of Virginia, L. Q. C. Lamar and William Barksdale of Mississippi, and the most radical of the South Carolinians: Miles, Boyce, and Keitt. In spite of the Kentucky bourbon and Chesapeake oysters she served her guests, these were not convivial gatherings. "These men held troubled consultations on the state of the country," Mrs. Pryor recalled long afterward. "The dawn would find them again and again with but one conclusion—they would stand together" in the defense of southern rights.[8]

As soon as the Congress adjourned in June, Keitt rushed home to prepare his district for secession. In mid-July, responding to a request from constituents, he wrote a public letter describing the threat posed by recent political developments and proposing an uncompromising solution.

It was futile to deny that the federal government was about to pass into the hands of the Republicans, Keitt warned his constituents, or that they would use its powers to cripple and ultimately to destroy slavery. Four years earlier, fanatical Republicans had declared that polygamy and slavery were "the twin relics of barbarism" and must be destroyed. Running on that platform, they came within a hair's breadth of seizing the government. Since that time, their strength had increased and the Democratic Party had broken in pieces, all but guaranteeing their success in November. The Republicans had reaffirmed their principles and nominated a man—Abraham Lincoln—whose vulgarity and ignorance guaranteed that he would be the mere instrument of their will, a man whose only achievements had been splitting rails and vilifying the Mexican War.[9]

Could the South permit a party "stained with treason, hideous with insurrection, and dripping with blood" to take command of the government? Could the South save itself from destruction when the Republican Party was successful in the coming election? Could the South afford to wait until the Republicans committed an overt act against its vital interests? To Keitt, the answer was obvious: the South must immediately dissolve the Union. He appealed to the rest of the southern states to defend their honor and answer the Republican victory by joining South Carolina in a new confederacy. "Loyalty to the Union," he insisted, "would be treason to the South" and everything it held dear. And if they refused to stand firm, South Carolina alone and at all hazards must secede from the Union. The governor must assemble the legislature, and it must take all steps necessary to protect the state from the vengeance of the Black Republicans. At the bar of history, Keitt assured his constituents, the state would stand justified. It would receive the plaudits of brave men for preserving their freedom and their praises for shattering a vile despotism.[10]

Keitt may have been the first prominent South Carolina politician to declare publicly that the state must answer Lincoln's election by seceding from the Union, even if it had to act alone.[11] In spite of its significance, his letter generated little editorial comment anywhere in the South. He had been campaigning for southern independence since the beginning of his public career. His latest pronouncement could not have surprised even the most guileless of his constituents. Still, it deserved more attention than it received.

In the North, however, Keitt's letter provoked an explosion. The editor of the *New York Times* warned that it was part of an elaborate bluff designed to wring concessions from timid northern voters and advance the author's political career in South Carolina. Keitt did not really expect the southern states to secede. Political power was passing to the North, and it would not be "chivalric" for him to let it go without protest. The South could no more "unite upon a scheme of secession, than a company of lunatics could conspire to break out of Bedlam." All in all, it was "a very silly production," all "bluster and bravado, false assumptions and shallow sophistries." This time, the North would not be taken in. Keitt had been a champion of secession so long and threatened secession so often the editor's suspicions must have seemed entirely justified.[12]

Horace Greeley's *New York Tribune* erupted in righteous indignation. If Keitt did not know it, it was high time somebody told him that treason was as much a crime as larceny, and just as promptly punished. From the start the federal government had been strong enough to crush any revolt, and it was stronger now than ever before. If Keitt attempted to put his theories into practice, Abraham Lincoln would introduce him to a jury of his peers who would make him a short but pointed speech about ropes and scaffolds and put an end to his blustering.[13] Only the *New York Herald* would concede that the southern radicals were capable of carrying out their threats. Editor James Gordon Bennett warned northern merchants to stop doing business with the South. They should collect their southern debts, he warned, and sell their southern securities before it was too late.[14]

Week after week, South Carolina's fire-eating politicians—aided by editors, clergymen, planters, and merchants—repeated their message. Lincoln would win, and when he did, South Carolina must leave the Union. Under the constant pounding, the state's traditional political divisions began to break down. The state's moderates found the ground cut out from under them, and men like James L. Orr and Durant Ashmore began deserting to the radicals. In his defense of the Union, Benjamin F. Perry stood almost alone.[15] Only questions about the mode of secession—alone or in cooperation with the rest of the South—remained to threaten the state's unity, and even there the separate secessionists were largely unchallenged.[16]

Still, unanimity was not quite complete. In the summer of 1860, the state's two senators, James Chesnut and James H. Hammond, had not committed themselves to separate secession.[17] Keitt wrote repeatedly to Hammond, urging him to endorse the radical position and warning that delay could endanger his political career. In a letter dated August 4, Keitt told the senator he must face the certainty that Breckinridge would be badly beaten. John Bell, the candidate of the Constitutional Union Party, was running well in the upper South, but he and Breckinridge would not carry enough states to force the election into the House. Even if they did, Breckinridge still could not win because Douglas would throw his support to Lincoln. A "wonderful feeling" was growing in the state, and even Orr had pronounced himself in favor of secession. Rhett wanted to return to the Senate, but if Hammond did not persist in "burning his fingers" as James Chesnut was doing, he had nothing to worry about. As for himself, Keitt concluded, he would "cut loose through fire and blood if necessary."[18]

In September, with Hammond stubbornly refusing to speak out in favor of secession, Keitt became increasingly concerned about his old friend. Hammond had cited ill health as an excuse for his failure to act, but Keitt was not impressed. "Dismiss your liver," he advised the Senator, "or make a man of it." Hammond had insisted that Breckinridge could win, and Keitt agreed, but only if he carried every southern state plus New York. And that, Keitt insisted, was all but impossible.

Over and over, Keitt insisted that if Hammond refused to speak out in favor of secession, he would lose his seat in the Senate. The new legislature would be dominated by radicals; even in traditionally conservative Marlborough District, "resistance spirit" was "mounting high." The implication was obvious; a radical legislature would not return a covert Unionist to office.[19]

Hammond must have been more than a little mystified by his young colleague's apparent concern for his political survival. If Lincoln was certain to win the presidency in November as Keitt insisted he was, and if South Carolina seceded from the Union as Keitt insisted it would, his reelection to the Senate would be irrelevant. Whatever the action of the legislature, he would not retain his seat. Perhaps Keitt was concerned that Hammond would not be elected to a seat in the Confederate Congress. Or perhaps he was playing on Hammond's hope that the Union would not dissolve to maneuver him into an alliance with the secessionists.

Keitt was himself facing a similar problem. In December 1859 he had announced that he would retire from Congress at the end of the session and take Sue back to Europe, but a month later he began to have second thoughts about his decision. He could not enter the field and campaign for reelection, Keitt told O. M. Dantzler, and three men were already running to succeed him, but if he were elected, he would cheerfully serve.[20] Almost immediately, Keitt found himself deluged with letters from friends and constituents urging him to stand for reelection. Resolutions passed by public meetings, editorials published by low-country newspapers, letters written by Third District voters all confirmed what Keitt already knew; he would have little trouble winning a fifth term in the Congress. On April 11, the Orangeburg *Southron* announced—perhaps without his formal permission—that he would run for reelection.[21]

The campaign to return Keitt to the House continued through the spring and summer of 1860, but without much help from the candidate himself. Early in July, William Gilmore Simms passed along to Porcher Miles the rumor that Keitt had withdrawn from the race.[22] Apparently Simms was right; at some time during the summer, Keitt must have recognized the absurdity of campaigning simultaneously for secession and reelection to his seat in the House. Or he may have realized that he could not decently back away from his decision to retire. Late in August, a mass meeting on Edisto Island endorsed him for a fifth consecutive term, and Keitt wrote to William M. Murray, the presiding officer at the meeting, confirming his intention to retire. Eighteen months earlier, he explained, "circumstances of a private nature" had induced him to announce that he would not stand for reelection. The circumstances had changed, but he would stand by his original decision.[23]

The hope others had entertained until recently, Keitt continued, that the South might defeat the Black Republican Party in the coming presidential election had vanished. The party would seize the government and subject the South to the rule of organized fanaticism and venality. Its speculations, falsehoods, usurpations, intrigues, and corruptions had disgraced every state it controlled. Its members had been expelled from Congress for bribery, its governors indicted for fraud, and its legislators convicted of embezzlement. Its judges had sold the law for a price; its leaders had provoked slaves to burn southern homes, poison southern wells, murder southern men and women, and then boasted of their atrocities. It pledged to continue its war against slavery, and only the South's degrading submission to its demands could assure the tranquility of the Union. The South could not look to the Congress or the Supreme Court for protection. It must take its safety into its own hands and do whatever was necessary to protect its vital interests.[24]

Since the birth of the republic, the South had tried to settle its disagreements with the North amicably, but in every instance—during the struggles over the admission of Missouri, the nullification of the tariff, the Mexican cession, the expansion of slavery into Kansas—it had failed. It would have been better if its statesmen had grappled boldly with the issues, but they had compromised with their enemies to obtain a precarious peace. Now, the South must pay the price for their failures.

Slavery, Keitt concluded, must remain solely in the keeping of the South, where it would be safe from the assaults of its enemies. When the Republicans elected the president and took control of Congress, they would deny slavery the protection of the federal government. They would use the power of the government to destroy slavery wherever it existed. Before that dread day arrived, the South must go to any length to defend the peculiar institution, even to the dissolution of the Union.[25]

In August, Keitt suddenly withdrew from active politics. Sue was ill—apparently having difficulty recovering from the birth of their daughter, Anna, in May—and her doctor prescribed rest and mountain air. He "bundled us off speedily," Keitt told Miles, "telling me that her health was fast sinking here, and that she could not stand out the summer this side of the mountains."[26]

On their way west, the Keitts stopped at the Congaree House in Columbia, where a crowd of well-wishers serenaded them. Inspired by the music and cheering, Keitt responded with an "eloquent and forceful" address that repeated the arguments in his letter to William Murray. He assailed the fanaticism that had seized northern voters and made the election of Abraham Lincoln all but certain. He would not wait for an overt act against the South, Keitt told his audience; he

Anna Keitt, carte de visite.
Courtesy of South Caroliniana Library, University of South Carolina.

would answer Lincoln's election with immediate secession. If the southern states would not go out together, he was for secession with as many states as possible. If none would go, he was for secession by South Carolina alone.[27] On their arrival at Glenn Springs on August 28, Keitt made still another fiery speech demanding that the state prepare to dissolve the Union, and with that, called a halt to political activity until fall.[28]

The letters Keitt wrote during his enforced vacation in the mountains and immediately following his return to St. Matthews reflected the peculiar combination of unreasoning fear and cool calculation with which he faced the future.

Reports of slaves rebelling, vigilance committees searching for "abolitionists," militia units arming and drilling drove him close to panic. In a letter to Hammond, he gave free rein to his emotions: "See—poison in the wells in Texas and fire for the houses in Alabama—our negroes are being enlisted in politics—with poison and fire—how can we stand it? I confess this new feature alarms me more than even everything in the past. If northern men get access to our negros [*sic*] to advise poison and the torch we must prevent it at every hazard. The future will not 'down' because we are blind."[29]

Keitt's fear of social revolution in the North matched his fear of servile insurrection in the South. "If we submit," he warned Miles a month before the election, "the South is undone. The concentration of Absolute power in the hands of the North will develop the wildest Democracy ever seen on this earth, unless it should have been matched in Paris in 1789. What of conservatism? What of order? What of social security or financial prosperity?"[30]

Keitt's prose was becoming increasingly hysterical, but his analysis of the problems that faced the South was essentially correct and his solution coldly calculated. He was convinced beyond all doubt that Lincoln would win the presidency and that the South had "no alternative but to meet his election with the sword." South Carolina must arm its militia, he told Miles, hold a state convention, and recall its representatives from Congress. Keitt understood that South Carolina could initiate the secession movement and that the other states of the lower South could not. "The absence of party spirit enables us to do so," he explained to Miles. "If we wait for Ala[bama] we will wait eternally. . . . She has no man strong enough." Yancey lacked ability; Jefferson Davis of Mississippi was more talented but also more cautious. South Carolina must rely on itself alone.[31]

After his return from the mountains late in September, Keitt threw himself into a last, desperate round of political activity, stumping his congressional district, following the circuit court from Orangeburg to Barnwell to Walterboro, haranguing his constituents, stirring up support for separate secession. Late in October, he tried one last time to persuade Hammond that to save his political career he had to endorse secession.[32] Keitt told the senator that he had to give up all hope that Breckinridge could win. If New York stood by him, Keitt admitted, victory was possible. New York City would give him a huge majority, but the rural districts would give the Republicans an even greater margin, and Lincoln would carry the state by forty thousand votes. Capital would carry the city, but fanaticism would carry the countryside. Douglas men in the free states would go for Lincoln to defeat Breckinridge, and Bell men would do the same. With them, the election was only "a new shuffle and cut of the cards"; with the South, it was a matter of life and death. The key to the outcome was fanaticism. In its economic interests, the rest of the country was closely linked to the South, but in the North, fanaticism was stronger than material concerns. Suppose we submit and the Republicans pass a law "declaring that every negro child born after 1880 will be free and every slave after 1900." That prospect doomed the Union to destruction.

He was in danger, Keitt warned the senator. He must tell the newspapers in Charleston that he considered the election of Lincoln a declaration of war against the South that would justify immediate secession. He must write nothing short of that; if he failed to support the movement without reservation, "they"—he meant the most extreme radicals: Rhett, Bonham, Gist—would "shoot you down."[33] Keitt was right; Hammond refused to cooperate with the secessionists and sat out the war years on his plantation at Beech Island, driven into retirement by legislators who refused to forgive his reluctance to champion secession.[34]

On election day, November 6, the nation's voters cast their ballots just as Keitt had predicted. Breckinridge carried the lower South; Douglas and Bell divided the border states; Lincoln won by a landslide in New England and by narrow margins in the rest of the North. He received only "a large third" of the popular vote, but enough to give him a substantial victory in the Electoral College.[35]

On November 7, when the news of the Republican victory reached South Carolina, the state gave itself up to an emotional orgy. Crowds thronged the streets of every city and town, whipped into a frenzy by mass meetings and parades, martial music and fiery oratory. Blue cockades appeared in every lapel, and palmetto flags waved from every rooftop.[36]

In Columbia the popular hysteria did not immediately communicate itself to the legislature, which was in the midst of a special session called to choose the state's presidential electors. After three days of debate between radicals who demanded immediate and separate secession and moderates who wanted to delay long enough to arrange a simultaneous secession of all of the cotton states, the two blocs reached a compromise. The legislature approved a bill that fixed January 8 for the election of delegates to a secession convention and January 15 for the first meeting of the convention.[37]

Outside the legislature, the decision generated unexpected opposition. A mass meeting in Charleston protested vehemently against the delay. A delegation of Georgians was in the city to celebrate the completion of a railroad between Charleston and Savannah. Members pledged that their state would follow South Carolina's lead and sent a three-man delegation by special train to urge the Georgia legislature to act at once. Robert Toombs telegraphed Keitt from Macon, announcing his resignation from the Senate and urging South Carolina to secede immediately: "I will sustain South Carolina in secession. . . . If you have power to act," he advised his friend, "act at once. We have bright prospects here."[38] Caught up in the emotion of the moment, both South Carolina senators resigned their seats, Chesnut on November 10 and Hammond the following day.[39] Keitt, like Boyce and Ashmore, was openly critical, insisting that the two men should have returned to Washington to push the rest of the South to secede and form a new confederacy. In Columbia secessionist orators—Rhett, Bonham, Edmund Ruffin of Virginia—hotly condemned the legislators' reluctance to take the state out of the Union without delay.[40]

On the evening of November 12, Keitt told a crowd of serenaders that South Carolina could not back away from secession without calling down on itself the curses of posterity. Interrupted by frequent applause, he demanded that the state take its destiny into its own hands and "shatter this accursed Union." It could establish its independence, alone if necessary, and if for some reason it failed, it could "throw its arms around the pillars of the Constitution and involve all of the states in common ruin.[41]

Reacting to the public clamor, the South Carolina legislature moved the election for delegates forward to December 6 and the first session of the convention to December 17. South Carolina would not leave the Union for more than a month, but by approving a new date for the convention, the legislature made its intention unmistakably clear. The vote the convention would cast for secession December 20 would be no more than a formality.[42]

His work in Columbia completed, Keitt left for Charleston, where he planned to visit friends and get a much-needed rest. In that he was quickly disappointed. On November 20, only hours after his arrival in the city, he was serenaded by a crowd of well-wishers who marched to his hotel behind a brass band. Responding to their persistent cheers, Keitt told his audience he had little more to say. The time for words had passed; the time for action had finally arrived. South Carolina was the sentinel on the southern watchtower. If the state hesitated, no matter how wildly the tempest might rage, others would lose heart. His district would cast every one of its sixteen hundred votes for secession. South Carolina had inaugurated the revolution, and now the state must carry it through to a successful conclusion.[43]

Keitt ridiculed the suggestion that the federal government would oppose secession with force. President Buchanan had pledged that he would allow South Carolina to secede in peace, and the state would hold him to his promise. Concluding with an oratorical flourish, Keitt left the crowd outside his hotel cheering hoarsely. The Black Republicans told them that fidelity to the Constitution was treason to the higher law, but he insisted that fidelity to the Union was treason to the South. The Republicans told them that resistance to the federal government was treason, but when he had to choose to be a traitor or a slave, God help him, he would be a traitor.[44]

The next day, Keitt conferred with prominent secessionists, ate dinner aboard the steamship *Columbia,* received a rifle disguised as a gutta percha cane from admirers, and addressed a torchlight parade organized by a young men's secession club.[45] Somehow, he found time to write to Hammond. He must go to Columbia for the convention, Keitt told his old friend. The secession of the state was settled, and nothing he could do could change it. He must guide his state's counsels and share her fate. The next governor would go down in history beside the heroes of the American Revolution, John Rutledge and Francis Marion. The honor was his if only he would seize it.[46] This time, Keitt was wrong; Hammond's political career was finished, and the old man was relieved that it had finally come to an end. It was an emotion Keitt would never experience and never understand.[47]

The South Carolina delegation returned to Washington on December 2, one day before Congress was scheduled to convene, and took rooms at Brown's Hotel. More than a month before, Keitt and his colleagues had agreed to remain in the House until South Carolina formally left the Union. The advantages were obvious; in the Congress, they could frustrate Republican attempts to prevent the secession of the upper South, cooperate with representatives from the other southern states, and draft plans for a new confederacy.[48] Early in the month, a caucus attended by twenty-six congressmen from eight states agreed unanimously that South Carolina should secede without delay. The resignation of the state's two senators in mid-November surprised and disappointed the congressmen but did not seriously disturb their plans.[49]

On December 8, the South Carolinians held the first of several crucial conversations with James Buchanan in which they tried to persuade him to evacuate Fort Sumter and the two smaller fortifications in Charleston harbor, Castle Pinckney and Fort Moultrie. From the start they assumed their mission would end in success. In his annual address to the Congress on December 3, Buchanan had denied that he possessed the authority to prevent states from seceding from the Union or to force them to return. He had done little to reinforce Fort Sumter and had allowed Secretary of War John B. Floyd to transfer arms and equipment to the southern states. Now more than ever, Keitt and his colleagues believed the president would acquiesce in the peaceful dissolution of the Union.[50]

Convinced that the administration would not resist secession, the South Carolinians were shocked by rumors circulating through the capital that the War Department was preparing to reinforce the forts. At their first meeting with the president, they had found him "much disturbed and moved." He had just completed "a painful interview" with Mrs. Robert Anderson, the wife of the officer in command of the federal troops in Charleston. The lady was afraid her husband was in danger from "an excited and lawless mob" and had asked the president to intervene.[51]

In their report to the convention, Keitt and Miles wrote that Buchanan had expressed concern for the safety of Major Anderson and his command. They had told him they did not believe Anderson was in any danger; the state convention was only ten days away, and the state would not attack the fort before it met. They could not say what the convention would do, but they believed it would first send commissioners to Washington to negotiate a peaceful settlement of the issues that were disturbing relations between the two governments. They emphasized that any change in the situation in Charleston harbor would "inevitably precipitate a collision." The president, the congressmen concluded, had not yet decided what course he would pursue.[52]

At the end of their interview, Buchanan asked the South Carolinians to prepare a written memorandum of their conversation. They drafted a statement on December 9 and presented it to the president the following day: "We now express to you our strong convictions that neither the constituted authorities, nor any body of the people of the State of South Carolina, will either attack or molest the United States forts in the Harbor of Charleston . . . provided that no re-enforcement shall be sent into those forts, and their relative military status shall remain as at present." The president objected to the word "provided" because it seemed to bind the federal government but left the government of South Carolina free to act as it saw fit. The congressmen disagreed; they were only expressing their belief that the state would not try to take the fort if he did not try to reinforce it. They insisted that Anderson must not move the main garrison from Fort Moultrie, a fortification on Sullivan's Island vulnerable to assault from land, to Fort Sumter out in the harbor. Such a move would be the equivalent of sending in fresh troops and could lead to the clash both sides wanted to avoid. In reply Buchanan assured the congressmen that he did not intend to make any change in the garrison.[53]

As the South Carolinians rose to leave, Buchanan remarked that he supposed no written record of their agreement was necessary. "After all, " he concluded, "this is a matter of honor among gentlemen. . . . We understand each other." At least one member of the delegation—Keitt and Miles did not reveal who it was—was not completely satisfied. "Mr. President," he said, "you have determined to let things stay as they are; . . . but suppose that you were hereafter to change your policy for any reason, what then?" In that case, Buchanan replied, pointing to the memorandum the congressmen had handed him at the start of their conversation, "I would first return you this paper."[54]

The South Carolinians left the White House convinced that they had successfully completed their mission. Buchanan had agreed not to send reinforcements to Fort Sumter or alter the military situation in Charleston harbor in any way. And he had strongly implied that the federal government would surrender the forts to commissioners appointed by the convention.

Less than a week after their meetings with Buchanan, three of the congressmen—Keitt, Miles, and Boyce—left Washington to attend the South Carolina secession convention. When they arrived in Columbia on December 17, they found smallpox raging in the city and a majority of the delegates ready to move to a safer location. Soon after the convention assembled for the first time—the legislature was in session and it had to meet in a nearby Baptist church—a resolution to adjourn to Charleston ran into unexpected opposition. A number of the delegates were determined to take the state out of the Union without delay. Miles opposed the move because delay might undermine support for secession in other southern states. In Washington sympathetic congressmen had told him that South Carolina must not hesitate, not even for a few days. The time for resolutions was over; the state must act at once.[55]

Keitt persuaded the delegates that a twenty-four-hour adjournment would cost them nothing. He agreed that prompt action was essential, and assured them he was ready to take South Carolina out of the Union and to burn every bridge behind him. But there was no reason the ordinance of secession had to be approved in Columbia. An ordinance enacted in Charleston would be equally valid. He was ready to risk his life, Keitt told the convention, if any gentleman could explain why he must stay in Columbia. He was ready to brave any peril, even death by smallpox. Still, if the god of battles were to call him to the tents the next day, he saw no reason why he should not sleep in a safe and comfortable bed that night.

Miles had argued that the convention should pass the ordinance of secession and then move, but Keitt thought that was unwise. The convention was about to pull down one government and raise up another, and must not act in haste. None of the delegates had a constitution in his trousers pocket, and none of them could write one in an evening. The convention must work carefully and diligently to enact legislation that would make secession more than an empty gesture. The work would take time; the loss of a day was not important.[56] Keitt's argument was decisive. The delegates agreed to move the convention to Charleston, but only after they had resolved unanimously that South Carolina should secede forthwith from the Union.[57]

Charleston welcomed the delegates, an unusually wealthy and talented group of men,[58] with pealing bells and booming cannon. They met first at the South Carolina Institute and then moved to St. Andrews Hall, where the facilities were more comfortable. There—while committees drafted an ordinance of secession, a declaration of causes, and an address to the slaveholding states—the rest of the delegates approved postal, customs, and other legislation necessary to make independence a reality.

On December 20, the committee submitted its draft of the ordinance of secession. It was brief and dignified, declaring that the "Union now subsisting between South Carolina and other states . . . is hereby dissolved." The convention adopted the proposal almost without debate and by a unanimous vote, 169–0.[59] Impatient radicals wanted the delegates to sign the ordinance at once, but again Keitt was able to persuade them to adopt a more deliberate course. Their act, he told the delegates, would live for ages to come, and must conclude with appropriate ceremony: "I have been engaged in this movement ever since I entered political life. I am content with what has been done today; and with what will take place tomorrow. We have carried the body of this Union to its last resting place, and now we will drop the flag over its grave. After that is done, I am ready . . . to leave the remaining ceremonies for tomorrow."[60] Impatient radicals agreed to the delay, but only for a few hours. That night, in the presence of the governor and both houses of the legislature, the delegates completed a two-hour ceremony by signing the ordinance.[61]

News of secession quickly spread through the city, leaving pandemonium in its wake. "Bells rang, men shouted, women wept, shops closed," one delegate reported to Hammond, "and almost everybody got drunk."[62] Artillery at the Citadel fired salute after salute. Volunteers donned their uniforms and wandered aimlessly about the streets. A special edition of the *Mercury*, prepared in advance and released five minutes after the final vote, quickly sold six thousand copies.[63] When the news reached Washington, all but one of the South Carolina congressmen immediately resigned. Their letter to the governor appeared in the *Mercury* the following day. They must have drafted and signed it in advance. On the day South Carolina seceded, Miles and Boyce were in Charleston, but McQueen, Bonham, and Ashmore were in Washington. Only Keitt did not sign the letter; he had resigned his seat on the seventeenth, jumping the gun by three days.[64]

For a time the delegates failed to agree on the best way to justify secession to the rest of the nation. The "Declaration of Immediate Causes" drafted by a committee led by Christopher Memminger was surprisingly blunt. It declared that South Carolina had a right to secede and had exercised that right to protest repeated northern violations of the Constitution. The North, it charged, had nullified the Fugitive Slave Law, permitted abolitionist societies to war against slavery, and encouraged servile revolts. It had denounced slavery as an evil and elected a president who declared that slavery must ultimately be destroyed.[65]

Because it frankly acknowledged that the state had seceded to protect slavery, the declaration encountered considerable opposition on the floor of the convention. Both Robert Barnwell Rhett and Maxcy Gregg argued that, by denouncing only northern attacks on slavery, the statement dishonored the memory of

South Carolinians who had fought against the protective tariff, the Bank of the United States, and federal appropriations for internal improvements. Their attempt to send the declaration back to the committee failed. The majority agreed with Keitt, who insisted that slavery was "the great central point from which we are now proceeding." He agreed that the power to tax was the most important power of any government, but the state had not dissolved the Union because the Congress had enacted economic legislation it strenuously opposed. Recent presidents had consistently vetoed internal improvements bills, and there had been no national bank for a quarter of a century. Every one of the state's senators and representatives had voted for the Tariff of 1857, and every member of the convention would have done the same. The tariff disturbed their relations with the federal government, Keitt concluded, but did not force them to dissolve the Union. Secession was the result of northern attacks on slavery, nothing more and nothing less. The delegates agreed and voted overwhelmingly, 124–31, to approve the declaration.[66]

With the preliminaries out of the way, the convention faced a host of problems. The delegates assumed that the state would soon be part of a southern confederacy, but until that time, they faced the task of making independence work. The convention had to amend the state's constitution, resume powers it had previously delegated to the federal government, replace laws enacted by the Congress, create an army and a navy, negotiate commercial treaties, collect customs duties, and deliver mail. Perhaps most important of all, it had to establish diplomatic relations with the nation from which it had just seceded.[67]

The very survival of the new government depended heavily on persuading the United States to acquiesce in secession and the rest of the slaveholding states to leave the Union and form a southern confederacy. Even before it ratified the ordinance of secession, the convention took steps to begin negotiations in Washington. On December 21, it agreed to send commissioners to demand that the Buchanan administration turn over to the state all of the property within its boundaries still held by the federal government. It also directed the commissioners to arrange for South Carolina to assume its share of the national debt and to make any other arrangements necessary to assure harmonious relations between the two countries.

The delegates immediately elected Robert W. Barnwell to the commission. In the balloting, Keitt received only four votes, evidence that his colleagues recognized that his lack of tact far overshadowed his knowledge of Washington personalities and politics and made him a particularly poor choice to carry out such delicate negotiations. The following day, December 22, the convention elected two additional commissioners, James L. Orr and James H. Adams.[68]

The commissioners reached Washington on December 26, the night Major Anderson spiked the guns in Fort Moultrie and moved the garrison to the relative safety of Fort Sumter. The news of his actions created chaos inside both governments. In Washington, Buchanan told the commissioners he had not ordered Anderson to transfer his command to Sumter but refused to order him back to the fort on Sullivan's Island. In Charleston the convention instructed Miles and Keitt to submit a report of their conversations with the president.[69]

Buchanan's actions infuriated Keitt. He and Miles had negotiated in good faith, he told the delegates. They had trusted the president; they had believed he wanted to avoid hostilities. They had made an agreement with him and had kept their part of the bargain, but he had violated his. He had pledged the faith of his government, and now he refused to redeem it.[70]

On the floor of the convention, Keitt introduced a resolution condemning the transfer of the Union garrison as a hostile act, approving the governor's seizure of Fort Moultrie and Castle Pinckney, and instructing the commissioners to demand that the president remove the troops from Charleston harbor. Under enormous pressure from his newly reorganized cabinet, Buchanan refused.[71]

At the same time, the convention began to consider ways to establish closer ties to the other seceding states. On December 31, it invited those states to send delegates to a convention that would create a new confederacy, and three days later, suggested that the convention meet in Montgomery on February 4. All of the seceding states accepted the proposal.

South Carolina selected a particularly strong delegation to represent the state. Only the delegation from Georgia, which included Alexander H. Stephens, Howell Cobb, and Robert Toombs, could match the South Carolinians in talent and experience. Keitt won a seat in the convention on the second ballot. His colleagues included two former senators, Barnwell Rhett and James Chesnut; three former congressmen, Miles, Boyce, and Barnwell; and a member of the legislature, Christopher Memminger. The eighth member of the delegation was Thomas J. Withers, a judge from Camden.[72]

The convention, its preliminary work completed, adjourned on January 5. Keitt, tired but in high spirits, remained in Charleston for at least a few days—he was in the city on January 9 when batteries on Morris Island prevented the *Star of the West* from reinforcing the federal garrison in Ft. Sumter—but soon after left for "Mandeville" for a much needed rest. For almost a month, he cut himself off from all political activity, spending the time with his wife and infant daughter. Toward the end of January, he wrote to A. G. Magrath, asking the judge to let him know when the southern congress would meet. He knew some of the states had suggested February 4, but doubted that Texas and Louisiana could be ready so soon. He commended Magrath for his skillful negotiations with Major Anderson; in the end, he predicted, he would have accomplished nothing. South Carolina would have to take Fort Sumter by force.[73]

Meanwhile, in the wake of the turmoil created by the Charleston convention, Sue Keitt was trying to explain—unsuccessfully, it seems—to her northern friends the reasons for her state's secession. Her letter to Mrs. Frederick Brown, a lady from Philadelphia she had met during her honeymoon tour of Europe, was probably the last in an exchange that had become increasingly rancorous. Mrs. Brown had written to congratulate Sue on the birth of her daughter, but their correspondence had apparently veered off into politics, and Sue had called down "a plague—yes the seven plagues of Egypt" on the Black Republicans who refused to leave the South in peace. Now something Mrs. Brown had written set off a great explosion. Keitt was in Montgomery, and Sue was at her parents' home with too little to do and too much time to stew over the events of the past months that had so unsettled her life.

Sue began the letter by laying out in terms the plantation elite would have approved the reasons the South would never accept Abraham Lincoln as president: "His vulgar facetiousness may suit the race of clock makers and woolen nutmeg venders—even Wall Street brokers . . . but never will he receive the homage of southern gentlemen. . . . The President Elect of the American people, on his triumphal march to the Capital, exhibits himself at railway depots, bandies jokes with the populace, kisses bold women from promiscuous crowds, . . . and to crown this disgusting progress, flees from an imaginary assassin, and under cover of night and in disguise, enters the Capital."[74] Midway through the letter, Sue's control over her emotions, tenuous from the start, cracked, and the anger and fear she had repressed came boiling up in a great flood. Who were these Black Republicans who will never lord it over the South? "A motley throng of Sans Culottes and Dames des Halles, infidels and free lovers, . . . Bloomer women, fugitive slaves and amalgamationists." And what were the South's conditions for returning to the Union? "Hang all your Redpaths, Garrisons, Greeleys, and Ward Beechers, incarcerate your Garrett Smiths, unite your Sumners and Sewards to ebony spouses and send them as resident ministers in perpetum [*sic*] to Timbuctoo, purge the halls of Congress and the White House of the odor of their presence and attach the death penalty to all future agitations of the slavery question."[75]

No doubt Mrs. Brown found it difficult to cut through Sue's emotional rhetoric and to understand what lay at the roots of her anguish. If only the men Sue railed at had recognized the depths of the South's anger and discarded the facile assumption that the South would recover its senses and voluntarily return to the

Union, the history of the United States might very well have played itself out far differently from how it in fact did. Now that people they hated and feared were about to take control of the federal government, southerners were convinced beyond all doubt that it was no longer safe for the region to remain inside the Union.

TEN

"True liberty is won by the blood of the brave"

The South Carolina delegation, minus Chesnut and Withers, reached Montgomery by rail on February 2, two days before the convention was scheduled to meet for the first time. Heavy rains had flooded rivers, washed out long sections of track, and made the trip even more treacherous than usual. In Atlanta the train carrying the South Carolinians was already twelve hours behind schedule, and three miles outside Montgomery, a collision with a horse and buggy delayed it even longer. For the next three months, the activities of the delegates revolved around the Exchange Hotel, where the rooms were dirty and the food almost inedible, and around the state capitol half a mile away. Until May, when they moved to Richmond, the delegates conducted business in the northern wing of the building, which in calmer times had been occupied by the Alabama Senate.[1]

All in all, the delegates sent to Montgomery by the seceded states were not a distinguished lot. Many leaders assumed that the convention would carry out only preliminary business and refused to attend. Others who understood its importance, men like John Slidell and Judah P. Benjamin of Louisiana and William L. Yancey of Alabama, lost out in their state conventions. Only Georgia and South Carolina sent delegates well qualified to create a government for the new nation. Unlike the members of the Confederate Congress, many of whom were elected to represent narrowly local interests or to oppose the centralizing activities of the Davis administration, all of the delegates from those two states were committed to the creation of a viable southern confederacy and worked together more or less harmoniously to lay its foundations, a record of success their successors were frequently unable to match.[2]

Keitt played only a modest role in the convention. He was active behind the scenes but curtailed his speech-making, much to the surprise of men who had known him in Washington. "He is quick as a flash," Mary Boykin Chesnut wrote in her famous diary, "always original and entertaining. He covers himself with words—the longest and the finest, as a garment. No one gets the better of him."[3] He was a heavy drinker, but in Montgomery he swore off entirely, an action that perhaps explains his unaccustomed behavior. Alexander H. Stephens wrote to his brother Linton: "Keit [*sic*] speaks seldom. He said his wife told him when he left home to keep his mouth shut and his hair brushed," and he was determined to follow her advice.[4]

Throughout his career in Congress, Keitt had refused to pledge allegiance to the Democratic Party or cooperate consistently even with the party's southern wing. He had almost no experience in formulating policy and drafting legislation, and in 1861 he was temperamentally unprepared to work constructively with men whose primary concern was to lay the foundations of the new nation. Like so many of the fire-eaters who had worked so long to break up the old Union, he found the transformation from obstructionist politician to creative statesman difficult and never fully succeeded in laying aside one role in favor of the other. This failure, and not his wife's admonitions alone, accounts for the modest part he played in establishing the Confederate government.

The delegates turned over the first session of the convention to preliminary business: prayers, welcoming speeches, the election of a president and a secretary. Late in the day, they authorized the presiding officer, Howell Cobb of Georgia, to appoint a committee of five to draft rules to govern the conduct of the convention. That evening, four members of the committee—Keitt, Stephens, James T. Harrison of Mississippi, and John Perkins of Louisiana—met in Stephens's rooms and adopted with only minor changes the set of twenty-nine rules their host proposed. The following day, after a brief debate, the convention approved the committee's recommendations.[5]

On the second day, February 5, the delegates agreed to expand significantly the powers the convention would exercise. Without exception, the state conventions had instructed their delegates to organize a provisional government and draft a constitution for the permanent government they assumed would be created later. From the start, however, circumstances forced the delegates to ignore the limits imposed by their instructions. Cautious delegates, among them Rhett and Boyce of South Carolina, argued that the convention should not erect even a provisional government until all of the southern states were represented or until they received specific instructions from their states, but a majority agreed with T. R. R. Cobb of Georgia that circumstances would not permit them to delay. Faced by the threat of military intervention from the North, the convention transformed itself into a Provisional Congress, adding the duties of a constituent assembly and an electoral college to its duties as a constitutional convention.[6]

Led by Chairman Christopher Memminger, a committee of twelve produced a draft of a new constitution that borrowed heavily from the Constitution of the United States, introducing changes only to incorporate slavery and state rights into the organic law. After only two days, the committee presented its proposals to the Congress. The delegates devoted only one day to debating the draft, made only a handful of changes, and on February 8 approved the Provisional Constitution by a unanimous vote. The length of time given over to debate accurately reflected the ability of the delegates to agree on the outlines of the new government, but also their determination to restore the functions routinely carried out by a central government as quickly as possible and their tacit agreement to postpone debate on such controversial issues as slavery and internal improvements until they drafted a permanent constitution.[7]

After approving the provisional constitution, the delegates put off the election of a president and vice-president until the following day. From the start the South Carolinians were badly divided. Rhett wanted the presidency and believed he deserved it, but did not have the support even of his own delegation. At least two of the members, Keitt and Chesnut, came to Montgomery determined to block his election. Keitt's low opinion of Rhett was widely shared. His arrogance, according to Hammond, made him "utterly odious" outside South Carolina. Henry Ravenel called him "the most untrustworthy politician in the state. . . . He wants judgment, and can never be relied on for statesmanship."[8] Ravenel could have added that Rhett was arrogant, condescending, and totally intolerant of dissent.[9] Stephens inferred from a conversation with Keitt that he would support Robert Toombs or Stephens himself, but the little Georgian was almost certainly wrong. Both Toombs and Stephens had opposed secession in 1850, and Stephens had continued his opposition until Georgia left the Union. Both men were old Whigs, and Toombs was notorious for his inability to remain sober for more than a few hours at a time. Keitt told Mary Boykin Chesnut that he preferred Howell Cobb, as did Miles and Boyce. Barnwell and Chesnut favored Jefferson Davis; Memminger and Withers were undecided.[10]

Rhett refused to call a caucus of his delegation, probably because he realized it would not support his candidacy, and the South Carolinians spent the early hours of February 9 conferring informally. Out of their deliberations a decision in favor of Davis slowly emerged. Chesnut "overpersuaded"—the phrase is Keitt's quoted by Mrs. Chesnut—Judge Withers, and Barnwell won over Rhett, though much "against his better judgment." Keitt supported Cobb to the end, but to no avail. The Georgia delegation failed to unite behind a candidate, and three others—Mississippi, Alabama and Florida—announced they would vote for Davis. Keitt said later that Rhett's conversion, coming as it did shortly after half of the states had committed themselves to Davis, was decisive. The four South Carolinians still supporting Cobb capitulated, and both Cobb and Toombs withdrew, leaving Davis as the only candidate. When the convention assembled later in the day, it elected Davis to the presidency and then, in a conciliatory gesture to the powerful Georgia delegation, elected Stephens to the vice-presidency.[11]

That night, a large crowd went to the Exchange Hotel to serenade the new vice-president. Stephens spoke briefly, and when he had finished, Keitt joined him on the balcony. He assured the jubilant crowd that the Provisional Congress had placed in the Confederacy's highest offices its greatest soldier and its wisest statesman, men distinguished for their ability and their service to the South. The old Union was dead, he continued, and in its place the South had raised up a new Confederacy. It was already more powerful than the thirteen American colonies when they declared their independence from Great Britain, and in the future, it would become more powerful still. The convention had not conducted an experiment in political science, nor had it adopted novel political theories. It had taken the Constitution of the founding fathers, cleansed it of its corruption, and put it to a nobler purpose. The new nation contained no factions that would conspire against its success; the harmony of its interests would protect it against the tyranny and fanaticism that had destroyed its predecessor.[12]

Only six stars then graced the firmament of the new Confederacy, Keitt admitted, but one after another, the slaveholding states would wheel into its galaxy until the very heavens were set ablaze. Their hopes and destinies were inextricably linked, and they must leave their faithless friends in the North or sink down in vassalage and wretchedness. They might come quickly, or they might come slowly, or they might not come at all. Whatever those states did, the separation of the cotton states from the Union was "final, absolute, and eternal." He prayed that the North would allow the South to leave the Union in peace, but even if it did not, the South would never shrink from the conflict, and never forget that "liberty . . . is but the blood of the brave."[13]

That night, Keitt wrote to his cousin David Jamison, describing the events of the past week. "We are getting along with great harmony," Keitt told him, "and I do not see anything to mar our unity." The convention had transformed itself into a congress; he had wanted to avoid that step, but the delegates from Georgia and Alabama were afraid the voters would repudiate them and had insisted it must be done. The other states had agreed to their demand. The new Constitution included a number of useful changes; he would send a copy as soon as the Congress removed the seal of secrecy. The election of Davis and Stephens had produced real satisfaction, and now the South could get on with the job of creating a great nation. If it could avoid war with the North, it could face the future with confidence.[14]

Jefferson Davis arrived in Montgomery on February 16, and his inauguration followed two days later. A few hours before, the members of the Congress had placed their signatures on the Provisional Constitution. The ceremonies properly disposed of, they could return to the difficult task of transforming the new government from ideal to reality.[15]

The following day, February 19, Davis began assembling his cabinet. He wanted Barnwell to be his secretary of state, but the South Carolina delegation had already agreed to recommend Memminger for the Treasury Department, and Barnwell rejected the offer. Davis wanted to make Toombs his secretary of the treasury but gave in to the wishes of the South Carolinians. Toombs got the State Department, a position he did not want, and Memminger got the Treasury Department. The Congress quickly approved Memminger, Toombs, and three of their four colleagues in the cabinet, Pope Walker as secretary of war, John H. Reagan as postmaster general, and Judah P. Benjamin as attorney general. Only the nomination of Stephen R. Mallory to be secretary of the navy encountered real opposition. Mallory's reluctance to endorse secession—along with his fondness for cavorting with prostitutes and then bragging about his performance—had made him unpopular with the radicals. Keitt had not yet lost his influence inside the administration; gossips speculated that Davis would make him ambassador to Spain.[16]

On the day it elected Davis to the presidency, the convention created a second committee of twelve to draft a permanent constitution and made Rhett chairman. For almost three weeks, the committee met nightly, borrowing heavily from the U.S. and Provisional Confederate constitutions, adding amendments to correct flaws, carefully redressing the balance of power between the state and central governments. Rhett presented the completed draft to the Congress on February 26, and debate began two days later.[17]

Keitt's contributions to the debate were modest. On the second day he tried unsuccessfully to eliminate the three-fifths clause from the draft proposed by the committee. His amendment would have based representation and direct taxation on the total population of a state, not on its free population plus three-fifths of its slaves.[18] Perhaps he was willing for South Carolina to pay more in taxes to the Confederate government in order to increase its representation in the Congress. Perhaps he believed, as he told Hammond, that Congress would never levy direct taxes because people would resist paying them. Taxes had to be hidden because people would rather "give ten dollars which they have never seen than one they have in their pockets."[19]

Keitt and the rest of the South Carolina delegation consistently supported amendments designed to restrict the authority of the Congress to levy taxes and appropriate money, and were among the convention's most persistent opponents of protective tariffs and internal improvements. During a congressional career that had spanned seven years, Keitt had rarely showed much interest in the tariff question. South Carolina exported almost everything it produced and imported almost everything it consumed, a situation that made him an advocate of free trade. In 1846, years before Keitt was first elected to Congress, the Walker Tariff had lowered duties on most products to revenue levels, and southern politicians and their constituents had turned their attention to more pressing problems. In Congress, Keitt had attacked the protective tariff only twice, and on both occasions had used the topic as a springboard to a subject he found both more congenial and more significant: the defense of slavery.

In theory Keitt was a free trader; in practice, he knew that the Confederacy could not abolish the tariff without risking economic disaster. In February he assured Hammond that the Confederacy would embark on no economic experiments. "As to free trade," he wrote, "we are all against it. Direct taxation would ruin us. The Confederacy must have a revenue tariff, Keitt concluded, because taxation must be indirect. The final draft of the Constitution authorized the Congress to enact tariffs, but only to raise revenue.[20]

Keitt supported the economic conservatives who worked successfully to prohibit the Congress from appropriating money for most internal improvements, even though the provision would force South Carolina to finance improvements in Charleston harbor. He was less successful when he tried to reopen debate on the twin issues of slavery and the international slave trade. The committee's draft forbade the importation of slaves from any foreign country except the United States and directed the Congress to enact laws to enforce the prohibition. Keitt was willing to grant Congress authority to prohibit the trade, but he wanted it to be free to reopen the trade later, probably because he believed an absolute prohibition cast a stigma on the peculiar institution. The delegates, many of them hoping to attract the border states into the Confederacy and to win the approval of the great powers of Europe, voted down his amendment.[21]

On the afternoon of March 11, after deliberating for more than two weeks, the delegates voted unanimously to approve the new Constitution and sent it on to the states for ratification. Keitt left Montgomery before the Congress adjourned, in part to be in Charleston when the state convention reconvened, but largely because he was miserable away from his wife and daughter and worried because both of them were seriously ill. He knew the work he was doing was important and consumed most of his time, he told Sue; the growth of a man was slow and painful, and so too was the growth of a nation, but when the work was done, he would "justly give way to my soul's longings, and fly right back to you."[22]

Like the rest of the South Carolinians, Keitt was dissatisfied in some degree with the work of the Provisional Congress, both for what it had done and what it had left undone. At least two—Keitt and Rhett—were prepared to continue their opposition in Charleston. Even before Keitt reached the city, the *Charleston Mercury* published a long commentary on the new Constitution that repeated many of his criticisms. The writer, who may have been Rhett or even Keitt himself, first conceded that the Constitution was "the best . . . ever devised by man"; its prohibition of protective tariffs and internal improvements made it far superior to the document it replaced. But, he insisted, it contained serious flaws that had to be corrected at once. The convention had retained some of the weakest provisions of the U.S. Constitution. Instead of creating an Electoral College, it should have transferred power to select the president and vice-president to the state legislatures. If the members of the legislatures elected the president, popular agitation and political expediency would no longer determine the results. Instead of retaining the three-fifths clause, it should have based representation in Congress on the total population of each state. If it counted women and children as "persons," it should count slaves as well. Instead of retaining the prohibition against the African slave trade, it should have referred the question to the Congress. It should not have prohibited Congress from appropriating funds not requested by the president or members of his cabinet. Finally, it should have forbidden the Congress to admit non-slaveholding states to the Confederacy.[23]

When the state convention reassembled on March 26, a majority of the delegates expressed serious concerns about defects in the completed Constitution. In spite of their objections and in spite of Keitt's "able and cunning arguments" in favor of voting it down, the delegates were unwilling to postpone ratification for more than a few days. On April 3, with the confrontation in Charleston harbor growing more threatening by the day, they voted to approve the Constitution and wait until the Confederacy was "securely established and in peaceful operation" before pushing for amendments. On April 3, Keitt and Rhett cast their ballots with the majority.[24]

Keitt was in Charleston late in March when Ward Lamon announced that Abraham Lincoln had sent him to arrange the evacuation of Fort Sumter. In his memoirs, Lamon described a confrontation with a mob that was threatening to lynch him. He was saved when Keitt arrived, recognized him, and took him off to the nearest bar, depriving the mob of its quarry and inspiring Lamon to declare his rescuer "cultivated, manly, noble, hospitable, brave, and generous," a description that would have dumbfounded all of Keitt's enemies and many of his friends.[25]

Two days after he reluctantly voted to ratify the new Constitution, Keitt learned that his father was seriously ill. He immediately obtained a leave of absence from the convention and started for home. George Keitt, sixty-six years old and badly crippled by arthritis, died April 19, soon after his son's arrival in St. Matthews.[26]

For Keitt it was a particularly frustrating time to be away from Charleston. After months of negotiation, the crisis in Charleston harbor had finally come to a head. For months Confederate officials had believed that Lincoln would order the evacuation of Fort Sumter, but on April 8, word reached the city that a relief expedition was on the way. After hurried consultations with his cabinet, Davis ordered Gen. P. G. T. Beauregard to seize the fort. The bombardment began early in the morning of April 12, continued all day, slackened that night, but increased in intensity the following morning. In mid-afternoon of the second day, convinced that continued resistance would be futile, Major Robert Anderson capitulated. His surrender set off wild celebrations all across the South.[27]

Keitt buried his father on April 20 and the following day left St. Matthews to attend the special session of the Confederate Congress scheduled to convene on April 29.[28] Back in Montgomery after an absence of almost three weeks, he joined in the work of preparing the country for war. Sitting almost continuously until May 21, the Congress enacted legislation critically important to the new Confederacy. On May 2, it recognized the existence of war with the United States, and over the next three weeks reorganized the army and navy, authorized the Treasury Department to issue interest-bearing bonds, debated imposing an embargo on cotton, and admitted the four southern states that left the Union when Lincoln called for troops. Finally, it moved the capital north to Richmond, squarely into the path of invading Yankee armies. Keitt took a significant part only in the debate over the embargo. After the Congress reconvened in July, he introduced a resolution instructing the Committee on Foreign Affairs to report a bill imposing an embargo on cotton, tobacco, and naval stores. He assumed that economic pressure would force England and France to intervene on the side of the Confederacy in order to restore the flow of cotton across the Atlantic. Davis feared that an embargo would alienate the government's European friends and undermine its European credit, and used his influence to defeat the bill before it emerged from the committee.[29]

In mid-May, Keitt took time from his legislative duties to write to Hammond, describing for his friend the activities of the Confederate government and speculating about the course the war would take. The curtain might rise at any moment, Keitt warned. Gen. Winfield Scott might try to recapture Norfolk or Harpers Ferry before the end of the summer, but it was more likely that fighting would not break out before the end of the year. Scott was too prudent to launch an invasion until he had at least forty thousand regulars, and it would be fall before he would be ready to move.[30]

Virginia, Keitt thought, would be the principal theater of the war, and the Confederacy would need a hundred thousand men to defend the state. They had men enough, he told Hammond, and courage enough, but far too little money. The administration was inefficient; it wasted time feuding over offices and patronage, and lacked sufficient energy to carry out the momentous task of defending the new nation. With leadership like theirs, he wondered, how could the country survive?[31]

On May 21, the Congress adjourned. Keitt spent a few weeks at "Mandeville" and then set out for Richmond, the new capital of the Confederacy. On the train going north, he was bitterly critical of the way Jefferson Davis was preparing for war. Even after James Chesnut and his wife boarded the train at Camden, he continued to berate the administration. Chesnut, now an aide-de-camp to the president, listened in silence. His wife found Keitt "original and entertaining," but when he pronounced Davis "a failure and his cabinet a farce," she was clearly amazed. Should he not reserve judgment until the administration had fairly gotten underway, she asked? Not at all, Keitt replied; the failure of the administration was "a foregone conclusion."[32]

Occasionally Keitt stopped abusing the government and amused his traveling companions with funny stories. In the one Mary Chesnut enjoyed most he imitated a Georgia man talking about volunteers for the Confederate Army. They tried their soldiers before they enlisted them, he said, to see if they were hot enough. If they did not "sizz" when recruiters threw water on them, "they won't do; their patriotism is too cool."[33]

Keitt's conversation with the Chesnuts marked the end of a critical transformation in his political philosophy. During his four terms in Congress, he had thrown himself wholeheartedly into the battle to limit the power of the federal government. During the constitutional convention in Montgomery, he had worked to create a government that would be too weak to interfere in the affairs of the states. But the outbreak of war brought about a striking change in his thinking. He began to assail Davis for failing to prosecute the war with greater energy and to advocate steps to increase the power of the central government that would have been all but inconceivable only a few weeks before, evidence that he was prepared to sacrifice ideological consistency to win the struggle for southern independence. Unfortunately for the Confederacy, this willingness to abandon the rights of the states and the freedoms of individual southerners was one that fire-eaters like Rhett and Yancey and moderates like Stephens were never willing to imitate.[34]

Soon after Keitt reached Richmond, his interest in the activities of the Congress cooled noticeably. Frustrated by his failure to influence the events of the past months, angered by what he considered the administration's inept preparations for war, jealous of friends who had exchanged politics for service in the field, he became increasingly eager to take a more active role in the war. In July, when a Union advance toward Centreville promised to bring on the first major engagement since the attack on Fort Sumter, he hurried north to get a firsthand look at the fighting.[35]

Back in Richmond after the battle of Manassas, Keitt wrote to Sue about his first taste of combat. The Confederate victory at Manassas had badly demoralized the enemy, he told her. All the fight was gone out of the Union, and the war should be over by January. If General Beauregard had only had fresh troops in reserve, he could have pursued the Yankees back to Washington and even occupied the city. Still, the capture of Washington would have meant very little; strategically, it had almost no value, and Beauregard had too few troops to hold it. The most important benefit of the battle, he thought, would be diplomatic. The Confederate commissioners in Europe had accomplished nothing, but now they could use the victory to force England and France to recognize southern independence.[36]

Confederate troops had handled themselves well during the battle, Keitt reported, but the Yankees had behaved like barbarians. During their march into Virginia, they had burned everything in their path, and after the battle, they left their wounded for Beauregard to care for. When he left the field, the Yankees had still not sent details to bury their dead. In the equipment they left behind on the battlefield, he had found ten wagons loaded with handcuffs, intended no doubt to shackle captured Confederate officers. However bad the behavior of the enemy, Keitt concluded, the South must always observe the laws of civilized warfare.[37]

After his trip to Manassas Junction, Keitt participated only sporadically in the work of the Congress, supported the losing side on most recorded votes, and left Richmond to return to Bennettville on August 21, ten days before it adjourned. The night before his departure, he wrote to Hammond to express his profound misgivings about the administration's prosecution of the war. The Confederacy, he wrote, was "building upon the most unsubstantial foundations." If the war lasted very long, the administration's economic policy would force the South into bankruptcy. Memminger was trying to run the Treasury Department like a small-town bank. He insisted on levying direct taxes, and Keitt could not imagine where South Carolina would get sixteen million dollars to pay its share. The government refused to take cotton in exchange for treasury notes but demanded notes in payment for taxes. If England would raise the Union blockade, South Carolina could easily get the money it needed, but if the blockade remained intact, the taxes would cause real distress among the people. If only one man in the ranks had his property sold because he could not pay his taxes, Keitt warned, the people would turn against the government. Economic hardship would force them to accept a dishonorable peace.[38]

The victory at Manassas had done the Confederacy little good in Europe, Keitt admitted. England and France would not recognize southern independence or raise the blockade until their interests required it. Almost half of the men in the army were sick; the hospitals were inadequate, and the "commissariat" was "wretched." The troops lacked shoes, woolen clothing, even gunpowder, and there was none to be had anywhere. If the government forced its soldiers to live from hand to mouth, the army would simply melt away. "We are fighting," he concluded bitterly, "with one hand tied behind our backs."[39] Keitt was never reluctant to express his opinions. In July, Mary Boykin Chesnut recorded William H. Trescot's comment that Keitt hated Jeff Davis, and a month later quoted the wife of Louis Wigfall, who had declared triumphantly that Keitt was part of a coalition opposed to Davis.[40]

The Provisional Congress convened for the last time on November 18. Keitt arrived in Richmond on December 14, attended two sessions and left again, called home by the birth of his second daughter, Stella Marie.[41] Two months before, he had announced that he would not stand for election to the first permanent Congress. Disappointed by his failure to contribute significantly to the work of the government and fascinated by dreams of military glory, he gave up his seat and returned to South Carolina. He did attend the third session of the state convention that met in late December, created an executive council, and gave it extraordinary powers over the state's military affairs. What he really wanted was to raise a regiment and lead it in battle. "Lance couched and banners flying," he would take his place among the heroes of the Confederacy.[42]

In mid-January 1862, Colonel Laurence Keitt arrived in Charleston to take command of his new regiment, the Twentieth South Carolina Volunteers. Earlier in the month, he had told Mary Chesnut her husband would command the regiment and he would be the executive officer. Unexpectedly Chesnut was appointed to the newly created state executive council, leaving Keitt in command of the regiment. He found the regiment, some eight hundred men in all, bivouacked on an old racetrack on the outskirts of the city. The unit had already reached its minimum authorized strength. Rumors that it was slated for garrison duty in South Carolina had lured into the ranks men who otherwise might have tried to avoid military service.[43]

The first meeting of the colonel and his men must have been an unsettling experience for both. Keitt confronted troops newly recruited from half a dozen up-country districts, rough, half-literate, fiercely independent, suspicious of their officers and unsure of themselves. They in turn faced a politician widely admired for his Yankee-baiting oratory and fiery temper, but a man who had almost no military experience. Keitt's friends habitually addressed him as "Colonel," but it was an honorary title, acquired years earlier during a brief term as an aide-de-camp on the staff of Gov. John L. Manning.[44]

On the day he arrived, the regiment elected Keitt its colonel and Olin Dantzler its lieutenant colonel.[45] With the formalities disposed of, Keitt launched his men into a round of activities intended to transform them from raw recruits into disciplined soldiers. Men in all wars have found the routine of camp life alternately boring and exhausting, and Keitt's men were no exception. For six weeks, one day passed very much like every other. Armed with Hardee's *Tactics,* an instructional manual, fledgling officers of both armies conducted never-ending drills: squad and company drill in the morning, regimental drill in the afternoon. Sergeants presided over never-ending details: guard mounts, sick calls, dress parades, and inspections.[46]

Unlike his men, Keitt found his new life in camp "stirring." "From 8 to 9," he explained to his wife, "I sign furloughs, either to go home or to go to the city. From 9 to ten I sign orders for rations. At 12 I get reports from officers. At 5 I review the regiment."[47] Keitt's troops complained openly about the quality of camp food. One company commander told his family of having to drink "pea coffee" and eat "floating batteries" for supper and again for breakfast. Keitt disagreed; the food, he said, was first-rate. He could requisition the commissary officer for anything he had. The beef was tough but plentiful, and nearby rivers and marshes yielded large quantities of fish and birds. No doubt the colonel was eating better than his men.[48]

Keitt would have had more difficulty rebutting the same officer when he quipped that the regiment had been stationed at the race grounds "for the purpose of getting measles." The camp's sanitary facilities were inadequate, preventive medicine was in its infancy, and unseasoned troops were highly susceptible to communicable diseases. Keitt's regiment was particularly hard hit. Victims of measles and varioloid filled Charleston's military hospitals and forced the colonel to keep many of his stricken men in camp. It was not until mid-February that the epidemic had run its course, and the unit was issued weapons and could begin training in earnest.[49]

Keitt begged Sue to visit him in Charleston before the regiment left for garrison duty on the coast. It could not move until it was supplied with weapons, he told her, and until more of his men were off the sick list. It would be "in first rate trim" in two weeks, and he wanted to show off his men before the sheen had worn off their new uniforms: gray jackets and trousers, and red flannel shirts. Apparently Sue did join her husband in the city for an extended visit. Keitt's letters home ended abruptly late in January and did not resume until early in April.[50]

In February the weather suddenly turned cold, rain fell in sheets, and Keitt's men had something more to complain about. The wind was blowing hard, an officer told his wife, and forcing sand into his tent. His cot had not floated away yet, but it would if the Ashley River rose much higher. There was no fire in his tent, and it was overcrowded, but at least he was eating better. He could buy plenty of cabbages, apple dumplings, and beefsteaks at the market, and oysters were plentiful. If she would send his heavy coat, a ham, and a few chickens, he could live "finely" for the rest of the winter.[51]

On March 4, Keitt and the Twentieth South Carolina left Charleston for garrison duty on the coast. For a time the regiment was stationed on James Island, southwest of the city. After about a month, it moved to the upper end of Sullivan's Island to fill a gap in the perimeter defenses of Charleston harbor created when the First South Carolina was transferred to Virginia.[52]

The Union assault on the Confederacy's Atlantic coast began in the fall of 1861. Confederate officials had long known the Yankees were coming, but the coast was long and cut by dozens of rivers; they had too few men and guns and could do little to counter the offensive. The forts guarding Port Royal fell November 7 after a battle that lasted only four hours. The defeat cost the South the best natural harbor on the entire coast. The fall of Roanoke Island on February 7 forced the evacuation of Norfolk and opened the James River to the Union Navy. By the end of March, every port on the Atlantic coast except Charleston and Wilmington was in federal hands or closed by federal blockade.[53]

Around Charleston, officers and men worked feverishly to prepare for the attack they knew was coming. Keitt spent much of his time strengthening Battery Marshall on Sullivan's Island, an earth-and-sod fort that anchored the northern flank of the Confederate line.[54] The first blockader arrived off Charleston in May 1861, and the Union Navy gradually increased the number of ships until December 1862, when the blockade was largely effective. Efforts to close the harbor by sinking a "stone fleet" in the ship channels failed when the wrecks sank into the mud.[55]

In spite of the growing Union threat, Keitt's letters home reflected more concern for the war in the West than the threat to Charleston harbor. "I am not . . . too sanguine," Keitt told his wife. Everybody in the city was celebrating the great Confederate victory at Shiloh. Albert Sidney Johnston had whipped Ulysses Grant and 35,000 Federal troops, but now Johnston was dead and Don Carlos Buell was bringing Grant 75,000 reinforcements. What would be the outcome of the next battle only time would tell. If the Confederates won, Keitt speculated, "the neck of the war is broken," but if they lost, it would be disastrous. Defeat would force them to give up the Mississippi Valley. The South could far better afford to lose Virginia and the government take to its heels than

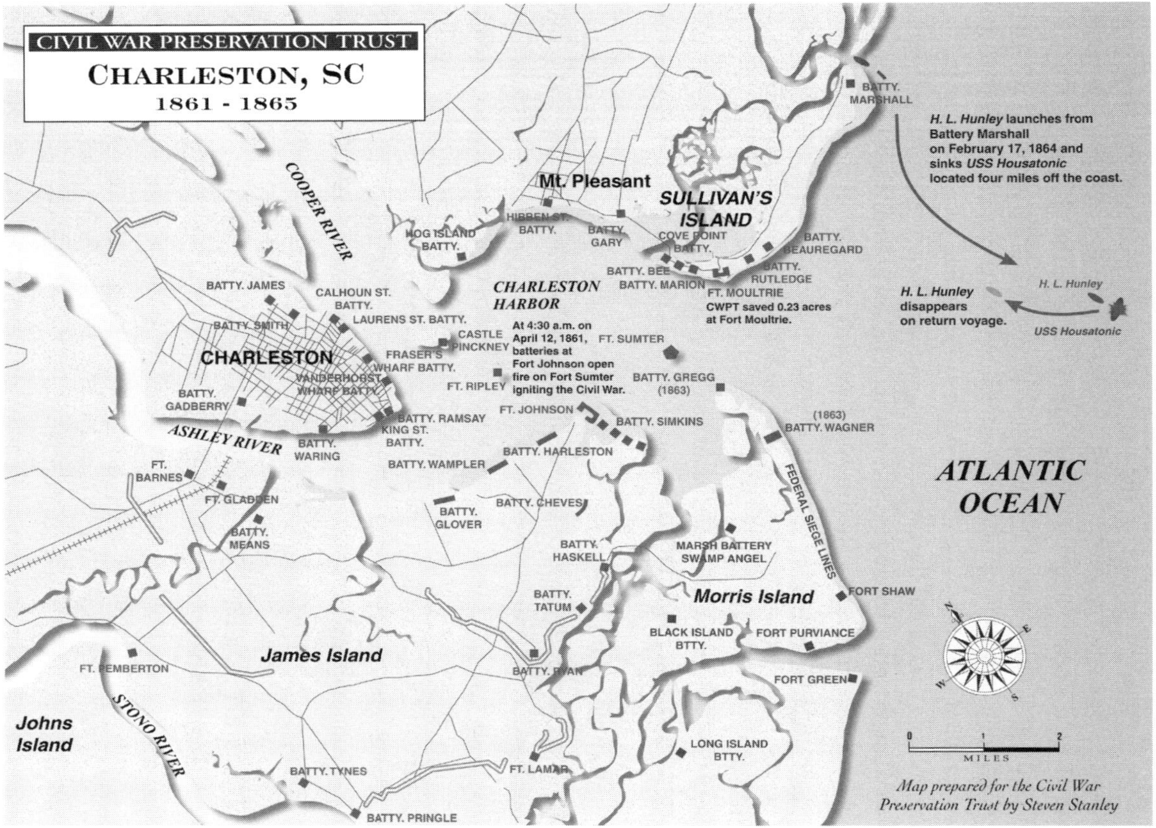

Defenses of Charleston Harbor, Civil War Trust. By permission of Mary Koik.

to lose the fight in Tennessee. He was afraid they were facing another loss as disastrous as Fort Donelson. The men were "enthusiastic, determined, and recklessly daring," Keitt continued, and led by the best generals in the Confederacy. They would win if it were in the power of so few to defeat so many.[56]

What Keitt did not know was that Buell had reinforced Grant at Shiloh with 25,000 men, counter-attacked, and forced P. G. T. Beauregard to retreat south to Corinth in northern Mississippi. What he did understand was the critical importance of the war in the West. What he did not recognize was the incompetence of the Confederate generals in the area.[57] Early in May, he assured Sue that the Confederates would retain control of the Mississippi Valley, and with God's help they would emerge victorious. If the enemy failed in the West, he would have to fight in Virginia, and if he lost there, the war would be over. "A little more marauding, a little more arson," a few more months to negotiate the border between the two countries, he assured her, and they would be together again.[58]

As time passed and their separation continued, Keitt's letters to Sue became increasingly tender. He realized that he would be absent from her for a long time, and might never see her again. Early in May he told her, "I feel more keenly than ever my love for you, and how much you are bound up with my existence." He feared she had become his very religion. He did not think he feared death more than a gentleman should. If death would not tear him away from her, he could be almost indifferent to it. He could part from his daughters, and his anguish would be terrible, but if he were separated from her for eternity, it would destroy his very soul.[59]

On May 4, 1862, Keitt reminded Sue that it was their eldest daughter's birthday and the month of their marriage three years before. If only the war would end, he could be with his family once more: "I hope, dark as the sky looks now, the end is nigh. . . . I think the war must end soon, or it must become internecine and almost endless. The latter is against the genius of civilization and the Christianity which underlies the conduct of modern nations."[60]

Keitt was not always so pessimistic, but his emotions did seem to fluctuate almost from minute to minute. Even after the fall of New Orleans, he insisted that the loss of its coastal cities would benefit the Confederacy because it would free the troops that were defending them to take the war into the North. But always he was bitterly critical of Jefferson Davis. The president had made himself "odious." To be a patriot, a man had to hate him. His imbecility was "as mischievous as treachery. . . . He ought to get a rope and hang himself."[61]

Keitt told Hammond much the same thing. Southern men were fighting with incredible heroism. At Ft. Donelson, they had fought in snow and sleet and rain and mud and surrendered only when they could fight no longer. Southern women were sacrificing their sons and their jewelry to the cause, but Davis's

Colonel L. M. Keitt. Courtesy of South Caroliniana Library, University of South Carolina.

"supreme imbecility" had "well nigh undone us." A great leader would have led us to victory long ago, but the administration "betrays and dwarfs everything." Hammond agreed: Davis was a "Polyphemus," but Keitt and his colleagues in the Congress had elected him even though he was obviously unfit to hold the position. He had imposed a tyranny on the people, and "neither the saintly Barnwell, nor Toombs the Cynic, nor the chivalric Keitt, nor honest Hunter, nor Memminger the Wise, nor rampant Wigfall" had warned the people of his treachery. Keitt was convinced the president was too weak to prosecute the war to a successful conclusion, and must have been amazed to learn that Hammond considered him a despot.[62]

In the same letter in which he condemned Davis as an imbecile, Keitt revealed a surprising ignorance of the military situation less than a dozen miles from Sullivan's Island. Only two days before the Union offensive got under way, he assured Hammond that Charleston was in no immediate danger. "I doubt if a serious attack is contemplated at this time," Keitt wrote. "It will come in time, I have no doubt, but not now." John C. Pemberton—the general commanding the Military District of South Carolina and Georgia, Keitt's immediate superior—thought the enemy had landed at least 10,000 men on James Island, but Keitt was certain Pemberton was wrong. The Confederates had 15,000 troops on the island, and there was too little room for more. "If we make it here a game of mechanics," Keitt continued, "Charleston will fall." The Confederates had too few big guns and too few men; if they dug in, the game was up. He had proposed that they open the fighting on the island tomorrow or the next day, but anything could change their plans and probably would.[63]

Early in June, the blow the Confederates had been expecting for months finally fell. On June 2, 12,000 Union troops under the command of Gen. Henry Benham landed on the southwestern tip of James Island and pushed rapidly inland. On the morning of the sixteenth, they assaulted Confederate lines west of Secessionville. The attack was badly coordinated, Union casualties were heavy, and after three hours of hand-to-hand fighting, Benham ordered a retreat. In July the Union pulled its troops off the island.[64]

The narrow escape convinced Pemberton that the defenses of Charleston were dangerously inadequate. As part of his reorganization of his command, Pemberton put Keitt in charge of Sullivan's Island, a position he held until May 1864. The island, a key to the Confederate defense of the harbor, was shaped like a crescent, almost four miles long but only a few hundred yards across at its widest point. At its southern end, where it hooked into the mouth of the harbor, it was heavily fortified; Battery Bee, Fort Moultrie, and Battery Beauregard mounted a total of forty guns. But for most of its length it was defended only by widely scattered rifle pits. At its northern end, Battery Marshall anchored the left flank of the city's defenses.[65]

"General Pemberton tells me that he means to work vigorously to make the city impregnable," Keitt told Sue in July. The general wanted to construct a sixteen-gun battery on Sullivan's Island and a similar battery on Morris Island on the opposite side of the harbor. When they were completed, the harbor would be ringed by two hundred guns, enough to sink the heaviest ship afloat. The city would be safe from any fleet the Yankees could send against it. If they could destroy the Yankee blockade, Keitt concluded, they would have earned the laurels that grateful citizens would shower down on them.[66]

After the Battle of Secessionville, the Union threat to Charleston eased, and work on the defenses of city continued, but the assault officials knew was coming did not occur. Charleston was quiet, Keitt told Sue, "unstirred by even the breath of rumor."[67] As the weeks passed and the Union army failed to renew its assault on the city, the strain of garrison life began to tell on Keitt and his men. Food was still the chief target for complaints. One man even criticized the chicken his wife sent from home: "We tried it for supper, then the boys biled it for breakfast, (you know it was roasted at home) then they stewed it for dinner. This time it was very good." Boredom created almost as many complaints as hunger. The regiment was "doing as near nothing here as men generally do in camp," blockade runners entering and leaving the harbor provided the only amusement, morale suffered, and one officer concluded that the colonel was rapidly losing the respect of his regiment. If only Keitt would resign, he wrote, it would be a blessing to the men. Unfortunately there was no hope he would take so wise a step. Keitt was staying in Mount Pleasant with his family, but his officers could not even get passes to visit the city. The regiment was still armed with ancient smoothbore muskets. At least there was little danger that the unit would go to Virginia, where the war was being fought in earnest. Keitt did not want to leave the island, and he had enough influence to keep his unit where it was.[68]

Keitt was not so sure. "The fire of battles is about to run all along our lines," he told Sue in December. The opposing armies had enacted only the opening scenes of the drama, and already many gallant leaders had fallen. Five thousand men—three regiments from Charleston and three more from Savannah—had just left for North Carolina to stop a Union drive to cut the railroad at Goldsboro. His regiment had not gone; it played too vital a role in the defense of the city.[69]

Keitt had told Hammond much the same thing a month earlier. The country was approaching a crisis. He was hopeful of the outcome, but first their state would experience a shock few of its people could even imagine. The Union would make a desperate effort to ward off intervention by European powers by attacking their cities. The blow would fall on Charleston in January.[70]

Little occurred to relieve the boredom of men preparing to meet an attack that never came. In the fall, Keitt's regiment received orders to repel a Union attempt to cut the Charleston and Savannah Railroad near Coosawatchie, just inland from the Union naval base at Port Royal. Confederate troops in the area forced the Yankee raiding party to withdraw before the unit could reach of the scene and deprived Keitt's men of their first taste of combat. Early the following year, two companies from the Twentieth participated in the capture of a Union gunboat in the Stono River. With those exceptions, nothing disturbed the monotony of life in garrison.[71]

In September 1862, Jefferson Davis relieved Pemberton from command of the Department of South Carolina and Georgia and appointed Gen. P. G. T. Beauregard to succeed him. After a brief inspection, Beauregard decided that his predecessor had bungled the defenses of Charleston harbor and took steps to repair the defects. In reorganizing his command, he greatly expanded Keitt's responsibilities. Early in January, he consolidated Sullivan's Island and the mainland between the Cooper and South Santee Rivers into a single department and placed it under Keitt's command.[72]

Keitt set out immediately on a four-day tour of the area. On January 9, he reported to Gen. Roswell Ripley that there was little danger that a Union thrust southward through Saint James Santee or Christ Church parishes could reach the city; the "facilities for defense against such a movement" were "too numerous and conclusive." But the area was extremely vulnerable to plundering and slave-stealing expeditions launched from the enemy fleet. The forty miles of coastline between the Cooper and Santee rivers were cut at frequent intervals by bays, creeks, inlets, and narrows, and posed severe problems for the defenders. Few white people remained on the plantations in the area, and small boats could land unnoticed at almost any point. Guided by slaves intimately acquainted with the coast, Union raiding parties could do untold damage and return to the fleet without encountering effective resistance. "Numbers of negroes . . . along the coast, have deserted to the enemy," Keitt reported, "and are known to have passed frequently between the fleet or the islands and the parishes of Christ-church and St. James Santee." Their knowledge of waterways and fortifications was enormously valuable to the enemy. It was almost as important to keep the slaves in as it was to keep the Yankees out.[73]

To guard the coast, Keitt reported, he had only a handful of troops: three companies of cavalry, two companies of infantry from the Twenty-sixth South Carolina, and a company of artillery, too few men even to patrol the countryside and provide early warning of Union raids. The five companies were continuously engaged in picketing the most vulnerable points along the coast, but many stretches of beach were entirely unguarded, and he had too few men to fill the gaps. Assuming correctly that Beauregard could give him no more men, Keitt suggested that the artillery company could be used more effectively. If it were broken into sections, the guns could fortify the largest creeks, closing them to all but federal ironclads. Beauregard flatly rejected Keitt's recommendation. The artillery must remain where it was, he told the colonel; small works inadequately defended would invite attack and could not easily be reinforced. He could spare no more troops to defend the mainland; Keitt would have to get along with what he had.[74]

After the failure of the landings on James Island, the Union Army abandoned its attempt to get into Charleston by the back door and turned over the job of taking the city to the navy. During the next nine months, Adm. Samuel F. DuPont assembled at Port Royal what was perhaps the most formidable fleet in the history of naval warfare up to that time: eight monitors and an ironclad frigate. On April 7, 1863, DuPont ordered the fleet into Charleston harbor in a daring attempt to batter down its defenses and force its surrender. For almost an hour, he pressed the attack against the forts but without success. The monitors took a terrible pounding from the Confederate guns and did little damage in return.[75]

When the battle opened, Keitt left Fort Moultrie, where he was conferring with Gen. James H. Trappier, and stationed himself at Battery Bee at the southern tip of Sullivan's Island. There, he believed, he would have a better view of the action. In his report, Keitt praised the "great precision" of the Confederate gunnery. He had seen "a large number" of ten-inch shot strike the three monitors that tried to engage the battery. The storm of metal that fell around the enemy "confused if it did not appall him." He could not accurately estimate the damage done to the three ships, but he was certain it had been severe. Keitt's assessment was on the mark. When the fleet gave up the fight, four of the monitors had been disabled and the frigate *Keokuk* so badly shot up that she sank the next morning. The ten thousand Union troops massed on Folly Island to follow up the naval assault never got into action.[76]

Keitt commended the officers and men of Battery Bee for the courage and skill with which they had fought. His own men, he added unnecessarily, had guarded the batteries at the upper end of Sullivan's Island. The enemy made no attempt to land troops anywhere on the island, and the Twentieth South Carolina took no part in the fighting.[77]

After the failure of the navy to batter its way into Charleston harbor, Union commanders decided to launch a coordinated land-and-sea assault against the city. Troops under Gen. Quincy A. Gillmore would land on Morris Island, bring up heavy artillery, and pound Fort Sumter into rubble. That accomplished, the fleet would run past the remaining forts ringing the harbor and force the city to surrender.[78]

To mask his preparations, Gillmore launched raids up the rivers south of the city. On May 9, Keitt received orders to take the Twentieth South Carolina to Seabrook Island some twenty miles southwest of Charleston to repel a Union raid. Before the regiment reached the island, the Federals withdrew, and Keitt's men returned to Charleston without firing a round.[79] Two weeks later, Keitt and the Twentieth South Carolina were again chasing Yankees. On June 2, several hundred federal troops supported by gunboats pushed up the Combahee River in an attempt to cut the Charleston and Savannah Railroad in the vicinity of Pocataligo. The Confederate commander in the area had too few men to repel the raiders and called for reinforcements. By the time Keitt and his men reached Green Pond five miles north of the river, the raiding party had completed its mission and withdrawn. In his report, Keitt noted that damage in the area was "very great." The Yankee "burning expedition" had destroyed four plantations and carried off at least seven hundred slaves. His regiment had arrived too late to engage the enemy.[80]

Gillmore finally unleashed his assault on the city early on the morning of July 10. In an attempt to divert Beauregard's attention from his primary objective, he landed troops on James Island west of the city and sent a raiding party to burn the railroad bridge over the Edisto River. At dawn, Union batteries on Folly Island supported by monitors began to bombard Confederate positions on the southern end of Morris Island, disabling most of the Confederate guns and inflicting heavy casualties. Three hours later, Union infantry in small boats crossed Lighthouse Inlet and quickly overwhelmed the defenders. Retreating up the island toward Battery Wagner, the Confederates lost all of their guns and almost half of their men. By mid-morning, Union troops were in control of two-thirds of the island.[81]

To plant their guns within range of Fort Sumter, the Federals had to take all of Morris Island, a more formidable task than they had anticipated. The island was approximately four miles long but only two hundred to three hundred yards wide. At its narrowest point, the Confederates had constructed Battery Wagner, a sand-and-earth fort riveted with sod and palmetto logs covering about three acres. Flanked on the east by the Atlantic Ocean and on the west by an impenetrable marsh, it could be approached only from the front along a narrow strip of beach cut by creeks and swept by artillery.[82]

Gillmore tried twice to take the fort by frontal assault. Before dawn on July 11, he sent troops from four regiments straight at the battery. The assault reached the parapet and stalled. In half an hour, it was over, smashed by repeated volleys of canister and musket fire at point-blank range.[83] The night after the attack, Keitt went to Morris Island to survey the damage. Confederate casualties had been extremely light, he reported, only twelve men killed and wounded. The Federals had lost more than a hundred. Damage to the battery had been negligible. Gillmore was bringing up artillery and mortars to shell the fort, and to protect the garrison he recommended that engineers begin constructing bombproofs, shelters constructed of pine logs and buried under twenty feet of sand, at once. The big guns mounted on the land face of the battery were vulnerable to Union artillery fire and should be moved to the sea face and replaced with smaller pieces that could be protected more easily. "A few mortars, large numbers of sandbags, and some reinforcements," Keitt concluded, would make the battery safe for some time to come. Beauregard implemented his recommendations, making the already formidable fortification even stronger and better able to withstand the Union assaults of the weeks ahead.[84]

A week later, Gillmore again tried to take the position by assault. At noon on July 18, Union batteries on Morris Island supported by monitors and gunboats from the fleet began a furious bombardment that continued for ten hours. Inside Battery Wagner, the garrison retired to the bombproofs and suffered few casualties. Just after sunset, the guns fell silent, and Gillmore massed fourteen regiments—a total of 6,000 men—and sent them against the battery. One regiment reached the top of the parapet, and parts of two other regiments penetrated the battery itself, but the defenders repelled both of them and inflicted heavy losses on the attacking columns. When Gillmore called off the assault, he had suffered more than 1,500 casualties, many of them mangled beyond recognition by point-blank artillery fire. Among the dead was Col. Robert Gould Shaw, the commanding officer of the Fifty-fourth Massachusetts, the first black regiment to see extensive action in the war. Confederate losses totaled 174.[85]

After two costly failures to overrun Battery Wagner, Gillmore decided to take the fort by siege. By constructing a network of zigzag trenches, he could push his guns slowly up the island, reduce the range to Sumter and Wagner, and batter both fortifications into rubble. After a week of preparations, he began driving his trenches toward the Confederate stronghold, the work slowed but never stopped by the dogged resistance of the garrison. As the trenches snaked steadily closer, fire from the Union artillery became increasingly effective, silencing the guns in the battery and allowing the sappers to work without interruption.[86]

Inside the battery, conditions became increasingly difficult. The Union bombardment forced the defenders to take cover in the bombproofs, where daytime temperatures soared and little air could circulate. Food and water were scarce; ammunition ran low; the incessant pounding of the Union artillery made sleep impossible and communication with the mainland increasingly difficult. Beauregard realized that troops could not stand up long under such conditions and, in spite of the obvious hazards, replaced the garrison every three days.[87]

On August 1, when Keitt assumed command of the beleaguered battery for the first time, Union troops had pushed their siege lines forward only to the second parallel, still almost nine hundred yards away, and he was able to employ the garrison at night to repair damage done to the battery during the day. When he completed his tour of duty on August 6, the fort had suffered relatively little damage from the bombardment. At the end of the tour, he proposed ways to improve conditions in the battery—increase the size of the bombproofs, lay a pipe to supply fresh water for the men, construct a covered way to the latrines, limit rations to salted meat (fresh meat spoiled in the heat and had to be buried). He refused to let conditions inside the battery undermine his morale. When Beauregard questioned his ability to hold out during a heavy bombardment, he replied, "Send some more limes, rum and sugar and a little water, we'll hold for another day."[88]

When Keitt returned to Morris Island on August 15, he found conditions inside Battery Wagner deteriorating rapidly. In his absence, the enemy had constructed a third parallel that reached within five hundred yards of the fort. Artillery fire from the new position, supported by half a dozen monitors, was doing more damage than the weary defenders could repair. Keitt was hard-pressed to

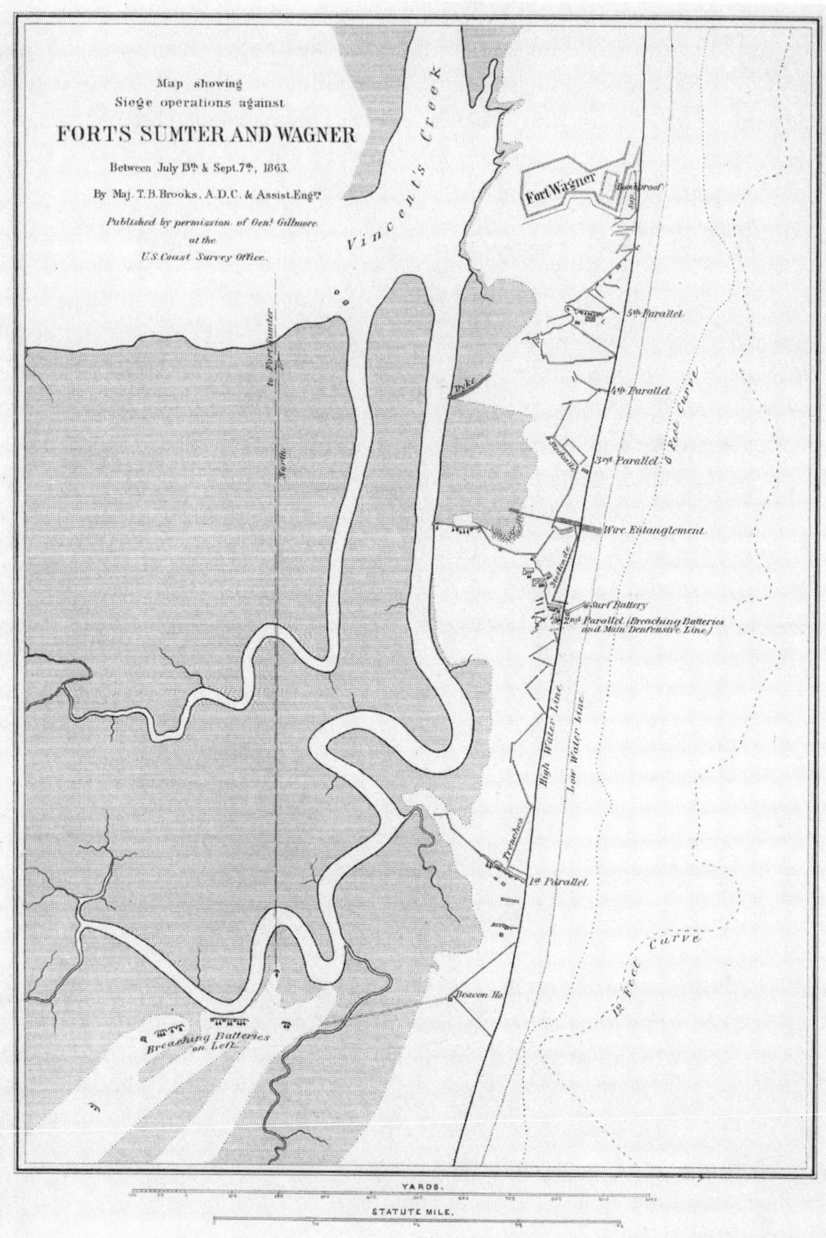

Morris Island. Courtesy of Library of Congress.

keep details at work remounting disabled guns and filling holes blasted in the parapet. Federal sappers working day and night threatened to overrun Confederate rifle pits only 240 yards in front of the parapet. Gen. Roswell Ripley, Keitt's immediate superior, praised his "constancy, bravery, and skill in the performance of . . . trying and arduous duties." Keitt's fears were well founded. The enemy did take the rifle pits on August 27 while he was on Sullivan's Island. The loss was "a great misfortune" because it meant an assault on the battery was not far off. He knew the defenders could not hold the position much longer.[89]

Beauregard realized now that he could not hold Morris Island. When the enemy's siege works reached Battery Wagner, he would have to evacuate the garrison or see it destroyed, but he was determined to hold on until new works on James and Sullivan's islands were complete. Playing for time, he gradually removed guns and men from the fort, leaving behind only a token force to slow the enemy advance. Gillmore, unaware that the Confederate were preparing to abandon the battery, continued to push his trenches forward.[90]

When Keitt returned to Battery Wagner for the last time, on September 2, the end was in sight. At dawn on September 5, Union artillery opened on the fort—causing heavy casualties, driving most of the garrison away from the guns and into the bombproofs, and doing major damage to the fort. There was very little food or water. It was impossible to bury the dead, and bodies decayed rapidly in the heat, fouling the air and making the water unfit to drink. The siege line had reached within fifty yards of the parapet, so close that the defenders could hear Union officers urging on their men. At night, calcium lights illuminated the entire area and made work inside the fort extremely dangerous. Casualties mounted rapidly; on September 5 alone, the garrison lost more than a hundred men.[91]

Keitt knew the battery was untenable. If he held his men inside the bombproofs, the enemy would overrun the fortification in a matter of hours; if he sent them to the parapet, they would be slaughtered by Union artillery and musket fire. After dark on September 5, he sent off a dispatch to Beauregard: "The parapet of the salient is badly breached. The whole fort is much weakened. A repetition to-morrow of today's fire will make the fort almost a ruin. The mortar fire is still very heavy and fatal, and no important work can be done. Is it desirable to sacrifice the garrison[?] To continue to hold it is to do so."[92] Beauregard had already prepared detailed instructions for evacuating the island, but he believed the time had not yet come to put them into operation. Early on the morning of the September 6, he ordered Keitt to hold the battery. Convinced that the general could not be aware of conditions inside Wagner, Keitt sent message after message describing the progress of the siege and demanding instructions: "Incessant fire. . . . Can't work negroes. . . . Had 30 or 40 soldiers wounded in an attempt to work. . . . Fear the garrison will be destroyed without injuring the enemy. . . . I hope that we may stand till to-night."[93]

Just before noon, Keitt dispatched a carefully detailed report to the commanding general. Artillery fire had breached the walls of the battery and was knocking down the bombproofs. The enemy's trenches were only fifty yards away and by nightfall would reach the moat surrounding the parapet. If the garrison were not evacuated that night, it would be killed or captured. Boats must be waiting at the northern tip of the island at dark.[94]

By mid-afternoon, Beauregard had still not replied, and Keitt sent off one last desperate plea for help: "The enemy's sap has reached the moat, and his bombardment has shattered large parts of the parapet. The retention of the post after tonight involves the sacrifice of the garrison. If the necessities of the service make this advisable, the men will cheerfully make it, and I will cheerfully lead them. I prefer to assault the enemy to awaiting an assault, and I will at 4 o'clock in the morning assail his works."[95] Keitt's final message, supported by a report by chief engineer Col. D. B. Harris, finally convinced the general that he could hold the battery no longer. Late on the afternoon of September 6, he sent Keitt orders to evacuate the island that night. Now began one of the most difficult operations in all of warfare, disengagement in the presence of the enemy. Keitt first sent away his sick and wounded, and then the rest of the troops left in the battery. Keitt himself remained at Wagner with a small rear guard, supervising the destruction of guns and equipment he could not carry off to the mainland. At about 1:30 A.M., he was among the last Confederates to leave the island.[96] The Confederates suffered their only losses when a Union gunboat captured two barges carrying troops to the mainland. Not until early in the morning of September 7 did the Union forces in front of the battery realize the Confederates had abandoned the position. Two aspects of the evacuation failed to go according to plan. Keitt's men did not successfully execute his orders to destroy the guns and ammunition they had to abandon. Gillmore reported that he captured nineteen pieces of artillery and a large supply of powder. Fuses laid to the powder magazine in the main bombproof failed to burn, and Union troops occupied a fort that was still partially intact and not a smoking ruin.[97]

Beauregard was generous in his praise of Keitt's conduct of the evacuation. If all had gone according to plan, he concluded, it would have been "one of the most memorable in history." In spite of Keitt's failure to blow up the battery, the operation had been "a signal success." His "coolness and discipline" had saved more than a thousand men for the Confederacy.[98]

The fall of Battery Wagner ended the first phase of Keitt's military education. He had transformed himself from a fire-eating politician into a competent infantry colonel, and compiled a solid though hardly distinguished record. He had raised, equipped, and trained the Twentieth South Carolina Volunteers, and led the regiment throughout the defense of Charleston harbor. For much of that time, he and his men had done little to set themselves apart from every other unit fighting to keep the Yankees out of the city. But in the battle for Battery Wagner, they had truly distinguished themselves. In the face of overwhelming odds, rapidly failing conditions, and almost certain defeat, they had fought gallantly until continued resistance had become suicidal, and had evacuated the island with enormous courage and skill.

Keitt's conduct during the harrowing days and weeks inside Fort Wagner had been truly heroic. He had proved to himself that he could face death without flinching, and that he could lead men in combat. But the men he led had fought from behind fortifications; he had not proved—had not had an opportunity to prove—that he could lead men in the field. When that opportunity at last arrived, he failed spectacularly.

ELEVEN

"Proudly the Southern Cross still floats to the breeze"

With the fall of Battery Wagner, Keitt's active role in the defense of Charleston harbor had almost come to an end. In mid-September, he moved the Twentieth South Carolina from Sullivan's Island, now within easy range of the Union guns, to a safer location on the mainland. For the next nine months, the regiment camped near Mount Pleasant on the grounds of the Moultrie House, a resort hotel patronized before the war by wealthy Charlestonians. From there it could support the batteries north of the harbor, shuttling troops between the mainland and the island at regular intervals, guarding against raids launched from the enemy fleet.[1]

Even at Mount Pleasant, Keitt's men were "living about as low down" as before. The water was pure, the air was fresh, and Union artillery was less threatening, but the lack of food was an everyday concern. There were no vegetables, and the only meat was bacon. Keitt would not let them go to Charleston to buy groceries, but that did not matter. There was almost nothing in the city for sale.[2]

With all of Morris Island in Union hands and Fort Sumter reduced to rubble, it should have been an easy matter for Quincy Gillmore to smash his way into the inner harbor and force the city to capitulate. He had only to plant artillery on the northern tip of the island, destroy the Confederate fortifications at long range, and open the harbor to the Union fleet. Instead, he decided to force the surrender of Fort Sumter before he attacked the city.

Three weeks before the Confederates evacuated Battery Wagner, Gillmore turned his guns against Sumter, bombarding the fort day and night without interruption. So destructive was the fire that Beauregard moved most of the guns and men from the fort to James and Sullivan's islands. The reduced fire from the fort convinced Gillmore that he could easily seize it. On the night of September 7, Admiral John Dahlgren sent sailors and marines to occupy the ruin in the harbor. The garrison resisted stubbornly, and the Yankees withdrew, leaving behind five boats and more than a hundred prisoners.[3] The bombardment resumed, and long before it ended in early December had reduced the fort to rubble, but Gillmore made no further attempt to occupy it.[4] With winter coming on and operations in the harbor largely suspended, Keitt could turn his attention to matters he had long neglected: his family and his military career.

From the beginning of his military service, Keitt was determined to be a general officer. Late in 1861, when he decided not to run for reelection to the Confederate Congress, he applied to the War Department for a commission as a brigadier general. He had earned the commission, Keitt was convinced, by his long and faithful service to his state and section. The government had commissioned hundreds of politicians without military training. It had made generals of Maxcy Gregg and James Chesnut; it should do as much for him.

In January 1862, Keitt had to be satisfied with a colonelcy. After he had organized the Twentieth South Carolina Volunteers and won election as its commanding officer, he withdrew his request for higher rank, but he never gave up his ambition to wear a wreath around his stars, and whenever he had the opportunity, he never failed to campaign for promotion.[5]

Early in the war, long before he had an opportunity to distinguish himself, Keitt's friends and political colleagues began bombarding the War Department with requests for his promotion. Petitions poured in: from Confederate congressmen Louis Wigfall of Texas and Thomas Bocock of Virginia, Governor John Letcher of Virginia, political allies Porcher Miles and William Boyce, and from generals P. G. T. Beauregard, Roswell S. Ripley, and John C. Pemberton. All of these men had antagonized Jefferson Davis at one time or another; none of them had any real influence with the War Department, and it cost the administration nothing to ignore their recommendations.[6]

After the fall of Battery Wagner, Keitt turned his full attention to securing a promotion. In a letter to Davis, he described his role in the defense of Charleston harbor and argued that he deserved to be promoted. For almost two years, Keitt told the president, his regiment had been a part of the Charleston garrison. On three occasions, he had volunteered his men for duty in the field, once during the Seven Days battles around Richmond and once when Lee began his invasion into Maryland. On both occasions, General Pemberton had turned down his request, explaining that the regiment was essential to the defense of Charleston. When the War Department sent Pemberton to Vicksburg, he had volunteered to take his regiment west, but again without success. Instead, he had retained his command of Sullivan's Island and the mainland parishes adjacent to it, a position that should have been held by a brigadier general. During the defense of Battery Wagner, he had shared command of that post with two general officers. He had conducted the evacuation of the battery and extricated the garrison without the loss of a man.[7]

In the same letter, Keitt defended himself against charges that he had violated the Conscription Act of February 1862. To avoid being drafted and sent to infantry regiments in the field, men commonly volunteered for less hazardous duty closer to home. Commanding officers frequently accepted the volunteers, even after their units had exceeded their authorized strengths. The most blatant offender, according to Superintendent of Conscription Col. John S. Preston, was Laurence Keitt.[8]

Before Congress had adopted the Conscription Act, Keitt reminded Davis, Secretary of War Judah P. Benjamin had given him permission to accept four companies of volunteers, even though they would increase the size of his regiment beyond the limits established by the War Department. Some months ago at the request of General Beauregard, he had mounted them as cavalry and assigned them to duty patrolling the coastline north of Charleston. At about the same time, he had organized a company of light artillery from men not liable to conscription. Secretary of War James A. Seddon had granted him permission to accept the volunteers, even though infantry regiments did not normally include cavalry or artillery.[9]

He was the senior colonel in the Department of South Carolina, Georgia, and Florida, Keitt concluded. For more than a year, he had been carrying out the duties of a general officer; he deserved to be promoted. If necessary, he would raise enough troops to expand his regiment into a brigade.[10]

Not satisfied by Davis's evasive reply to his letter—the president tried to encourage him to raise additional troops but refused to promise him a promotion—Keitt secured a ten-day leave and went to Richmond. There, he enlisted the aid of old friends and paid a brief visit to the War Department.[11] The trip was not successful, and in mid-December 1863, less than two weeks after his return to Charleston, Keitt wrote to Seddon. He noted that the secretary had granted him permission to raise another regiment and proposed that he organize a cavalry regiment instead of the infantry regiment Seddon had originally authorized. The topography of the South Carolina coast required a larger force of cavalry, Keitt argued, and he could recruit cavalry more quickly than infantry. The army's shortage of horses would not pose a problem because the men would provide their own mounts. Seddon agreed to the change but stipulated that Keitt could not accept men liable to conscription under existing laws.[12]

Apparently Keitt found recruiting a new regiment in war-ravaged South Carolina more difficult than he had expected. Late in December, he wrote to Adjutant

General Thomas Jordan, and in January 1864 directly to Davis, this time asking for the command of a brigade already in service. During a recent conversation, Keitt told the president, Secretary Seddon had assured him that he would be promoted as soon as he took command of a brigade. That brigade could be created by uniting his Twentieth South Carolina Volunteers—now composed of ten companies of infantry, six of cavalry, and one of artillery—with the First South Carolina Infantry and another unbrigaded regiment stationed in Charleston. Altogether, the three regiments would number at least three thousand men, enough for a regulation-size brigade.[13]

Keitt's letter must have taken Davis and Seddon by surprise. Both men were probably amazed that Keitt could openly criticize the president and then ask him for promotion. He could not recall the exact language he had used in his conversation with Colonel Keitt, Seddon told Davis. He had led Keitt to believe that only the lack of a brigade had prevented his promotion and suggested that he try to raise one. If he were successful, he could expect to be promoted immediately. In any event, Seddon bluntly reminded his chief, he had acted "strictly in the line chalked out by yourself."[14]

Less than a week later, Davis found an excuse to deny the promotion Keitt wanted so desperately. The Department of South Carolina, Georgia, and Florida included four brigades commanded by generals John Wise, Nathan G. Evans, Johnson Hagood, and Alfred Colquitt. In all, thirteen brigadier generals were serving in the department, nine of them without commands. It would not be possible, he concluded, to create additional general officers at that time.[15]

As late as February 1864, Keitt still believed he would be promoted as soon as Seddon could give him a brigade. "I got a letter from Richmond," he told Sue, "kindly in its expressions . . . assuring me that it will soon be fixed." He had already told Davis he would not take the brigade commanded by Nathan Evans. It was "utterly spoiled," and the war would end before he could get it back into fighting trim. Beauregard would have to make up a new one for him.[16] In spite of his optimism, Keitt could not deceive himself much longer. In mid-February, he had still not heard from the president. Davis had decided not to promote him, he told Sue bitterly, and lacked the courage to tell him so.[17]

Long after the war, Sue Keitt tried to explain why her husband had not received the promotion she thought he deserved. It was, she wrote—expressing a belief Keitt no doubt had shared—"because human nature being not perfect, a great man's personal vanity being offended, prejudice had engendered a great injustice." In 1862, when the Provisional Confederate Congress elected a president, Keitt had supported Robert Toombs, and Davis had never forgiven him. Every man who had endorsed Toombs fell into disfavor, and his services, no matter how great, won him no recognition. Again and again, Beauregard and Ripley had recommended Keitt for promotion, but always without success. Davis's vanity was "immovable."[18]

Sue refused to concede that combat had severely reduced the number of men in the ranks, that the army had become top heavy with general officers, and that even when vacancies did occur, colonels who had commanded troops in the field had a stronger claim to the promotion than her husband. Politics and prejudice played a part in Keitt's failure to be promoted, but they were hardly the only or even the most important factors.

In mid-October, soon after he had moved his regiment to new quarters near Mount Pleasant, Keitt began begging Sue to visit him. Union forces were shelling Charleston, he admitted, but he would rent rooms for her at the northern edge of the city, beyond the range of the guns.[19] A week later, Keitt assured his wife that the enemy had turned their attention from Charleston to Fort Sumter. The bombardment was very heavy, and the Union forces would probably flatten the fort completely in three weeks. When it finally collapsed, the siege of Charleston would begin in earnest. Until then, it would be safe for her to stay in the city.[20] Apparently Keitt's attempt to convince Sue to join him was successful. His letters to her stopped in late October and did not resume until January 1864. When they did, he repeatedly begged her to return.

In his first letters after her visit, Keitt told Sue that he had just "crushed out" a mutiny among the troops defending Sullivan's Island. He had investigated and realized that reports of the incident were exaggerated, but he had put a few men under arrest. If he had temporized, the situation could easily have gotten out of hand. Their pretext for the mutiny, he reported, was "short rations."[21]

Keitt would have been hard pressed to find men in the garrison who agreed that hunger was only a pretext for dissatisfaction. Only days after the evacuation of Morris Island, a captain in the Twentieth South Carolina complained that the men in his company were living as "low down" as was humanly possible. It was useless to go to Charleston for groceries; there was almost nothing there to buy.[22]

As winter approached and rations became even scarcer, the captain's attention focused increasingly on food. Late in September, he asked his wife to send him some potatoes.[23] Later in the fall, he reported that his men were "almost crazy" for meat. They were eating "beef tripe, tongues, livers, heads, feet," and anything else they could get their hands on. He had just finished off a "wasted goose" that had left a great deal to be desired. Most of the time, he had only bacon, greens, and rice, and rye coffee without sugar. He asked his wife for more potatoes and a suit of blue jeans; a complete officer's uniform was selling for a thousand dollars, and he did not have the money to buy one. At least she did not need to worry that the regiment might be sent to the West. Keitt would not allow the War Department to move it away from Charleston.[24]

In mid-December, the same officer told his wife he had eaten his Christmas feast a week early. A lady had presented him a cabbage, a soldier had given him a roasted chicken and a custard, and another man had given him a wild duck and a big potato. If she were wondering what to give him for Christmas, she should send food. Bread and butter, potatoes, chickens, and sausages would do very well.[25]

Keitt admitted that the men were not to blame for protesting the short rations. The Confederate commissary was wretchedly managed, but Davis clung stubbornly to Commissary General Lucius Northrup and the "poor creatures" who worked under him. They were incapable of learning from their mistakes, Keitt raged, and their incapacity was jeopardizing the entire Confederacy.[26]

The Keitts, at least, were in no danger of going hungry. During a quick trip to Orangeburg in January 1864, Keitt found the town crowded—an entire family was living in his old law office—and his plantation prospering. His cattle and sheep were fat; his slaves were healthy and seemingly contented; his potato crop was the largest ever, and his overseer had just butchered twelve thousand pounds of pork. The place was in good order; the war was still far away.[27]

The condition of his plantation convinced Keitt that the war had not fatally undermined slavery, as many of his colleagues feared. The peculiar institution played too conspicuous a part in the transactions of every southerner; it was too thoroughly embedded in southern politics and society. Come what might, it would emerge from the war unshaken. Still, he told his wife, he would bow to her judgment and buy no more slaves. He already owned 115; that was enough.[28]

With the Yankees doing little to push the siege of Charleston to a successful conclusion, Keitt had time to speculate about the war outside South Carolina. The summer of 1864, he was certain, would bring an end to the fighting. The old Union would collapse in ruins; its final agony would be brief but terrible.[29] Foreign intervention on the side of the Confederacy, he told Sue, was increasingly probable. Only the Confederacy's defense of slavery had kept the great powers of Europe out of the war, but the selfish interests of the Europeans would soon overcome their objections to the institution. Maximilian was in Mexico, and the stability of his government would rest heavily on the success of the Confederacy.[30] Spain too was deeply interested; southern failure would mean the abolition of slavery in Cuba and the loss of huge amounts of property there. Austria would sustain the Hapsburgs, and France would join in when the time was right. Sooner or later, European politics would force the French to come to their aid.[31]

Keitt's optimism did not blind him to the enormous difficulties facing the Confederacy. Dissatisfaction with the government in Richmond was growing steadily, he thought, largely as a result of the "awkward and vexacious [*sic*] manner" in which it was impressing war supplies. There was no real scarcity in the country as a whole, but the army was always short of food, and in some areas people were actually starving. Farmers were unwilling to sell even a part of their crops for fear that commissary officers would seize everything they owned. Interference with property was always dangerous. The government could suspend the writ of habeas corpus, and men would only grumble, but when it invaded their corn cribs, they invariably resisted: "Women may give up their butter and eggs, as well as their sons, to the needs of the country; but men are apt to give up the child and hold on to the granary." The government was to blame for the economic ruin of the country. The "gross and criminal incapacity" of a handful of "impracticable and visionary men" threatened to sacrifice a great people and a noble cause. The sight of so much folly struck like a dagger to his heart.[32]

By the spring of 1864, Keitt had decided the administration's attack on habeas corpus was too serious to ignore. In April he told Alexander Stephens he agreed that the suspension of the writ was unconstitutional. All power was passing into the hands of the president. His promise of "Independence now, liberty hereafter," was unacceptable.[33]

Late in January, Keitt told Sue that her cousin Calhoun Sparks was dead, shot down from ambush by Union troops concealed in the basement of a deserted house. Every war was cruel, he conceded, and the enemy had robbed this war of all of its chivalry, all of its nobility, all of its manliness, and had made it little more than butchery. Sooner or later, the wrath of heaven would strike down the Yankee pillagers and assassins and free the South from their barbarities.[34]

He was certain, Keitt told Sue, that the war would end that year. Neither side could endure the butchery much longer. The North was heartily sick of it, and if the people of the South could hold out just a little longer, if the army could win in the spring, the North would sue for peace. The curtain was about to rise on the last act of the drama.[35]

Robert Toombs had taken to the stump in Georgia, Keitt reported a week later, and was arraigning President Davis "in a terrible manner." He had always feared that quarrels would spring up among their leaders. Too many politicians put their own selfish interests ahead of the welfare of the country. Their armies had repeatedly defeated the enemy, and yet the Confederacy stood in mortal peril from the inability of southerners to govern themselves. They were fighting a bloody war to establish their independence, and yet they were acting as if they had never left the Union. They had a worthless government, but they had to support it, if only because they could not safely replace it in the midst of war. Toombs was threatening to pull it down; if he succeeded, he would almost certainly destroy their last hope for independence.[36]

But then Keitt did what he had just condemned Toombs for doing, what he himself had done since the early days of the war. He attacked the administration, condemning its "crazy imbecility," its "gross and criminal incapacity," its failure to inspire the people of the South. The administration was "impracticable and visionary." The Congress was full of "idiots."[37]

The president and the Congress were about to reach an agreement on a new currency act,[38] Keitt continued, that would confiscate two-thirds of all the paper money in the Confederacy. He feared it would leave too little in circulation to carry on the business of the country and cause ever greater suffering among the people. He did not understand how it "could enter into the brain of the Congress to adopt such a crazy scheme." They must endure the government's "criminal imbecilities" until the war was over, he concluded; only then would they have an opportunity to carry out necessary reforms.[39]

Early in February 1864, events in Charleston harbor forced Keitt to turn his attention back to the war closer to home. On the night of February 1, the blockade runner *Presto* collided with a partially submerged wreck and ran aground near Fort Moultrie on the southern tip of Sullivan's Island. The next morning, Keitt crossed over to the island to investigate. The enemy had discovered the wreck and was firing on it to prevent the Confederates from salvaging the cargo. A monitor "took the notion to fire at me," Keitt told Sue. A shell passed about twenty feet in front of him; if it had burst, "You would have had to hunt up someone else to complain about. . . . I have no especial use for shells, yet I am a little accustomed to them, and as I was taking it quietly, the monitor thought that it wouldn't pay to continue the fire."[40]

When he arrived on the island, Keitt discovered that Major Robert deTreville, the commanding officer of Fort Moultrie, had allowed his men to pillage the ship. They had removed several barrels of whiskey, and a "grand drunk" was under way. Outraged, Keitt placed deTreville under arrest and sent his men back to the fort. It might be well to hang a number of the men, he blustered, to discourage pillaging in the future.[41]

The cargo of the *Presto*—shoes, blankets, flannels, pork, beef—was the property of the Confederate government, and Keitt was determined to recover as much of it as possible, both from the wreck and from the pillagers. He sent officers to search the camps on the island and seize all the stolen property they could find. One man had paid $120 for eight pairs of shoes, and others had bought blankets for $8 each. Search parties forced the men to give up their booty only minutes after they had purchased it. At first Keitt was reluctant to risk the lives of his men to save the cargo still onboard the ship, but the Union artillery fire was ineffective, and during the next few days he was able to get most of it ashore.[42]

A week after the *Presto* piled up on the beach, Keitt decided its cargo should be distributed to his men. Many of them had not eaten meat in weeks, and many more were without shoes or blankets and had to stand guard on the beach barefoot and shivering. The vessel was stranded; the captain and his crew had abandoned it; his men had ignored enemy fire to remove the cargo, and now commissary officers were preparing to send the desperately needed supplies to Virginia. The news set off a commotion among the men. He ordered them back to their camps and threatened to punish severely anyone who hesitated. They told him they were sorry they had done anything to "disoblige" him and obeyed at once. He had protested the decision to send the supplies north, Keitt told Sue; what the result would be he did not know.[43]

Perhaps it was his realization that his men would not get the food and clothing they so desperately needed that sobered the usually optimistic colonel. Perhaps it was his belief that Davis would not grant him the promotion he was certain he deserved. Or perhaps it was his realization that the Confederates would not turn back the invading Union armies as he had so often proclaimed. Whatever the reason, the letter Keitt wrote to Sue in mid-February was unusually introspective. He had been thinking over the events of the past month, he told her. He had done as much as anyone to bring on the war, and if the Confederacy lost, he would have to accept the consequences, whatever they might be. The men around him knew nothing about the causes of the war, had little at stake, and stood to gain little or nothing as a result of their sacrifices. Slave owners had started the war; slave owners had led ordinary men into it, often without their consent, and now those ordinary men were doing the bulk of the fighting and the dying. As long as the war lasted, he would do his duty fully and promptly and without complaint. When it was over, if he survived, he would try to make amends for the errors he had made and the damage he had done. Until that time arrived, he would do his duty to the best of his ability.[44]

Belatedly Keitt had realized that the war was indeed "a rich man's war and a poor man's fight." True, planters and their sons were fighting and dying, but many as officers, not as enlisted men, many of them with body servants to make their lives less onerous. True, many of them lost mansions, animals, and crops to invading Union armies, but in the end they at least retained their land. True, they lost their slaves, but ordinary men had no slaves to lose.

A quarter of a million southerners died; countless more were horribly mangled physically and emotionally, and most of them were ordinary men. The wives and daughters they left at home suffered at the hands of tax collectors and impressment agents and foragers and bummers. Many of them lost everything they owned and, after the war, found themselves tenant farmers, sharecroppers, and day laborers.

Keitt and men like him had dominated the government of South Carolina, determined its policies, and led the state out of the Union and into devastation and defeat. What an appalling realization that must have been for a man who knew he had done so much to bring on the tragedy. What a remarkable admission of responsibility for the tragedy he had helped to bring about.

Early in 1864, Keitt guessed correctly that he and his regiment would leave Charleston in the spring when the armies broke camp and returned to active campaigning. At first he thought they would be sent to Florida, where a Union expedition had seized Jacksonville and was pushing westward into the interior. He knew that, if it were successful, the thrust would cut the state off from the rest of the Confederacy.[45]

In mid-February, Keitt revealed to Sue that Beauregard was in a "state of great despondency." He had too few troops around Charleston to defend the city against a determined Union assault, and had received orders to send a part of the garrison to counter the enemy offensive in Florida. Beauregard thought the expedition under General Truman Seymour was part of a two-pronged campaign against Mobile, Seymour approaching the city from the east and William Tecumseh Sherman from the north. Keitt was skeptical. Why would an enemy march across hundreds of miles of thinly settled, insufficiently provisioned country, he wondered, when he could reach Mobile much more easily by water? Beauregard was preparing to send most of the troops in the Department to Mobile. If he were wrong about the enemy's intentions, if he stripped the city's defenses and the enemy launched a full-scale assault, Charleston would surely fall.[46]

In the end, Keitt's fears proved groundless. Late in February, troops from the Charleston garrison—but not Keitt or the Twentieth South Carolina—met the Union expedition at Olustee in northern Florida, inflicted heavy casualties, and forced it back to Jacksonville. Keitt assumed—this time incorrectly—that Sherman was trying to take Mobile from the north, and the failure of the Union army to reach the city convinced him that Confederate victory in 1864 was still possible. If James Longstreet could take Knoxville and march north into Kentucky, he would force Sherman to fall back from Chattanooga to the Ohio River and free Joe Johnston to operate against Memphis. If Longstreet had twenty thousand more men, he could regain control of the lower Mississippi Valley and close the river to the enemy. If Lee could crush Grant and move back into Pennsylvania, the war would certainly end in a great victory before the end of the fall.[47]

Keitt's optimism rested on his ignorance of the military situation outside of South Carolina. The Confederacy had all but exhausted its reserves of men and materiel. Grant was preparing to launch the Overland campaign that forced Lee back into the fortifications around Richmond and Petersburg and ultimately into the retreat that ended at Appomattox. Sherman had already set out on the giant turning movement that took him from Chattanooga to Atlanta and Savannah and then north through the Carolinas. The end of the war was in sight, but Keitt did not yet recognize the signs of impending disaster.[48]

When Keitt realized that Beauregard was not going to send his regiment to Florida, he wrote repeatedly to Sue, begging her to join him in Charleston. He had learned that an epidemic of measles had broken out in the neighborhood of "Mandeville," Keitt told his wife, and it would be dreadful if she or the children were infected. They should come to Charleston where they would be safe. It would be difficult to find rooms, but he was sure he could make them "tolerably comfortable." It would be better to accept a little inconvenience than to risk catching a serious disease.[49]

Almost two weeks later, Sue had not replied, and Keitt wondered if she were hiding bad news from him. He was afraid his family had contracted measles and she was refusing to tell him. Charleston was not really safe, he admitted. The Union forces had resumed shelling the city, but they were doing very little damage. He had heard of several cases of smallpox, and it was becoming increasingly "troublesome to live." Beauregard had ordered all blockade runners to carry out cargoes of government-owned cotton, but the ship captains had refused and put an end to all traffic in the harbor. The city, of course, depended on them for goods no longer available inside the Confederacy. He had sold his shares in the blockade runners months earlier and no longer had an interest in any of the steamers, but he was sorry to see the traffic interrupted. The railroads brought nothing into the city, and there was little to be had in the markets. Very poor beef sold for three dollars a pound, but fish would be in soon, Keitt added optimistically, and he was certain he could provide for her, if only she would come.[50]

Sue did join Keitt in Charleston for a few weeks during the early spring. Toward the end of her visit, she wrote to Dudley Mann in Europe, describing "the wonderful siege of Charleston, and its glorious defense." From her rooms in Mount Pleasant, Sue told him, she could look out at

> the distant city, all the islands and their gun-crowned hills, the forts rising from the waters, and Fort Sumter dismantled but defiant still. Proudly the Southern Cross still floats to the breeze, and sure as sets the sun comes the loud peal across the waters that Sumter salutes her flag with the voice of her enemy's gun;[51] and all around for miles—front, right, and left—come back the faithful echoes. How beautiful this scene. . . . To the seaward lie the insolent beasts in their ironclad ships of war; and fronting me now the vengeful guns of Morris Island are hurling on the hated city and coveted fort their bursting balls. Sharp and thundering they fall. Anon, one goes screeching on its way, and soon a cloud of smoke and an echoing sound tells it has reached the city. Yet despite of this, how calm and beautiful the bay; no boat disturbs the waters, and they sleep like those of a midland sea.[52]

Toward the end of the letter, Sue suddenly abandoned the romantic portrait of the war she had been painting for her old friend. "I teach my children daily to hate the Yankees," she wrote. She told them of their "noble kindred" killed in battle, pointed out the crippled soldiers who thronged the streets, and said, "children, the Yankees did this." They must never forgive the Yankees for what they had done. In Europe, where men observed the amenities of war, where they fought according to the code of civilized warfare, no one could imagine the ravages of the enemy. When Bedford Forrest stormed Fort Pillow, he gave no quarter, and she was glad of it. The South had been merciful to its enemies all too long; it must make the enemy feel the thrust of southern steel.[53]

In mid-April 1864, the War Department ordered Beauregard to send the Twentieth South Carolina to Dalton in northwest Georgia, where Gen. Joseph E. Johnson's Army of Tennessee was attempting to block Sherman's march toward Atlanta. The order moved slowly down the chain of command, and it was not until early May that Ripley instructed Col. William Tabb of the Fifty-ninth Virginia to report to Sullivan's Island to relieve Keitt of his command.[54] Two weeks later, before he could complete preparations to move the Twentieth to Georgia, the War Department suddenly altered Keitt's destination.[55]

Early in May, Robert E. Lee had caught Ulysses S. Grant trying to push his army through the Wilderness, a densely wooded area west of Fredericksburg. Aware that Grant was in an untenable position, Lee had hit him head on, pulled back, and hit him again. In two momentous battles—one in the Wilderness, the other outside Spotsylvania Court House—Lee inflicted enormous losses on the Union Army and temporarily checked its drive toward Richmond. After two such bloody battles, any other Union general would have allowed his army to rest and refit. Grant refused to retreat and resumed his dogged attempt to envelop Lee's right flank and open the road to the Confederate capital. Hard pressed, Lee called on the War Department for reinforcements.[56]

On May 18, while the Battle of Spotsylvania Court House was still raging, Keitt received orders to take his regiment north to Richmond "with the greatest possible expedition."[57] In spite of the urgency of the orders and his eagerness for service in the field, Keitt could not start immediately for Virginia. First, Samuel Jones—since March the commanding general of the Department of South Carolina, Georgia, and Florida—tried unsuccessfully to prevent the War Department from transferring any more troops out of his command. Then, realizing that the Confederates were sending troops from the Charleston garrison to reinforce the Army of Northern Virginia, the Union forces launched a series of raids on the islands south of the city.[58]

For a time the Union attacks prevented Jones from sending the regiment north. Twice Keitt loaded his men onto railroad cars for the trip to Virginia, and twice Jones stopped the train and sent them back to James Island to oppose the Union landings. On May 24, after two days and nights of fruitless marching, the regiment—now tired and hungry—returned to Charleston and set out on its long-delayed trip to Virginia.[59]

Keitt and the Twentieth South Carolina arrived in Richmond late on the night of May 29. At a meeting with Jefferson Davis early the next morning, Keitt asked the president to send him to the brigade commanded by his friend Joseph Kershaw. Davis gave him a note addressed to Lee asking the general to grant the request. Davis had treated him with real kindness, Keitt told Sue; if he could only survive the next battle, he was certain the president would promote him. He also visited Gov. William Smith, who invited Sue to stay at the mansion when she came to Richmond to visit her husband.[60]

Keitt reached Kershaw's Brigade early on the morning of May 31. The brigade had lost its commanding officer when Kershaw had taken over the division previously commanded by Lafayette McLaws. Keitt, as the senior colonel, automatically assumed command. Keitt had performed competently—at times heroically—during the siege of Charleston, but he had no experience handling large numbers of troops in the field, and was unfamiliar with the infantry tactics employed by the Army of Northern Virginia. Keitt's regiment was very large; it probably outnumbered the rest of the brigade, which had suffered heavy losses since the start of Grant's spring offensive. Compared to the rest of Lee's army, it was in good condition. One observer later recalled, perhaps with some exaggeration, that it was "as healthy, well clad and well fed a body of troops as anyone would wish to see." But the men were unaccustomed to hard campaigning and completely unfamiliar with the tactics that had become routine late in the war.[61]

Keitt joined his new brigade near Cold Harbor, a village some eight miles northeast of Richmond. He was immediately impressed by the men under his command. "I wish you could see the confidence of our troops," he wrote Sue; "they feel as led by the hand of Providence." The enemy soldiers they captured were frequently intoxicated, made so by their officers. Union prisoners said that the only way Grant could get them to attack Confederate fortifications was to get them drunk.[62]

Less than a week before Keitt's arrival, Lee had again stopped Grant at the Battle of the North Anna River, and Grant had again attempted to reach Richmond by sidling around Lee's right flank. Lee had anticipated the maneuver and, on May 31, the two armies faced each other at Cold Harbor. Hoping to smash the Union left before Grant could get his entire army onto the field, Lee ordered Richard H. Anderson's First Corps to attack at dawn. Federal cavalry held the crossroads in the village, and Lee expected Anderson to take it back.[63] Keitt's brigade would lead the assault.

Early the next morning, June 1, Keitt received orders to reconnoiter the thickly wooded area to his front. He could have located the enemy position and sustained only minor losses by pushing forward a line of skirmishers until it met serious resistance. Instead, he formed his entire brigade in line of battle along the old road to Beulah Church. Writing years later, a veteran recalled that the men instantly recognized their colonel's "inexperience and want of self control." Keitt was preparing for battle "like a knight of old," determined to cut his way through the Union Army as if he were Alva or Turenne.[64]

After considerable confusion and delay, Keitt finally got his men into line and at about eight o'clock ordered them forward. The brigade advanced across an old field toward a patch of dense woods. Keitt, mounted on an iron-gray charger and waving his saber, rode in front. The crossroads was held by only six hundred Union cavalrymen, but they were dismounted, dug in, and armed with breech-loading Sharps and magazine-fed Spencer carbines. The troopers allowed the attack to get within two hundred yards of their position and opened fire. Union Capt. Theodore Rodenbough described the horror they unleashed on the Confederates: "A sheet of flame came from the cavalry line, and for three or four minutes the din was deafening. . . . The whole thing was over in five minutes."[65] On the left of the brigade, the Twentieth South Carolina faltered and then broke. Facing enemy fire in the open for the first time, some of the men huddled behind trees or in depressions in the ground; the rest turned and ran. In their flight, they carried along the veteran regiments on their right. Keitt attempted to rally his old regiment but without success. In the chaos, he was an inviting target for enemy marksmen and was seriously wounded.[66]

Men from his regiment carried Keitt to a farmhouse several hundred yards behind the Confederate lines. There the regimental surgeon, Maj. A. S. Salley, dressed his wounds. Salley told Keitt that he was gravely wounded—a round was lodged in his liver—and his chances for recovery were not good. He administered morphine and whiskey to relieve Keitt's pain and had the wounded man placed on a stretcher and carried three miles to a house out of range of the Union guns. At first the surgeon thought Keitt was growing stronger, but the next morning he began to bleed internally, and Salley told him he did not have long to live. Keitt listened quietly; such, he told the doctor, was the fate of soldiers. Dr. Theodoric Pryor, the regimental chaplain, came to see him, and the two men talked about religious matters. After a few minutes of conversation, Keitt called for Sue and died.[67]

Accompanied by a military escort, Keitt's body traveled by train from Richmond to Orangeburg. He arrived there June 7 and was buried a few days later, "amidst peals of thunder and a downpour of rain," at Tabernacle Methodist Church a few miles outside of St. Matthews. Years later, after Sue had become an Episcopalian, she had his body moved to the public cemetery on the edge of town. Keitt rests there today with his wife and daughters.[68]

Obituaries published in South Carolina newspapers and a resolution adopted by the South Carolina legislature reviewed Keitt's services to his state and nation and fondly recalled his many virtues: his genial manner, which "threw an atmosphere of cheerfulness around him" and won the love of a host of friends; his "energetic and indomitable will"; the fiery rhetoric that distinguished his career as legislator and congressman; the courage that carried him through every crisis on the field of battle.[69]

Obituaries commonly reveal more by what they omit than by what they include. Virtually all focus on achievements and gloss over failures. Certainly that was true of notices of Keitt's death in combat. A fuller, more objective account would have paid far more attention to a political career so contentious that it provoked criticism by friends as well as enemies. He was, as the *Charleston Mercury* acknowledged, a leader of "the strictest sect of Southern Rights politicians." His determination to defend the interests of his state and section, whatever the cost, coupled with his fiery temper, led him into confrontations with Democrats, Know Nothings, and Republicans alike, some of them violent, some of them he later came to regret. The caning of Charles Sumner by his friend Preston Brooks was only the most notorious. He regularly employed his "inexhaustible eloquence" and "readiness in debate" to defend slavery against the assaults of its critics. He was totally convinced that they posed an unacceptable threat to the way of life he held dear, and that the only rational response was secession. He devoted his public career to preparing the people of South Carolina to leave the Union, and then led them into a defeat so devastating that the state required almost a century to recover. Shortly before he died, he seemed to realize that the Confederacy would not win its war for independence, that slavery was doomed, that the appalling loss of life and property was all in vain. He realized too that he had done as much as any man to bring on the debacle, and if he survived, he had a duty to make amends for his many mistakes. It was perhaps the crowning moment of his short but tumultuous life.

Epilogue

"I will not lose my land"

After Keitt's death at Cold Harbor in June 1864, records reveal all too little about Sue and her two daughters. Shortly after the close of the war, the editor of the Boston *Atlas* noted that she was living in poverty. Before the war, Keitt had boasted that he had married the daughter of a wealthy planter, not a merchant or industrialist or speculator whose assets could vanish overnight during a panic. Now, the editor gloated, Keitt's former slaves owned the land and his widow was penniless. He may not have been entirely mistaken. Sue still owned the land, but as a local historian recorded about that time, "desolation [had] flapped his wings over this beautiful ridge, and Cinderella-like, raggedness and poverty now claim it as their own."[1]

Poverty and defeat did little to change Sue's hatred of the Yankees and everything they stood for. Benjamin F. Perry, formerly the Unionist editor of the Greenville *Patriot,* now provisional governor of South Carolina, advised her to take the oath of allegiance to the federal government in order to protect her property, but she adamantly refused. She was not ready, she told Perry, to "bow . . . at Andy Johnson's footstool." If sacrifices were the consequence of her loyalty to the principles of her dead husband, she was willing to endure them. She was not afraid of the Yankees. For two years she had lived in the midst of their bombardment of Charleston. She had defied Sherman's drunken soldiery while they plundered her plantation. They might hang her, but they could not change her heart: "I hate, hate the Yankee nation. They have inflicted upon me every wrong it was in their power to inflict. My children are fatherless, my home a ruin, and every treasure dear from inheritance and association swept away. Not even the blood-stained uniform, precious as my own soul, was spared me. And now . . . I must . . . bow myself an humble supplicant at Andy Johnson's mercy seat. O! Sir! I cannot, cannot do it."[2] Concluding, she begged Perry, "Save me from the dreadful necessity" of swearing allegiance to the government that had made orphans of her children. Was there no other way to save their inheritance?[3]

Perry no doubt told Sue that she had no choice in the matter. The Radical Republicans were rapidly gaining strength. Andrew Johnson was her only hope. Her reply was even more frantic than before: "The President you trust is a man to be . . . dreaded. His life is a tissue of betrayals of the South." He had celebrated his inauguration by hanging an innocent woman.[4] He might do justice to the South if the Democratic Party could sustain him, but if the Republicans won the battle for control of the government, he would hand the South over to her tormentors. What, she wailed, was to be the fate of herself and her daughters? Would the radicals confiscate her plantations? And what was "to be done with the demoralized race in our midst?" Her heart quailed at "the thought of the midnight torch and the poison bowl."[5]

The news that her brother-in-law Col. Ellison Keitt was preparing to run for Congress sent her into a rage. His "Union proclivities" and his "antagonism to the political principles of [his] distinguished brother" filled her with "sorrow and mortification." No southern man of honor could hold office under the federal government. Such men were "a laughing stock, . . . tools and butts of the Yankees, . . . regarded with contempt by the people at home." He had an honorable name, intimately associated with the principles on which the Confederacy rose and fell—"Southern Rights, State Sovereignty, Southern Independence. And Southern Union." She implored him not to drag his brother's name through "the disgraceful orgies now enacted in Washington. . . . wait patiently the future. You are young yet and the time may come when with respect to your brother's memory, respect for yourself, and in all honor and dignity, you can hold office and high estate."[6]

Keitt did run unsuccessfully for a seat in the House of Representatives in 1872. Whatever his true political beliefs then, by the middle of the 1870s, he had become an ally of Wade Hampton, an advocate of the Lost Cause, an outspoken critic of industrial capitalism, a leader in the state Farmers Alliance, and a caretaker of his brother's legacy.[7]

To Sue, the succession of tragedies she had to endure must have seemed unending. On February 18, 1866, Stella, the younger of her two daughters, died at "Mandeville" at the age of four. Newspaper accounts said nothing about the cause of her death. Sue's mother died in 1870, and a decade later "Mandeville," her girlhood home, burned to the ground. She, her father, and her surviving daughter, Anna, escaped the fire unharmed but saved almost none of their possessions.[8]

Sue's father, Samuel Sparks, died in 1875, and the following year, the Probate Court of Marlboro County ordered his land sold to pay his debts. Sue borrowed money from William A. Carrigan, the owner of a store in Society Hill, bought the plantation at public auction, and set about paying off the mortgage and restoring the productivity of land that had been declining since Sherman's men swept over it.[9]

The relationship of the widow and the store keeper must have been contentious. At the start, Sue was fearful she would lose Mandeville and almost pathetically grateful when Carrigan provided the money she needed to save the land. She knew little about the day-to-day operation of a cotton plantation, and depended heavily on his advice and support as she set about finding tenants and putting the land back into production. She filled her letters to him with accounts of repairing old tenant houses and building new ones, establishing boundaries between farms, erecting fences, acquiring mules and plows, preparing the land for spring plowing, increasing the amount of land under cultivation. She was "battling against great odds," she told him, and asked for his patience and understanding. Without his help, she could accomplish nothing.[10]

Early in their relationship, Sue decided that Carrigan was not the true friend she had first believed him to be. She objected to the rate of interest on the loan, and accused him of "asking me to sign my own death warrant," but she had no choice and reluctantly agreed to the terms he imposed. In the spring of 1879, she assured him, "It will not be your fault if I cannot save my old inheritance. I will feel that I at least made the effort to do so, and will thank you for the chance given [me]."[11] By mid-summer, she was aware that, if she failed to pay off the mortgage, Carrigan would acquire the land for a fraction of its true value. She had agreed to pay 18 percent interest on the mortgage itself and from 24 to 40 percent on the money she borrowed to improve the plantation and support herself and her young daughter. The difficulty she experienced in paying off those short-term notes made her doubt that she could pay the five annual installments on the mortgage when they came due.[12]

Just as she feared, Sue found it impossible to make the first payment; Carrigan threatened to seize the land, and Sue alternately begged for more time and threatened to fight him through every court in the state. She had gotten off to a bad start, she admitted. If only he would give her another chance, another eight months, she could make the plantation as prosperous as it had been before the war. She had worked hard; she was "trustworthy and irrepressible as to energy and brain work." The price of cotton was rising and pushing up the value of good land. Her mortgage was a good investment for him. If he would give her another year to put the plantation in working order, both of them would benefit. If he refused, she would enter a convent.[13]

When her pleas failed to move her creditor, Sue flew into a rage. Why had he encouraged her, she demanded; why had he promised to be lenient; why had he taken advantage of her hard work when he knew he would take the land at the end of the year? She could scarcely believe he was serious. Surely he was only testing her courage and determination. She had turned over every bale of cotton and every bushel of corn. She had even handed over the silver she had rescued from the fire that destroyed her home. She would refuse to leave the land, and every one of her tenants would stand behind her. She would spend her last breath to defeat him. Would it be "peace or war" between them? Would they be "good friends or enemies . . . to the bitter end?"[14]

Carrigan relented, and Sue immediately began demanding privileges that would let her do business with the advantages of a man. "If I am to do the work of a man, I must have the tools" of a man. He must provide her with the money she needed at 18 percent, and not at "special premium rates." He must stop interfering with her tenants; he must give her control of the sale of her cotton. Remarkably Carrigan agreed to her demands.[15]

Sue did avoid one problem that plagued most planters caught up in the difficult transition from slavery to free labor. With few exceptions, her relations with her tenants were harmonious. She had the respect of the men who worked her land, she assured Carrigan. Most of them had been her father's slaves and did "just what I told them to do." She treated them fairly and kept them happy by providing them substantial houses, mules, provisions, and equipment. For one tenant, "a grand, old time, faithful serving man," "she even bought a coat. In return they were "contented . . . industrious . . . orderly . . . thrifty," and paid their rents when they were due. She had more applicants than she had farms to rent.

All over the state, Sue reminded Carrigan, planters were losing their tenants, but he "need have no apprehension of the Exodus." The black migration to Kansas was "already played out." Whatever panic there might be elsewhere, they had nothing to fear. Planters who abused the "ignorance and humanity" of their tenants lost them to more enlightened masters. Her father and men like him had "lived in daily association and sympathy with their slaves." Wherever their sons and daughters treated the freedmen justly, the result was a "better, kinder tempered, more contented population" than could be found anywhere else in the South.[16]

Sue's methods were not invariably successful. With two brothers, they were conspicuous failures. The men had refused to turn over her share of the cotton at the end of the season, and her "forebearance" had made them "insolent." She ordered them off her land; they had refused to go, and she had called the sheriff to put them off. The brothers had gone off to get drunk and "raise a crowd of roughs" to resist the sheriff. They had left without a fight but threatened to burn down her house. For two months she had sat up all night guarding her property. "I will . . . be mistress of it," she vowed, even "if an army of Hyatts [were] camped around it."[17]

In spite of all the failures, in spite of all the disappointments, Sue persevered and prospered. She endured the world-shattering events of Reconstruction and Restoration, regained control of both her father's and her husband's plantations and doubled their productivity. She joined the Episcopal Church, saw to her daughter's education at the Augusta Female Seminary, now Mary Baldwin College, in Staunton, Virginia, and introduced her into society. Gossip columnists reported that Sue, now "a stately, high bred dame," and her daughter frequented spas in Virginia and balls in New York and Washington. Anna was the belle of the Pee Dee, just as her mother had been a generation before. One writer gushed over Miss Keitt, "the noted South Carolina Beauty," lovingly describing her golden hair, dark eyes, long lashes, exquisite mouth, pale skin, and gracious manners. Rumor had it that Sue tried to marry her off to President Grover Cleveland shortly before he wed Frances Folsom. Anna never married; perhaps she was as hard to please as her mother had been a quarter-century before.[18]

The two women traveled extensively in Europe and North Africa, fulfilling the dreams Sue had cherished early in her marriage. A physician who knew them commented that the income from the two plantations was "enormous, [and] they lived up to their limit." Sue died in January 1915 and was buried in St. Matthews next to her husband. Her daughter died only four years later. The sale of the plantations at auction brought the estate more than $270,000, a substantial sum for women once left almost penniless by the war.[19]

NOTES

Introduction

1. Schultz, *Nationalism and Sectionalism,* 3–25; Barney, *Road to Secession,* 85–100; Barney, *Secessionist Impulse,* 88–95; Takaki, *Pro-Slavery Crusade,* 10–22.

2. Barney, *Road to Secession,* 85. For an effective demonstration that there was no "typical" fire-eater, see Walther, *Fire-Eaters.*

Chapter 1: "See that you rear a new Union"

1. Herd, "Chapters from the Life," 187–88.

2. Herd, "Chapters from the Life," 9–10; U.S. Census, 1850, Agriculture, Orangeburg District, South Carolina; U.S. Census, 1850, Population, Orangeburg District, South Carolina, both microfilm, University of North Carolina, Chapel Hill; unidentified newspaper clipping, December 18, 1952, Keitt Collection South Caroliniana Library, University of South Carolina, Columbia.

3. Unidentified newspaper· clipping, December 18, 1952, Keitt Collection, South Caroliniana Library. The author visited "Puritan Hall" in 1973, and has described it from photographs he made at that time.

4. F. H. Foster to L. M. Keitt, January 26, 1859, Laurence M. Keitt Papers, Duke University, hereafter cited as Keitt Papers, Duke.

5. Charles Moore, comp., Alumni Records, University of South Carolina, vol. 6: n.p.

6. Hollis, *University of South Carolina* 1: 264–69; Schultz, *Nationalism and Sectionalism,* 8. Thornwell was professor of sacred literature and Christian evidences. LaBorde taught logic, rhetoric, and belles lettres; Henry taught metaphysics, moral and political philosophy. See also Sugrue, "'We Desired Our Future Rulers to Be Educated Men,'" 91–114; Pace, *Halls of Honor.*

7. Hollis, *University of South Carolina* 1: 269.

8. Hollis, *University of South Carolina* 1: 181–87; Berry, "Francis Lieber," 31; Herd, "Chapters from the Life," 10–11; Freidel, *Francis Lieber,* 115–288.

9. Hollis, *University of South Carolina* 1: 230–54; "Subjects for Debate," Euphradian Society; McKissick, *Clariosophic and Euphradian Societies,* 60.

10. Hollis, *University of South Carolina* 1: 234, 244; "Treasurer's Book, 1838–1840" and "Treasurer's Book, 1841–1842," Euphradian Society; McKissick, *Clariosophic and Euphradian Societies,* 37.

11. Clipping, [*Charleston Courier*?], June 6, 1864. One contemporary recalled many years later that Keitt graduated third in his class (Dickert, *History of Kershaw's Brigade,*

374). A biographical sketch published during the secession crisis noted that he had "graduated with Highest Honors" (*Harper's Weekly,* December 22, 1860, 1). The author has been unable to confirm either statement.

12. O'Neall, *Biographical Sketches of the Bench and Bar of South Carolina* 2: 38–44, 609. Dickert, *History of Kershaw's Brigade,* 374. Hamilton, "James Louis Petigru," 314–15. *Charleston Mercury,* April 30, 1849, 2; June 20, 1864, 2. L. M. Keitt to John C. Calhoun, October 25, 1848, *Papers of John C. Calhoun,* ed. Wilson and Cook, vol. 26: 109–10.

13. Barrett, *Sherman's March Through the Carolinas,* 58–59 and passim.

14. *Charleston Mercury,* October 13, 1848, 2.

15. *Journal of the House of Representatives of South Carolina, 1848,* 110, 187; *1849,* 35, 58, 82, 198; *1850,* 104, 133–34; *1851,* 6, 21, 120–21; *1852,* 5–6, 42.

16. Smith, *Economic Readjustment,* 201–2; Sharp, *Jacksonians versus the Banks,* 277–79.

17. Sharp, *Jacksonians versus the Banks,* 279.

18. *Charleston Mercury,* August 5, 1848, 2.

19. *Charleston Mercury,* August 5, 1848, 2; L. M. Keitt to Sue Sparks, January 20, 1855, Keitt Papers, Duke.

20. *Charleston Mercury,* December 13, 1849, 2.

21. L. M. Keitt to Sue Sparks, January 20, 1855, Keitt Papers, Duke.

22. *Journal of the House of Representatives of the State of South Carolina, 1850,* 56–58; *Reports and Resolutions, South Carolina General Assembly, 1850,* 158.

23. Keitt, *Address of Lawrence M. Keitt, Esq., on Laying the Corner-Stone of the Fire-Proof Building at Columbia, Dec. 15, 1851,* 7–9.

24. Keitt, *Address of Lawrence M. Keitt, Esq., on Laying the Corner-Stone of the Fire-Proof Building at Columbia,* 9; *Charleston Mercury,* December 18, 1851, 2; *Black River Watchman,* February 7, 1852.

25. Boucher, "Secession and Cooperation Movements in South Carolina, 1848 to 1852," 67–70; Hamer, *Secession Movement in South Carolina,* 22–37; Potter, *Impending Crisis,* chap. 2. For recent accounts of the war with Mexico, see Eisenhower, *So Far from God;* Wheelan, *Invading Mexico;* and Clary, *Eagles and Empire.* Rhett's congressional district included Beaufort, Colleton, Barnwell, and Orangeburg districts. In 1852, when South Carolina lost a seat in the House of Representatives, the district remained intact but was renumbered. Keitt represented the Third District from 1853 to 1860.

26. In the Federal Census of 1850, Orangeburg District had a total population of 23,582: 8,120 whites, 78 free blacks, and 15,384 slaves (U.S. Census, Population and Slave Schedules, South Carolina, 1850).

27. *Charleston Mercury,* November 9, 1848, 2; November 17, 1848, 2; December 7, 1848, 2; December 11, 1848, 2. *Journal of the House of Representatives of the State of South Carolina, 1848,* 60, 95, 122. Boucher, "Secession and Cooperation Movements in South Carolina," 71–74.

28. Boucher, "Secession and Cooperation Movements in South Carolina," 83–84; Nevins, *Ordeal of the Union* 1: 247–50.

29. *Charleston Mercury,* November 29, 1849, 2; December 1, 1849, 2; December 5, 1849, 2; December 10, 1849, 2; December 20, 1849, 2.

30. *Charleston Mercury,* December 8, 1849, 2; December 22, 1849, 2. *Journal of the House of Representatives of the State of South Carolina, 1849,* 108–9, 240. The four states that had enacted personal liberty laws were Massachusetts, Rhode Island, Vermont, and Pennsylvania. L. M. Keitt to John C. Calhoun, October 1, 1847 in *Papers of John C. Calhoun,* ed. Wilson and Cook, vol. 24: 589–90.

31. *Charleston Mercury,* January 28, 1850, 2; March 27, 1850, 2; May 10, 1850, 2. Boucher, "Secession and Cooperation Movements in South Carolina," 95–96.

32. Clay proposed to admit California to the Union as a free state; organize the rest of the territory acquired from Mexico without reference to slavery; draw a new boundary between Texas and New Mexico, and compensate Texas by assuming its state debt; prohibit the slave trade in the District of Columbia; and approve a more effective fugitive slave act. Finally he asked the Congress to declare that it would not abolish slavery in the District of Columbia without the consent of the people of Maryland and Washington, nor without compensation to the owners, and that it had no power to interfere with the interstate slave trade (Nevins, *Ordeal of the Union* 1: 265–66).

33. Nevins, *Ordeal of the Union* 1: 264–301; Hamilton, *Prologue to Conflict,* 1–117.

34. Nevins, *Ordeal of the Union* 1: 314–18; Boucher, "Secession and Cooperation Movements in South Carolina," 97–98. The convention also approved by a narrow margin a radical manifesto written by Robert Barnwell Rhett. Rhett repeated Calhoun's argument that for Congress to admit California as a free state would be the equivalent of it approving the Wilmot Proviso.

35. For accounts of the passage of the Compromise of 1850, see Nevins, *Ordeal of the Union* 1: 318–45, and Hamilton, *Prologue to Conflict,* 118–65.

36. *Charleston Mercury,* October 16, 1850, 2; Boucher, "Secession and Cooperation Movements in South Carolina," 99–100.

37. *Journal of the House of Representatives of the State of South Carolina, 1850,* 46–48 and passim; Boucher, "Secession and Cooperation Movements in South Carolina," 111–12.

38. *Journal of the House of Representatives of the State of South Carolina, 1850,* 46–48, 167–94, 279; Boucher, "Secession and Cooperation Movements in South Carolina," 113–14; Schultz, *Nationalism and Sectionalism,* 28; Nevins, *Ordeal of the Union* 1: 362–64.

39. Nevins, *Ordeal of the Union* 1: 366–70.

40. *Charleston Mercury,* May 6, 1851, 2; June 19, 1851, 2; September 4, 1851, 2; September 20, 1851, 2. *Black River Watchman,* July 26, 1851. Boucher, "Secession and Cooperation Movements in South Carolina," 115–29. Schultz, *Nationalism and Sectionalism,* 28–30.

41. *Charleston Mercury,* October 29, 1851, 2; Boucher, "Secession and Cooperation Movements in South Carolina," 128–29. In the Seventh Congressional District, the vote was 3,262 to 1,851 in favor of the immediate secessionists. In South Carolina as a whole, it was 24,909 to 17,471 against them.

42. *Journal of the House of Representatives of the State of South Carolina, 1851,* 68–69.

43. *Journal of the House of Representatives of the State of South Carolina, 1851,* 118. *Charleston Mercury,* December 8, 1851, 2; December 9, 1851, 2; December 10, 1851, 2. Boucher, "Secession and Cooperation Movements in South Carolina," 131–32. Schultz, *Nationalism and Sectionalism,* 33–35.

44. Boucher, "Secession and Cooperation Movements in South Carolina," 133–36; Schultz, *Nationalism and Sectionalism,* 33–35.

45. L. M. Keitt to James Chesnut, February 22, 1853, Williams-Chesnut-Manning Papers, South Caroliniana Library. *Charleston Mercury,* November 19, 1852, 2; November 20, 1852, 2. *Lancaster Ledger,* July 6, 1853, 2. O. M. Dantzler to W. J. Keitt, November 30, December 1, 1852; W. J. Keitt to O. M. Dantzler, November 30, 1852 (2); J. W. Cantey, James Chesnut, and T. S. McGowan to T. W. Howell and W. A. Owens, December 1, 1852; J. H. Means to W. A. Owens, December 3, 1852; M. A. Jones et al., to ?, December 7, 1852, all in Olin M. Dantzler Papers. Schultz, *Nationalism and Sectionalism,* 52–56.

46. *Charleston Mercury,* December 9, 1852, 2; January 18, 1853, 2. Boucher, "Sectionalism, Representation, and the Electoral Question in Ante-Bellum South Carolina," 15–16 and passim.

47. *Charleston Mercury,* February 4, 1853, 2; *Black River Watchman,* December 25, 1853; Davidson, *Last Foray,* 186–87; *Biographical Directory of the American Congress,* 769.

48. *Charleston Mercury,* March 7, 1853, 2; April 11, 1853, 2; April 29, 1853, 2; May 6, 1853, 2; May 10, 1853, 2. *Abbeville Banner,* April 14, 1853, 2; May 12, 1853, 2. *Black River Watchman,* April 1, May 13, 1853. L. M. Keitt to James Simons, July 5, 1853, South Carolina Legislative System, Messages and Petitions, South Carolina Department of Archives and History, Columbia.

Chapter 2: "Trample upon your hosannas to the Union"

1. For a description of the English Compromise, see Nichols, *Disruption of American Democracy,* 175–56; Freehling, *Road to Disunion,* 2: 142–44.

2. A clergyman who heard Keitt speak in the legislature wrote that he had invoked "thunder and lightning" in the morning and "heaven and hell" in the afternoon (Lancaster *Ledger,* July 6, 1853, 2).

3. *Congressional Globe,* 33rd Congress, 1st sess.: 2.

4. *Congressional Directory,* 33rd Congress, 1st sess.

5. Nevins, *Ordeal of the Union,* 2: 93–98; Johannsen, *Stephen A. Douglas,* 401–15; Etcheson, *Bleeding Kansas,* 9–14.

6. Nevins, *Ordeal of the Union* 2: 122–32; Johannsen, *Stephen A. Douglas,* 418–34, 439–47; Etcheson, *Bleeding Kansas,* 6, 16–19, 23.

7. Nevins, *Ordeal of the Union* 2: 111–12, 132–35; Johannsen, *Stephen A. Douglas,* 418–34, 441–42. For a description of the reactions of southern senators to the Kansas-Nebraska Bill, see Wolff, "Party and Section: The Senate and the Kansas-Nebraska Bill," 295–99; Etcheson, *Bleeding Kansas,* 25–26. For the "Appeal of the Independent Democrats," see *Congressional Globe,* 33rd Congress, 1st sess.: 281–82.

8. Laurence M. Keitt to O. M. Dantzler, April 18, 1854, Keitt Collection, Newspaper Clippings.

9. *Charleston Mercury,* March 7, 1854, 2.

10. *Congressional Globe,* 33rd Congress, 1st sess.: app. 463–66.

11. The doctrine, called "popular sovereignty" by its friends and "squatter sovereignty" by its enemies, was originated by Lewis Cass of Michigan and exploited by Stephen A.

Douglas. In the bill organizing the Kansas and Nebraska territories, Douglas purposely omitted any direct reference to slavery, and left the problem of establishing or prohibiting the institution to be solved by local governments. He left the time at which the decision would be made unspecified, satisfying northern Democrats and southern Democrats alike and encouraging both to vote in favor of the bill. During the debate, northern representatives argued that territorial legislatures could act on the question immediately after they were elected, assuming that the earliest settlers would be small farmers hostile to slavery. Like Keitt, southern representatives argued that only a state legislature could act on the question, assuming that the interval between territorial organization and admission to the Union would allow slaveholding planters time to settle and dominate the area.

12. *Congressional Globe,* 33rd Congress, 1st sess.: 467–68.

13. *Charleston Mercury,* April 3, 1854, 2; April 4, 1853, 2; April 10, 1854, 1–2; April 11, 1854, 1–2. *Charleston Courier,* April 3, 1854, 2; April 4, 1854, 1. *Black River Watchman,* April 7, 1854. *Southern Quarterly Review* 10 (July 1854): 261.

14. Senator John M. Clayton, a Whig from Delaware, had introduced an amendment to the Kansas bill that prevented aliens from voting or holding office in the territory. The Congress had placed no such restriction on Illinois, Wisconsin, Iowa, or Michigan when those states had been territories. Southerners wanted to apply the restriction to Kansas to prevent its immigrant population from voting to exclude slavery. Some supported it because they were both nativists and proponents of slavery (Nevins, *Ordeal of the Union* 2: 128).

15. L. M. Keitt to O. M. Dantzler, April 18, 1854, Keitt Collection, Newspaper Clippings.

16. *Congressional Globe,* 33rd Congress, 1st sess.: 1072–74.

17. *Congressional Globe,* 33rd Congress, 1st sess.: 1099–1100.

18. *Charleston Courier,* April 17, 1854, 1; May 16, 1854, 1.

19. *Congressional Globe,* 33rd Congress, 1st sess.: 1254, app. 425–29; Russel, "The Issues in the Congressional Struggle over the Kansas-Nebraska Bill, 1854," in his *Critical Studies in Antebellum Sectionalism,* 209; Nevins, *Ordeal of the Union* 2: 154–57; Etcheson, *Bleeding Kansas,* 19–20.

20. Etcheson, *Bleeding Kansas,* 28–35, 42–49. For a description of the attitudes of the settlers toward slavery and other issues, see Berwanger, *Frontier against Slavery,* 97–101.

21. Craik, "Southern Interest in Territorial Kansas," 334–451; Schultz, *Nationalism and Sectionalism,* 106–10.

22. Craik, "Southern Interest in Territorial Kansas," 415–18. Boucher, "South Carolina and the South," 99. *Charleston Mercury,* March 8, 1856, 2; May 12, 1856, 2; July 11, 1856, 2; July 31, 1855, 2. *Sumter Watchman,* September 3, 1856, 2.

23. Orangeburg *Southron,* May 21, June 4, 11, 1856.

24. Craik, "Southern Interest in Territorial Kansas," 414; *Charleston Mercury,* March 5, 1856, 2; Columbia *Carolina Times,* March 4, 1856, Keitt Collection, Newspaper Clippings; *Abbeville Banner,* March 13, 1856, 2.

25. L. M. Keitt to Sue Sparks, May 10, 1856, Keitt Papers, Duke.

26. Schultz, *Nationalism and Sectionalism in South Carolina,* 108–10; Boucher, "South Carolina and the South," 99.

27. Nevins, *Ordeal of the Union* 2: 380–411; Berwanger, *Frontier against Slavery,* 101–15; Freehling, *Road to Disunion* 2: 75; Potter, *The Impending Crisis,* 204; Etcheson, *Bleeding Kansas,* chaps. 3–4.

28. Overdyke, *Know Nothing Party,* 33, 70, 95–96; Schultz, *Nationalism and Sectionalism,* 78–80; Boucher, "South Carolina and the South," 108; White, "The National Democrats in South Carolina," 372; Anbinder, *Nativism and Slavery,* esp. chaps. 7–8.

29. Shultz, *Nationalism and Sectionalism,* 80–81.

30. Overdyke, *Know Nothing Party,* 70; Schultz, *Nationalism and Sectionalism,* 80–81; Boucher, "South Carolina and the South," 108; White, "National Democrats in South Carolina," 372; Anbinder, *Nativism and Slavery,* 105–6.

31. Overdyke, *Know Nothing Party,* 70, 95–96.

32. White, "National Democrats in South Carolina," 372–73.

33. Schultz, *Nationalism and Sectionalism,* 81.

34. Chauncey S. Boucher argued that formal opposition to the Know Nothing movement did not appear in South Carolina until August 1855, when Preston Brooks addressed a mass meeting in his congressional district. Brooks's speech followed Keitt's by more than seven months ("South Carolina and the South," 108).

35. *Congressional Globe,* 33rd Congress, 2nd sess.: app. 66.

36. *Congressional Globe,* 33rd Congress, 2nd sess.: 67, 69.

37. *Congressional Globe,* 33rd Congress, 2nd sess.: 67–69.

38. *Congressional Globe,* 33rd Congress, 2nd sess.: 68. Less than a year before, Keitt had argued that settlers could not exclude slavery from the territories. For him, logical consistency was not necessarily a virtue. If he realized that each of his assertions about the right of Americans to shape their domestic institutions contradicted the other, he was not greatly troubled by it. Keitt was transparently honest and believed every statement he made at the time he made it. But he was apt to judge any argument by its usefulness as well as its consistency.

39. *Congressional Globe,* 33rd Congress, 2nd sess.: 69.

40. Murray, *Letters from the United States,* 158; *Charleston Mercury,* January 11, 1855, 2; *Black River Watchman,* January 19, 1855; Goodwin, "Amelia Matilda Murray," *Dictionary of National Biography* 13: 1243–44.

41. *Congressional Globe,* 33rd Congress, 2nd sess.: 183.

42. *Congressional Globe,* 33rd Congress, 2nd sess.: 183.

43. *Charleston Mercury,* January 15, 1855, 2; Boston *American Celt,* n.d., and *Baltimore Argus,* January 20, 1855, both clippings, Keitt Collection, Newspaper Clippings. For similar comments, see *Charleston Mercury,* January 9, 1855, 2; January 11, 1855, 2; January, 15, 1855, 2; *Charleston Courier,* January 8, 1855, 1; January 9, 1855, 1; Abbeville *Independent Press,* January 19, 1855, 1, Keitt Collection, Newspaper Clippings; *Black River Watchman,* January 19, 1855.

44. Overdyke, *Know Nothing Party,* 248.

45. L. M. Keitt to Sue Sparks, January 20, 1855, Keitt Papers, Duke.

46. L. M. Keitt to James Chesnut, February 9, 1855, Williams-Chesnut-Manning Collection, South Caroliniana Library.

47. L. M. Keitt to Sue Sparks, March 16, 1855, Keitt Papers, Duke; *Abbeville Banner,* March 29, 1855, 2.

48. L. M. Keitt to Sue Sparks, May 30, 1855, Keitt Papers, Duke.

49. *Charleston Courier,* July 18, 1855, 1. *Charleston Mercury,* July 19, 1855, 2; August 16, 1855, 2. Spartanburg *Carolina Spartan,* August 23, 1855. Keitt Collection, Newspaper Clippings. L. M. Keitt to Sue Sparks, September 19, 1855, Keitt Papers, Duke.

50. *Charleston Mercury,* October 18, 1855, 2.

51. L. M. Keitt to Sue Sparks, February 29, 1856, Keitt Papers. Duke University.

52. Potter, *Impending Crisis,* 255.

53. L. M. Keitt to Sue Sparks, September 19, 1955, Keitt Papers, Duke.

54. Orangeburg *Southron,* October 31, 1855.

55. Herd, "Chapters from the Life," 49.

56. *Congressional Globe,* 34th Congress, 1st sess.: 25; Nevins, *Ordeal of the Union* 2: 413–16.

57. *Congressional Globe,* 34th Congress 1st sess.: 71–72; L. M. Keitt to Sue Sparks, January 3, 1856, Keitt Papers, Duke.

58. *Charleston Courier,* January 19, 1856, 1; *Sumter Watchman,* January 23, 1856, 1.

59. *Congressional Globe,* 34th Congress, 1st sess.: 155.

60. *Congressional Globe,* 34th Congress, 1st sess.: 157–58.

61. *Congressional Globe,* 34th Congress, 1st sess.: 157–58. *Charleston Mercury,* January 14, 1856, 2; January 15, 1856, 2. See also Staunton *Republican Vindicator,* January 19, 1856, 1; *Abbeville Banner,* February 7, 1856, 2.

62. L. M. Keitt to Sue Sparks, January 10, 1856, Keitt Papers, Duke.

63. *Congressional Globe,* 34th Congress, 1st sess.: 335–37.

64. Richardson antagonized southern congressmen when he hedged on the Wilmot Proviso. Orr won back the southern votes, but his attacks on nativism prevented him from attracting the Know Nothing votes necessary to win (Harrington, "The First Northern Victory," 198–202).

65. L. M. Keitt to Sue Sparks, February 2, 1856, Keitt Papers, Duke.

66. *Congressional Globe,* 34th Congress, 1st sess.: 335–37.

67. *Congressional Globe,* 34th Congress, 1st sess.: 296–98; Nevins, *Ordeal of the Union* 2: 416–17; Nichols, *Disruption of American Democracy,* 441–43; Etcheson, *Bleeding Kansas,* 91–92.

68. Nevins, *Ordeal of the Union* 2: 426–27. Etcheson, *Bleeding Kansas,* 95–97.

69. An anonymous correspondent described the speaker for the *Charleston Mercury*: he was dressed in a dark blue coat with large shiny "plantation style" buttons. His nervous gestures, his shifting expression, his restless pacing suggested that he was suffering from a series of electric shocks. His eloquence was more florid than Calhoun's, but even men who disagreed with his opinions had to acknowledge his "generous ardor, brilliant intellect and glowing diction" (*Charleston Mercury,* April 15, 1856, 2).

70. *Congressional Globe,* 34th Congress, 1st sess.: app. 442–46.

71. *Congressional Globe,* 34th Congress, 1st sess.: app., 443.

72. Keitt, *Politics of the Country;* L. M. Keitt to Sue Sparks, April 13, 1856, Keitt Papers, Duke University.

73. *Baltimore Republican,* April 9, 1856, 1; *Mobile Daily Register,* April 15, 1856, 2. See also: *Washington Union,* April 11, 1856, 2; *Charleston Courier,* April 11, 1856, 1; April 12, 1856, 1; Abbeville *Independent Press,* April 18, 1856, 1; Staunton *Republican Vindicator,* April 12, 1856, 2; *Charleston Mercury,* April 12, 1856, 2; April 18, 1856, 2; April 19, 1856, 2.

74. *Congressional Globe,* 34th Congress, 1st sess.: 937–38.

Chapter 3: "He who dallies is a dastard"

1. Schultz, *Nationalism and Sectionalism,* 84–85.

2. Schultz, *Nationalism and Sectionalism,* 87–96, 101–2.

3. Schultz, *Nationalism and Sectionalism,* 83–84.

4. Schultz, *Nationalism and Sectionalism,* 96–101; Boucher, "South Carolina and the South," 112; Takaki, *Pro-Slavery Crusade,* 196; Orangeburg *Southron,* October 31, 1855.

5. Orangeburg *Southron,* October 31, 1855; *Charleston Mercury,* October 18, 1855, 2; Abbeville *Independent Press,* February 15, 1856, 1.

6. Schultz, *Nationalism and Sectionalism,* 102–3; Boucher, "South Carolina and the South," 112.

7. *Congressional Globe,* 34th Congress, 1st sess., app. 444–45.

8. *Congressional Globe,* 34th Congress, 1st sess., app. 937–38.

9. L. M. Keitt to Sue Sparks, May 10, 1856, Keitt Papers, Duke.

10. Schultz, *Nationalism and Sectionalism,* 121; L. M. Keitt to Sue Sparks, June 8, 1856, Keitt Papers, Duke University.

11. L. M. Keitt to Messrs. Salley, Glover, and Marchant, June 28, 1856, in *Abbeville Banner,* July 17, 1856, 2.

12. *Charleston Courier,* May 9, 1856, 1; May 12, 1856, 1; May 14, 1856, 1; May 16, 1856, 1.

13. L. M. Keitt to Sue Sparks, May 10, 1856, Keitt Papers, Duke.

14. *Congressional Globe,* 34th Congress, 1st sess.: 1228–29. *Charleston Courier,* July 14, 1856, 2; July 15, 1856, 1; July 16, 1856, 1; July 17, 1856, 1; July 18, 1856, 1; July 19, 1856, 1; July 21, 1856, 1; July 22, 1856, 2; July 23, 1856, 1. *New York Times,* July 10, 1856, 1; July 11, 1856, 4; July 12, 1856, 1; July 14, 1856, 3; July 15, 1856, 4; July 16, 1856, 1; August 1, 1856, 3. Orangeburg *Southron,* May 21, 1856.

15. Nevins, *Ordeal of the Union,* 2: 437–38. For an excellent account of the entire affair, see Donald, *Charles Sumner,* 2: 279–311; for an analysis of Sumner's strengths and weaknesses, see esp. chap. 1.

16. For the text of Sumner's speech, see *Congressional Globe,* 34th Congress, 1st sess.: app. 529–44.

17. *Congressional Globe,* 34th Congress, 1st sess.: app. 530.

18. *Congressional Globe,* 34th Congress, 1st sess.: app. 543.

19. Judged by the standards of South Carolina politics, Butler was a moderate. He had championed nullification, the Fugitive Slave Law of 1850, and the Lecompton constitution, and opposed the admission of California. But he represented upcountry South Carolina. In the early 1850s he argued against secession or any form of separate state

action (Gaines, "Andrew Pickens Butler," *Dictionary of American Biography* 3: 355–56; Mathis, "Preston Smith Brooks," 296–310).

20. John S. Preston to John L. Manning, May 19, 1856, Chesnut-Williams-Manning Collection, South Caroliniana Library; Walmsley, "Preston S. Brooks," *Dictionary of American Biography* 3: 88; Donald, *Charles Sumner* 1: 289–90.

21. "Recollections of Sumner," 482. For an unusually perceptive analysis of Brooks's behavior, see Freehling, *Road to Disunion,* 2: 80–84.

22. J. G. Mittag to the Editor, *Charleston Courier,* June 2, 1856, 2. For the details of the caning, see Donald, *Charles Sumner,* 1: 289–97, and *Congressional Globe,* 34th Congress, 1st sess.: 1352–67, "The Journal of the Committee Appointed to Investigate the Assault." The journal was also published as Report No. 182, *Reports of Committees of the House of Representatives during the First Session of the Thirty Fourth Congress,* 1–142.

23. Brooks wrote to his brother, J. Hamilton Brooks, "It would not take much to have the throats of every abolitionist cut" (letter, May 23, 1856, *South Carolina Historical and Genealogical Magazine,* 1–4).

24. L. M. Keitt to Sue Sparks, May 29, 1856, Keitt Papers, Duke.

25. *Congressional Globe,* 34th Congress, 1st sess.: 1279–80, 1317. Members of the committee were Senators James A. Pearce of Maryland, Philip Allen of Rhode Island, Henry Dodge of Wisconsin, Henry S. Geyer of Missouri, and Lewis Cass of Michigan.

26. *Congressional Globe,* 34th Congress, 1st sess.: 1289–93. Members of the committee were Republicans Francis E. Spinner of New York, A. C. M. Pennington of New Jersey and Lewis D. Campbell of Ohio, and Democrats Howell Cobb of Georgia and Alfred B. Greenwood of Arkansas.

27. *Boston Atlas,* May 23, 1856, 2; *New York Tribune,* May 23, 1856, 4; *New York Herald,* May 23, 1856, 4; May 26, 1856, 4; *New York Times,* May 28, 1856, 4.

28. *Boston Atlas,* June 11, 1856, 2; June 18, 1856, 2; Orangeburg *Southron,* June 11, 1856.

29. Orangeburg *Southron,* June 11, 1856.

30. *Richmond Whig,* May 23, 1856, 2; Richmond *Enquirer,* June 12, 1856; Orangeburg *Southron,* May 28, 1856.

31. Columbia *South Carolinian,* July 30, 1856, 2; *Sumter Watchman,* June 4, 1856, 2. For other expressions of approval, see Craven, *Coming of the Civil War,* 374–77.

32. *Charleston Mercury,* June 13, 1856; *Charleston News,* June 10, 1856.

33. Newspapers reported meetings at Orangeburg, Edgefield, Bishopville, Ninety-Six, Chester, Hamburg, Newberry, Anderson, Columbia, Bamburg, and Fairfield. Doubtless there were others (Keitt to Sue Sparks, June 8, May 28, 1856, 2; May 31, 1856, 2; 1856; *Charleston Mercury,* Columbia *Carolina Times,* June 2, 5, 11, 1856; Orangeburg *Southron,* June 18, 1856).

34. *Charleston Mercury,* May 29, 1856, 2.

35. *Congressional Globe,* 34th Congress, 1st sess.: 1306, app. 631; Orangeburg *Southron,* June 4, 1856.

36. *Congressional Globe,* 34th Congress, 1st sess.: 1348–49.

37. *Congressional Globe,* 34th Congress, 1st sess.: 1349–52.

38. *Congressional Globe,* 34th Congress, 1st sess.: app. 805–9; *New York Times,* July 10, 1856, 1.

39. Donald, *Charles Sumner* 1: 308; *Biographical Directory of the American Congress,* 672–3.

40. *Congressional Globe,* 34th Congress, 1st sess.: app. 655.

41. *Congressional Globe,* 34th Congress, 1st sess.: app. 655.

42. *Congressional Globe,* 34th Congress, 1st sess.: app. 656.

43. *New York Times,* June 24, 1856, 1; Donald, *Charles Sumner* 1: 308.

44. *Boston Atlas,* July 10, 1856. For an account of the trial, see *Charleston Courier,* July 10, 1856, 1; July 14, 1856, 1.

45. *Congressional Globe,* 34th Congress, 1st sess.: 1628, 1641, app. 833–38. Only two congressmen from slave states voted to censure Keitt, one from West Texas, one from Delaware. Twenty congressmen from free states voted against censure—14 Democrats, 2 Know Nothings, and 4 members of "The Opposition" who would soon call themselves Republicans. Seven represented Philadelphia, New York, or their suburbs. Four came from "Little Dixie," the southernmost districts of Ohio and Indiana. See Martis, *Historical Atlas of United States Congressional Districts,* 88–89, and Martis, *Political Atlas of Political Parties in the United States,* 108–9.

46. *Congressional Globe,* 34th Congress, 1st sess.: app. 653–56, 833–34; *New York Tribune,* July 18, 1856, 4.

47. *Congressional Globe,* 34th Congress, 1st sess.: app. 838.

48. *Charleston Mercury,* July 17, 1856, 2; *Charleston Courier,* July 21, 1856, 2.

49. *Abbeville Banner,* July 24, 1856, 2; *Charleston Courier,* July 25, 1856, 2; *Yorkville Enquirer,* July 24, 1856, 2.

50. *Charleston Mercury,* July 25, 1856, 2.

51. *Charleston Mercury,* July 25, 1856, 2.

52. *Edgefield Advertiser,* August 27, 1856, 1.

53. *Charleston Mercury,* July 24, 1856, 2; July 31, 1856, 2; August 6, 1856, 2. *Charleston Courier,* July 28, 1856, 2. *Abbeville Banner,* July 24, 1856, 2.

54. *Edgefield Advertiser,* August 13, 1856, 4; Columbia *Carolina Times,* August 6, 1856.

55. Orangeburg *Southron,* July 31, 1856.

56. *Congressional Globe,* 34th Congress, 1st sess.: 1944, 1948.

57. *Congressional Globe,* 34th Congress, 3rd sess.: 501–2; *Charleston Mercury,* February 2, 1857, 1; *Charleston Courier,* January 29, 1857, 1; Abbeville *Independent,* February 6, 1857, 2; *Sumter Watchman,* February 4, 1857, 2.

58. *New York Tribune,* June 12, 1856, 4. See also L. M. Keitt to Sue Sparks, June 19, 1956, Keitt Papers, Duke.

59. *Lexington Gazette,* July 22, 1858, 2.

60. Lexington *Valley Star,* July 10, 1856, 1.

61. Keitt, *Address Delivered before the Two Literary Societies,* 1–26.

62. Keitt, *Address Delivered before the Two Literary Societies,* 1–26.

63. Lexington *Valley Star,* July 10, 1856, 1. *Lexington Gazette,* July 10, 1856, 1; July 22, 1858, 2.

64. Keitt to Sue Sparks, June 8, 1856, Keitt Collection, Newspaper Clippings.

65. *New York Herald,* September 21, 1856, 1–2.

66. *Charleston Courier,* September 25, 1856, 1.

67. *New York Times,* September 22, 1856, 2; September 26, 1856, 2; September 29, 1856, 3.

68. *New York Times,* September 29, 1856, 5. *New York Herald,* September 22, 1856, 4; October 2, 1856, 4–5.

69. *Lynchburg Virginian,* September 13, 1856, 2, 3.

70. *Richmond Examiner,* September 23, 1856, 1.

71. *Charleston Mercury,* November 29, 1856, 2; Abbeville *Independent Press,* October 24, 1856, 2.

72. *New York Times,* October 14, 1856, 3.

73. *Charleston Mercury,* October 23, 1856, 2; November 13, 1856, 2. *Sumter Watchman,* November 5, 1856, 1.

74. Keitt, "Patriotic Services of the North and the South," 491–508; *Charleston Mercury,* October 17, 1856, 2.

75. Nevins, *Ordeal of the Union,* 2: 487–514; Schultz, *South Carolina,* 124.

Chapter 4: "Shake the Federal temple from turret to foundation stone"

1. Stampp, *America in 1857,* 6–7; *Congressional Globe,* 34th Congress, 1st sess.: 77; *Messages and Papers of the President* 5: 397–407.

2. *New York Times,* December 8, 1856, 1.

3. *Congressional Globe,* 34th Congress, 1st sess.: 77–78.

4. *Congressional Globe,* 34th Congress, 1st sess.: 77–78.

5. *Congressional Globe,* 34th Congress, 1st sess.: 77–78.

6. *Congressional Globe,* 34th Congress, 1st sess.: 77–78.

7. For the court's decision, see *Dred Scott v. John F. A. Sandford,* 19 Howard 393 (1857). The most useful analysis is Fehrenbacher, *The Dred Scott Case.* For a recent and persuasive interpretation, see Freehling, *Road to Disunion,* 2: chap. 9; the footnotes are especially useful.

8. Nevins, *Emergence of Lincoln* 133–40; Stampp, *America in 1857,* 5, 146–158; Etcheson, *Bleeding Kansas,* 131–42.

9. Nevins, *Emergence of Lincoln* 1: 144–47, 150–54; Nichols, 106–8, 111–24; Etcheson, *Bleeding Kansas,* 143–51; Freehling, *Road to Disunion* 2: 128–133.

10. Nevins, *Emergence of Lincoln* 1: 144–47, 150–54; Nichols, 106–8, 111–24; Etcheson, *Bleeding Kansas,* 143–51; Freehling, *Road to Disunion* 2: 128–33.

11. *Cheraw Gazette,* May 27, 1857.

12. *Cheraw Gazette,* May 27, 1857.

13. *Cheraw Gazette,* May 27, 1857.

14. *Cheraw Gazette,* May 27, 1857; Cheraw *Herald,* May 26, 1857; *Sumter Watchman,* June 3, 1857, 2; *Charleston Mercury,* June 6, 1857, 2; *Charleston Courier,* June 1, 1857, 1; *Lexington Gazette,* June 11, 1857, 1.

15. L. M. Keitt to William Porcher Miles, June 17, 1857, Miles Papers.

16. *Richmond Examiner,* June 26, 1857, 2.

17. *Richmond Examiner,* June 26, 1857, 2. The editor was alluding to a political theory widely shared by advocates of slavery that the South could best defend its peculiar institution by supporting the Democratic Party. The South could overcome its minority position

in the nation by dominating the majority party, and through it determine the shape of national legislation. The strategy was generally successful until 1860 when the lower South bolted the Charleston convention, split the party, and destroyed its usefulness. See Nichols, "Why the Democratic Party Divided," in Knowles, ed., *Crisis of the Union*, 30–50.

18. *Richmond Examiner*, July 3, 1857, 2. See also *Charleston Courier*, July 9, 1857, 1; *Charleston Mercury*, July 10, 1857, 2; *Sumter Watchman*, July 15, 1857, 2; Abbeville *Independent Press*, July 17, 1857, 2; *New York Herald*, July 6, 1857, 2; *New York Times*, July 7, 1857, 2.

19. *New York Herald*, July 6, 1857, 4.

20. Among the betrayals Keitt charged to the northern democracy were its support of the protective tariff, internal improvements, and the Wilmot Proviso; its votes to dismember Texas, admit California, and abolish the slave trade in the District of Columbia; its refusal to extend the Missouri Compromise line to the Pacific Ocean; its vote against the Kansas-Nebraska bill and its cooperation with Free Soilers in the territories. To Keitt the southerner who placed his confidence in the Democratic Party was a mad man or a fool.

21. *Marion Star*, n.d., in *Sumter Watchman*, August 19, 1857, 2; *New York Times*, August 17, 1857, 5.

22. Ibid. For a convincing argument that Buchanan was far more sympathetic to the South and slavery than Keitt believed, see Freehling, *Road to Disunion* 2: 97–108, 131–39.

23. *New York Times*, August 17, 1857, 4; *New York Herald*, August 17, 1857, 4.

24. Nevins, *Emergence of Lincoln* 1: 168–75, 239–47; Nichols, *Disruption of American Democracy*, 104–8, 133–38, 160.

25. Nevins, *Emergence of Lincoln* 1: 161–62, 229–36; Nichols, *Disruption of American Democracy*, 129–33; Etcheson, *Bleeding Kansas*, 141–56.

26. Nevins, *Emergence of Lincoln* 1: 173, 264–69; Nichols, *Disruption of American Democracy*, 125–28, 161; Etcheson, *Bleeding Kansas*, 152–64.

27. In one of his first appointments, Orr made Keitt chairman of the House Committee on Public Buildings and Grounds (*Congressional Globe*, 35th Congress, 1st sess.: 23).

28. *Congressional Globe*, 35th Congress, 1st sess.: app. 1–7; Nevins, *Emergence of Lincoln* 1: 248–49; Nichols, *Disruption of American Democracy*, 159; Stampp, *American in 1857*, 299–301, 324–25.

29. L. M. Keitt to James H. Hammond, December 18, 1857, Hammond Papers, Library of Congress.

30. Nevins, *Emergence of Lincoln* 1: 275–79, 284–87; Nichols, *Disruption of American Democracy*, 167–70; Etcheson, *Bleeding Kansas*, 174.

31. Nevins, *Emergence of Lincoln* 1: 287–88; Nichols, *Disruption of American Democracy*, 161–67.

32. Nevins, *Emergence of Lincoln* 1: 287–88; Nichols, *Disruption of American Democracy*, 164–65.

33. Various accounts list twenty-three congressmen as participants: Keitt and John McQueen of South Carolina; Reuben Davis, William Barksdale, L. Q. C. Lamar, and John Quitman of Mississippi; Thomas Bocock of Virginia; James Stallworth of Alabama; Augustus Wright of Georgia; Burton Craige of North Carolina; Galusha Grow, John Cavode and William Montgomery of Pennsylvania; Cadwallader Washburne, Owen Lovejoy, and William Kellogg of Illinois; John Potter and Elihu Washburne of Wisconsin;

John Haskin of New York; Richard Mott of Ohio; David Wallbridge of Michigan; and Israel Washburne of Maine. Doubtless there were others.

34. *Charleston Mercury,* February 6, 1858, 2; February 8, 1858, 2; February 10, 1858, 2; February 13, 1858, 2; *Sumter Watchman,* February 10, 1858, 2; February 17, 1858, 2; *Abbeville Banner,* February 11, 1858, 2. Abbeville *Independent Press,* February 12, 1858, 2; February 19, 1858, 2; *New York Times,* February 6, 1858, 1; February 8, 1858, 4; February 9, 1858, 1; *New York Herald,* February 7, 1858, 4–5; February 9, 1858, 1; Nevins, *Emergence of Lincoln* 1: 288. Nichols, *Disruption of American Democracy,* 165; Mayes, ed., *Lucius Q. C. Lamar,* 74–75; Parker, *Life and Public Services of Justin Smith Morrill,* 68–70; Davis, *Recollections of Mississippi and Mississippians,* 371–72; Poore, *Perley's Reminiscences* 1: 5, 32–35; Cox, *Three Decades of Federal Legislation,* 75–76.

35. *Congressional Globe,* 35th Congress, 1st sess.: 623.

36. L. M. Keitt to Ellison S. Keitt, February 17, 1858, in Charles Colcock Jones, "Autograph Letters and Portraits of the Signers of the Constitution of the Confederate States."

37. *New York Times,* February 8, 1858, 4; *Charleston Courier,* February 16, 1858, 2; *Charleston Mercury,* February 8, 1858, 2. Grow's biographers state, without providing evidence, that Keitt sent a friend to Grow to explain his statement in the House. If Keitt acknowledged that Grow had hit him, he would be forced to cane him. Grow declined to press the issue, but "often said laughingly afterward, 'I wonder what it was that made Keitt drop?'" (DuBois and Matthews, *Galusha A. Grow,* 182). See also Ilisevich, *Galusha Grow,* 163–65.

38. *New York Times,* February 8, 1858, 4–5.

39. *Ithaca* (New York) *Journal,* February 10, 1858; Charles Town *Virginia Free Press,* February 11, 1858, both in Herd, "Chapters from the Life," 117; Abbeville *Independent Press,* February 19, 1858, 2; *New York Times,* February 13, 1858, 1. William W. Freehling agreed with Greeley. He called the episode "more comic than tragic." See Freehling, *Road to Disunion* 1: 139–40.

40. *Sumter Watchman,* February 17, 1858, 2; Abbeville *Independent Press,* February 19, 1858, 2; *Charleston Mercury,* February 13, 1858, 2; Raleigh *Standard,* February 17, 1858, in Herd, "Chapters from the Life," 119.

41. David F. Jamison to James H. Hammond, February 22, 1858, in Hammond Papers, Library of Congress.

42. Benjamin Evans to William Porcher Miles, March 4, 1858, and Allan McFarlan to William Porcher Miles, February 14, 1858, in Miles Papers.

43. William Henry Trescott to William Porcher Miles, February 7, 1858, Miles Papers.

44. [Oliver Wendell Holmes?], "The Fight Over the Body of Keitt," 100; Nevins, *Emergence of Lincoln* 1: 288. The extent to which alcohol affected Keitt's conduct is impossible to determine. He clearly had had too much to drink on the evening he attacked Grow. William Gilmore Simms reported that he was intoxicated during his speech at the dedication of the Calhoun monument in Charleston the following month. He could have been drinking on other occasions when his behavior shocked friends and enemies alike. The consumption of alcohol was a conspicuous feature of American life in the mid-nineteenth century. Whether Keitt drank more than other men is a question without an answer. The possibility that Keitt was emotionally unstable is also impossible

to determine. His temper was volatile, and he occasionally lost control of it. His rhetoric was frequently bombastic and his behavior violent. It seems probable, however, that his actions were shaped less by alcohol or mental instability than by the culture in which he lived. See Wyatt-Brown, *Yankee Saints and Southern Sinners,* chap. 7, and Wyatt-Brown, *Shaping of Southern Culture,* chap. 8.

45. James H. Hammond to William Gilmore Simms, February 7, 1858, Hammond Papers, Library of Congress; Nevins, *Emergence of Lincoln* 1: 288–92; Nichols, *Disruption of American Democracy,* 165–71.

46. *Congressional Globe,* 35th Congress, 1st sess.: 1009–13.

47. *Congressional Globe,* 35th Congress, 1st sess.: 1009–13.

48. *Charleston Mercury,* March 13, 1858, 2; *Abbeville Banner,* March 18, 1858, 2. See also: *Sumter Watchman,* March 24, 1858, 2; Abbeville *Independent Press,* March 19, 1858, 2.

49. Nevins, *Emergence of Lincoln* 1: 292–93; Nichols, *Disruption of American Democracy,* 171–73; Etcheson, *Bleeding Kansas,* 176.

50. *New York Herald,* April 2, 1858, 1; Nevins, *Emergence of Lincoln* 1: 295–97; Windle, *Life in Washington,* 349–50, Nichols, *Disruption of American Democracy,* 173–74.

51. Nevins, *Emergence of Lincoln* 1: 296–301; Nichols, *Disruption of American Democracy,* 172–80. Etcheson, *Bleeding Kansas,* 168–84.

52. *Congressional Globe,* 35th Congress, 1st sess.: 1863–64, 1886. At the conclusion of his remarks on the Lecompton constitution and the English Compromise, Keitt launched a vicious attack on the constitution of Minnesota that was about to come before the House for approval. It was, he insisted, "deformed, disfigured, disgraced by base imposture, by driveling philanthropy, by whining hypocracy, and by a practical amalgamation of the white and black races . . . [a] miserable and rickety thing."

53. William Porcher Miles to James H. Hammond, November 10, 1858, Hammond Papers, Library of Congress.

54. *Charleston Mercury,* May 1, 1858, 2; *Sumter Watchman,* May 12, 1858, 2; Nevins, *Emergence of Lincoln* 1: 300–301.

Chapter 5: "Like mildew and blast, like pestilence and famine"

1. W. A. Owens to James H. Hammond, May 11, 1858, Hammond Papers, Library of Congress.

2. *Charleston Mercury,* July 12, 1858, 2; July 19, 1858, 2; *Sumter Watchman,* July 21, 1858, 2; Oliphant and others, eds., *Letters of William Gilmore Simms* 4: 86n.

3. William Gilmore Simms to James H. Hammond, June 26, 1858, in Oliphant and others, eds., *Letters of William Gilmore Simms* 4: 72. Simms obviously considered Keitt an intellectual lightweight, an opinion seemingly shared by his scholarly friends. It is disappointing that Simms did not explain what he wanted Keitt to become. He was probably right when he told Hammond that Keitt was vain and clearly right when he called his rhetoric flowery, but he was wrong when he insisted that Keitt lacked purpose. He had, after all, devoted his public career to wrenching South Carolina out of the Union.

4. *Charleston Mercury,* June 29, 1858, 2; *Charleston Courier,* June 29, 1858, 2; *Sumter Watchman,* July 14, 1858, 2.

5. *Charleston Mercury,* June 29, 1858, 2.

6. W. G. Simms to J. H. Hammond, July 16, 1858, in *Letters of William Gilmore Simms,* ed. Oliphant and others, vol. 4: 80. The story is open to question. Apparently Simms was quoting a rumor that was making the rounds in Charleston, not reporting an incident he had witnessed. Nowhere in his correspondence does Keitt refer to such an event. Highly detailed accounts of the day's activities published in Charleston newspapers —not always a reliable source of information—do not suggest that he experienced difficulty in completing his address or participating in the closing ceremonies that followed. More than anything else, Simms's story resembles a smear circulated by Keitt's enemies calculated to reduce his vote in October.

7. L. M. Keitt to W. P. Miles, July 1, 1858, Miles Papers.

8. *Charleston Mercury,* June 29, 1858, 2; *Sumter Watchman,* July 14, 1858, 2; Abbeville *Independent Press,* July 2, 1858, 2.

9. For outstanding analyses of the role of Old Republican ideology in South Carolina politics, see Faust, *James Henry Hammond,* 40–43, 148–49, 222–23, 331–34; Freehling, *Road to Disunion* 2: 170–71, 293–94, 353–54; and Greenberg, *Masters and Statesmen,* chaps. 3–4.

10. L. M. Keitt to J. H. Hammond, June 23, 1858, Hammond Papers, Library of Congress.

11. L. M. Keitt to J. H. Hammond, July 5, 1858, Hammond Papers, Library of Congress.

12. Abbeville *Independent Press,* August 13, 1858, 1.

13. L. M. Keitt to J. H. Hammond, August 9, 1858, Hammond Papers, Library of Congress.

14. *Sumter Watchman,* July 14, 1858, 2.

15. *Charleston Mercury,* August 9, 1858, 2; August 16, 1858, 2. *Charleston Courier,* August 14, 1858. Abbeville *Independent Press,* August 13, 1858, 2.

16. Columbia *South Carolinian,* Orangeburg *Southron, Abbeville Banner, Anderson Gazette, Unionville Journal,* no dates, in *Charleston Courier,* August 13, 1858, 2; September 6, 1858, 2. Unidentified clippings, Keitt Collection, Newspaper Clippings.

17. Kibler, *Benjamin F. Perry,* 291.

18. [James D. Tradewell], *An Appeal to the State Rights Party of South Carolina,* in Schultz, *Nationalism and Sectionalism,* 172.

19. *Charleston Mercury,* August 25, 1858, 2.

20. W. G. Simms to J. H. Hammond, March 27, 1858, and J. H. Hammond to W. G. Simms, April 3, 1858, in *Letters of William Gilmore Simms,* ed. Oliphant and others, vol. 4: 43–44. I. W. Hayne to J. H. Hammond, April 17, 21, 1858, Hammond Papers, Southern Historical Collection, University of North Carolina. W. H. Trescott to W. P. Miles, May 30, 1858, Miles Papers; L. M. Keitt to W. P. Miles, July 1, 1858, Miles Papers.

21. L. M. Keitt to W. P. Miles, October 6, 8, 1858, Miles Papers.

22. *Charleston Mercury,* October 13, 1858, 2.

23. *Charleston Mercury,* October 13, 1858, 2; *Lancaster Ledger,* October 20, 1858, 2. The *New York Herald* observed that swamps were charged with deadly gases. Whippy Swamp was the ideal site for Keitt's "pestilential exhalations" (quoted in *Charleston Mercury,* October 27, 1858, 2).

24. *Charleston Mercury,* October 15, 1858, 2.

25. *Sumter Watchman,* November 2, 1858, 2; November 16, 1858, 2.

26. *Abbeville Banner,* June 18, 1857, 2; *Yorkville Enquirer,* October 15, 1857, 2; *Charleston Mercury,* December 1, 1857, 2.

27. John Cunningham to J. H. Hammond, June 20, 1857; M. C. M. Hammond to J. H. Hammond, December 2, 3, 1857; Peyton G. Bonner to J. H. Hammond, January 24, 1858, Hammond Papers, Library of Congress.

28. J. H. Hammond to M. C. M. Hammond, May 16, 1858, Hammond Papers, Library of Congress.

29. L. M. Keitt to J. H. Hammond, August 9, 1858, Hammond Papers, Library of Congress.

30. Richmond *South,* July 24, 1858, 2; *Charleston Mercury,* July 28, 1858, 1; *Sumter Watchman,* August 4, 1858, 2.

31. Schultz, *Nationalism and Sectionalism,* 175–77.

32. Schultz, *Nationalism and Sectionalism,* 176; Takaki, *Pro-Slavery Crusade,* 192; *Charleston Mercury,* December 17, 1858, 2; Abbeville *Independent Press,* December 3, 1858, 2; December 10, 1858, 2.

33. Politicians who announced their willingness to fill Keitt's seat included William A. Owens, Lewis M. Ayer, George P. Elliott, John E. Tobin, William H. Barnwell, and Robert Barnwell Rhett Sr. (*Charleston Courier,* December 15, 1858, 1; *Charleston Mercury,* December 17, 1858, 2; January 3, 1859, 2; February 24, 1859, 2; March 24, 1859, 1; August 8, 1859, 1; August 30, 1859, 1; *Sumter Watchman,* December 21, 1858, 2; Orangeburg *Southron,* March 9, 1859; W. H. Trescott to W. P. Miles, November 8, 20, 1859, Miles Papers).

Chapter 6: "Lance couched, helmet on, visor down"

1. The secondary literature on the defense of slavery is voluminous. The most valuable works include Jenkins, *Pro-Slavery Thought in the Old South*; Fredrickson, *The Black Image in the White Mind,* 43–70; Faust, ed., *The Ideology of Slavery,* esp. 1–20; Faust, *A Sacred Circle,* 112–31; Finkelman, *Defending Slavery,* esp. 19–44; and Tise, *Proslavery.*

2. On Fitzhugh, see Genovese, *World the Slaveholders Made,* part 2; on Simms, see Wakelyn, *The Politics of a Literary Man,* esp. chap. 8; on Dew, see Root, *All Honor to Jefferson,* chap. 7; on Thornwell, see Farmer, *Metaphysical Confederacy,* esp. 216–33.

3. Windle, *Life in Washington,* 40–42; *Charleston Courier,* January 31, 1857, 4. For a similar account by the same author, see *Charleston Courier,* June 5, 1858, 1.

4. *Congressional Globe,* 33rd Congress, 1st sess.: app. 467–68; 34th Congress, 1st sess.: app. 442–44; 34th Congress, 3rd sess.: app. 140. *Charleston Mercury,* April 17, 1855, 2; April 18, 1855, 2; August 16, 1855, 2.

5. *Congressional Globe,* 33rd Congress, 1st sess.: app. 467–68; 34th Congress, 1st sess.: app. 442–44; 34th Congress, 3rd sess.: app. 140. *Charleston Mercury,* April 17, 1855, 2; April 18, 1855, 2; August 16, 1855, 2.

6. *Congressional Globe,* 34th Congress, 3rd sess.: app. 140–42. See also *Charleston Mercury,* April 14, 1857, 2; *Charleston Courier,* April 30, 1857, 1.

7. *Congressional Globe,* 36th Congress, 1st sess.: app. 94.

8. *Congressional Globe,* 36th Congress, 1st sess.: app. 94.

9. *Congressional Globe,* 34th Congress, 1st sess.: app. 443.

10. *Congressional Globe,* 34th Congress, 1st sess.: app. 443.

11. *Congressional Globe,* 33rd Congress, 1st sess.: app. 130; 35th Congress, 1st sess., app. 404–6.

12. Ibid.

13. *Congressional Globe,* 35th Congress, 1st sess., app. 405.

14. *Congressional Globe,* 35th Congress, 1st sess.: app. 407, 409. For similar arguments, see *Congressional Globe,* 35th Congress, 2nd sess.: app. 270–75.

15. *Congressional Globe,* 33rd Congress, 1st sess.: app. 130. Keitt used the same argument in his defense of slavery at the Virginia Military Institute in Lexington, Virginia, *Address Delivered before the Two Literary Societies of the Virginia Military Institute, July 4, 1856,* 1–26.

16. *Congressional Globe,* 35th Congress, 2nd sess.: app. 370; 36th Congress, 1st sess.: app. 94.

17. *Congressional Globe,* 33rd Congress, 1st sess.: app. 467.

18. *Congressional Globe,* 36th Congress, 1st sess.: app. 94.

19. *Congressional Globe,* 34th Congress, 1st sess.: app. 444.

20. On the debate between advocates of single and plural creations, see Fredrickson, *Black Image in the American Mind,* chap. 3.

21. *Congressional Globe,* 34th Congress, 3rd sess.: app. 143–44; 36th Congress, 1st sess.: app. 97.

22. May, *Southern Dream of a Caribbean Empire,* chap. 8; Freehling, *Road to Disunion,* 2: 155–59.

23. *Congressional Globe,* 33rd Congress, 1st sess.: app. 130–33; Keitt, *Tonnage Duties.* See also *Speech of Hon. Lawrence M. Keitt, of South Carolina, on the Acquisition of Cuba.*

24. In October 1854, the three principal American diplomats in Europe—Pierre Soulé, James M. Mason, and James Buchanan—met first at Ostend and later at Aix-la-Chapelle to draft the Ostend Manifesto. The federal government, they announced, should immediately attempt to buy Cuba from Spain. If Spain rejected the offer and if its possession of Cuba threatened American peace and security, the government should take the island, by force if necessary (Nevins, *Ordeal of the Union,* 2: 348–63; May, *Southern Dream of a Caribbean Empire,* 67–71).

25. *Charleston Mercury,* October 17, 1854, 2.

26. L. M. Keitt to Sue Sparks, February 14, 1855, [May 1855], Keitt Papers, Duke.

27. *Congressional Globe,* 33rd Congress, 2nd sess.: app. 91–94.

28. L. M. Keitt to James Chesnut, February 9, 1855, Williams-Chesnut-Manning Papers, South Caroliniana Library, University of South Carolina, Columbia, South Carolina.

29. May, *Southern Dream of a Caribbean Empire,* 203–5. Freehling, *Road to Disunion* 2: 152–59. Boucher, "South Carolina and the South," 100n. *Charleston Mercury,* January 18, 1855, 2; January 23, 1855, 2; April 2, 1855, 2.

30. May, *Southern Dream of a Caribbean Empire,* 203–5, 234–35; Channing, *Crisis of Fear,* 162–63.

31. Schott, *Alexander H. Stephens,* 269; May, *Southern Dream of a Caribbean Empire,* 186.

32. *Charleston Mercury,* April 17, 1855, 2; April 18, 1855, 2. L. M. Keitt, *Speech of Hon. Lawrence M. Keitt Delivered at Orangeburg, South Carolina, Monday, April 16, 1855.*

33. Keitt, *Speech of Hon. Lawrence M. Keitt Delivered at Orangeburg, South Carolina, Monday, April 16, 1855.*

34. Keitt, *Speech of Hon. Lawrence M. Keitt Delivered at Orangeburg, South Carolina, Monday, April 16, 1855.*

35. *Charleston Mercury,* April 17, 1855, 2; April 19, 1855, 2; April 28, 1855, 2.

36. A. D. Mann to L. M. Keitt, June 1, 1855; L. M. Keitt to Sue Sparks, June 6, 1855, Keitt Papers, Duke.

37. Nevins, *Ordeal of the Union* 2: 361–63; May, *Southern Dream of a Caribbean Empire,* 69–71.

38. *Messages and Papers of the Presidents* 5: 509–11.

39. Nevins, *Ordeal of the Union* 2: 423, 445–49; May, *Southern Dream of a Caribbean Empire,* 163–89; Nichols, *Disruption of American Democracy,* 231–33.

40. *Congressional Globe,* 35th Congress, 2nd sess.: 453–57. Keitt had first used the argument during a speech on slavery and southern resources delivered January 15, 1857. See *Congressional Globe,* 34th Congress, 3rd sess.: app. 140–45.

41. *Congressional Globe,* 35th Congress, 2nd sess.: 456; *Speech of Hon. Lawrence M. Keitt, of South Carolina, on the Acquisition of Cuba.*

42. *Charleston Mercury,* February 28, 1859, 2; May, *Southern Dream of a Caribbean Empire,* 186–89.

43. May, *John A. Quitman,* 270–95; May, *Manifest Destiny's Underworld,* 47–52; May, *Southern Dream of a Caribbean Empire,* 46–53; Brown, *Agents of Manifest Destiny,* 117–44.

44. May, *Southern Dream of a Caribbean Empire,* 77–135.

45. May, *Southern Dream of a Caribbean Empire,* 114–17; *Charleston Courier,* January 9, 1858, 1; May, *John A. Quitman,* 336–37.

46. *Congressional Globe,* 35th Congress, 1st sess.: 216–17.

47. *Congressional Globe,* 35th Congress, 1st sess.: 197–99.

48. *Charleston Mercury,* January 8, 1858, 2; *Charleston Courier,* January 9, 1858, 1.

49. *Congressional Globe,* 35th Congress, 1st sess.: 213.

50. *Congressional Globe,* 35th Congress, 1st sess.: 213, 299.

51. *Congressional Globe,* 35th Congress, 2nd sess.: 318; May, *Southern Dream of a Caribbean Empire,* 124–25. See also Brown, *Agents of Manifest Destiny,* 267–447.

52. Takaki, *Pro-Slavery Crusade,* 1–2; Freehling, *Road to Disunion* 2: 168–77.

53. Takaki, *Pro-Slavery Crusade,* 103–33.

54. In *The Counterrevolution of Slavery,* 127, Manisha Sinha incorrectly includes Miles and Keitt on her roster of men who wanted to reopen the African slave trade.

55. Takaki, *Pro-Slavery Crusade,* 11.

56. Smith, *Economic Readjustment,* esp. 22–25, 62, 106, 209; Freehling, *Road to Disunion* 2: 171, 293, 363–64.

57. Freehling, *Road to Disunion* 2: 177–80.

58. *Congressional Globe,* 34th Congress, 3rd sess.: 123.

59. *Congressional Globe,* 34th Congress, 3rd sess.: 123–25.

60. *Congressional Globe,* 34th Congress, 3rd sess.: 125–26; Schultz, *Nationalism and Sectionalism,* 131–32.

61. Nevins, *Emergence of Lincoln,* 1: 434–35; Takaki, *Pro-Slavery Crusade,* 212–36.

62. Nevins, *Emergence of Lincoln* 1: 435–37; Takaki, *Pro-Slavery Crusade,* 202–12; Freehling, *Road to Disunion* 2: 183–84.

63. *Congressional Globe,* 35th Congress, 2nd sess.: 615. *Charleston Mercury,* January 29, 1859, 2; February 1, 1859, 2.

64. For a more objective description of the American Colonization Society, see Staudenraus, *The African Colonization Movement, 1816–1865.*

65. *Congressional Globe,* 35th Congress, 2nd sess.: 615.

Chapter 7: "Take the fetters from your heart"

1. Nevins, *Ordeal of the Union,* 1: 51–53; Nevins, *Emergence of Lincoln,* 1: 119–29; Nichols, *Disruption of American Democracy,* 17.

2. Nevins, *Ordeal of the Union* 2: 54–58; *Congressional Directory,* 33rd Congress, 1st sess.; Sterling, ed., *Belle of the Fifties,* chap. 3.

3. Nevins, *Ordeal of the Union* 2: 54. On the president's bizarre reputation as a drunkard, see Nichols, *Franklin Pierce,* 86–87, 291.

4. Nevins, *Ordeal of the Union* 2: 54–56.

5. *Charleston Courier,* January 24, 1854, 2; *Abbeville Banner,* February 2, 1854, 2; Sterling, *Belle of the Fifties,* 95; Ellet, *Court Circles of the Republic,* 496.

6. L. M. Keitt to "My Dear Sister" [Anna Keitt Whaley], December 13, 1853, Keitt Papers, Duke.

7. Thomas, *A History of Marlboro,* 34–35; Dudley, "History of Bennettville," 21; Davidson, *Last Foray,* 252; U.S. Census, South Carolina, Marlborough District, Slave Schedule, 1850; U.S. Census, South Carolina, Marlborough District, Agriculture Schedule, 1850; L. M. Keitt to Sue Sparks, July 29, 1855; Keitt Papers, Duke.

8. *Anderson Gazette,* December 20, 1854, Keitt Collection, Newspaper Clippings. See also Robert F. W. Allston to Adele Pettigrew Allston, December 1, 1851, in *South Carolina Rice Plantation,* ed. Easterby, 111. Describing a South Carolina College commencement, Allston wrote: "One of the prettiest girls was Miss Sparks from Marlborough, but poor child she was laced up like a wasp."

9. Greenville *Southern Patriot,* August 16, 1855, Keitt Collection, Newspaper Clippings; L. M. Keitt to Sue Sparks, September 11, 19, 1855, Keitt Papers, Duke

10. L. M. Keitt to Sue Sparks, January 20, February 14, September 19, 1855, January 10, 1856, Keitt Papers, Duke; Lately Thomas [Robert V. P. Steele], *Between Two Empires,* 158–63.

11. L. M. Keitt to Sue Sparks, January 20, 1855, Keitt Papers, Duke.

12. L. M. Keitt to Sue Sparks, February 14, 1855, Keitt Papers, Duke.

13. L. M. Keitt to Sue Sparks, [June 1855?], Keitt Papers, Duke.

14. L. M. Keitt to Sue Sparks, July 11, 1855, Keitt Papers, Duke.

15. L. M. Keitt to Sue Sparks, [June 1855], Keitt Papers, Duke.

16. L. M. Keitt to Sue Sparks, July 29, 1855, Keitt Papers, Duke.

17. L. M. Keitt to Sue Sparks, July 29, 1855, Keitt Papers, Duke. In spite of the absence of evidence, it is tempting to speculate about the books Keitt might have read during the time he spent in the mountains. In the mid-nineteenth century, scholars often used the terms "metaphysics" and "philosophy" interchangeably, a practice that makes speculation particularly problematic. Keitt sprinkled his speeches with references to ancient history, and he may have returned to authors he had read when he was studying with Francis Lieber and Robert Henry at South Carolina College—Tacitus and Cicero. Or he may have spent time reading British philosophers—John Locke, David Hume, and Francis Hutcheson. But he may also have focused on American political philosophers—the authors of the *Federalist,* John Taylor of Caroline, or John C. Calhoun. Unfortunately his letters to Susanna Sparks do not identify the books he read that might have helped to shape his thinking during his years in Congress.

18. L. M. Keitt to Sue Sparks, September 11, 1855, Keitt Papers, Duke.

19. L. M. Keitt to Sue Sparks, March 16, September 19, 1855, Keitt Papers, Duke.

20. L. M. Keitt to Sue Sparks, January 20, September 19, October 13, 1855; May 10, 29, June 8, 19, 1956, Keitt Papers, Duke.

21. L. M. Keitt to Sue Sparks, January 20, October 4, 1855, Keitt Papers, Duke. Herd says Keitt was earlier engaged to a girl who died. I can find no evidence to support his assertion ("Chapters from the Life," 143). On courtship and marriage practices in the antebellum South, see Jabour, *Scarlet's Sisters,* chaps. 4–6; Clinton, *Plantation Mistress,* chap. 4.

22. L. M. Keitt to Sue Sparks, February 14, 1855; [February 1855]; May 3, 9, 1855, Keitt Papers, Duke.

23. L. M. Keitt to Sue Sparks, [April 1855], May 9, 1855, [May 1855], Keitt Papers, Duke.

24. L. M. Keitt to Sue Sparks, [April 1855], Keitt Papers, Duke.

25. L. M. Keitt to Sue Sparks, [May 1855], May 3, 1855, Keitt Papers, Duke.

26. L. M. Keitt to Sue Sparks, May 9, September 26, 1855, Keitt Papers, Duke.

27. L. M. Keitt to Sue Sparks, [May 1855], June 6, July 29, 1855, Keitt Papers, Duke.

28. L. M. Keitt to Sue Sparks, September 26, 1855, Keitt Papers, Duke.

29. L. M. Keitt to Sue Sparks, October 4, November 6, 29, 1855, Keitt Papers, Duke.

30. L. M. Keitt to Sue Sparks, January 3, 10, 1856, Keitt Papers, Duke.

31. L. M. Keitt to Sue Sparks, February 2, 17, March 9, 1856, Keitt Papers, Duke.

32. For an analysis of Sue Sparks's reluctance to marry, see Berry, *All That Makes a Man,* 59–64, 227–28.

33. L. M. Keitt to Sue Sparks, February 2, March 9, April 13, 1856, Keitt Papers, Duke.

34. The best Washington families, Keitt explained, kept Lent strictly because it was fashionable to do so. But "traveling persons" had no religion to speak of, and festivities continued in all the big hotels (Keitt to Sue Sparks, March 23, 1856, Keitt Papers, Duke).

35. L. M. Keitt to Sue Sparks, March 9, 23, April 13, 30, 1856, Keitt Papers, Duke.

36. L. M. Keitt to Sue Sparks, May 10, June 19, 1856, Keitt Papers, Duke.

37. L. M. Keitt to Sue Sparks, July 7, 1856, Keitt Papers, Duke.

38. Herd, "Chapters from the Life," 149; Windle, *Life in Washington,* 61–62, 144, 271, 327, 343; Ellet, *Court Circles of the Republic,* 496; Sterling, ed., *Belle of the Fifties,* 95;

Forney, *Anecdotes of Public Men* 1: 283–84, 332; Cox, *Three Decades of Federal Legislation,* 410–11; Lately Thomas [Robert V. P. Steele], *Between Two Empires,* 158–63; *Harper's Weekly,* February 26, 1859, 134; Nevins, *Emergence of Lincoln* 1: 431; Alfred Huger to W. P. Miles, February 18, 1858, Robert Bunch to W. P. Miles, February 18, 1858, M. L. Bonham to W. P. Miles, January 30, 1858, Miles Papers.

39. Ellet, *Court Circles,* 506–9; Sterling, *Belle of the Fifties,* 95, 114–15; Pryor, *Reminiscences of Peace and War,* 53–55, 65; Poore, *Perley's Reminiscences* 2: 47, 507–8, 523; Nevins, *Emergence of Lincoln* 1: 120; *Charleston Mercury,* March 26, 1858, 2.

40. On the way to port, the couple stopped off in Washington, where Keitt had trouble convincing James Buchanan he was really married (*Charleston Mercury,* May 24, 1859, 4; *Yorkville Enquirer,* May 26, 1859, 2; *Abbeville Banner,* May 26, 1859, 2; L. M. Keitt to W. P. Miles, May 18, 1859 and John McQueen to W. P. Miles, September 28, 1859, Miles Papers; Buchanan to Harriet Lane, May 20 [1859] in *Works of James Buchanan,* ed. Moore, vol. 12: 214.

41. L. M. Keitt to J. H. Hammond, August 19, 1859, Hammond Papers, Library of Congress; L. M. Keitt to O. M. Dantzler, August 22, 1859, Dantzler Papers.

42. Ibid.

43. Ibid.

44. Ibid.

45. Sue Keitt to "Dear Mar" [Mrs. Ann H. Sparks], August 9, 1859; Charlotte A. Brown to Sue Keitt, September 8, 1859; Sue Keitt to "My Dear Father" [Samuel Sparks], [September 1859], all in Keitt Collection, Newspaper Clippings.

46. Sue Keitt to "My Dear Carrie" [Caroline W. Keitt, October 1859], Keitt Collection, Newspaper Clippings; *Charleston Mercury,* November 15, 1859.

Chapter 8: "Style, beauty, and high training"

1. *Charleston Mercury,* November 15, 1859, 2; December 6, 1859, 2; *Charleston Courier,* November 16, 1859, 4; Sue Keitt to "Dear Mar" [Ann H. Sparks], December 4, 1859, Keitt Papers, Duke.

2. Nevins, *Emergence of Lincoln,* 2: 98–112; Channing, *Crisis of Fear,* passim; Oates, *To Purge This Land With Blood,* 318–19. For a survey of southern reactions to John Brown's raid, see Wallenstein, "Incendiaries All, 149–73. For recent studies of John Brown, see McGlone, *John Brown's War against Slavery,* and David S. Reynolds, *John Brown, Abolitionist.*

3. Nevins, *Emergence of Lincoln* 2: 116–23; Nichols, *Disruption of American Democracy,* 273–76.

4. *Congressional Globe,* 36th Congress, 1st sess.

5. *Congressional Globe,* 36th Congress, 1st sess., 21; Brown, *Southern Outcast,* 156–59.

6. *Congressional Globe,* 36th Congress, 1st sess.: 23–24; Pryor, *Reminiscences of Peace and War,* 94.

7. Nichols, *Disruption of American Democracy,* 271–76; Nevins, *Emergence of Lincoln* 2: 116–124; Brown, *Southern Outcast,* 152–79.

8. *Congressional Globe,* 36th Congress, 1st sess.: 219–20.

9. *Congressional Globe,* 36th Congress, 1st sess.: 220.

10. *Charleston Courier,* December 26, 1859, 1; see also *Charleston Mercury,* December 28, 1859, 1.

11. Nevins, *Emergence of Lincoln* 2: 112–23.

12. W. H. Gist to W. P. Miles, December 29, 1859, Miles Papers.

13. Telegram, George N. Sanders to W. P. Miles and L. M. Keitt, December 16, 1859; G. N. Sanders to W. P. Miles, December 24, 1859, Miles Papers; Channing, *Crisis of Fear,* 107–8n26.

14. *Congressional Globe,* 36th Congress, 1st sess.: 235, 246.

15. Sue Keitt to "Dear Carrie" [Caroline W. Keitt, December, 1859], Keitt Papers, Duke.

16. Sue Keitt to William J. Keitt, December 9, 1859, Keitt Collection, South Caroliniana Library, University of South Carolina.

17. Sue Keitt's guests were congressmen Roger A. Pryor of Virginia and Thomas L. Clingman of North Carolina, and Assistant Secretary of State A. Dudley Mann.

18. Sue Keitt to Alex Sparks, [December 1859?], Keitt Papers, Duke.

19. Sue Keitt to "Dear Carrie," [December 1859], Keitt Papers, Duke.

20. Sue Keitt to "Dear Mother," December 22, 1859, Keitt Papers, Duke. Buchanan had a defect in one eye that impaired his sight. To compensate for it, he tilted his head slightly forward and sideways (Klein, *President James Buchanan,* 21).

21. Sue Keitt to "Dear Mother," December 22, 1859, Keitt Papers, Duke. On Sanders, see Curti, "George N. Sanders—American Patriot of the Fifties," 79–87.

22. Hammond had married Catherine Fitzsimons "out of ambition rather than love." She was wealthy but unusually homely. Young men insisted "they would not marry the girl even if every pimple on her face was worth a million dollars." Hammond did marry her because he needed her money and connections to launch his political career. He never grew to love her and was repeatedly unfaithful to her (Faust, *James Henry Hammond,* 58–61, 241–45, 303, 314–20).

23. Sue Keitt to "Dear Mother," December 26, 1859; Sue Keitt to ?, [January 1860?], Keitt Papers, Duke; *Congressional Globe,* 36th Congress, 1st sess.: 235, 246.

24. Sue Keitt to "Ma Belle Soeur" [Caroline W. Keitt], January 17, 1860, Keitt Papers, Duke.

25. Sue Keitt to "Dear Mother," December 26, 1859, Keitt Papers, Duke.

26. Sue Keitt to "Dear Mother," December 26, 1859; Sue Keitt to "My Dear Father," January 26, 1860; Sue Keitt to [Caroline W. Keitt], February 2, 11, 1860, Keitt Papers, Duke.

27. L. M. Keitt to "Ma Belle Soeur" [Carrie Sparks], January 17, 1860, Keitt Papers, Duke.

28. Sue Keitt to "My Dear Father," January 26, 1860; Sue Keitt to [Carrie Sparks], February 2, 11, 1860, Keitt Papers, Duke.

29. L. M. Keitt to "Ma Belle Soeur," January 17, 1860, Keitt Papers, Duke.

30. *Congressional Globe,* 36th Congress, 1st sess.: 368, 390.

31. L. M. Keitt to O. M. Dantzler, January 15, 1860, Dantzler Papers.

32. *Congressional Globe,* 36th Congress, 1st sess.: app. 93–97.

33. *Congressional Globe,* 36th Congress, 1st sess.: app. 93–97.

34. *Charleston Mercury,* January 28, 1860, 1; January 30, 1860, 4; February 4, 1860, 4; *Charleston Courier,* January 28, 1860; *Sumter Watchman,* February 15, 1860, 2; Orangeburg *Southron,* February 15, 1860; Keitt, *Speech of Hon. L. M. Keitt, of South Carolina, on the Organization of the House.*

35. *Congressional Globe,* 36th Congress, 1st sess.: 618–21; Nevins, *Emergence of Lincoln* 2: 123.

36. *Charleston Mercury,* February 2, 3, 1860, 1; Nevins, *Emergence of Lincoln* 2: 124. Keitt attracted two votes on the twenty-fifth ballot for Speaker, one on the twenty-eighth, and one on the thirty-second (*Congressional Globe,* 36th Congress, 1st sess.: 338, 360, 386).

37. *Congressional Globe,* 36th Congress, 1st sess.: 651–52.

38. Sue Sparks to "Carrie, Dear" [Carrie Sparks], February 2, 1860, Keitt Papers, Duke.

39. Keitt died February 19. A neighbor, Thomas C. Bauskett, wrote to Robert Barnwell Rhett Jr. the following day. Rhett telegraphed the news to Porcher Miles on February 24. Miles informed Keitt on February 25 (telegram, Robert Barnwell Rhett to W. P. Miles, [February] 24, 1860; George S. Bryan to W. P. Miles, February 24, 1860, Miles Papers).

40. L. M. Keitt to Sue Keitt, February 29, 1860, Keitt Papers, Duke; Caroline W. Keitt to Thomas B. Wadlington, March 20, 1860, Ellison S. Keitt Papers, Duke University; *Sumter Watchman,* March 7, 1860, 2.

41. Woodward, ed., *Mary Chesnut's Civil War,* 218. The white powder may have been calomel, a laxative if taken in small doses but fatal if taken in larger quantities. See Stern, *Mary Chesnut's Civil War Epic,* 125.

42. L. M. Keitt to Sue Keitt, February 29, 1860, Duke University; *Sumter Watchman,* March 7, 1860, 2; Orangeburg *Southron,* March 21, 1860; unidentified clipping, Keitt Collection, Calhoun County Museum and Cultural Center.

43. *Charleston Courier,* April 14, 1860. *Sumter Watchman,* February 22, 1860, 2; March 7, 1860, 2.

44. Sue Keitt to "Dear Carrie" [Carrie Sparks, December, 1860]; Sue Keitt to A. D. Banks and George N. Sanders, March 1, 1860, Keitt Papers, Duke.

45. Sue was referring to Mrs. Jacob Thompson, wife of the secretary of the interior and a noted Washington hostess; Mrs. Jefferson Davis, wife of the senator from Mississippi; Mrs. Clement C. Clay, whose husband was a senator from Alabama; and Mrs. William M. Gwin, wife of the senator from California and hostess of many of the capital's most fashionable parties.

46. Sue Keitt to A. D. Banks and G. N. Sanders, March 1, 1860, Keitt Papers, Duke.

47. Sue Keitt to "My Dear Father," March 25, 1860, Keitt Papers, Duke; Herd, "Chapters from the Life," 168–69.

Chapter 9: "Fidelity to the Union is treason to the South"

1. Nevins, *Emergence of Lincoln* 2: 188–96.

2. *Congressional Globe,* 36th Congress, 1st sess.: 746–47, 776, 1419, 2020, 2255–56, 2798–99; *Charleston Mercury,* February 14, 1860, 4; February 20, 1860, 4.

3. *Congressional Globe,* 36th Congress, 1st sess.: 1521–23; app. 195–98. *Charleston Mercury,* April 9, 1860, 1; *Charleston Courier,* April 9, 1860, Keitt Collection, Newspaper Clippings.

4. After insisting for more than a decade that the Congress lacked authority to exclude slavery from the territories, southern leaders now insisted that the Congress must enact legislation to protect it there. At Charleston, they demanded that the Democratic Party include in its platform a plank endorsing a federal slave code for the territories. When the northern Democrats refused, a majority of the southern delegates and a few northern sympathizers bolted the convention. See Bestor, "State Sovereignty and Slavery," 117–80.

5. Perry, *Biographical Sketches,* 186–89; Nevins, *Emergence of Lincoln* 2: 203–28; Nichols, *Disruption of American Democracy,* 288–308; Freehling, *Road to Disunion,* 2: 269, 278–308.

6. Freehling, *Road to Disunion* 2: 311–12.

7. Channing, *Crisis of Fear,* 232–33; Schultz, *Nationalism and Sectionalism,* 219–22; Nevins, *Emergence of Lincoln* 2: 262–72; Nichols, *Disruption of American Democracy,* 308–18; Freehling, *Road to Disunion* 2: 309–22.

8. Pryor, *Reminiscences of Peace and War,* 102–3; Nevins, *Emergence of Lincoln* 2: 287–90, 306–9.

9. *Charleston Mercury,* July 20, 1860, 4.

10. *Charleston Mercury,* July 20, 1860, 4.

11. White, *Robert Barnwell Rhett,* 172.

12. *New York Times,* July 24, 1860, 4.

13. *New York Tribune,* July 27, 30, 31, 1860; *Charleston Mercury,* August 3, 1860, 4.

14. *New York Herald,* July 24, 1860, Keitt Collection, Newspaper Clippings.

15. James Louis Petigru, Alfred Huger, John B. O'Neal, Isaac Hayne, and a few others held stubbornly to their faith in the Union but kept their views largely to themselves (Channing, *Crisis of Fear,* 241–44).

16. Channing, *Crisis of Fear,* 234–40. Perry, *Biographical Sketches,* 171–85; *Charleston Mercury,* August 4, 1860, 3; August 10, 1860, 4; August 21, 1860, 1; August 23, 1860, 1; Abbeville *Independent Press,* August 24, 1860, 1. For an account that emphasizes the problems the radicals had to overcome to unite the state, see Freehling, *Road to Disunion* 2: 309–423. For one that focuses on the success of the fire-eaters' demagogic tactics, see McCurry, *Confederate Reckoning,* 38–53.

17. Cauthen, *South Carolina Goes to War,* 49–50; Cauthen, "South Carolina's Decisions to Lead the Secession Movement," 360–72; Faust, *James Henry Hammond,* 349–51, 357–58.

18. L. M. Keitt to J. H. Hammond, August 4, 1860, Hammond Papers, Library of Congress.

19. L. M. Keitt to J. H. Hammond, August 7, October 23, 1860, Hammond Papers, Library of Congress.

20. The candidates for Keitt's seat in the House were Lewis M. Ayer, George P. Elliott, and William H. Barnwell (Orangeburg *Southron,* February 13, March 9, 1860).

21. L. M. Keitt to O. M. Dantzler, January 16, 1860, Dantzler Papers. L. M. Keitt to "Ma Belle Soeur," January 17, 1860, Keitt Papers, Duke. Orangeburg *Southron,* April 11, 1860. Abbeville *Independent Press,* January 13, 1860, 2. *Charleston Mercury,* January 5, 1860, 2; September 5, 1860, 4. Herd, "Chapters from the Life," 166.

22. W. G. Simms to W. P. Miles in *Letters of William Gilmore Simms,* ed. Oliphant and others, vol. 3: 230.

23. *Charleston Mercury,* September 5, 1860, 4; September 27, 1860, 4. In mid-October, Lewis M. Ayer won a substantial victory over George P. Elliott in a two-way race for the seat Keitt had reluctantly vacated (*Charleston Mercury,* October 11, 1860, 2; October 12, 1860, 2; October 13, 1860, 1). Barnwell apparently dropped out before the end of the campaign.

24. *Charleston Mercury,* September 27, 1860, 4.

25. *Charleston Mercury,* September 27, 1860, 4.

26. L. M. Keitt to W. P. Miles, October 3, 1860, Miles Papers.

27. *Charleston Mercury,* August 23, 1860, 4.

28. J. D. Ashmore to J. H. Hammond, August 30, 1860, Hammond Papers, Library of Congress.

29. L. M. Keitt to J. H. Hammond, September 10, 1860, Hammond Papers, Library of Congress.

30. L. M. Keitt to W. P. Miles, October 3, 1860, Miles Papers.

31. L. M. Keitt to W. P. Miles, October 3, 1860, Miles Papers.

32. *Charleston Mercury,* September 27, 1860, 4; *Charleston Courier,* October 22, November 3, 1860; W. G. Simms to James Lawson, October 16, 1860; *Letters of William Gilmore Simms,* ed. Oliphant and others, vol. 4: 248–49; W. G. Simms to J. H. Hammond, October 9, 1860, Hammond Papers, Library of Congress.

33. L. M. Keitt to J. H. Hammond, October 23, 1860, Hammond Papers, Library of Congress.

34. Merritt, *James Henry Hammond,* 141; Faust, *Hammond,* 357–59.

35. Nevins, *Emergence of Lincoln* 2: 312–13.

36. Nevins, *Emergence of Lincoln* 2: 318–19.

37. Cauthen, *South Carolina Goes to War,* 54–60; Nevins, *Emergence of Lincoln* 2: 319–32.

38. *Charleston Mercury,* November 16, 1860, 1; Thompson, *Robert Toombs of Georgia,* 147; Cauthen, *South Carolina Goes to War,* 57–58; Freehling, *Road to Disunion* 2: 406–14.

39. Cauthen, *South Carolina Goes to War,* 61; Freehling, *Road to Disunion* 2: 416.

40. Cauthen, *South Carolina Goes to War,* 53–58; Nevins, *Emergence of Lincoln* 2: 318–20; Nichols, *Disruption of American Democracy,* 370–71; Kibler, "Unionist Sentiment in South Carolina in 1860," 346–66; J. D. Ashmore to W. P. Miles, November 15, 1860, Miles Papers; Abbeville *Independent Press,* November 30, 1860, 2.

41. *Charleston Mercury,* November 13, 1860, 3.

42. Cauthen, *South Carolina Goes to War,* 60–61.

43. *Charleston Mercury,* November 21, 1860, 3; *Charleston Courier,* November 21, 1860.

44. Ibid. The irony of men who owned slaves and insisted repeatedly that slavery provided slaves "benefits"—food, clothing, shelter, medical care, discipline—they could not provide themselves, but objected violently to being "enslaved" by the Federal government is too obvious to require comment.

45. *Charleston Mercury,* November 23, 1860, 2.

46. L. M. Keitt to J. H. Hammond, November 22, 1860, Hammond Papers, Library of Congress.

47. In a letter to his brother, Hammond compared his resignation to Japanese harakiri; for him, it was the easiest way out of an intolerable situation (J. H. Hammond to M. C. M. Hammond, November 12, 1860, Hammond Papers, Library of Congress).

48. J. D. Ashmore to W. P. Miles, November 15, 20, 1860, Miles Papers; Abbeville *Independent Press,* November 30, 1860, 2; *Charleston Mercury,* December 3, 1860, 3; *Congressional Directory,* 36th Congress, 2nd sess.; *War of the Rebellion,* ser. 1, vol. 1: 93–94.

49. *War of the Rebellion,* ser. 1, vol. 1: 93–94; Nichols, *Disruption of American Democracy,* 371, 399.

50. Channing, *Crisis of Fear,* 278–80; Nevins, *Emergence of Lincoln* 2: 352–54, 357; *Works of James Buchanan,* ed. Moore, vol. 12: 7–25.

51. *War of the Rebellion,* ser. 1, vol. 1: 125; Nichols, *Disruption of American Democracy,* 403.

52. *War of the Rebellion,* ser. 1, vol. 1: 125–26.

53. *War of the Rebellion,* ser. 1, vol. 1: 126–27.

54. *War of the Rebellion,* ser. 1, vol. 1: 126.

55. Buchanan's version of the conversation was somewhat different. On the back of the memorandum composed by Keitt and his colleagues, he wrote: "I objected to the word 'provided,' as this might be construed into an agreement on my part *which I would never make* [emphasis added]. They said nothing was further from their intention. They did not so understand it, and I should not so consider it. Afterwards Messrs. McQueen and Bonham, in behalf of the delegation, returned and gave me the most positive assurance that the forts and public property would not be molested until after commissioners had been appointed to treat with the Federal Government in relation to the public property, and until the decision was known. I informed them that what would be done was a question for Congress and not for the Executive." Buchanan did not believe that he had pledged not to reinforce the forts; nor did he believe he had the authority to do so (*Works of James Buchanan,* ed. Moore, vol. 11: 56–57). The original memorandum is in the Miles Collection. For the report written by Keitt and Miles, see *Journal of the Convention of the People of South Carolina,* 372–77, and *War of the Rebellion,* ser. 1, vol. 1: 125–28. For accounts of the negotiations, see Cauthen, *South Carolina Goes to War,* 94–95; Channing, *Crisis of Fear,* 278–79; Nichols, *Disruption of American Democracy,* 403; Nevins, *Emergence of Lincoln* 2: 357; *Charleston Mercury,* December 18, 1860, 1; December 19, 1860, 4.

56. *Charleston Mercury,* December 19, 1860, 4; December 21, 1860, 4; Abbeville *Independent Press,* December 21, 1860, 2.

57. Cauthen, *South Carolina Goes to War,* 69; *Journal of the House of Representatives of the State of South Carolina,* 11–13.

58. The convention included seven past or future governors, four senators and five congressmen, plus the most eminent of the state's educators, businessmen and planters. Ninety percent owned at least one slave, 60 percent owned at least twenty, and 16 percent owned one hundred or more (Wooster, *Secession Conventions,* 15–16; Freehling, *Road to Disunion* 2: 422).

59. *Journal of the House of Representatives of the State of South Carolina,* 44.

60. *Journal of the House of Representatives of the State of South Carolina,* 45; *Charleston Mercury,* December 22, 1860, 4; Greeley, *American Conflict* 1: 845.

61. Cauthen, *South Carolina Goes to War,* 70–71. In her memoirs, Mrs. Roger Pryor described the arrival of the news in Washington. The city's elite was assembled for a wedding. After the ceremony, she was talking quietly with President Buchanan when their conversation was interrupted by a disturbance in a nearby hallway. The president sent her to find out what was happening. She found Keitt, "leaping in the air, shaking a paper over his head, and exclaiming, 'Thank God! Oh, thank God!'" She grabbed the congressman: "Mr. Keitt, are you crazy? The President hears you, and wants to know what is the matter." Keitt replied, "South Carolina has seceded! Here's the telegram. I feel like a boy let out of school." Mrs. Pryor informed the president, who called for his carriage and left at once for the White House. Mrs. Pryor's fascinating story is unfortunately fictitious; on December 20, Keitt was in Charleston (*Reminiscences of Peace and War,* 111–12; *My Day,* 153–54).

62. A. P. Aldrich to J. H. Hammond, December 21, 1860, Hammond Papers, Library of Congress.

63. *Charleston Mercury,* December 21, 1860, 2.

64. *Charleston Mercury,* December 20, 1860, 3; December 28, 1860, 1; Cauthen, *South Carolina Goes to War,* 70n.

65. *Journal of the House of Representatives of the State of South Carolina,* 461–66.

66. *Journal of the House of Representatives of the State of South Carolina,* 75–77; *Charleston Mercury,* December 22, 1860, 4; Cauthen, *South Carolina Goes to War,* 74; Cox, *Three Decades of Federal Legislation,* 110.

67. Cauthen, *South Carolina Goes to War,* 79–84.

68. Cauthen, *South Carolina Goes to War,* 97; *Journal of the House of Representatives of the State of South Carolina,* 55–56.

69. *War of the Rebellion,* ser. 1, vol. 1: 109–10, 115–18. See also Nevins, *Emergence of Lincoln* 2: 365–72, 376–79; Cauthen, *South Carolina Goes to War,* 97–102.

70. *War of the Rebellion,* ser. 1, vol. 1: 127–28.

71. *Journal of the House of Representatives of the State of South Carolina,* 118.

72. Cauthen, *South Carolina Goes to War,* 84.

73. L. M. Keitt to A. G. Magrath, January 28, 1861, F. W. Pickens Papers, Duke University.

74. Sue Keitt to Mrs. Frederick Brown, [January 1861,] March 4, 1861, Keitt Papers, Duke.

75. Sue Keitt to Mrs. Frederick Brown, March 4, 1861, Keitt Papers, Duke.

Chapter 10: "True liberty is won by the blood of the brave"

1. *Charleston Mercury,* February 6, 1861, 1; Nichols, *Disruption of American Democracy,* 456–57; Yearns, *Confederate Congress,* 11–12; Lee, *Confederate Constitutions,* 51–52; Davis, *"A Government of Our Own,"* 31–39.

2. Yearns, *Confederate Congress,* 9–10; Nichols, *Disruption of American Democracy,* 455–56; Lee, *Confederate Constitutions,* 47–50. For a contrary opinion, see Davis, *"A Government of Our Own,"* 74–75.

3. Woodward, ed., *Mary Chesnut's Civil War,* 274.

4. Alexander H. Stephens to Linton Stephens, March 3, 1861, in Lee, *Confederate Constitutions,* 27; Davis, *"A Government of Our Own,"* 47.

5. *Journal of the Congress of the Confederate States of America, 1861–1865* 1: 16–19: Lee, *Confederate Constitutions,* 54–55; Davis, *"A Government of Our Own,"* 65–67, 75–81.

6. *Journal of the Congress of the Confederate States of America* 1: 19–22; Yearns, *Confederate Congress,* 22–24; Lee, *Confederate Constitutions,* 55–59; Davis, *"A Government of Our Own,"* 81–84.

7. Lee, *Confederate Constitutions,* 62–72; Yearns, *Confederate Congress,* 24–29; Nichols, *Disruption of American Democracy,* 457–458; Davis, *"A Government of Our Own,"* 83–89, 98, 102–9.

8. Freehling, *Road to Disunion,* 2: 382.

9. Davis, *Rhett,* 580.

10. Freehling, *Road to Disunion* 2: 382; Nichols, *Disruption of American Democracy,* 459–61; Davis, *"A Government of Our Own,"* 67–68, 91–102, 106–8; Woodward, ed., *Mary Chesnut's Civil War,* 6; Davis, *Rhett,* 423–25.

11. Cauthen, *South Carolina Goes to War,* 86; Von Abele, *Alexander H. Stephens,* 193–94; Davis, *Rhett,* 425–33; Lee, *Confederate Constitutions,* 72–78; Yearns, *Confederate Congress,* 30–32; Davis, *"A Government of Our Own,"* 110–22; Rhett, "The Confederate Government at Montgomery," *Battles and Leaders of the Civil War* 1: 101–3.

12. *Charleston Mercury,* February 11, 1861, 3; February 18, 1861, 4.

13. Ibid.

14. L. M. Keitt to David F. Jamison, February 9, 1861, Jamison Papers, Leyburn Library, Washington and Lee University.

15. Lee, *Confederate Constitution,* 79–81; Davis *"A Government of Our Own,"* 148–66.

16. *Charleston Mercury,* February 26, 1861, 1; Lee, *Confederate Constitutions,* 85–86; Patrick, *Jefferson Davis and His Cabinet,* 48–55; Davis, *"A Government of Our Own,"* 169–83.

17. Lee, *Confederate Constitutions,* 82–84, 87–122; Davis, *"A Government of Our Own,"* 224–29, 237–57.

18. *Journal of the Congress of the Confederate States of America* 1: 861–62, 889; Lee, *Confederate Constitutions,* 91; Davis, *"A Government of Our Own,"* 238–40, 244–57.

19. L. M. Keitt to J. H. Hammond, February 13, 1861, Hammond Papers, Library of Congress.

20. L. M. Keitt to J. H. Hammond, February 13, 1861, Hammond Papers, Library of Congress; Lee, *Confederate Constitutions,* 94–95, 99–101; Yearns, *Confederate Congress,* 26–27; Nichols, *Disruption of American Democracy,* 463; *Journal of the Congress of the Confederate States of America* 1: 864–65, 868, 871.

21. *Journal of the Congress of the Confederate States of America* 1: 865, 868, 891–92; Lee, *Confederate Constitutions,* 64–65, 95–96.

22. L. M. Keitt to Sue Keitt, February 19, 1861, Keitt Papers, Duke; *Journal of the Congress of the Confederate States of America* 1: 896; Lee, *Confederate Constitutions,* app. C. At the top of a copy of the Constitution in the Keitt Papers at the Calhoun County Historical Commission, Sue Keitt wrote, "This constitution was mainly written by Col. Laurence M. Keitt."

23. *Charleston Mercury,* March 15, 1861, 1.

24. The convention did agree to work for five amendments to the Constitution: to repeal the three-fifths clause; to abolish the authority of Congress to borrow money except in time of war; to require that all expenditures in excess of revenues derived from customs duties—not to exceed 15 percent *ad valorum*—be paid by direct taxes; to repeal the prohibition against the international slave trade; to allow admission of free states to the Confederacy only after a unanimous vote of the state legislatures. Cauthen, *South Carolina Goes to War,* 87–91; Lee, *Confederate Constitutions,* 134–36; Yearns, *Confederate Congress,* 29–30; *Journal of the Convention of the People of South Carolina,* 539.

25. Lamon, *Recollections of Abraham Lincoln,* 76–78. Just what led Lamon to believe he spoke for Lincoln or that the president had ordered the evacuation of the fort no historian has been able to discover.

26. *Journal of the House of Representatives of the State of South Carolina,* 265; Herd, "Lawrence M. Keitt's Letters from the Provisional Congress of the Confederacy, 1861," 23.

27. Nevins, *War for the Union,* 37–66; Cauthen, *South Carolina Goes to War,* 17–133. See also Potter, *Lincoln and His Party,* 336–75, and Stampp, *And the War Came,* 263–86.

28. *Charleston Mercury,* April 23, 1861, 1; May 2, 1861, 4.

29. Owsley, *King Cotton Diplomacy,* 25–42; Yearns, *Confederate Congress,* 102–5, 165–68, 184–91; *Journal of the Congress of the Confederate States of America* 1: 180–244, 288, 308, 328–65, 375; Nevins, *War for the Union* 1: 98–100.

30. L. M. Keitt to J. H. Hammond, May 15, 1861, Hammond Papers, Library of Congress.

31. L. M. Keitt to J. H. Hammond, May 15, 1861, Hammond Papers, Library of Congress.

32. Woodward, ed., *Mary Chesnut's Civil War,* 79.

33. Woodward, ed., *Mary Chesnut's Civil War,* 79.

34. For the unwillingness or inability of obstructionist politicians to become creative statesmen, and champions of state rights to become advocates of centralized power, see Thomas, *Confederacy as a Revolutionary Experience,* 23–42, 58–78; Walther, *Fire-Eaters,* chaps. 2, 4.

35. Unidentified newspaper clipping, Keitt Collection, Calhoun County Museum and Cultural Center.

36. L. M. Keitt to Sue Keitt, July 26, 1861, Keitt Papers, Duke.

37. L. M. Keitt to Sue Keitt, July 26, 1861, Keitt Papers, Duke. It is highly unlikely that Keitt had seen wagons loaded with handcuffs. He was probably repeating one of the many rumors that circulated after the battle. See Davis, *Battle at Bull Run,* 239.

38. L. M. Keitt to J. H. Hammond, August 20, 1861, Hammond Papers, Library of Congress.

39. L. M. Keitt to J. H. Hammond, August 20, 1861, Hammond Papers, Library of Congress.

40. Woodward, ed., *Mary Chesnut's Civil War,* 121, 139.

41. *Journal of the Congress of the Confederate States of America* 1: 573–77.

42. Cauthen, *South Carolina Goes to War,* 141–42. *Charleston Mercury,* September 10, 1861, 1; September 21, 1861, 1; December 9, 1861, 1. I have found no evidence of Keitt's

activities during this period. It seems likely that he spent his time away from Congress raising and equipping his regiment and putting his personal affairs in order.

43. Paul A. McMichael, Diary, and P. A. McMichael to his wife, January 11, 1862, Paul A. McMichael Papers; *Charleston Courier,* January 21, 1862.

44. *Charleston Mercury,* December 17, 1852, 2.

45. *Charleston Mercury,* January 13, 1862, 2.

46. Wilson, *Confederate Soldier,* 30; Wiley, *Life of Johnny Reb,* chaps. 1 and 4; Robertson, *Soldiers Blue and Gray,* chaps. 3–4.

47. L. M. Keitt to Sue Keitt, January 21, 1862, Keitt Papers, Duke.

48. P. A. McMichael to his wife, January 15, 1862, McMichael Papers; L. M. Keitt to Sue Keitt, January 21, 1862, Keitt Papers, Duke.

49. L. M. Keitt to Sue Keitt, January 21, 1862, Duke University; *War of the Rebellion,* ser. 1, vol. 6: 387.

50. L. M. Keitt to Sue Keitt, January 21, 1862, Keitt Papers, Duke.

51. P. A. McMichael to his wife, February 9, 16, 19, 1862, McMichael Papers.

52. *Charleston Mercury,* March 5, 1862, 2; March 14, 1862, 1; April 22, 1862, 2.

53. McPherson, *Battle Cry of Freedom,* 370–73.

54. P. A. McMichael to his wife, March 19, April 7, 1862, McMichael Papers.

55. Burton, *Siege of Charleston,* 84–89, 126.

56. L. M. Keitt to Sue Keitt, April 10, 1862, Keitt Papers, Duke.

57. McPherson, *Battle Cry of Freedom,* 405–16.

58. L. M. Keitt to Sue Keitt, May 1, 1862, Keitt Papers, Duke.

59. L. M. Keitt to Sue Keitt, May 1, 1862, Keitt Papers, Duke.

60. L. M. Keitt to Sue Keitt, May 4, 1862, Keitt Papers, Duke.

61. L. M. Keitt to Sue Keitt, May 4, 1862, Keitt Papers, Duke.

62. L. M. Keitt to J. H. Hammond, June 14, 1862; J. H. Hammond to L. M. Keitt, June 27, 1862, Hammond Papers, Library of Congress.

63. L. M. Keitt to Sue Keitt, June 14, 1862, Keitt Papers, Duke.

64. For details of the battle, see Burton, *Siege of Charleston,* 98–114; Johnson, *Defense of Charleston Harbor,* 25; *War of the Rebellion,* ser. 1, vol. 14: passim.

65. *War of the Rebellion,* ser. 1, vol. 14: 591.

66. L. M. Keitt to Sue Keitt, July 30, 1862, Keitt Papers, Duke.

67. L. M. Keitt to Sue Keitt, July 30, 1862, Keitt Papers, Duke, July 30, 1862. For a description of the defenses erected around the city, see Wise, *Gate of Hell,* chap. 1; Burton, *Siege of Charleston,* 132–35.

68. P. A. McMichael to his wife, May 30, July 9, August 1, 7, December 31, 1862, McMichael Papers. A captain in the Seventeenth South Carolina Infantry called Keitt's unit the "Pound Cake Regiment," a derisive reference to the fact that the Twentieth South Carolina had remained close to home throughout the war, so close that wives and mothers could easily take the men cake and other delicacies (Stone, ed., *Wandering to Glory,* 99–101, 275n28).

69. L. M. Keitt to Sue Keitt, December 15, 1862, Keitt Papers, Duke.

70. L. M. Keitt to J. H. Hammond, November 4, 1862, Hammond Papers, Library of Congress.

71. Burton, *Siege of Charleston,* 120–23; Johnson, *Defense of Charleston Harbor,* 26–28; P. A. McMichael to his wife, October 23, 24, 1862, February 10, 1863, McMichael Papers; *War of the Rebellion,* ser. 1, vol. 14: 199–204.

72. Williams, *P. G. T. Beauregard,* 166–68; *War of the Rebellion,* ser. 1, vol. 14: 609–37, 748, 776; Burton, *Siege of Charleston,* 114–19.

73. *War of the Rebellion,* ser. 1, vol. 14: 743–45.

74. *War of the Rebellion,* ser. 1, vol. 14: 743–45; McCurry, *Confederate Reckoning,* 295–96.

75. Williams, *P. G. T. Beauregard,* 174–78; Burton, *Siege of Charleston,* 131–41; Johnson, *Defense of Charleston Harbor,* 43–61; *War of the Rebellion,* ser. 1, vol. 14: 240–80.

76. *War of the Rebellion,* ser. 1, vol. 14: 271–72; *Charleston Mercury,* April 11, 1863, 1. In describing the battle, a reporter for the *Mercury* wrote that Keitt was "as full of fire and energy in the field as when he was fighting the battle of the Constitution in the House of Representatives, and . . . quite as eager to encounter in the 'deadly breach,' the same foe he so often vanquished on the floor of the Congress." Keitt would not be satisfied until he could "take part in a little blood-letting here in sight . . . of his own home, and the graves of his ancestors."

77. *War of the Rebellion,* ser. 1, vol. 14: 272.

78. Williams, *P. G. T. Beauregard,* 185; Gillmore, "The Army before Charleston in 1863," 54–55; Burton, *Siege of Charleston,* 148–50; Wise, *Gate of Hell,* 33–37.

79. P. A. McMichael to his wife, May 13, 1863, McMichael Papers.

80. *War of the Rebellion,* ser. 1, vol. 14: 290–91, 963; P. A. McMichael to his wife, June 2, 5, 1863, McMichael Papers.

81. Johnson, *Defense of Charleston Harbor,* 83–92; Burton, *Siege of Charleston,* 151–61; Wise, *Gate of Hell,* 66–72.

82. Williams, *P. G. T. Beauregard,* 185–87; Burton, *Siege,* 151–52; Wise, *Gate of Hell,* 59–61.

83. Johnson, *Defense of Charleston Harbor,* 93–96; Burton, *Siege of Charleston,* 157–59; Wise, *Gate of Hell,* 76–79.

84. *War of the Rebellion,* ser. 1, vol. 28, pt. 1: 453.

85. *War of the Rebellion,* ser. 1, vol. 28, pt. 1: 76–77; Burton, *Siege,* 162–71; Johnson, *Defense of Charleston Harbor,* 100–107; Williams, *P. G. T. Beauregard,* 188–89; Wise, *Gate of Hell,* 92–118. Wise puts the number of Confederate casualties at 222.

86. Burton, *Siege of Charleston,* 171–78; Johnson, *Defense of Charleston Harbor,* 107–8, 147–48; Wise, *Gate of Hell,* 119, 138–48.

87. Salley, "Life in Battery Wagner," 351–55; Izlar, *Sketch of the War Record of the Edisto Rifles,* 38–44.

88. *War of the Rebellion,* ser. 1, vol. 28, pt. 1: 377, 411–12, 454–66; Ashe, "Life at Fort Wagner," 255. The story about Keitt and the ingredients for a rum toddy is almost certainly apocryphal.

89. *War of the Rebellion,* ser. 1, vol. 28, pt. 1: 387–91, 466–78, 533–35, 545–54; pt. 2, 293–94. *Charleston Mercury,* August 17, 1863, 2; August 19, 1863, 2. L. M. Keitt to Sue Keitt, August 29, 1963, Keitt Papers, Duke.

90. Williams, *P. G. T. Beauregard,* 190–93.

91. *War of the Rebellion,* ser. 1, vol. 28, pt. 1: 479–82; Burton, *Siege of Charleston,* 178; Johnson, *Defense of Charleston Harbor,* 148–51; Izlar, *Sketch of the War Record of the Edisto Rifles,* 38–44; Salley, "Life in Battery Wagner," 351–55.

92. *War of the Rebellion,* ser. 1, vol. 28, pt. 1: 482.

93. *War of the Rebellion,* ser. 1, vol. 28, pt. 1: 89, 106–8.

94. *War of the Rebellion,* ser. 1, vol. 28, pt. 1: 89, 106–8.

95. *War of the Rebellion,* ser. 1, vol. 28, pt. 1: 89, 103, 107, 482–83. All of Keitt's messages exist in two or more versions; apparently he sent them by both flag and messenger to assure that at least one would reach Beauregard in Charleston.

96. *War of the Rebellion,* ser. 1, vol. 28, pt. 1: 90–91, 483–88. *Charleston Mercury,* September 7, 1863, 1; September 8, 1863, 2; September 11, 1863, 2.

97. *War of the Rebellion,* ser. 1, vol. 28, pt. 1: 91, 206; pt. 2: 86.

98. *War of the Rebellion,* ser. 1, vol. 28, pt. 1: 488. For a more detailed description of the evacuation of Battery Wagner, see Wise, *Gate of Hell,* 195–202.

Chapter 11: "Proudly the Southern Cross still floats to the breeze"

1. Paul A. McMichael to his wife, September 15, 19, 1863, McMichael Papers.

2. Paul A. McMichael to his wife, September 15, 19, 1863, McMichael Papers.

3. Williams, *P. G. T. Beauregard,* 190–96; Burton, *Siege of Charleston,* 183–206; Johnson, *Defense of Charleston Harbor,* 115–64; *War of the Rebellion,* ser. 1, vol. 33, pt. 1, 724–27; L. M. Keitt to Sue Keitt, October 27, 30, 1863, Keitt Papers, Duke.

4. L. M. Keitt to Sue Keitt, October 27, 30, 1863, Keitt Papers, Duke; P. A. McMichael to his wife, October 13, 19, 1863, McMichael Papers; Williams, *P. G. T. Beauregard,* 199–201; Burton, *Siege of Charleston,* 200–207; Johnson, *Defense of Charleston Harbor,* 165–85.

5. Note, n.p., n.d., in "Compiled Service Records of Confederate Soldiers Who Served in Organizations from South Carolina. Twentieth Infantry," microfilm, copy #267, reel #313, South Carolina Department of Archives and History, Columbia.

6. William W. Boyce and James L. Orr to George W. Randolph, September 1, 1862, Compiled Service Records. L. M. Keitt to Louis Wigfall, January 26, 1863 in King, *Louis T. Wigfall,* 164. William W. Boyce et al. to James A. Seddon, January 17, 1863; Roswell S. Ripley to the Secretary of War, n.d.; John C. Pemberton to Jefferson Davis, April 21, 1863; John C. Pemberton to L. M. Keitt, November 11, 1863; John Letcher to Jefferson Davis, December 22, 1868, all in Compiled Service Records. Sue Keitt wrote to John L. Manning, governor of South Carolina, 1852–54, asking him to support Keitt's promotion (Sue Keitt to J. L. Manning, no date, Williams-Manning-Chesnut Alliance Papers, South Carolina Department of Archives and History).

7. L. M. Keitt to Jefferson Davis, October 1, 1863, Compiled Service Records.

8. *War of the Rebellion,* ser. 4, vol. 2: 811–18.

9. In 1863 a full-strength Confederate infantry regiment included a headquarters and ten infantry companies. Its maximum authorized strength was 1,025. Keitt's regiment had fifteen companies and approximately 1,600 men (Boatner, *Civil War Dictionary,* 610–13).

10. L. M. Keitt to Jefferson Davis, October 1, 1863, CSR. Around the same time, Capt. P. A. McMichael, a company commander in Keitt's regiment, commented, "Col. Keitt is no General yet, and when he gets to be one, I expect to be president" (McMichael to Margaret McMichael, [October?] 10, 1863, McMichael Papers).

11. L. M. Keitt to William F. Nance, November 23, 1863, Compiled Service Records; John Letcher to Jefferson Davis December 22, 1863, Compiled Service Records. Mary Chesnut wrote, "Our old tempestuous Keitt breakfasted with us yesterday. . . . Mr. Chesnut has now gone with him to the War Department" (Woodward, ed., *Mary Chesnut's Civil War,* 493).

12. L. M. Keitt to James A. Seddon, December 11, 1863, Compiled Service Records.

13. L. M. Keitt to Thomas Jordan, December 30, 1863; L. M. Keitt to Jefferson Davis, January 4, 1864, Compiled Service Records.

14. Ibid., second endorsement, J. A. Seddon to J. Davis, January 16, 1864, Compiled Service Records.

15. Jefferson Davis to Samuel Cooper, n.d. and first endorsement, S. Cooper to J. Davis, January 22, 1864, Compiled Service Records.

16. L. M. Keitt to Sue Keitt, February 2, 19, 1864, Keitt Papers, Duke. On the condition of Evans's Brigade, see *War of the Rebellion,* ser. 1, vol. 28, pt. 1: 583–90: 1, 35, 545–46, 642. Evans was an alcoholic. Beauregard severely criticized his brigade's lack of discipline and training. Inspector General Alfred Roman reported that he was frequently absent from the unit, never attended drills, and was never with the unit when it went into combat. His officers did not know their duties and did not see to the maintenance of their arms and equipment or the police of their camps. One regiment had not drilled in fifteen months.

17. L. M. Keitt to Sue Keitt, February 11, 1864, Keitt Papers, Duke.

18. Sue Keitt, "L. M. Keitt," typescript, Keitt Papers, Calhoun County Museum and Cultural Center. Sue Keitt was almost certainly wrong. Davis did have many faults. He was often petty and vindictive, and nurtured feuds with politicians like Alexander H. Stephens and Robert Toombs, generals like Joseph E. Johnston and P. G. T. Beauregard, and editors like Edward A. Pollard. But he appointed Toombs as secretary of state, a position for which he was temperamentally unsuited, and brigadier general, a position for which he was unqualified. I have found no evidence that Davis discriminated against men because they had wanted to make Toombs president of the Confederacy.

19. L. M. Keitt to Sue Keitt, October 20, 1863, Keitt Papers, Duke.

20. L. M. Keitt to Sue Keitt, October 27, 30, 1863; January 13, 15, 17, 22, 27; February 6, 8, 1864, Keitt Papers, Duke.

21. L. M. Keitt to Sue Keitt, October 20, 1863; L. M. Keitt to Sue Keitt, January 13, 17, 1864, Keitt Papers, Duke.

22. P. A. McMichael to his wife, September 15, 1863, McMichael Papers.

23. P. A. McMichael to his wife, September 19, 1863, McMichael Papers.

24. P. A. McMichael to his wife, October 9, November 13, 19, 1863, McMichael Papers.

25. P. A. McMichael to his wife, December 19, 1863, McMichael Papers.

26. L. M. Keitt to Sue Keitt, January 17, 1864, Keitt Papers, Duke.

27. L. M. Keitt to Sue Keitt, January 17, 1864, Keitt Papers, Duke. The war had not seriously hurt Keitt's estate. In December he had written to James H. Hammond, asking him to join a group of politicians and businessmen who were trying to buy the *Charleston Mercury.* The newspaper was for sale for $200,000, a large sum "but infinitely smaller in Memminger's currency." Keitt would contribute $40,000; Boyce, Orr, and others would join him in the venture. In the end, the deal fell through (L. M. Keitt to James H. Hammond, December 11, 1863, Hammond Papers, Library of Congress).

28. L. M. Keitt to Sue Keitt, January 22, 1864, Keitt Papers, Duke.

29. L. M. Keitt to Sue Keitt, January 15, 27, February 8, 1864, Keitt Papers, Duke.

30. In June 1863, a French army had occupied Mexico City and installed Archduke Ferdinand Maximilian as emperor, part of Louis Napoleon's inept attempt to reestablish the French empire in the Western Hemisphere. The project foundered; the French withdrew their troops, and the Juaristas executed Maximilian in June 1867 (Crook, *The North, The South, and the Powers,* 333–43).

31. L. M. Keitt to Sue Keitt, January 22, 1864, Keitt Papers, Duke.

32. L. M. Keitt to Sue Keitt, January 22, 1864, Keitt Papers, Duke; see also L. M. Keitt to James H. Hammond, December 11, 1863, Hammond Papers, Library of Congress.

33. L. M. Keitt to A. H. Stephens, April 13, 1864, in Eicher, *Dixie Betrayed,* 218.

34. L. M. Keitt to Sue Keitt, January 24, 1864, Keitt Papers, Duke.

35. L. M. Keitt to Sue Keitt, January 15, 22, 27, 1864, Keitt Papers, Duke.

36. L. M. Keitt to Sue Keitt, January 31, 1864, Keitt Papers, Duke.

37. L. M. Keitt to Sue Keitt, January 15, 22, 1864, Keitt Papers, Duke.

38. For a discussion of the Currency Act of February 17, 1864, designed to reduce the amount of paper money in circulation and so increase its value, see Ball, *Financial Failure and Confederate Defeat,* 187–89.

39. L. M. Keitt to Sue Keitt, January 27, [February ?] 1864, Keitt Papers, Duke.

40. L. M. Keitt to Sue Keitt, February 2, 1864, Keitt Papers, Duke.

41. L. M. Keitt to Sue Keitt, February 2, 1864, Keitt Papers, Duke.

42. L. M. Keitt to Sue Keitt, February 2, 6, 1864, Keitt Papers, Duke; P. A. McMichael to his wife, February 3, 7, 1864, McMichael Papers; *War of the Rebellion,* ser. 1, vol. 35, pt. 1: 103–4; pt. 2: 40.

43. L. M. Keitt to Sue Keitt, February 6, 1864, Keitt Papers, Duke.

44. L. M. Keitt to Sue Keitt, February 11, 1864, Keitt Papers, Duke. For contrasting interpretations of the role of class conflict in Confederate defeat, see Gallagher, *The Confederate War,* chap. 1, and Freehling, *South vs. The South,* pt. 2.

45. L. M. Keitt to Sue Keitt, February 8, 1864, Keitt Papers, Duke.

46. L. M. Keitt to Sue Keitt, February 19, 26, 1864, Keitt Papers, Duke. In fact, the expedition was intended only to encourage Unionist resistance to Confederate authority in the northern quarter of the state (*War of the Rebellion,* ser. 1, vol. 35, pt. 1: 276).

47. L. M. Keitt to Sue Keitt, February 26, March 6, 9, 1864, Keitt Papers, Duke; *War of the Rebellion,* ser. 1, vol. 35, pt. 1: 274–356; Jones, "The Battle of Olustee, or Ocean Pond, Florida," 79.

48. For the military situation in the spring of 1864, see McPherson, *Battle Cry of Freedom,* 718–24, 743–44.

49. L. M. Keitt to Sue Keitt, March 3, 9, 1864, Keitt Papers, Duke.

50. L. M. Keitt to Sue Keitt, March 15, 1864, Keitt Papers, Duke.

51. The Confederates had salvaged the signal gun at Fort Sumter from the wreck of the Union ironclad *Keokuk* that they had sunk when Admiral DuPont tried to enter Charleston harbor in April 1863.

52. Sue Keitt to A. Dudley Mann, [May 1864?], Keitt Papers, Duke. Sue was praising Maj. Gen. Nathan Bedford Forrest, the Confederate cavalryman whose men overran Ft. Pillow, a Union outpost on the Mississippi River, and massacred an undetermined number of black soldiers after they had surrendered. See Cimprich, *Fort Pillow,* 129.

53. Sue Keitt to A. D. Mann, March 15, 1864, Keitt Papers, Duke.

54. *War of the Rebellion,* ser. 1, vol. 32, pt. 3: 493, 792.

55. *War of the Rebellion,* ser. 1, vol. 32, pt. 2: 461; vol. 36, pt. 2: 1012.

56. For details of the battles of the Wilderness and Spottsylvania Court House, and the campaign that followed, see Freeman, *R. E. Lee* 3: 259ff. and Freeman, *Lee's Lieutenants* 3: 342ff.

57. *War of the Rebellion,* ser. 1, vol. 35, pt. 2: 484; or vol. 36, pt 3: 850.

58. *War of the Rebellion,* ser. 1, vol. 35, pt. 2: 500–503.

59. L. M. Keitt to Sue Keitt, May 23, 24, 1864, Keitt Papers, Duke; *War of the Rebellion,* ser. 1, vol. 35, pt. 2: 500–503.

60. L. M. Keitt to Sue Keitt, May 30, 1864, Keitt Papers, Duke; *War of the Rebellion,* ser. 1, vol. 36, pt. 3: 850.

61. L. M. Keitt to Sue Keitt, May 31, 1864, Keitt Papers, Duke; Dickert, *History of Kershaw's Brigade,* 365–68.

62. L. M. Keitt to Sue Keitt, May 31, 1864, Keitt Papers, Duke.

63. For details of the events that immediately preceded the battle of Cold Harbor, see Freeman, *R. E. Lee* 3: 362–77, and Freeman, *Lee's Lieutenants* 3: 496–506.

64. Dickert, *History of Kershaw's Brigade,* 369. Turenne was Henri de la Tour d'Auvergne, Vicomte de Turenne, the seventeenth-century French marshal whom Napoleon ranked among the seven greatest generals in history. Alva was Fernando Alvarez de Toledo, Third Duke of Alba, the sixteenth-century Spanish general and governor of the Netherlands—notorious for his cruelty.

65. Rosenbough, "Sheridan's Richmond Raid," 193.

66. Dickert, *History of Kershaw's Brigade,* 369–70; Hagood, *Memoirs of the War of Secession,* 257; Stiles, *Four Years Under Marse Robert,* 273–74; Freeman, *R. E. Lee* 3: 377–78; Freeman, *Lee's Lieutenants* 3: 506; Trudeau, *Bloody Roads South,* 266–67; Hess, *Trench Warfare Under Lee and Grant,* 145–46; Furguson, *Not War but Murder,* 87–93; *War of the Rebellion,* ser. 1, vol. 36, pt. 1: 1059.

67. A. S. Salley to Alexander Sparks, June 8, 1864, Keitt Papers, Duke; S. D. Hammond to Sue Keitt, June 5, 1864, Hammond Papers, South Caroliniana Library.

68. *Charleston Mercury,* June 7, 1864, 2; *Camden Journal,* June 10, 1864; clipping, n.p., n.d., "Lawrence Keitt: The Fire-eater Who Practiced What He Preached," by T. H. Dreher, Keitt Collection, Newspaper Clippings.

69. *Charleston Mercury,* June 20, 1864, 1; *Charleston Courier,* December 5, 8, 1864.

Epilogue: "I will not lose my land"

1. Boston *Evening Transcript,* October 21, 1865, 1; Dudley, "History of Bennettville."

2. Sue Keitt to Benjamin F. Perry, October 25, 1865, Benjamin F. Perry Collection, Alabama Department of Archives and History, Montgomery.

3. Sue Keitt to Benjamin F. Perry, October 25, 1865, Perry Collection. For an eyewitness account of the sack of "Mandeville," see Rutledge, ed., "Elizabeth Jamison's Tale of War," 327–32.

4. Sue was referring to the execution of Mrs. Mary Surratt for her involvement in the assassination of Abraham Lincoln. See Kauffman, *American Brutus,* 373–84; Leonard, *Lincoln's Avengers,* 133–34.

5. Sue Keitt to B. F. Perry, November 29, 1865, Perry Collection.

6. Sue Keitt to Ellison S. Keitt, February 29, 1867, Ellison S. Keitt Papers, South Caroliniana Library, University of South Carolina.

7. Poole, *Never Surrender,* 86.

8. Cawthen, *Inevitable Guest,* 209–10, 293.

9. Sue Keitt to William A. Carrigan, January 18, April 9, 1879, 4 additional letters, undated, Suzanne Mandeville Sparks Keitt Papers.

10. Sue Keitt to W. A. Carrigan, January 13, 18, 20; April 9, 26; May 2, 4; June 13; July 1, 25; October 11, 31; December 1, 8, 15, 23, 1879; February 27, April 24, 1880, 4 additional letters, undated, Suzanne Mandeville Sparks Keitt Collection.

11. Sue Keitt to W. A. Carrigan, March 12, 1879, 2 undated, Suzanne Mandeville Sparks Keitt Papers.

12. Sue Keitt to W. A. Carrigan, April 7, May 10, 20, December 24, 1879, 4 additional letters, undated, Suzanne Mandeville Sparks Keitt Papers.

13. Sue Keitt to W. A. Carrigan, October 29, December 24, 1879, 4 additional letters, undated, Suzanne Mandeville Sparks Keitt Papers.

14. Sue Keitt to W. A. Carrigan, May 20, 1879, 2 additional letters, undated, Suzanne Mandeville Sparks Keitt Papers.

15. Sue Keitt to W. A. Carrigan, December 24, 1879, 3 additional letters, undated, Suzanne Mandeville Sparks Keitt Papers.

16. Sue Keitt to W. A. Carrigan, January 18, April 9, May 22, June 3, September 13, 22, November 20, December 1, 1879, April 24, June 29, 1880, 1 additional letter, undated, Suzanne Mandeville Sparks Keitt Papers.

17. Sue Keitt to W. A. Carrigan, November 18, 1879, 1 additional letter, undated, Suzanne Mandeville Sparks Keitt Papers.

18. Ibid.; unidentified newspaper clippings, Keitt Collection, South Caroliniana Library.

19. Columbia State, January 22, 1915, 3; Anna Keitt, "Will," Apartment #15, Package #288, Probate Judge's Office, Calhoun County Court House, St. Matthews, South Carolina.

BIBLIOGRAPHY

Primary Sources

Archival Sources

Chesnut-Miller-Manning Papers. South Carolina Historical Society, Charleston.

Clement C. Clay Papers. Duke University, Durham, N.C.

Compiled Service Records of Confederate Soldiers Who Served in Organizations from South Carolina. Twentieth Infantry. Microfilm, South Carolina Department of Archives and History, Columbia.

Olin M. Dantzler Papers. Calhoun County Museum and Cultural Center, St. Matthews, S.C.

Dudley, C. W. "History of Bennettville." Typescript. Southern Historical Collection, University of North Carolina, Chapel Hill.

James H. Hammond Papers. Library of Congress, Washington, D.C.

James H. Hammond Papers. South Caroliniana Library, University of South Carolina, Columbia.

David F. Jamison Papers. Duke University, Durham, N.C.

David F. Jamison Papers. Washington and Lee University, Lexington, Va.

Charles Colcock James Papers. Autograph letters and portraits of the signers of the Constitution of the Confederate States, collected by Charles Colcock Jones, Jr. Duke University, Durham, N.C.

Anna Keitt. Will. Report of ex. in re estate of Anna Keitt, deceased. Apartment #15, Package #288, Probate Judge's Office, Calhoun County Court House, St. Matthews, S.C.

Laurence M. Keitt Collection. Newspaper Clippings. Calhoun County Museum and Cultural Center, St. Matthews, S.C.

Laurence M. Keitt Collection. Calhoun County Historical Commission, St. Matthews, S.C.

———. Papers. Duke University Library, Durham, N.C.

Laurence M. Keitt Collection. "Laurence Massillon Keitt, Statesman and Soldier." Typescript, L. M. Keitt Papers, Calhoun County Historical Commission.

Suzanne Mandeville Sparks Keitt Collection. South Caroliniana Library, University of South Carolina, Columbia.

McMichael, Paul A. Diary. Southern Historical Collection, University of North Carolina, Chapel Hill.

Paul A. McMichael Papers. Southern Historical Collection, University of North Carolina, Chapel Hill.

W. Porcher Miles Papers. Southern Historical Collection, University of North Carolina, Chapel Hill.

Alumni Records. Typescript. 7 vols. Compiled by Charles Moore. South Caroliniana Library, University of South Carolina, Columbia.

Pettigrew Family Papers. South Carolina Department of Archives and History, Columbia.

Francis W. Pickens Papers. Duke University, Durham, N.C.

John A. Quitman Papers. Southern Historical Collection, University of North Carolina, Chapel Hill, N.C.

South Carolina Legislative System, Southern Congress, 1851. South Carolina Department of Archives and History, Columbia.

"Subjects for Debate." Euphradian Society, South Carolina College. South Caroliniana Library, University of South Carolina, Columbia.

"Treasurer's Book, 1838–1840" and "Treasurer's Book, 1841–1842." Euphradian Society, South Carolina College. South Caroliniana Library, University of South Carolina, Columbia.

Wigfall Family Papers. Library of Congress, Washington, D.C.

Williams-Manning-Chesnut Alliance Papers. South Carolina Department of Archives and History, Columbia.

Newspapers and Magazines

Abbeville Banner, 1848–60.

Anderson Gazette, 1854.

Baltimore Republican, 1856.

Black River Watchman (Sumter), 1850–55. Keitt Collection, Newspaper Clippings.

Boston Atlas, 1856.

Boston Evening Transcript, 1865.

Camden Journal, 1864.

Carolina Spartan (Spartanburg, S.C.), 1855.

Carolina Times (Columbia, S.C.), 1856. Keitt Collection, Newspaper Clippings.

Charleston Courier, 1848–64.

Charleston Mercury, 1848–64.

Charleston News, 1856. Keitt Collection, Newspaper Clippings.

Cheraw Gazette, 1857. Keitt Collection, Newspaper Clippings.

Cheraw Herald, 1857. Keitt Collection, Newspaper Clippings.

Edgefield Advertiser, 1852–61.

Harper's Weekly, 1856–60.

Herald (Cheraw, S.C.), 1857.

Independent Press (Abbeville, S.C.), 1854–61.

Lancaster Ledger, 1853–61.

Lexington Gazette (Lexington, Va.), 1856–57.

Lynchburg Virginian, 1856.

Mobile Daily Register, 1856.

New York Herald, 1854–60.

New York Times, 1854–60.
New York Tribune, 1856.
Richmond Examiner, 1856–57.
Richmond Whig, 1856.
South (Richmond), 1858.
South Carolinian (Columbia), 1848–61.
Southern Patriot (Greenville, S.C.), 1855.
Southern Quarterly Review, 1854.
Southron (Orangeburg), 1856–60. Keitt Collection, Newspaper Clippings.
State (Columbia, S.C.), 1915.
Sumter Watchman, 1855–64. Keitt Collection, Newspaper Clippings.
Times (Calhoun, S.C.), 1930.
Valley Star (Lexington, Va.), 1856.
Washington Union, 1856.
Yorkville Enquirer, 1853–61.

Books and Articles

Beauregard, P. G. T. "The Defense of Charleston." In *Battles and Leaders of the Civil War,* ed. Johnson and Buel. Vol. 4: 1–23.

Biographical Directory of the American Congress, 1774–1971. Washington, D.C.: Government Printing Office, 1971.

Cawthon, John. *Inevitable Guest: Life and Letters of Jemima Darby.* San Antonio: Naylor Co., 1965.

Chesnut, Mary Boykin. *Diary from Dixie,* ed. Ben Ames Williams. Boston: Houghton Mifflin Co., 1949.

———. *Mary Chesnut's Civil War,* ed. C. Vann Woodward. New Haven, Conn.: Yale University Press, 1981.

Congressional Directory. 1st Sess., 33rd Congress–1st Sess., 36th Congress. Washington, D.C.: G. S. Gideon, 1854–60.

Congressional Globe. 1st Sess., 33rd Congress–1st Sess., 36th Congress. Washington, D.C.: John C. Rives, 1853–60.

The Correspondence Between the Commissioners of the State of So. Ca. to the Government at Washington and the President of the United States; Together with The Statement of Messrs. Miles and Keitt. Charleston, S.C.: Evans & Cogswell, 1861.

Cox, Samuel S. *Three Decades of Federal Legislation, 1855–1885.* Providence, R.I.: J. A. & R. A. Reid, 1885.

Davis, Reuben. *Recollections of Mississippi and Mississippians.* Boston: Houghton, Mifflin and Co., 1891.

DeLeon, Thomas C. *Belles, Beaux and Brains of the 60's.* New York: G. W. Dillingham, 1907.

———. *Four Years in Rebel Capitals: An Inside View of Life in the Southern Confederacy, from Birth to Death.* Mobile, Ala.: Gossip Printing Co., 1892.

Dickert, D. Augustus. *History of Kershaw's Brigade.* Newberry, S.C.: E. H. Aull Co., 1899.

DuBose, Henry K. *The History of Company B, Twenty-First Regiment (Infantry), South Carolina Volunteers.* Columbia, S.C.: R. L. Bryan, 1909.

Easterby, J. H., ed. *The South Carolina Rice Plantation as Revealed in the Letters of Robert F. W. Alston.* Chicago: University of Chicago Press, 1945.

Ellet, Elizabeth F. *Court Circles of the Republic: Or the Beauties and Celebrities of the Nation.* Philadelphia: Philadelphia Publishing Co., 1872.

Featherstonhaugh, G. W. *Excursion Through the Slave States from Washington on the Potomac to the Frontier of Mexico: With Sketches of Popular Manners and Geological Notices.* New York: Harper & Brothers, 1844.

Forney, John W. *Anecdotes of Public Men.* 2 vols. New York: Harper & Brothers, 1881.

Gilchrist, Robert C. *The Confederate Defense of Morris Island by the Troops of South Carolina, Georgia, and North Carolina in the Late War Between the States.* Charleston, S.C.: News and Courier Book Presses, 1884.

Gillmore, Quincy A. "The Army before Charleston in 1863." In *Battles and Leaders of the Civil War,* ed. Johnson and Buel. Vol. 4: 52–71.

Greeley, Horace. *The American Conflict: A History of the Great Rebellion.* 2 vols. Hartford, Conn.: O. D. Case & Co., 1864.

Hagood, Johnson. *Memoirs of the War of Secession.* Columbia, S.C.: State Co., 1910.

Harleston, John. "Battery Wagner on Morris Island." *South Carolina Historical Magazine* 57 (January 1956): 1–13.

Herd, Elmer D. "Lawrence M. Keitt's Letters from the Provisional Congress of the Confederacy, 1861." *South Carolina Historical Magazine* 61 (January 1960): 19–25.

[Holmes, Oliver Wendell.] "The Fight over the Body of Keitt." *Punch* 34 (March 1858): 100.

Izlar, William V. *A Sketch of the War Record of the Edisto Rifles, 1861–1865.* Columbia, S.C.: State Co., 1914.

Jacobs, Thornwell, ed. *Diary of William Plumer Jacobs.* Oglethorpe: Oglethorpe University Press, 1937.

Johnson, John. *The Defense of Charleston Harbor, Including Fort Sumter and the Adjacent Islands, 1863–1865.* Charleston, S.C.: Walker, Evans & Cogswell Co., 1890.

Johnson, Robert U., and Clarence C. Buel, eds. *Battles and Leaders of the Civil War.* 4 vols. New York: Century Co., 1887–88.

Jones, Samuel. "The Battle of Olustee, or Ocean Pond, Florida." In *Battles and Leaders of the Civil War,* ed. Johnson and Buel. Vol. 4: 76–79.

———. *The Siege of Charleston and the Operations on the South Atlantic Coast in the War Among the States.* New York: Neale Publishing Co., 1911.

Journal of the Congress of the Confederate States of America, 1861–1865. 7 vols. Washington, D.C.: Government Printing Office, 1904.

Journal of the Convention of the People of South Carolina Held in 1860, 1861, and 1862, Together with the Ordinances, Reports, Resolutions, Etc. Columbia, S.C.: R. W. Gibbes, 1862.

Journal of the House of Representatives of the State of South Carolina, 1848–1853. Columbia, S.C.: I. C. Morgan, 1848–53.

Journal of the South Carolina Executive Councils of 1861 and 1862, ed. Charles A. Cauthen. Columbia: South Carolina Archives Department, 1956.

LaBorde, Maximilian. *History of South Carolina College.* Charleston, S.C.: Walker, Evans & Cogswell, 1874.

Lamon, Ward Hill. *Recollections of Abraham Lincoln, 1847–1865.* Washington, D.C.: By the author, 1911.

Keitt, L. M. *Address Delivered before the Two Literary Societies of the Virginia Military Institute, July 4, 1856.* Richmond: MacFarlane and Ferguson, 1856.

———. *Address of Lawrence M. Keitt, Esq. on Laying the Cornerstone of the Fire-Proof Building at Columbia, Dec. 15, 1851.* Columbia, S.C.: I. C. Morgan, 1851.

———. "Patriotic Services of the North and the South." *DeBow's Review* 21 (November 1856): 491–508.

———. *Politics of the Country: Speech of Hon. L. M. Keitt, of South Carolina, in the House of Representatives, April 7, 1856. Delivered in the Committee of the Whole on the State of the Union.* N.p., n.d.

———. *Speech of Hon. Lawrence M. Keitt Delivered at Orangeburg, South Carolina, Monday, April 16, 1855.* N.p., n.d.

———. *Speech of Hon. L. M. Keitt, of S. Carolina, on the Kansas and Nebraska Bill. Delivered in the House of Representatives, March 30, 1854.* Washington, D.C.: Congressional Globe, 1854.

———. *Speech of Hon. Lawrence M. Keitt, of South Carolina, on the Acquisition Of Cuba Delivered in the House of Representative, January 19, 1859.* Washington, D.C.: Lemuel Towers, 1859.

———. *Speech of Hon. Lawrence Keitt, of South Carolina, on the Organization of the House, Delivered in the House of Representatives, January 25, 1860.* Washington, D.C.: Thomas McGill, 1860.

———. *Speech of Hon. Lawrence M. Keitt, of South Carolina, on Resigning His Seat. Delivered in the House of Representatives, July 16, 1856.* N.p., n.d.

———. *Speech of Hon. Lawrence M. Keitt, of South Carolina, on Slavery and the Resources of the South; Delivered in the House of Representative, January 15,* Washington, D.C.: Office of the Congressional Globe, 1857.

———. *Tonnage Duties: Speech of Hon. L. M. Keitt, of South Carolina, in the House of Representatives, January 19, 1854.* N.p., n.d.

McPherson, Edward. *The Political History of the United States of America During the Great Rebellion.* Washington, D.C.: Philip & Solomons, 1854.

Meriwether, Robert L., ed. "Preston Brooks on the Caning of Charles Sumner." *South Carolina Historical and Genealogical Magazine* 51 (October 1950): 1–4.

Messages and Papers of the Presidents. 10 vols. Washington, D.C.: Government Printing Office, 1897.

Moore, John Bassett, ed. *The Works of James Buchanan.* 12 vols. Philadelphia: J. B. Lippincott Co., 1910.

Murray, Amelia M. *Letters from the United States, Cuba and Canada.* New York: G. P. Putnam & Co., 1856.

[Nicholls, Sarah Ashton, ed.] *In Memoriam: A Selection from the Letters of the Late John Ashton Nicholls.* N.p., 1862.

Oliphant, Mary C. Simms, Alfred Taylor Odell, and T. C. Duncan Eaves, eds. *The Letters of William Gilmore Simms.* 5 vols. Columbia: University of South Carolina Press, 1954.

O'Neall, John Belton. *Biographical Sketches of the Bench and Bar of South Carolina.* 2 vols. Columbia, S.C.: S. G. Courtenay & Co., 1859.

Pencil, Mark [Mary M. Hagner]. *The White Sulphur Papers, or Life at the Springs of Western Virginia.* New York: Henry Colman, 1839.

Perry, Benjamin F. *Biographical Sketches of Eminent American Statesmen, with Speeches, Addresses and Letters by Ex-Governor B. F. Perry of Greenville, S.C.* Philadelphia: Ferree Press, 1887.

———. *Reminiscences of Public Men.* Philadelphia: John D. Avil & Co., 1883.

Pierce, Edward L. *Memoir and Letters of Charles Sumner.* 4 vols. Boston: Roberts Brothers, 1893.

Poore, Ben Perley. *Perley's Reminiscences of Sixty Years in the National Metropolis.* 2 vols. Philadelphia: Hubbard Brothers, 1886.

Pryor, Mrs. Roger A. *My Day: Reminiscences of a Long Life.* New York: Macmillan Co., 1909.

———. *Reminiscences of Peace and War.* New York: Macmillan Co., 1904.

"Recollections of Charles Sumner." *Scribner's Monthly* 8 (August 1874): 475–90.

Rhett, Robert Barnwell. "The Confederate Government at Montgomery." In *Battles and Leaders of the Civil War,* ed. Johnson and Buel. Vol. 1: 101–3.

Rogers, C. R. P. "DuPont's Attack at Charleston." In *Battles and Leaders of the Civil War,* ed. Johnson and Buel. Vol. 4: 32–47.

Rutledge, David J., ed. "Elizabeth Jamison's Tale of War." *South Carolina Historical Magazine* 99 (October 1998): 312–39.

[Salley, A. S.?] "Life in Battery Wagner." *Land We Love* 2 (March 1867): 351–55.

Scarborough, William K., ed. *The Diary of Edmund Ruffin.* 3 vols. Baton Rouge: Louisiana State University Press, 1972–89.

Stanton, Henry B. *Random Recollections.* New York: Harper & Brothers, 1887.

Sterling, Ada, ed. *A Belle of the Fifties: Memoirs of Mrs. Clay of Alabama.* New York: Doubleday, Page and Co., 1904.

Stiles, Robert. *Four Years Under Marse Robert.* New York: Neale Publishing Co., 1903.

Stone, DeWitt Boyd, Jr., ed. *Wandering to Glory: Confederate Veterans Remember Evans's Brigade.* Columbia: University of South Carolina Press, 2002.

Tenney, W. J. *The Military and Naval History of the Rebellion.* New York: D. Appleton & Co., 1865.

U.S. Congress. House of Representatives. Miscellaneous Document #76, 33rd Congress, 1st Session. Washington, D.C.: A. O. P. Nicholson, 1854.

———. Report #182. 34th Congress, 1st Session. Washington, D.C.: Cornelius Wendell, 1856. 1–142.

———. Reports of Committees. 33rd Congress, 1st sess. Washington, D.C.: A. O. P. Nicholson, 1854.

Wallace, Sarah Agnes, and Frances Elma Gillespie, eds. *The Journal of Benjamin Moran.* 2 vols. Chicago: University of Illinois Press, 1948.

War of the Rebellion: A Compilation of the Official Records of the Union and Confederate Armies, comp. Fred C. Ainsworth and Joseph W. Kirkley. 128 vols. Washington, D.C.: Government Printing Office, 1880–1901.

Wilson, Clyde N., and Shirley B. Cook, eds. *The Papers of John C. Calhoun.* 28 vols. Columbia: University of South Carolina Press, 1998, 2001.

Windle, Mary J. *Life in Washington.* Philadelphia: J. B. Lippincott & Co., 1859.

Woodward, C. Vann, ed. *Mary Chesnut's Civil War.* New Haven, Conn.: Yale University Press, 1981.

———, and Elizabeth Muhlenfeld, eds. *The Private Mary Chesnut: The Unpublished Civil War Diaries.* New York: Oxford University Press, 1984

Secondary Sources

Abraham, James L. *The Men of Secession and Civil War, 1859–1861.* Wilmington, Del.: Scholarly Books, 2000.

Alexander, Thomas B. and Richard T. Beringer. *The Anatomy of the Confederate Congress.* Nashville, Tenn.: Vanderbilt University Press, 1972.

Anbinder, Tyler. *Nativism and Slavery: The Northern Know Nothings and the Politics of the 1850s.* New York: Oxford University Press, 1992.

Anderson, J. P. "Public Education in Ante-Bellum South Carolina." *South Carolina Historical Association Proceedings* (1933): 3–11.

Ashe, S. A. "Life at Fort Wagner." *Confederate Veteran* 35 (July 1927): 254–56.

Ball, Douglas B. *Financial Failure and Confederate Defeat.* Urbana: University of Illinois Press, 1991.

Barney, William L. *The Road to Secession: A New Perspective on the Old South.* New York: Praeger Publishers, 1972.

———. *The Secessionist Impulse: Alabama and Mississippi in 1860.* Princeton, N.J.: Princeton University Press, 1974.

Barnwell, John. *Love of Order: South Carolina's First Secession Crisis.* Chapel Hill: University of North Carolina Press, 1982.

Barrett, John G. *Sherman's March Through the Carolinas.* Chapel Hill: University of North Carolina Press, 1956.

Beringer, Richard E. and Thomas B. Alexander. *The Anatomy of the Confederate Congress: A Study of the Influences of Member Characteristics on Legislative Voting Behavior, 1861–1865.* Nashville, Tenn.: Vanderbilt University Press, 1972.

Bernstein, Barton J. "Southern Politics and Attempts to Reopen the African Slave Trade." *Journal of Negro History* 51 (January 1960): 16–35.

Berry, Hester. "Francis Lieber as a Teacher and Political Writer in the South Carolina College." Master's thesis, University of South Carolina, 1943.

Berry, Stephen W. *All That Makes a Man: Love and Ambition in the Civil War South.* New York: Oxford University Press, 2003.

Berwanger, Eugene H. *The Frontier against Slavery: Western Anti-Negro Prejudice and the Slavery Extension Controversy.* Urbana: University of Illinois Press, 1967.

Bestor, Arthur. "State Sovereignty and Slavery: A Reinterpretation of Proslavery Constitutional Doctrine, 1846–1860." *Journal of the Illinois State Historical Society* 54 (Summer 1961): 117–80.

Bleser, Carol, ed. *The Hammonds of Redcliffe.* New York: Oxford University Press, 1981.

———. *Secret and Sacred: The Diaries of James Henry Hammond, A Southern Slaveholder.* New York: Oxford University Press, 1988.

Boatner, Mark Mayo, comp. *The Civil War Dictionary.* New York: David McKay Co., 1959.

Boney, F. N. *John Letcher: The Story of Virginia's Civil War Governor.* University: University of Alabama Press, 1966.

Botkin, Theodosius. "Life Among the Sovereign Squats." *Transactions of the Kansas State Historical Society* 7 (1901–2): 418–41.

Boucher, Chauncey S. "The Secession and Cooperation Movements in South Carolina, 1848–1852." *Washington University Studies* 5, pt. 3, no. 2 (April 1918): 67–138.

———. "Sectionalism, Representation, and the Electorial Question in Ante-Bellum South Carolina." *Washington University Studies* 4, pt. 2, no. 1 (October 1916): 3–62.

———. "South Carolina and the South on the Eve of the Secession Crisis." *Washington University Studies* 6, no. 2 (1919): 81–144.

Brewster, Lawrence. *Summer Migrations and Resorts of South Carolina Low-Country Planters.* Durham, N.C.: Duke University Press, 1947.

Brown, Charles H. *Agents of Manifest Destiny: The Lives and Times of the Filibusters.* Chapel Hill: University of North Carolina Press, 1980.

Brown, David. *Southern Outcast: Hinton Rowan Helper and the Impending Crisis of the South.* Baton Rouge: Louisiana State University Press, 2006.

Buchanan, James. *Mr. Buchanan's Administration on the Eve of the Rebellion.* New York: D. Appleton, 1866.

Burton, E. Milby. *The Siege of Charleston, 1861–1865.* Columbia: University of South Carolina Press, 1970.

Calonius, Erik. *The Wanderer: The Last American Slave Ship and the Conspiracy that Set Its Sails.* New York: St. Martin's, 2006.

Capers, Henry D. *The Life and Times of C. G. Memminger.* Richmond: Everett Waddy Co., 1893.

Carr, Albert Z. *The World and William Walker.* New York: Harper & Row, 1963.

Cash, Wilbur J. *The Mind of the South.* New York: Alfred A. Knopf, 1941.

Cate, Wirt A. *Lucius Q. C. Lamar: Secession and Reunion.* Chapel Hill: University of North Carolina Press, 1935.

Cauthen, Charles E. *South Carolina Goes to War, 1860–1865.* Chapel Hill: University of North Carolina Press, 1950.

———. "South Carolina's Decision to Lead the Secession Movement." *North Carolina Historical Review* 18 (October 1941): 360–72.

Channing, Stephen A. *Crisis of Fear: Secession in South Carolina.* New York: Simon & Schuster, 1970.

Cimprich, John. *Fort Pillow, A Civil War Massacre, and Public Memory.* Baton Rouge: Louisiana State University Press, 2005.

Clary, David A. *Eagles and Empire: The United States, Mexico, and the Struggle for a Continent.* New York: Bantam Books, 2009.

Clinton, Catherine, *The Plantation Mistress: Woman's World in the Old South.* New York: Pantheon, 1982.

Cooper, William J. *Jefferson Davis: American.* New York: Alfred A. Knopf, 2000.

———. *Liberty and Slavery: Southern Politics to 1860.* New York: Alfred A. Knopf, 1983.

———. *The South and the Politics of Slavery, 1828–1856.* Baton Rouge: Louisiana State University Press, 1978.

Coulter, E. Merton. *College Life in the Old South.* New York: Macmillan Co., 1928.

———. *The Confederate States of America, 1861–1865.* Baton Rouge: Louisiana State University Press, 1950.

Craik, Elmer L. "Southern Interest in Territorial Kansas." *Collections of the Kansas State Historical Society* 15 (1919–22): 334–451.

Craven, Avery O. *Civil War in the Making, 1815–1860.* Baton Rouge: Louisiana State University Press, 1959.

———. *The Coming of the Civil War.* Chicago: Macmillan, 1942.

———. *Edmund Ruffin, Southerner: A Study in Secession.* New York: D. Appleton and Co., 1932.

———. *The Growth of Southern Nationalism, 1848–1861.* Baton Rouge: Louisiana State University Press, 1953.

———. *The Repressible Conflict.* Baton Rouge: Louisiana State University Press, 1939.

Crenshaw, Ollinger. *The Slave States in the Presidential Election of 1860.* 2nd ed. Gloucester: Peter Smith, 1969.

———. "The Speakership Contest of 1859–1860. John Sherman's Election a Cause of Disruption?" *Mississippi Valley Historical Review* 29 (December 1942): 323–38.

Crook, D. P. *The North, The South, and The Powers, 1861–1865.* New York: John Wiley & Sons, 1974.

Curti, Merle. "George N. Sanders—American Patriot of the Fifties." *South Atlantic Quarterly* 27 (January 1928): 79–87.

Curtis, George Ticknor. *Life of James Buchanan, Fifteenth President of the United States.* 2 vols. New York: Harper & Brothers, 1883.

Davidson, Chalmers G. *The Last Foray: The South Carolina Planters of 1860: A Sociological Study.* Columbia: University of South Carolina Press, 1971.

Davis, William C. *Battle at Bull Run: A History of the First Major Campaign of the Civil War.* New York: Doubleday, 1977.

———. *Breckinridge: Statesman, Soldier, Symbol.* Baton Rouge: Louisiana State University Press, 1974.

———, ed. *A Fire-Eater Remembers: The Confederate Memoir of Robert Barnwell Rhett.* Columbia: University of South Carolina Press, 2000.

———. *"A Government of Our Own": The Making of the Confederacy.* New York: Free Press, 1994.

———. *Jefferson Davis: The Man and His Hour.* New York: Harper Collins, 1991.

———. *Look Away! A History of the Confederate States of America.* New York: Free Press, 2002

———. *Rhett: The Turbulent Life and Times of a Fire-Eater.* Columbia: University of South Carolina Press, 2001.

———. *The Union that Shaped the Confederacy: Robert Toombs and Alexander H. Stephens.* Lawrence: University Press of Kansas, 2001.

DeCredico, Mary A. *Mary Boykin Chesnut: A Confederate Woman's Life.* Madison, Wis.: Madison House, 1996.

Detzer, David. *Allegiance: Fort Sumter, Charleston, and the Beginning of the Civil War.* New York: Harcourt, 2001.

Dew, Charles B. *Apostles of Disunion: Southern Secession Commissioners and the Causes of the Civil War.* Charlottesville: University Press of Virginia, 2001.

Donald, David H. *Charles Sumner and the Coming of the Civil War.* New York: Alfred A. Knopf, 1967.

———. "The Proslavery Argument Revisited." *Journal of Southern History* 37 (February 1971): 3–18.

Dowdey, Clifford. *Lee.* Boston: Little, Brown and Co., 1965.

DuBois, James T., and Gertrude S. Matthews. *Galusha A. Grow: Father of the Homestead Law.* Boston: Houghton Mifflin Co., 1917.

DuBose, John W. *The Life and Times of William Lowndes Yancey.* 2 vols. Birmingham: Roberts and Son, 1892.

Dumond, Dwight L. *The Secession Movement, 1860–1861.* New York: Macmillan Co., 1931.

Edgar, Walter B. "Lawrence Keitt." In *Encyclopedia of the Confederacy,* ed. Richard N. Current. 4 vols. New York: Simon and Schuster, 1993. Vol. 2: 876–79.

———. *South Carolina: A History.* Columbia: University of South Carolina Press, 1998.

Edmunds, John B. *Francis W. Pickens and the Politics of Destruction.* Chapel Hill: University of North Carolina Press, 1986.

Eicher, David J. *Dixie Betrayed: How the South Really Lost the Civil War.* New York: Little Brown, 2006.

Eisenhower, John S. D. *So Far from God: The U.S. War with Mexico, 1846–1848.* New York: Random House, 1989.

Emilio, Luis F. *A Brave Black Regiment: History of the Fifty-Fourth Regiment of Massachusetts Volunteer Infantry, 1863–1865.* Boston: Boston Book Co., 1894.

Etcheson, Nicole. *Bleeding Kansas: Contested Liberty in the Civil War Era.* Lawrence: University Press of Kansas, 2004.

Farmer, James Oscar, Jr. *The Metaphysical Confederacy: James Henley Thornwell and the Synthesis of Southern Values.* Macon, Ga.: Mercer University Press, 1986.

Faust, Drew Gilpin, ed. *The Ideology of Slavery: Proslavery Thought in the Antebellum South, 1830–1860.* Baton Rouge: Louisiana State University Press, 1981.

———. *James Henry Hammond and the Old South: A Design for Mastery.* Baton Rouge: Louisiana State University Press, 1982.

———. *Mothers of Invention: Women of the Slaveholding South in the American Civil War.* Chapel Hill: University of North Carolina Press, 1996.

———. *A Sacred Circle: The Dilemma of the Intellectual in the Old South,* Baltimore: Johns Hopkins University Press, 1977.

———. *This Republic of Suffering: Death and the American Civil War.* New York: Alfred A. Knopf, 2008.

Fehrenbacher, Don E. *Constitutions and Constitutionalism in the Slaveholding South.* Athens: University of Georgia Press, 1989.

———. *The Dred Scott Case: Its Significance in American Law and Politics.* New York: Oxford University Press, 1978.

———. *The Slaveholding Republic: An Account of the United States Government's Relations to Slavery.* New York: Oxford University Press, 2001.

Finkelman, Paul. *Defending Slavery: Proslavery Thought in the Old South.* Boston: Bedford/St. Martin's, 2003.

Fite, Emerson D. *The Presidential Campaign of 1860.* New York: Macmillan Co., 1911.

Fitts, Albert N. "The Confederate Convention. Part I: The Provisional Constitution." *Alabama Review* 2 (April 1949): 83–101.

———. "The Confederate Convention. Part II: The Constitutional Debate." *Alabama Review* 2 (July 1949): 189–210.

Foner, Eric. *Free Soil, Free Labor, Free Men: The Ideology of the Republican Party Before the Civil War.* New York: Oxford University Press, 1970.

Foner, Philip S. *A History of Cuba and Its Relations with the United States.* 2 vols. New York: International Publishing Co., 1962–1963.

Ford, Lacy K., Jr. *Deliver Us from Evil: The Slavery Question in the Old South.* New York: Oxford University Press, 2009.

———. *Origins of Southern Radicalism: The South Carolina Upcountry, 1800–1860.* New York: Oxford University Press, 1988.

Foulke, William Dudley. *Life of Oliver P. Morton.* 2 vols. Indianapolis: Bowen-Merrill Co., 1899.

Fox-Genovese, Elizabeth and Eugene D. Genovese. *The Mind of the Master Class: History and Faith in the Southern Slaveholders' Worldview.* Cambridge, U.K.: Cambridge University Press, 2005.

———. *Slavery in Black and White: Class and Race in the Southern Slaveholders' New World Order.* Cambridge, U.K.: Cambridge University Press, 2008.

Fredrickson, George M. *The Black Image in the American Mind: The Debate on Afro-American Character and Destiny, 1817–1914.* New York: Harper and Row, 1971.

Freehling, William W. *Prelude to Civil War: The Nullification Controversy in South Carolina, 1816–1836.* New York: Harper & Row, 1966.

———. *The Road to Disunion.* Vol. 1: *Secessionists at Bay, 1776–1854.* New York: Oxford University Press, 1990.

———. *The Road to Disunion.* Vol. 2: *Secessionists Triumphant, 1854–1861.* New York: Oxford University Press, 2007.

———. *The South vs. The South: How Anti-Confederate Southerners Shaped the Course of the Civil War.* New York: Oxford University Press, 2001.

Freeman, Douglas Southall. *Lee's Lieutenants.* 3 vols. New York: Charles Scribner's Sons, 1942–44.

———. *R. E. Lee.* 4 vols. New York: Charles Scribner's Sons, 1940–43.

Freidel, Frank. *Francis Lieber: Nineteenth Century Liberal.* Baton Rouge: Louisiana State University Press, 1948.

Furguson, Ernest B. *Not War But Murder: Cold Harbor, 1864.* New York: Alfred A. Knopf, 2000.

Gaines, Francis P. "Andrew Pickens Butler." In *Dictionary of American Biography,* ed. Allen Johnson and Dumas Malone. 26 vols. New York: Charles Scribner's Sons, 1929. Vol. 3: 355–56.

Gallagher, Gary W. *The Confederate War: How Popular Will, Nationalism, and Military Strategy Could Not Stave Off Defeat.* Cambridge, Mass.: Harvard University Press, 1999.

Genovese, Eugene D. *The Political Economy of Slavery.* New York: Alfred A. Knopf, 1961.

———. *Roll, Jordan Roll: The World the Slaves Made.* New York: Pantheon, 1974.

———. *The Slaveholders' Dilemma: Freedom and Progress in Southern Conservative Thought, 1820–1860.* Columbia: University of South Carolina Press, 1992.

———. *The World the Slaveholders Made: Two Essays in Interpretation.* New York: Random House, 1969.

Gienapp, William E. "The Crime against Sumner: The Caning of Charles Sumner and the Rise of the Republican Party." *Civil War History* 25 (September 1979): 218–45.

———. *The Origins of the Republican Party, 1852–1856.* New York: Oxford University Press, 1986.

Goodwin, Gordon. "Amelia Matilda Murray." In *Dictionary of National Biography,* ed. Leslie Stephen and Sidney Lee. 22 vols. London: Oxford University Press, 1908–9. Vol. 13: 1243–44.

Graebner, Norman A., ed. *Politics and the Crisis of 1860.* Urbana: University of Illinois Press, 1961.

Greenberg, Kenneth S. *Masters and Statesmen: The Political Culture of American Slavery.* Baltimore: Johns Hopkins University Press, 1985.

Hamer, Philip May. *The Secession Movement in South Carolina, 1847–1852.* Allentown, Pa.: H. Ray Haas & Co., 1918.

Hamilton, Holman. *Prologue to Conflict: The Crisis and Compromise of 1850.* Lexington: University of Kentucky Press, 1964.

Hamilton, James G. deR. "James Louis Petigru." In *Dictionary of American Biography,* ed. Allen Johnson and Dumas Malone. 26 vols. New York: Charles Scribner's Sons, 1929. Vol. 14: 314–15.

Hamlin, Charles. *The Life and Times of Hannibal Hamlin.* Cambridge, U.K.: Riverside Press, 1899.

Harrington, Fred H. "The First Northern Victory." *Journal of Southern History* 5 (May 1939): 186–205.

Hartz, Louis. *The Liberal Tradition in America: An Interpretation of American Political Thought Since the Revolution.* New York: Harcourt, Brace & World, 1955.

Hattaway, Herman, and Richard E. Beringer. *Jefferson Davis: Confederate President.* Lawrence: University Press of Kansas, 2002.

Heidler, David S. *Pulling Down the Temple: The Fire-Eaters and the Destruction of the Union.* Darby, Pa.: Diane Publishing Co., 1994.

Henderson, G. B. "Southern Designs on Cuba." *Journal of Southern History* 5 (August 1939): 371–85.

Herd, Elmer Don, Jr. "Chapters from the Life of a Southern Chevalier: Lawrence Massillon Keitt's Congressional Years." Master's thesis, University of South Carolina, 1958.

Hess, Earl J. *Trench Warfare Under Grant and Lee: Field Fortifications in the Overland Campaign.* Chapel Hill: University of North Carolina Press, 2007.

Hollis, Daniel W. *University of South Carolina.* Vol. 1: *South Carolina College.* Columbia: University of South Carolina Press, 1951.

Holt, Michael F. *The Political Crisis of the 1850s.* New York: W. W. Norton, 1978.

———. *The Rise and Fall of the American Whig Party.* New York: Oxford University Press, 1999.

Huston, James L. *Calculating the Value of the Union: Slavery, Property Rights, and the Economic Origins of the Civil War.* Chapel Hill: University of North Carolina Press, 2003.

———. *The Panic of 1857 and the Coming of the Civil War.* Baton Rouge: Louisiana State University Press, 1987.

Ilisevich, Robert D. *Galusha Grow: The People's Candidate.* Pittsburgh: University of Pittsburgh Press, 1989.

Jabour, Anya. *Scarlet's Sisters: Young Women in the Old South.* Chapel Hill: University of North Carolina Press, 2007.

Jenkins, William S. *Pro-Slavery Thought in the Old South.* Chapel Hill: University of North Carolina Press, 1935.

Johannsen, Robert J. *Stephen A. Douglas.* New York: Oxford University Press, 1973.

Kauffman, Michael W. *American Brutus: John Wilkes Booth and the Lincoln Conspiracies.* New York: Random House, 2004.

Keegan, John. *The Face of Battle.* New York: Viking, 1976.

———. *The Mask of Command.* New York: Viking, 1987.

Kibler, Lillian A. *Benjamin F. Perry: South Carolina Unionist.* Durham, N.C.: Duke University Press, 1946.

———. "Unionist Sentiment in South Carolina in 1860." *Journal of Southern History* 4 (August 1938): 346–66.

King, Alvy L. *Louis T. Wigfall: Southern Fire-eater.* Baton Rouge: Louisiana State University Press, 1970.

Kirwan, Albert D. *John J. Crittenden: The Struggle for the Union.* Lexington: University of Kentucky Press, 1962.

Klein, Philip S. *President James Buchanan: A Biography.* University Park: Pennsylvania State University Press, 1962.

Klein, Rachel N. *Unification of a Slave State: The Rise of the Planter Class in the South Carolina Backcountry* 1760–1808. Chapel Hill: University of North Carolina Press, 1990.

Knoles, George H., ed. *The Crisis of the Union, 1860–1861.* Baton Rouge: Louisiana State University Press, 1965.

Lander, Ernest M. *Reluctant Imperialists: Calhoun, the South Carolinians, and the Mexican War.* Baton Rouge: Louisiana State University Press, 1979.

Lee, Charles Robert, Jr. *The Confederate Constitutions.* Chapel Hill: University of North Carolina Press, 1963.

Leemhuis, Roger P. *James L. Orr and the Sectional Conflict.* Washington, D.C.: University Press of America, 1979.

Leonard, Elizabeth D. *Lincoln's Avengers: Justice, Revenge, and Reunion after the Civil War.* New York: W. W. Norton, 2004.

Martis, Kenneth C. *The Historical Atlas of Political Parties in the United States, 1789–1989.* New York: Macmillan, 1989.

———. *The Historical Atlas of United States Congressional Districts, 1789–1982.* New York: Free Press, 1982.

Mathis, Robert N. "Preston Smith Brooks: The Man and His Image." *South Carolina Historical Magazine* 79 (October 1978): 296–310.

May, John A. and Joan R. Faunt, *South Carolina Secedes.* Columbia: University of South Carolina Press, 1960.

May, Robert E. *John A. Quitman: Old South Crusader.* Baton Rouge: Louisiana State University Press, 1985.

———. *Manifest Destiny's Underworld: Filibustering in Antebellum America.* Chapel Hill: University of North Carolina Press, 2002.

———. "Psychobiography and Secession: The Southern Radical as Maladjusted Outsider." *Civil War History* 34 (March 1988): 46–69.

———. *The Southern Dream of a Caribbean Empire, 1854–1861.* Baton Rouge: Louisiana State University Press, 1973.

Mayes, Edward, ed. *Lucius Q. C. Lamar: His Life, Times and Speeches.* Nashville, Tenn.: Publishing House of the Methodist Episcopal Church, South, 1896.

McCardell, John. *The Idea of a Southern Nation: Southern Nationalists and Southern Nationalism, 1830–1860.* New York: W. W. Norton, 1979.

McCash, William B. *Thomas R. R. Cobb: The Making of a Southern Nationalist.* Macon, Ga.: Mercer University Press, 1983.

McCurry, Stephanie. *Confederate Reckoning: Power and Politics in the Civil War South.* Cambridge, U.K.: Harvard University Press, 2010.

———. *Masters of Small Worlds: Yeoman Households, Gender Relations, and the Political Culture of the Antebellum South Carolina Low Country.* New York: Oxford University Press, 1995.

McGlone, Robert E. *John Brown's War against Slavery.* Cambridge, U.K.: Cambridge University Press, 2009.

McKissick, James R. *The Clariosophic and Euphradian Societies, 1806–1931.* Columbia, S.C.: Epworth Orphanage Press, [1931].

McKitrick, Eric L., ed. *Slavery Defended: The Views of the Old South.* Englewood Cliffs, N. J.: Prentice-Hall, 1963.

McPherson, James M. *Battle Cry of Freedom: The Civil War Era.* New York: Oxford University Press, 1988.

Merk, Frederick. *Manifest Destiny and Mission in American History: A Reinterpretation.* New York: Alfred A. Knopf, 1963.

Merritt, Elizabeth. *James Henry Hammond, 1807–1864.* Johns Hopkins University Studies in Historical and Political Science, vol. 61. Baltimore: Johns Hopkins Press, 1923.

Mitchell, Betty L. *Edmund Ruffin: A Biography.* Bloomington: Indiana University Press, 1981.

Montgomery, Horace. *Howell Cobb's Confederate Career.* Tuscaloosa, Ala.: Confederate Publishing Co., 1959.

Morrison, Chaplain W. *Democratic Politics and Sectionalism: The Wilmot Proviso Controversy.* Chapel Hill: University of North Carolina Press, 1967.

Morrison, Michael A. *Slavery & the American West.* Chapel Hill: University of North Carolina, 1997.

Morrison, Ralph E. "The Proslavery Argument Revisited." *Mississippi Valley Historical Review* 48 (June 1961): 79–94.

Muhlenfeld, Elizabeth. *Mary Boykin Chesnut: A Biography.* Baton Rouge: Louisiana State University Press, 1981.

Nevins, Allan. *The Emergence of Lincoln.* Vol. 1: *Douglas, Buchanan and Party Chaos, 1857–1859.* New York: Charles Scribner's Sons, 1950.

———. *The Emergence of Lincoln.* Vol. 2: *Prologue to Civil War, 1859–1861.* New York: Charles Scribner's Sons, 1950.

———. *Ordeal of the Union.* Vol. 1: *A House Dividing, 1852–1857.* New York: Charles Scribner's Sons, 1947.

———. *Ordeal of the Union.* Vol. 2: *Fruits of Manifest Destiny, 1847–1852.* New York: Charles Scribner's Sons, 1947.

———. *The War for the Union.* Vol. 1: *The Improvised War, 1861–1862.* New York: Charles Scribner's Sons, 1959.

———. *The War for the Union.* Vol. 2: *War Becomes Revolution, 1862–1863.* New York: Scribners, 1971.

———. *The War for the Union.* Vol. 3: *The Organized War to Victory, 1864–1865.* New York: Scribners, 1971.

Nichols, Roy F. *The Disruption of American Democracy.* New York: Macmillan Co., 1948.

———. *Franklin Pierce: Young Hickory of the Granite Hills.* Philadelphia: University of Pennsylvania Press, 1931.

Niven, John. *John C. Calhoun and the Price of Union: A Biography.* Baton Rouge: Louisiana State University Press, 1988.

Oates, James. *The Ruling Race: A History of American Slaveholders.* New York: Alfred A. Knopf, 1982.

———. *Slavery and Freedom: An Interpretation of the Old South.* New York: Alfred A. Knopf, 1990.

Oates, Stephen B. *To Purge This Land With Blood: A Biography of John Brown.* New York: Harper & Row, 1970.

O'Brien, Michael and David Moltke-Hansen, eds. *Intellectual Life in Antebellum Charleston.* Knoxville: University of Tennessee Press, 1986.

Overdyke, W. Darrell. *The Know Nothing Party in the South.* Baton Rouge: Louisiana State University Press, 1950.

Owsley, Frank L. *King Cotton Diplomacy.* Chicago: University of Chicago Press, 1931.

Pace, Robert F. *Halls of Honor: College Men in the Old South.* Baton Rouge: Louisiana State University Press, 2004.

Parker, William Belmont. *The Life and Public Services of Justin Smith Morrill.* Boston: Houghton Mifflin Co., 1924.

Patrick, Rembert W. *Jefferson Davis and His Cabinet.* Baton Rouge: Louisiana State University Press, 1944.

Pease, William H. and Jane Pease. *James Louis Petigru: Southern Conservative, Southern Dissenter.* Athens: University of Georgia Press, 1995.

Pemberton, John C. *Pemberton: Defender of Vicksburg.* Chapel Hill: University of North Carolina Press, 1942.

Phillips, Jason. *Diehard Rebels: The Confederate Culture of Invincibility.* Athens: University of Georgia Press, 2007.

Phillips, Ulrich Bonnell. *The Life of Robert Toombs.* New York: Macmillan Co., 1913.

Poole, W. Scott. *Never Surrender: Confederate Memory and Conservatism in the South Carolina Upcountry.* Athens: University of Georgia Press, 2004

Potter, David M. *The Impending Crisis, 1848–1861.* New York: Harper & Row, 1976.

———. *Lincoln and His Party in the Secession Crisis.* New Haven, Conn.: Yale University Press, 1942.

Power, J. Tracy. *Lee's Miserables: Life in the Army of Northern Virginia from the Wilderness to Appomattox.* Chapel Hill: University of North Carolina Press, 1998.

Rable, George C. *Civil Wars: Women and the Crisis of Southern Nationalism.* Urbana: University of Illinois Press, 1989.

———. *The Confederate Republic: A Revolution against Politics.* Chapel Hill: University of North Carolina Press, 1994.

Ranck, James Byrne. *Albert Gallatin Brown: Radical Southern Nationalist.* New York: D. Appleton-Century Co., 1937.

Randall, James G. "The Blundering Generation," *Mississippi Valley Historical Review* 27 (June 1940): 3–28.

———. "The Civil War Restudied." *Journal of Southern History* 6 (November 1940): 439–57.

———. "When the War Came in 1861." *Abraham Lincoln Quarterly* 1 (March 1940): 3–42.

Rauch, Basil. *American Interest in Cuba, 1848–1855.* New York: Columbia University Press, 1948.

Rawley, James A. *Race and Politics: "Bleeding Kansas" and the Coming of the Civil War.* Philadelphia: J. B. Lippincott, 1969.

Reynolds, David S. *John Brown, Abolitionist: The Man Who Killed Slavery, Sparked the Civil War, and Seeded Civil Rights.* New York: Alfred A. Knopf, 2005.

Rhodes, James Ford. *History of the United States from the Compromise of 1850 to the Final Restoration of Home Rule at the South in 1877.* New York: Macmillan Co., 1910.

Robertson, James I., Jr. *Soldiers Blue and Gray.* Columbia: University of South Carolina Press, 1998.

Rogers, Tommy W. "The Great Population Exodus from South Carolina, 1850–1860." *South Carolina Historical Magazine* 68 (January 1967): 14–21.

Root, Erik S. *All Honor to Jefferson? The Virginia Slavery Debate and the Positive Good Thesis.* Lanham, Md.: Lexington Books, 2008.

Rosenbough, Theodore F. "Sheridan's Richmond Raid." In *Battles and Leaders of the Civil War,* ed. Johnson and Buel. Vol. 4: 188–93.

Russel, Robert R. *Critical Studies in Antebellum Sectionalism: Essays in American Political and Economic History.* Westport, Conn.: Greenwood Publishing Co., 1972.

———. *Economic Aspects of Southern Sectionalism, 1840–1861.* New York: Russell & Russell, 1924.

Schaper, William A. "Sectionalism and Representation in South Carolina." *Annual Report of the American Historical Association* 1 (1900): 239–463.

Schott, Thomas E. *Alexander H. Stephens of Georgia: A Biography.* Baton Rouge: Louisiana State University Press, 1988.

Schultz, Harold S. *Nationalism and Sectionalism in South Carolina, 1852–1860.* Durham, N.C.: Duke University Press, 1950.

Shallope, Robert S. "Race, Class, Slavery, and the Antebellum Southern Mind." *Journal of Southern History* 37 (November 1971): 557–74.

Sharp, James R. *The Jacksonians versus the Banks: Politics in the States after the Panic of 1837.* New York: Columbia University Press, 1970.

Simonowicz, Vincent J. "History of the 20th South Carolina Volunteer Infantry." http://20scvi.org/history/simonowicz/html (accessed May 19, 2008).

Simpson, Craig M. *A Good Southerner: The Life of Henry A. Wise of Virginia.* Chapel Hill: University of North Carolina Press, 1985.

Sinha, Manisha. *The Counterrevolution of Slavery: Politics and Ideology in Antebellum South Carolina.* Chapel Hill: University of North Carolina Press, 2000.

Skipper, Ottis C. *J. D. B. DeBow: Magazinist of the Old South.* Athens: University of Georgia Press, 1958.

Smith, Alfred Glaze, Jr. *Economic Readjustment of an Old Cotton State: South Carolina, 1820–1860.* Columbia: University of South Carolina Press, 1958.

Smith, Elbert B. *The Presidency of James Buchanan.* Lawrence: University Press of Kansas, 1975.

Stampp, Kenneth M. *America in 1857: A Nation on the Brink.* New York: Oxford University Press, 1990.

———. *And the War Came.* Chicago: University of Chicago Press, 1950.

Staudenraus, P. J. *The African Colonization Movement, 1816–1865.* New York: Columbia University Press, 1961.

Stephenson, N. W. "Southern Nationalism in South Carolina in 1851." *American Historical Review* 36 (January 1931): 314–35.

Stern, Julia A. *Mary Chesnut's Civil War Epic.* Chicago: University of Chicago Press, 2010.

Strode, Hudson. *Jefferson Davis.* 3 vols. New York: Harcourt Brace and Co., 1955–64.

Sugrue, Michael. "'We Desired Our Future Rulers to Be Educated Men': South Carolina College, the Defense of Slavery, and the Development of Secessionist Politics." In *The American College in the Nineteenth Century,* ed. Roger Geiger. Nashville, Tenn.: Vanderbilt University Press, 2000.

Sydnor, Charles S. "The Southerner and the Laws." *Journal of Southern History* 6 (February 1940): 3–23.

Takaki, Ronald T. "The Movement to Reopen the African Slave Trade in South Carolina." *South Carolina Historical Magazine* 66 (January 1966): 38–54.

———. *A Pro-Slavery Crusade: The Agitation to Reopen the African Slave Trade.* New York: Free Press, 1971.

Taylor, Rosser H. *Ante-Bellum South Carolina: A Social and Cultural History.* Chapel Hill: University of North Carolina Press, 1942.

———. "The Gentry of Ante-Bellum South Carolina." *North Carolina Historical Review* 17 (April 1940): 114–31.

Thomas, Emory M. *The Confederacy as a Revolutionary Experience.* Englewood Cliffs, N.J.: Prentice-Hall, 1970.

———. *The Confederate Nation, 1861–1865.* New York: Harper & Row, 1979.

Thomas, J. A. W. *A History of Marlboro County, with Traditions and Sketches of Numerous Families.* Atlanta: Foote and Davise Co., 1897.

Thomas, Lately [Steele, Robert V. P.]. *Between Two Empires: The Life Story of California's First Senator, William McKendree Gwin.* Boston: Houghton Mifflin, 1969.

Thompson, William Y. *Robert Toombs of Georgia.* Baton Rouge: Louisiana State University Press, 1966.

Tise, Larry. *Proslavery: A History of the Defense of Slavery in America, 1701–1840.* Athens: University of Georgia Press, 1987.

Trudeau, Noah H. *Bloody Roads South: The Wilderness to Cold Harbor, May–June 1864.* Boston: Little Brown, 1989.

Tucker, Robert C. "James Henry Hammond: South Carolinian." Ph.D. diss., University of North Carolina, 1958.

Van Deusen, John G. *Economic Bases of Disunion in South Carolina.* New York: Columbia University Press, 1928.

Vandiver, Frank E. *Their Tattered Flags: The Epic of the Confederacy.* New York: Harper's Magazine Press, 1970.

Von Abele, Rudolph. *Alexander H. Stephens: A Biography.* New York: Alfred A. Knopf, 1946.

Wakelyn, Jon. *The Politics of a Literary Man: William Gilmore Simms.* Westport, Conn.: Greenwood Press, 1973.

Wallace, David D. *History of South Carolina.* 3 vols. Chapel Hill: University of North Carolina Press, 1934.

———. *The History of South Carolina.* 4 vols. New York: American Historical Society, 1934.

———. "Social Classes and Customs in South Carolina, 1830–1860." *Americana* 29 (1935): 57–97.

Wallenstein, Peter. "Incendiaries All: Southern Politics and the Harpers Ferry Raid." In *His Soul Goes Marching On: Responses to John Brown and the Harpers Ferry Raid,* ed. Paul Finkelman. Charlottesville: University Press of Virginia, 1995.

Walmsley, James E. "Preston S. Brooks." In *Dictionary of American Biography,* ed. Dumas Malone and Allen Johnson. 26 vols. New York: Charles Scribner's Sons, 1929. Vol. 3: 88.

Walther, Eric H. *The Fire-Eaters.* Baton Rouge: Louisiana State University Press, 1992.

———. *The Shattering of the Union: America in the 1850s.* Wilmington, Del.: Scholarly Resources, 2004.

———. *William Loundes Yancey and the Coming of the Civil War.* Chapel Hill: University of North Carolina Press, 2006.

Weinburg, Albert K. *Manifest Destiny: A Study of Nationalist Expansionism in American History.* Baltimore: Johns Hopkins Press, 1935.

Wheelan, Joseph. *Invading Mexico: America's Continental Dream and the Mexican War.* New York: Carroll & Graf, 2007.

———. "Membership of the South Carolina Secession Convention." *South Carolina Historical Magazine* 55 (October 1978): 296–310.

White, Laura A. "The National Democrats in South Carolina, 1852 to 1860." *South Atlantic Quarterly* 28 (October 1929): 370–89.

———. *Robert Barnwell Rhett: Father of Secession.* New York: Century Co., 1931.

Wiley, Bell I. *The Life of Johnny Reb: The Common Soldier of the Confederacy.* New York: Bobbs Merrill Co., 1943.

Williams, Jack K. "The Code of Honor in Ante-Bellum South Carolina." *South Carolina Historical Magazine* 54 (July 1953): 113–28.

Williams, T. Harry. *P. G. T. Beauregard: Napoleon in Gray.* Baton Rouge: Louisiana State University Press, 1955.

Wilson, Clyde N. *Carolina Cavalier: The Life and Mind of James Johnston Pettigrew.* Athens: University of Georgia Press, 1990.

Wilson, LeGrand James. *The Confederate Soldier,* ed. James W. Silver. Memphis: Memphis State University Press, 1973.

Wiltse, Charles M. *John C. Calhoun: Sectionalist, 1840–1850.* New York: Bobbs-Merrill Co., 1945.

Wise, Stephen R. *The Gates of Hell: Campaign for Charleston Harbor, 1863.* Columbia: University of South Carolina Press, 1994.

Wolff, Gerald W. "Party and Section: The Senate and the Kansas-Nebraska Bill." *Civil War History* 18 (December 1972): 293–311.

Woodson, Mrs. A. A. "South Carolina's Representatives in the Confederate Congress." *Confederate Veteran* 35 (January 1927): 16–19.

Wooster, Ralph A. "An Analysis of Secession Conventions in the Lower South." *Journal of Southern History* 24 (August 1958): 360–68.

———. "Membership of the South Carolina Secession Convention." *South Carolina Historical Magazine,* 55 (October 1954): 185–97.

———. *The Secession Conventions of the South.* Princeton, N.J.: Princeton University Press, 1962.

Wyatt-Brown, Bertram. *Honor and Violence in the Old South.* New York: Oxford University Press, 1986.

———. *The Shaping of Southern Culture: Honor, Grace, and War, 1760s–1890s.* Chapel Hill: University of North Carolina Press, 2001.

———. *Southern Honor: Ethics and Behavior in the Old South.* New York: Oxford University Press, 1982.

———. *Yankee Saints and Southern Sinners.* Baton Rouge: Louisiana State University Press, 1985.

Yearns, Wilfred Buck. *The Confederate Congress.* Athens: University of Georgia Press, 1960.

INDEX

Page numbers in italic type indicate illustrations.